ENTREPRENEURIAL MANAGEMENT AND PUBLIC POLICY

SECOND EDITION

ENTREPRENEURIAL MANAGEMENT AND PUBLIC POLICY

SECOND EDITION

VAN R. JOHNSTON

EDITOR

Nova Science Publishers, Inc.
New York

ENTREPRENEURIAL MANAGEMENT AND PUBLIC POLICY
SECOND EDITION

Claire-Lauren Schulz
Assistant to the Editor

Library of Congress Cataloging-in-Publication Data

Entrepreneurial management and public policy / Johnston, Van R. (Editor). -- 2nd ed.
    p. cm.
 Includes bibliographical references and index.
 ISBN-13: 978-1-60021-886-6 (hardcover)
 ISBN-10: 1-60021-886-5 (hardcover)
 1. Industrial management. 2. Industrial policy. 3. Deregulation. 4. Privatization. 5. Contracting out. 6. Competition. 7. Entrepreneurship. I. Johnston, Van R.
HD31.E657 2006
338.9'25--dc22
                          2007030157

Published by Nova Science Publishers, Inc. ✤ New York

For My Family and Friends
and
For My Students and Supportive Colleagues

It is not the critic who counts, not the one who points out how the strong one stumbled or how the doer of deeds might have done them better. The credit belongs to the one who is actually in the arena; whose face is marred with sweat and dust and blood; who strives valiantly; who errs and comes up short again and again; who knows the great enthusiasms, the great devotions, and spends himself in a worthy cause; and who, if he fails, at least fails while bearing greatly so that his place shall never be with those cold and timid souls who know neither victory nor defeat.

Theodore Roosevelt

CONTENTS

PREFACE
TO THE SECOND EDITION

Van R. Johnston

The first edition of ENTREPRENEURIAL MANAGEMENT AND PUBLIC POLICY was published in 2000. Subsequent events have proven that the contents, theories and lessons of this book have been on target. Our world of business and public policy has continued to move towards more competition and efficiency, and away from collaboration and effectiveness.

The lure of private sector and market based decision models has given us more freedom and innovation, but it has also increased our risk. We have sacrificed safety and security along the way, leading us to experience the consequences of catalytic events like: the terrorist attacks of September 11, 2001; NASA's Columbia space shuttle disaster; FEMA's collapse with Hurricane Katrina; and the financial ethics scandals involving Enron, Andersen, Qwest, and so many more.

As we begin 2008, our political leadership across the land has continued to lean towards efficiency, economy, competition, and customer and market based practices to solve our business and public policy problems and issues. President Jimmy Carter led the way into the paradigm shift when he deregulated air transportation in the late seventies. President Ronald Reagan followed with Reaganomics starting in 1980. Bush 41 continued Reagan's approach, policies and strategies. President Bill Clinton, while a liberal on social policies, was a fiscal conservative as evidenced by his turnaround of the federal government with Reinventing Government (the public sector rendition of reengineering), and his support for bringing Mexico into an expanded and more conservative NAFTA. Bush 43, our first MBA President, has championed the efficiency and competition paradigm. He has made his positions clear on a wide range of stakeholder issues from privatizing social security to global warming and the environment, and on to a privatized and contract based war machine built to fight in Iraq and Afghanistan with Halliburton and numerous other contractors performing significant roles.

The national elections, in November 2006, brought large numbers of democrats back to Congress, changing its balance significantly towards democratic control. Nancy Pelosi, a democrat, became Speaker of the House, third in succession for the Presidency. While there are a number of issues voters were expressing themselves on in that election; from the war in Iraq, to FEMA's collapse in Hurricane Katrina, and even global warming and beyond, there are other lessons to be learned here as well.

Across America, there appears to be increasing concern about a business and public policy arena which many experienced as too efficiency and competition oriented. There has been an increasingly serious lure for more collaboration, cooperation and effectiveness over the last few years. Scholars and practitioners in both the private and public sectors are making the case for more balanced analysis of complex systems for answers to the increasing number of catalytic events which have been precipitated by over reliance on the efficiency and competition based decision models.

In developing this Second Edition of ENTREPRENEURIAL MANAGEMENT AND PUBLIC POLICY, all of the authors in the first edition were contacted and asked if they wanted to have their chapters published in the second edition, with updates and adjustments as appropriate. Every author said yes. Each author was then given the opportunity to make such changes in their manuscripts. There were some changes in the first part of the book: Privatization, Competition, Deregulation and Entrepreneurial Management. There were more adjustments in the second part of the book: Entrepreneurship, Reinventing Government, Franchising and Contracting Out. The third part of the Book: Entrepreneurial Quality, Ethics, and Governance had significant changes. And, a new fourth part of the book has been added: Implementing the Entrepreneurial Management and Public Policy Model. This new Part IV develops a more integrated, complex and mature model than was in the first edition of the book.

Major additions and adjustments were made by Arie Halachmi in Part II in his chapter on Agency Theory and Transaction Analysis in Government. A new chapter was also added in Part II by Johnston and Schulz on FEMA and Katrina. This was necessary to balance the analysis in the FEMA chapter by Bert Useem which was done after the Northridge, California Earthquake.

Part III had more changes. Linda de Leon updated her chapter on Ethics and Entrepreneurship to include references to risky business behaviors and performance by those involved in ethics scandals like: Enron, Andersen, Qwest, and more. Bill Waugh added to and adjusted his manuscript on the potential for evil in entrepreneurialism and managerialism. He also added a section on the perceived evils following Katrina in academic governance in southern universities. Al Hyde shifted gears significantly. He is collaborating in the second edition with Dorothy Olshfski for a chapter titled: Service Quality in the Public Sector in the Internet Society. This major adjustment demonstrates the significance of our advances in the electronic environment. We also have a new and most significant cutting edge chapter by Dan Mazmanian and Daniel Press titled: The Greening of Industry through Government Supervised Self Regulation. The analysis and managerial advances demonstrated in this chapter show not only improvements made to date, but the potential for enhanced quality and collaboration in the future.

Part IV, The Entrepreneurial Management and Public Policy Model, features a new chapter by Wendy Haynes and Robert Wright using the integrated analytical model to analyze the development of the Department of Homeland Security. Haynes and Wright do an exceptional job of demonstrating how the logic of the model was employed to optimize the merging of over 20 federal agencies to create a mega agency to fight terrorism in America. Chapter 18 by Johnston uses the Model to analyze four catalytic events which have occurred since the first edition was published in 2,000. These catalytic events are: Terrorism and the response to September 11, 2001; NASA and the Columbia disaster; FEMA and Katrina; and, entrepreneurial management and ethics, and risky business cases like Enron, Andersen and Qwest. Finally, at the end of chapter 18, in Part IV, Johnston analyzes our struggle to balance competition and collaboration for more optimal results. The Entrepreneurial Management and Public Policy Model will be adjusted to provide lessons and insights for more optimal theory to practice results.

The book has contributed to a number of professional awards. Early on, it received the Wildavsky Book Award from the Policy Studies Organization. It also received the Discovery Award for theoretical research at the Daniels College of Business at the University of Denver. Later, the Application Award for theory to practice applications was received from the Daniels College of Business. This award focused on the more integrated models developed for later research on this topic, including the ones used in this second edition of the book. The material in the book also contributed to a Top Professor teaching award for the Stakeholders Issues Course at the Daniels College of Business. This award was given by Mortar Board, the National Senior Honor Society. That course has evolved and is now called Public Policy and Business. Over 1,200 students have now had this course at the University of Denver with this book. It is also used in other universities that have similar courses on public policy and business.

I want to take this opportunity to thank the authors who are contributing to this book. To all the returning authors, I must say how pleased I am to have you back as contributors again. Your work has been very well received. The awards listed above are a testament to the value of your contributions. The book review by *Public Administration Review* (January/February, 2002, 62(1), pp. 119-120) concluded: "*Entrepreneurial Management and Public Policy* has a considerable amount to offer...the essays are well-written and easily read and digested. It is a text rich in information for all those interested in exploring the numerous issues surrounding the world of privatization, reinvention, and entrepreneurship…..

One of our authors is no longer with us. Stuart Nagel, who founded the Policy Studies Organization, passed a few years ago now. He was instrumental in luring so many young scholars to write in quality journals like PSO's premier journals: *Policy Studies Journal*, and *Policy Studies Review* (now the *Review of Policy Research*) which helped set standards of excellence for publications in this field.

I also want to thank our new authors for contributing their chapters. They will enhance our book with their targeted contributions. Wendy Haynes is President of the American Society for Public Administration and an Associate Professor and Department Chair at Bridgewater State College in Massachusetts. Dan Mazmanian is immediate past Dean at the School of Policy Planning and Development at the University of Southern

California where he is now Director of the Governance Center. Dan is also President of NASPAA. Dorothy Olshfski has been Managing Editor of *Public Performance and Management Review* and a Professor at Rutgers University. Daniel Press is a Department Chair at the University of California at Santa Cruz. Claire Schulz is a law student, with an MBA and an MS in Management from the Daniels College of Business at the University of Denver. She is also a co-author and Assistant Editor of this book. And Robert Wright is a doctoral candidate, and a chapter co-author with Wendy Haynes.

Van R. Johnston
Denver, 2008

INTRODUCTION: THE ENTREPRENEURIAL MANAGEMENT TRANSFORMATION

Van R. Johnston

Entrepreneurial Management is transforming the world we live and work in. Public policy and administration as we have known it has been under siege for three decades now. Traditional public policy and administration has clearly undergone a significant paradigm shift (Kuhn, 1972), leaving many without the standards and practices of the past while searching for guidelines for the future. There are even those who argue that the sectors and their management have become blurred (Bozeman, 1987).

Early signals were California's Proposition 13 and the deregulation of the airlines, both in 1978. Proposition 13 urgently required public managers to become more efficient and innovative. Deregulation of the airlines sent the message that competition was being infused into the regulatory system in order to create more economy and to grow the industry. This sort of political economy (Halachmi and Boydston, 1994) was to be increasingly witnessed and experienced in the following years as the public sector and its organizations were either driven or lured towards the business and market model of the private sector.

The decade of the eighties was dominated by the conservative bent of Reaganomics. Mergers, acquisitions, hostile takeovers, and reengineering (Hammer and Champty, 1993) were regular events in the private sector. In the public sector, privatization (Donahue, 1989; Savas, 1987), public-private partnerships, outsourcing and/or contracting out (Kettl, 1993), load shedding, franchising (Halachmi, 1996) and restricted services became common place.

Privatization's lure traditionally revolved around the logic stream that concluded that smaller government is better. It was argued that privatization helps stimulate the economy and lower taxes. Government agencies are considered less efficient than private firms. Many believe that private sector managers manage better than public sector managers. Government monopolies don't typically have the necessary incentives to manage well. Government should not be in the business of delivering services provided by the private sector. And, public agencies, being political, are less efficient than private firms (O'Brien, 1989).

Privatization is also considered to have a number of disadvantages. Arguments against privatization typically point to: fraud, corruption, less accountability to citizens, loss of benefits of capital investment, lack of competition leading to increased costs, quality control problems, service cost increases due to taxes and liability insurance, and the political considerations involved in privatization (Palumbo and Maupin, 1989; O'Brien, 1989).

By the nineties we were well into identity shifting behaviors, both for individuals and for organizations. Citizens were beginning to think of themselves as customers. They began to wonder about their sovereign constitutional protections (Johnston, 1995; Moe, 1994; Moe and Stanton, 1989).

As this experience unfolded, the Clinton-Gore regime launched its **reinventing** government agenda (Osborne and Gaebler, 1991). Based upon the four bedrock principles of Gore's National Performance Review (Gore, 1993), entrepreneurship was injected into public management. Red tape was cut and accountability to rules shifted to accountability for results. Customers were to be put first by adopting business and market type competition. Authority was decentralized by empowering employees. And there was to be a shift towards the basics by simplifying, modernizing and putting an end to special privileges (Gore, 1993).

Based upon those significant adjustments, former Vice President Gore came out with a freshly reinvented profile for federal executives. The new federal executive would: empower employees, create a team environment, create a clear and more shared vision, cut red tape, put the customer first, communicate with employees, and create clear accountability (Gore, 1994).

Competition is traditionally seen as a function of private markets; e.g., vs. public monopolies. When competition is healthy, efficiency and economy are experienced and valued (Kettl, 1993). Where competition is missing, organizations and governments can appear to be lazy, inefficient, or even primarily focused on building and using its monopoly-like power. Under increasingly competitive conditions, quality and choice become more important as well.

As government continues to become more involved in working with the private sector, and becomes more like it, contracting becomes a larger factor. Developing skills in this expanding arena leads scholars and practitioners alike to explore the developing principal-agent theory in greater depth (Halachmi, 1996).

Governance has also become a significant concern. Citizens are increasingly aware of being treated as customers rather than as citizens. They wonder who is guarding their constitutional and sovereignty based rights (Johnston, 1990, Johnston, 1995). Many may still believe the government has the public interest as a priority, but it is increasingly difficult to understand how that interest is translated into practice in the world of entrepreneurial management. Citizens wonder about due process, equity, participation and predictable rules among other values (Nagel, 1989; Goodsell, 1993).

As we continue to experience these changes and adjustments, we increasingly notice the shifting priorities, from citizens towards customers, as follows (Johnston, 1995).

From Citizens	*Towards Customers*
Accountability	Reinvent
Public Interest	Reengineer
Legitimacy	Redesign
Constitutions	Efficiency
Legal Rights	Downsizing
Due Process	Customer Satisfaction
Stewardship	Empowerment
Effectiveness	Decentralized
Equity	Adaptive
Sovereignty	Competitive
Authority-Responsibility Links	Lean
Political Feasibility	Creative
Governance	Flexible
Fairness	Streamlined
Public Values	Contracts/Outsourcing
Administrative Management	Franchising
Legislative Direction	Consultants
Political Accountability	Privatizing
Elected Leaders	Public-Private Partnerships
Public Law	Total Quality Management
Agencies Delivering Services	Reduced Rules and Regulations
Employee Protections	Rework Performance Measures
Employee Benefits	Outcomes vs. Inputs
-health	Market Systems
-pensions	Survey Customers
- vacation	Secrecy
Checks and Balances	Entrepreneurship

Many increasingly wonder about authority, responsibility and accountability linkages. Implementation of the customer oriented market model changes the rules of the game. A great deal is at risk in the metamorphosis. There are new winners and new losers. Goal displacement and predatory practices can and do occur. We need to be increasingly skilled and vigilant if we want to optimize our opportunities as both citizens and customers (Johnston, 1995). The unfolding world of entrepreneurial management forces us to focus more clearly on quality, choice, governance, ethics, and professional performance priorities in a transformed political, economic and managerial environment.

Having transitioned the century and millennium, we discover a new frontier for professional and ethical entrepreneurial managers. It revolves around building visionary professional organizations of substance; built for producing value for both external and internal constituencies and stakeholders. Neither citizens or customers on the one hand, nor employees and professionals on the other should have to protect themselves against hollow organizations impacted by goal displacement, missing resources, or deceptive practices.

Citizens in the public sector have generally traditionally had a covenant-like (high trust) relationship with their governments. As the market model has become more prominent, and we find ourselves dealing more with issues like provision vs. production of services, contracts (lower trust and legal agreements) become more significant. The private sector can find itself reifying "ownership", and the related misuse of power often associated with the concept. If not filtered by reciprocal constraints or enlightened leadership and management, modern versions of nepotism can spring up; such as power mentoring on a more subtle level, or blatant cronyism on a more basic level. They usually manifest themselves as factions which can't lose, controlling both the resources and other factions which can't win, regardless of the performance involved. The role and power of the dollar should not be forgotten when private sector influences are increasing.

Trust, accordingly, becomes a more important factor with increased, and often zero sum competition for organizational analysts and practitioners as well (Wicks, Berman, and Jones, 1999). Cynicism follows when trust fails (Berman, 1997). And, when both trust and control of cynicism fail, credibility is on the line (Kouzes and Posner, 1993). Nuclear power failed in this country due to such concerns. Later, air transportation was investigated (Johnston, 1999; Petzinger, 1996), and a Passenger Bill of Rights was raised in Congress (Wyden *et al., 1999)*. These, however, are but two examples of problems resulting from inconsistent guidelines provided by both the private and the public sectors. Interestingly, in both of these cases, the conflict of providing for safety conflicted with requirements to promote the industry as well.

Entrepreneurial management is significantly more complex than the administration we have traditionally known and understood in this arena. The continuing emergence of entrepreneurship also confronts citizens with different sets of values, which many find uncomfortable. Pool and skim, and power and control can manifest themselves quite differently than shared vision, representative governance and the public interest. To optimize public policy in the future, with increasing levels of entrepreneurial management, we will need to develop more sophisticated competition and collaboration skills (Johnston, Haynes and Schulz, 2006); be more vigilant, responsible and ethical (de Leon, chapter 14); and focus on a more appropriate mix of public and private sector professional performance priorities (Johnston, chapter 16).

This book presents and analyzes the increasingly large and significant domain of entrepreneurial management. Its authors focus on investigating its various contributions, tradeoffs, problems, issues, dimensions and theories in considerable and meaningful depth.

Each of the four parts of this book also has an introduction which integrates the theme of the chapters found therein. These introductions will also highlight the thematic entrepreneurial management contributions, point out problems and issues, note relationships to theory, and highlight the authors primary focuses and contributions.

REFERENCES

Berman, E. M. 1997. "Dealing With Cynical Citizens," *Public Administration Review*, 57 (2), 105-112.

Bozeman, Barry. 1987. *All organizations are Public: Bridging Public and Private Organizational Theories.* San Francisco: Jossey-Bass.

Donahue, John. 1989. *The Privatization Decision: Public Ends, Private Means.* New York: Basic Books, Inc., Publishers.

Goodsell, Charles T. 1993. "Reinvent Government or Rediscover It," *Public Administration Review*, 53 (1): 85-87.

Gore, Al E., Jr. 1993. *From Red Tape To Results: Creating A Government That Works Better and Costs Less.* Washington, DC: United States Government Printing Office.

Gore, Al E., Jr. 1994. 'The New Job of the Federal Executive," *Public Administration Review*, 54 (4): 317- 321.

Halachmi, Arie. 1994. "The Challenge of a Competitive Sector," In *The Enduring Challenges in Public Management: Surviving and Excelling in a Changing World.* San Francisco: Jossey-Bass, 220 – 223.

Halachmi, Arie. 1996. "Franchising in Government: Can a Principal – Agent Perspective Be the First Step in the Development of a Theory?" *Policy Studies Journal*, 24 (3), 478 – 494.

Halachmi, Arie and Boydston, R. 1994. "The Political Economy of Outsourcing," In Kahn, A. and Hildreth, B. *Public Budgeting and Financial Management.* Dubuque, Iowa: Kendall Hunt Publishing Company.

Hammer, Michael and Champty, J. 1993. *Reengineering the Corporation.* New York: Harper Business Books.

Johnston Van R. 1990. "Privatization of Prisons: Management, Productivity and Governance Concerns," *Public Productivity and Management Review*, 14 (2), 189- 201.

Johnston, Van R. 1995. "Caveat Emptor: Customers vs. Citizens," The *Public Manager – The New Bureaucrat.* 24 (Fall), 11 –14.

Johnston, Van R. 1996. "Optimizing Productivity Through Privatization and Entrepreneurial Management," Policy *Studies Journal*, 24 (3), 444 – 463.

Johnston, Van R. (Ed.) 1996. "Privatization and Entrepreneurial Management," A Symposium in *Policy Studies Journal*, 24 (3): 437 – 510.

Johnston, Van R. 1999. "Trust, Cynicism and Credibility in Air Transportation Policy and Administration," A Professional Paper for the National Conference of the American Society for Public Administration, Orlando FL, April.

Johnston, Van R., and Wendy Haynes, and Claire-Lauren Schulz. Summer, 2006. "The T-REX Megaproject: Denver's Showcase for Innovation and Collaboration," *The Public Manager*, 35(2), 3-8.

Kettl, Donald F. 1993. *Sharing Power: Public Governance and Private Markets.* Washington, DC: The Brookings Institution.

Kouzes, James M., and Posner, Barry Z. 1993. *Credibility: How Leaders Gain and Lose It, Why People Demand It*. San Francisco: Jossey Bass.

Kuhn, Thomas S. 1972. *The Structure of Scientific Revolutions*. 2d ed., Chicago: University of Chicago Press.

Martin, John. 1993. "Reengineering Government," *Governing*, March, 26-30.

Moe, Ron C. 1987. "Exploring the Limits of Privatization," *Public Administration Review*, 47 (6), 453 – 460.

Moe, Ron C. 1994. "The 'Reinventing Government' Exercise: Misinterpreting the Problem: Misjudging the Consequences," *Public Administration Review*, 54 (2), 111 – 122.

Moe, Ron C. and Stanton, T.H. 1989. "Government Sponsored Enterprises as Federal Instruments: Reconciling Private Management with Public Accountability," *Public Administration Review*, 49 (4), 321 – 329.

Nagel, Stuart S. 1989. *Higher Goals For America*. Lonham, MD: University Press of America, Inc.

O'Brien, T.M. 1989. *Privatization in Colorado State Government*. Denver: Colorado Office of State Auditor.

Osborne, David and Gaebler, Ted. 1991. *Reinventing Government: How the Entrepreneurial Spirit is Transforming Government*. New York: Addison Wesley.

Palumbo, Dennis J. and Maupin, J. 1989. "The Political Side of Privatization," *Journal Of Management Science and Policy Analysis*, 6 (2): 25 – 40.

Petzinger, Thomas Jr. 1996. *Hard Landing: The Epic Contest for Power and Profits That Plunged the Airlines into Chaos*. New York: Times Business, Random House.

Savas, E.E. (Ed.) 1977. *Alternatives for Delivering Public Services: Toward Improved Performance*. Boulder, CO: Westview Press.

Wicks, Andrew C., Berman, Shawn L., and Thomas L. Jones. 1999. "The Structure of Optimal Trust: Moral and Strategic Implications," *Academy of Management Review*, 24 (1), 96-115.

Wyden, Ron, McCain, John, Bryen H. and Olympia J. Snowe. 1999. *Airline Passenger Fairness Act*. S. 383, 106th Congress, 1st Session. http:// www.congress.gov/cgi-lis/query/z?c106:s.383:.

PART I

PRIVATIZATION, COMPETITION, DEREGULATION AND ENTREPRENEURIAL MANAGEMENT

Part I of this book deals with the shift towards efficiency and economy as productivity continues to become more important. This is manifested in increasing competition and a variety of entrepreneurial management configurations which will be reviewed and analyzed in this part of the book. Privatization, certainly one of the more significant forms of entrepreneurial management, will be looked at in depth in Part I.

Chapter 1, *Optimizing Productivity through Privatization and Entrepreneurial Management*, by Johnston, analyzes both private and public sector productivity and demonstrates how the two have come together in the increasingly entrepreneurial world we are encountering. The author links efficiency and effectiveness to this analysis and shows that the merging of the models has contributed to privatization and other forms of entrepreneurial management including reinventing and reengineering. Part of this developing infrastructure is based on Total Quality Management and that analysis is woven in here and later on as well. The virtual organization is yet another emerging model that is focused on.

Johnston then studies applications of privatization and entrepreneurial management at the federal, state and local levels. He also generates public sector caveats and warns us about endangered public sector governance priorities. His chapter concludes with an entrepreneurial management productivity optimization model and sets the stage for the following chapters.

Chapter 2 is *Privatization: Trends, Interplay of Forces, and Lessons Learned* by Paul Seidenstat of the Privatization Institute at Temple University. In this chapter he defines privatization and shows how it has come into prominence. He distinguishes between contracting out and the other privatization practices. There is also a focus on and analysis of the political coalition of forces behind the scenes.

Seidenstat emphasizes the cost containment and quality enhancement benefits that have come from privatization. He ends by identifying numerous significant lessons, and charts the future path of privatization.

In Chapter 3, *Privatization of Government Services as a Reinventing Tool; Developments into the 21st Century*, Seidenstat continues his in-depth analysis of privatization with particular emphasis on privatization in the 21st century. Delving into his extensive research and experience with the Privatization Institute, he shows how privatization became and remains a response to cost containment, tax resistance, and cuts in service. Privatization has offered organizations advantages of flexibility, speed of adjustment, access to expertise, and innovation.

Seidenstat then links the growth of privatization efforts to the reinventing movement. He analyzes the significant distinction between provision and production of services. And, he provides a classification system for privatization processes. Such processes include: service shedding; asset sales; franchising; vouchers, grants and subsidies; public-private partnerships; volunteer activities; contracting in; contracting out; managed competition; and competitive contracting. He then demonstrates how predominant contracting has become, and where it is used most.

Seidenstat also analyzes both the political and practical factors involve in privatization and deals with cost containment, public-private competition, and quality. Privatization continues to be a useful management option for government managers and elected officials, but privatization failures (e.g., Atlanta water system contracts and 9/11 airport security) have become more apparent as we have moved into the 21st century. Seidenstat then analyzes the basis for improved performance based upon exogenous and management factors. The author also develops a force field model which he uses to analyze privatization.

He concludes with a discussion of future developments for privatization in the 21st century. The author anticipates that privatization, though void of much of its ideological appeal, will remain a popular management tool as governmental deficit spending increases.

In Chapter 4, *Deregulation, Privatization and Competition in Telecommunications*, Roberto Evaristo shows how the enormously increasing competition being experienced both in the United States and abroad is linked to both privatization and deregulation. He has selected telecommunications as an area to apply his analysis. In this chapter, the author develops a model to provide guidance for those affected by increasing entrepreneurial policy and administration as competitive forces significantly impact stakeholders.

The final chapter in Part I is by Stuart Nagel. It is entitled *Privatization, Competition, and Organizing the Economy*. In this chapter, Nagel analyzes the relationship between the private and public sectors. He also looks at how having numerous competitors in each sector can encourage competition, rather than having just one large firm or agency. Nagel, like Evaristo before him, expands the analysis beyond our American boundaries and provides a rich, encompassing, and in-depth national and international analysis.

Dr. Nagel provides a serious review of privatization and competition and leads up to a super optimum solution. Monopolies are also explored. Yet, he comes back to the significance of appropriate competition and cooperation in various relevant real world and theoretical environments.

The author also spends time and attention on creating innovative ideas regarding competition. He notes problems experienced by both liberals and conservatives. Then he delves into the struggle over consolidation vs. competition in public organizations such as: police departments, public schools and political parties. Nagel ends with an analysis of the public and private sectors, and political and economic competition as they deal with prosperity and super optimum solutions.

Chapter 1

Optimizing Productivity through Privatization and Entrepreneurial Management

Van R. Johnston

Efficiency and economy have become the forces driving both public and private organizations as we transition into the new millennium. Competition and legal mandates constrict managers' abilities to use their traditional options in delivering goods and services to their citizens and customers. Privatization and entrepreneurial management are being utilized increasingly to improve productivity. This is creating a genuine transformation in the way we manage our organizations. It also changes the nature of the relationship between our organizations and their citizens, clients, and customers.

In this chapter we explore this unfolding transformation and analyze its significance. An entrepreneurial management productivity optimization model is also developed. Productivity is explored in terms of efficiency and effectiveness. The mechanisms for improving productivity, privatization, and entrepreneurial management are then examined. After noting the changing roles that public policy and competition now play, the more prominent managerial models are explored, including reinventing and reengineering.

The chapter then presents examples of federal, state, and local entrepreneurial strategies and innovations. It concludes by alerting us to endangered public policy priorities and sets forth significant public management caveats to which we should increasingly become sensitive. The entrepreneurial management productivity optimization model has been developed to assist in clarifying and analyzing the issues involved in this chapter. It should also help those working in this arena to formulate optimal choices when building entrepreneurial management models for their own organizations or for those of their citizens, clients, or customers.

The entire nation took note when even the Republican presidential candidates were complaining about the problems with organizational downsizing for American workers in the 1996 presidential campaign. Reinventing, reengineering, privatization, and other entrepreneurial management efforts have brought the realities of losing jobs to middle-class Americans. The fallout of these adjustments translates into lost medical coverage, pensions, and vacations. Competition, legal mandates, and efficiency-consciousness in the United States have come, for many, to mean working two jobs at significantly less pay and with far fewer benefits. The loyalty of organizations to their workers is becoming an increasingly hotly debated issue. Many who have been laid off could not even find meaningful employment.

American managers, policymakers, and organizational strategists have been struggling with the pressures and uncertainties of enormous turbulence and change. The private sector has been forced to downsize and become more efficient due to increasing competition both at home and abroad. Emerging from the mergers, acquisitions, deregulation, and privatization of the 1980s, and 1990s, and approaching the end of the first decade of the 21st century, business, industry, and governments are also being confronted with new international realities as well. Eastern Europe and the socialist bloc have collapsed. The European Union has become a reality, and is emerging into a potent force. The Pacific Rim is booming. The North American Free Trade Agreement has been expanded to include Mexico, creating both problems and opportunities. Increasing quality and productivity have become serious and ubiquitous enough that even major business publications are bemoaning the plight of surviving bosses who are identified as victims of the restructuring under way, as business and industry seek to maximize quality and productivity (Smith, 1994).

Demands have also been placed upon public-sector managers as well. Some come from proactive efforts to adjust public-sector organizations toward premier-level, cutting-edge institutions in their field. More typically, however, public-sector organizations have been forced towards private-sector-like entrepreneurial management and privatization by budget and policy constraints imposed upon them. Privatization has become a classic coping strategy (Johnston, 1999; Johnston, 2002; Johnson, Haynes, and Schulz, 2006; Johnston and Seidenstat, 2007).

Notification was delivered in 1978 that the traditional public-sector administrative management paradigm was going to shift. On June 6 of that year, California voters passed Proposition 13. With local property taxes cut in half, the fiscal pressure on public managers soared. More recently in the 1990s, Colorado voters approved Amendment 1, which limits government spending to local population growth and inflation. Any excess money raised must be returned to the voters. The November 3, 1992 amendment has taken years to interpret, litigate, and implement. It quickly becomes obvious that the rules of the game have changed. Yet, citizens continue to make demands for improved services.

The tax revolt has spread across the country, and with it citizens/customers (Johnston, 1995a) have become much more vocal about increasing administrative efficiency and improving the quality of managerial operations at all levels of government. Entrepreneurial management has begun to emerge as a strategic alternative oriented towards doing more with increasingly limited resources. Alternative service delivery mechanisms such as public/private partnerships, vouchers, privatization, total quality management, volunteers, and contracting out, among others, became the core of Osborne and Gaebler's entrepreneurially oriented *Reinventing Government* (Osborne & Gaebler, 1992).

Shortly after publishing this book, David Osborne was recruited by the Clinton White House to help Vice President Al Gore with the entrepreneurially oriented National Performance Review (Gore, 1993), among other tasks. At the state level, we then received the Winter Commission Reports on State and Local Public Service (Elling, 1994). The entrepreneurial arguments of Osborne and Gaebler were well represented in the report, even though it provides caveats to the effect that privatization is far from being a cure-all.

PRODUCTIVITY, EFFICIENCY, AND EFFECTIVENESS

At the theoretical level, the adjustment towards entrepreneurial management represents a shift from the public sector's effectiveness orientation towards the private sector's efficiency orientation. Along the way there arise some concerns regarding public-sector values, rights, and protections.

Productivity in the public sector usually is thought of in terms of output over standards (liberal vs. conservative, for instance). Services are produced. These typically have a qualitative orientation and emerge from a dominant political system. They are based in the public or not-for-profit environment. We typically refer to it as effectiveness. This is shown in Figure 1.

Figure 1
Public-Sector Productivity

Productivity	=	Effectiveness
		Output
		Standards (e.g., liberal or conservative)
	=	Services
	=	Qualitatively Measured
	=	Political Systems
	=	Nonprofit Organizations
	=	Public Organization

Productivity in the private sector is simpler. It is viewed as output over input, as summarized in Figure 2. Typically, discrete goods that can be packaged and sold are produced. Measurement is in quantitative terms. Such products are based traditionally in the private sector and play a role in the supply and demand of the market system. The organizational base is found in the private sector. We call this sort of private-sector system "efficiency."

Figure 2
Private-Sector Productivity

Productivity	= Efficiency
	= $\dfrac{\text{Output}}{\text{Input}}$
	= Products/Goods
	= Quantitative Measurements
	= Market Systems
	= Private Firms
	= Private Industry

In reality, most organizations emphasize both efficiency and effectiveness, as shown in Figure 3. A predominance of their emphasis, however, usually occurs on either the private or the public side of the equation. It is helpful to understand roughly what percentage of an organization's productivity is perceived to be efficiency vs. effectiveness based.

Figure 3
Productivity = Efficiency + Effectiveness

Productivity	=	Efficiency	+	Effectiveness
	=	$\dfrac{\text{Output}}{\text{Input}}$	+	Output / Standards
	=	Products/Goods	+	Services
	=	Quantitative Measures	+	Qualitative Measures
	=	Market Systems	+	Political Systems
	=	Private Firms	+	Nonprofit Organizations
	=	Private Industry	+	Public Organizations
	=	%	+	%

As we increasingly adopt private-sector-oriented entrepreneurial management, we move more towards the efficiency model or equation. As we move away from the more traditional public-sector administrative management model, we begin to lose our grounding in public-sector standards. Such values as sovereign rights, equity, the public interest, legitimacy, due process, and accountability increasingly become eroded. There are mechanisms, such as by guarding these values in contracts, that we can use to attempt to preserve them. At this time, however, we are not yet very skilled in this arena.

PRIVATIZATION AS EMERGING ENTREPRENEURIAL MANAGEMENT

This chapter now will explore how public-sector organizations are evolving towards more entrepreneurial management. What are the more significant managerial models being used? What is happening at the various levels of government, and what caveats should we be heeding in order to preserve our public-sector rights and safeguards?

Privatization was one of the first alternatives opted for when governments were forced to become more efficient. Contracting out typically worked well and was not too complicated. Later, privatizing whole organizations was attempted. This proved to be much more complex (Johnston, 1990; Johnston, Hayes, and Schulz, 2006; Seidenstat, 2007). Among the more practical arguments for privatization are the following: costs can be reduced; short-term projects can be optimized economically; services can be provided more frugally; limited resources can be compensated for; and some would argue that government operations typically are improved.

Formidable ideological arguments include the following: because of their political realities, government agencies are less efficient and economical; they also are monopolies, without incentives to manage well; smaller government is better; government should not deliver services that the private sector offers; and privatization can assist in lowering taxes and in stimulating the economy (O'Brien, 1989).

Policymakers and managers alike must weigh the trade-offs in their pursuit of efficiency and economy. Palumbo (1986) warned that in certain cases, like privatizing prisons, we may forget about some of the more serious questions while profitmaking becomes a priority. In such cases, it is possible that efficiency and economy would be considered a priority; while many serious, yet complicated, management, constitutional, and ethical problems would be put off for consideration at a later time. John Donahue (1989) cautioned us about the potential for warping public choices and monitoring accountability, even if efficiency is improved significantly.

Those who warn us about the risks of privatizing argue that once private firms begin delivering public services, accountability drops and the public interest is threatened. Often there is also an increase in the cost of delivering services. It is not unusual for policymakers and managers to misjudge increased costs due to liability insurance, taxes, and markets too small to assure competitive pricing and the other realities found in genuinely competitive situations. There can be labor strikes and profit declines, which can cause a loss of control over the quality of service delivery. The potential loss of capital investment cannot be forgotten, either, and there is no guarantee that political considerations can or will be overcome by privatizing (Palumbo & Maupin, 1989, pp. 25–40).

Linowes (1988) found that private-sector delivery of public services, which continues to increase well into the first decade of the 21st century, can improve quality and performance and contribute to more effective government. We see it being used reactively to fill budget gaps and downsizing needs, such as with education and prison systems (Johnston, 1993b). The Iraq War has a privatized support structure far beyond any in history, relying on private companies like Haliburton and Blackwater. We also see it being used proactively to develop national- and world-class teaching, research, and administrative organizations, as has been the case with the reorganization of Colorado's University Hospital (Johnston, 1993a). While it took time to develop and evolve University Hospital to its much more professional and successful entrepreneurial status in the latter years of the first decade of the new millennium, it has become a role model for other similar organizations attempting to be world class professional entrepreneurial organizations. On the international scene, Savas (1993) provided an update and analysis of the different kinds of privatization being attempted in the Central and Eastern European postsocialist countries.

Overall, whether proactively or reactively, many consider privatization, both in the United States and in many other nations around the world, to be a very viable way to pursue increased efficiency, quality, performance, and productivity in the delivery of public-sector services. It is viewed as an alternative that can be attempted immediately. At certain times and in certain places, it is optional; in others it is not. Whatever the circumstances, there are arguments for and against it. In the long run, efficiency and economy should be balanced by the public interest and accountability.

COMPETITION, PUBLIC POLICY, AND ENTREPRENEURIAL MANAGEMENT

Competition and public policy mandates forced public-sector managers to search seriously for more management options to enable them dramatically to enhance efficiency and economy. Market-oriented mechanisms were employed as they geared up for more entrepreneurially oriented management. Roles began to be adjusted. Citizens began to be treated more as customers. Historically and academically, we use theories based on political economy and efficiency to provide guidance in adjusting the course (Halachmi & Boydston, 1994). Competition leverages the pressure to optimize the adjustments (Halachmi, 1994). We have now come to recognize Total Quality Management (TQM), reinventing, reengineering, and other entrepreneurially oriented models as the managerial extension of the efficiency-based political economy model (Johnston, 1995a).

TQM AND BEYOND: THE MANAGERIAL MODELS

TQM

Emerging from the early private-sector quality improvement efforts of Deming (Walton, 1990; Juran, 1988; and Crosby, 1984), total quality management became a centerpiece of organizational efforts to improve performance and productivity in the 1990s. Forced to adapt to their increasingly hostile fiscal environment, public-sector managers reached out to the private sector and innovatively brought back a creatively adapted TQM. As work with this model of management progressed, the public sector proudly developed its own renditions, as can be witnessed in the Federal Quality Institute's operating practices, the President's Award for Quality and Productivity (President's Council on Management Improvement, 1991), and the Baldrige award given to private-sector organizations (Garvin, 1991).

Many TQM-based concepts were used in developing more entrepreneurially oriented models such as reinventing, reengineering, and the virtual organization that were to follow. Among the more significant for developing performance and productivity are those listed in Figure 4. These key TQM-based concepts form a baseline for developing other managerial models to be utilized herein.

Figure 4
TQM: Key Concepts
Johnston

1. Quality	9. Training
2. Productivity	10. Goals and Plans
3. Customers	11. Teams, Boards, and Councils
4. Empowerment	12. Communication
5. Top Management Support	13. Developing a Quality Culture
6. Built-in Quality vs. Finding Defects	14. Employee Involvement
7. Constant Improvements	15. Performance Recognition
8. Education	16. Documenting Quality

Reinventing

Reinventing Government was a primary catalytic agent that blended TQM and entrepreneurial management. It has had a transformational impact on the way public-sector agencies operate. Emphasizing efficiency as well as effectiveness, this market system based model proactively highlights innovation and creativity.

As the model is increasingly embraced, we hear more about the paradigm shift occurring in public-sector management. Public-sector managers at the federal, state, and local levels are learning about and experiencing more of the model as it continues to unfold. As represented in the following twin figures (Figures 5 and 6), reinventing can be seen as a new paradigm, and in terms of its primary approaches (Osborne & Gaebler, 1992).

Figure 5
Reinventing: The New Paradigm

1. Decentralized	6. Customer Oriented
2. Flexible	7. Creative
3. Adaptive	8. Lean
4. Competitive	9. Streamlined
5. Learning	

Figure 6
Reinventing: Approaches

1. Contracting Out	6. Vouchers
2. Privatization	7. Volunteers
3. Public-Private Partnerships	8. Participatory Management
4. Load Shedding	9. Empowerment
5. Alternative Service Delivery	10. Total Quality Management

Reengineering

Reengineering is noted for its emphasis on the development of parallel processes from sequential, bureaucratic processes. This model typically concentrates on innovative, holistic jobs and team processes. It reorganizes and redesigns jobs, and enhances participatory management and empowerment. Developed to a great extent by Michael Hammer, a Cambridge Massachusetts management consultant, reengineering is an organizational model that typically eliminates the old and redesigns, or reengineers, something completely new (Martin, 1993). It is oriented towards being able to deliver services to clients more efficiently. It focuses on adapting business and engineering concepts to management practices.

Reengineering has been most successful in the private sector. It has enabled companies to downsize substantially and it has raised some public policy caveats, too. For instance, reengineering contributes to the contingency workforce. Increasing numbers of workers are impacted negatively by lost pensions, vacations, and medical care. Reengineering and its contribution of increased efficiency do drop substantial numbers of employees from the regular workforce (Ehrbar, 1993). The temporary workforce, meanwhile, continues to grow. Contractors, disposable workers, leased employees, per diem workers, and supplementals are among those adding to the contingency workforce (Fierman, 1994).

A Hammer-based reengineering model (Martin, 1993) can be set up as indicated in Figure 7.

Figure 7
A Reengineering Model

1. Important to fit management needs and government purposes
2. Focuses on eliminating the old and redesigning or reengineering something new
3. Links are formed between engineering and organizations
4. Grounded in information technology and oriented toward constant change
5. Create parallel processes from sequential, bureaucratic processes
6. Emphasize empowerment, work teams, and participatory decisionmaking
7. Important to project number of workers to be laid off
8. Helpful to have a clear and workable problem
9. Visionary leaders are an asset
10. Timing is critical
11. Opportunities for retraining or early retirement
12. Reexamine and redetermine organization's mission and goals

Virtual Organizations

The virtual organization is another alternative in the beyond-TQM dimension. In this context, "virtual" emerges from the early days of computing when we began to realize that computers could act as if they had more storage capacity than they really did (Byrne, 1993). The concept has been adapted to explain our efforts to get organizations to act similarly by focusing vision and energy through projects and teams. Increasing quality, service, and productivity through managerial and organizational adjustments is the goal of the virtual organization.

Virtual organizations are structures on the verge of losing their structural edges. They are perceived to be in continuous change. Their products and services are adapted to client, customer, and citizen needs and demands. Teams based on trust and dependent relationships focus their performance by utilizing temporary projects and joint ventures (Byrne, Brandt, & Post, 1993). They often are identified as best-skill teams. Virtual organization endeavors typically become more productive and quality oriented. The virtual organization model can be set forth as Figure 8 (Davidson & Malone, 1992).

Figure 8
The Virtual Organization

1. Flatter organization structure with modern communication networks
2. More self-managing work teams having true power and responsibility
3. Products are developed that have been partly designed by customers and suppliers
4. Workers are well educated, trainable, and flexible enough to lcarn new tasks and skills frequently
5. Close relationship with their suppliers
6. Top executives have detailed knowledge of how the organization really operates

FEDERAL, STATE, AND LOCAL ENTREPRENEURIAL STRATEGIES AND INNOVATIONS

Federal Entrepreneurial Innovations

The National Performance Review (NPR) took place from March to September, 1993. President Clinton launched it and assigned Vice President Gore to lead the effort. The Vice President created teams of experienced government professionals whose assignment was to identify problems, offer solutions, and generate ideas for cost savings. Each Cabinet secretary was asked to set up reinvention teams and to experiment with reinvention laboratories, to find new ways of doing business. The goal was to create a government that works better and costs less (Gore, 1993). Reinventing government, therefore, became a mechanism for transforming our government from the traditional administrative management model to an innovative entrepreneurial management model. It represents a genuine paradigm shift (Kuhn, 1970).

The National Performance Review also looked at success experiences from the private sector and from state and local governments (Gore, 1993). The reviewers concluded that the successful organizations cut red tape. Accountability to rules was shifted to accountability for results. Such organizations put customers first. Market competition, therefore, became more important. Empowered employees get results by decentralized authority. Finally, NPR's successful organizations cut back to basics. They modified, simplified, and ended special privileges.

To make sure that results become a baseline for evaluating federal performance, the Government Performance and Results Act (GPRA) was passed in 1993 (Public Law 103-62, 1993). It required federal agencies to develop strategic plans prior to Fiscal Year (FY) 1998, to prepare annual plans setting performance goals beginning in FY 1999, and to report annually on actual performance compared to goals. The first report was due in March, 2000.

The Department of Defense (DoD) was used as an example of how reinventing could be applied by the federal government. DoD was responsible for 67% of federal contract awards in 1993. Secretary of Defense William J. Perry believed that DoD could save up to $10 billion a year with such changes by 1999. That represented approximately 10% of DoD procurement outlays.

Additional savings came from a reduction in the number of federal procurement employees. NPR estimated that there were over 72,500 federal acquisition personnel. DoD had over 49,000, and there were over 70,000 accountants and auditors working at the federal level, about half at DoD. Since President Clinton targeted over 250,000 federal jobs for extinction, many at DoD were eliminated in a downsizing military environment. DoD targeted the release of about 50,000 civilians and over 85,000 military in 1994 (Gregory, 1994).

Some of DoD's entrepreneurially oriented changes actually got under way toward the end of the Bush Administration when TQM was used to press for reorganizing action and more efficiency (Johnston & D'Amico, 1992). After the Gulf War and the collapse of the

Soviet Union and the Warsaw Pact, DoD began downsizing and looking for innovative ways to integrate entrepreneurial management and optimal privatization into the defense acquisition system (Johnston & D'Amico, 1993).

When Clinton and Gore were elected, and reinventing came into focus. Entrepreneurial management efforts were launched. Among the key thrusts being observed to date in acquisition reform are the following.

The administration pressed hard for new federal acquisition legislation in 1994. It encouraged purchasing off-the-shelf products, and waivers where necessary. Administrative actions were taken to do away with milspecs (military specifications) in equipment ordering. Pilot projects for new acquisition methods are being promoted. More electronic commerce is being encouraged, both to pay for and to order products, and the threshold for simplified acquisition procedures is being raised from $25,000 to $100,000. These improvements in DoD acquisitions save very significant amounts of money. They are also designed to enhance accountability, simplify procedures, and empower employees (Gregory, 1994).

Figure 9
Reinventing Federal Procurement

PROC 01--Reframe acquisition policy

PROC 02--Build an innovative procurement workforce

PROC 03--Encourage more procurement innovation

PROC 04--Establish new simplified acquisition threshold and procedures

PROC 05--Reform labor laws and transform the labor department into an efficient partner for meeting public policy goals

PROC 06--Amend protest rules

PROC 07--Enhance programs for small business and small disadvantaged business concerns

PROC 08--Reform information technology procurements

PROC 09--Lower costs and reduce bureaucracy in small purchases through the use of purchase cards

PROC 10--Ensure customer focus in procurement

PROC 11--Improve procurement ethics laws

PROC 12--Allow for expanded choice and cooperation in the use of supply schedules

PROC 13--Foster reliance on the commercial marketplace

PROC 14--Expand electronic commerce for federal acquisition

PROC 15--Encourage best value procurement

PROC 16--Promote excellence in vendor performance

PROC 17--Authorize a two-phase competitive source selection process

PROC 18--Authorize multiyear contracts

PROC 19--Conform certain statutory requirements for civilian agencies to those of defense agencies

PROC 20--Streamline buying

Clinton and Gore recognized the importance of military acquisitions and procurement enough to select it out for special attention. Reinventing federal procurement was reviewed, and acquisition policy was changed. The reframing can be seen in the first 20 recommendations made to reinvent federal procurement (Walsh, 1994). They are shown in Figure 9.

Results again become much more important than traditional rigid rules. Employees become empowered to innovate. Interagency programs are developed with enhanced roles for civilian employees. Innovative tests are set up for new procurement methods, and procurement information becomes more widely disseminated. An electronic bulletin board is established to enhance small-business access and contracting information opportunities. Credit card utilization for small purchases is expanded, and electronic commerce and data interchange are examined in a pilot program. Promoting vendor performance excellence will also become an increasing priority (Walsh, 1994).

Emerging from the turbulent adjustments made in the federal system was the new federal executive. Vice President Gore noted that two developments changed significantly the premises upon which both private- and public-sector management have been grounded. First, we now have an increasing understanding of how best to employ human capacity. Second, information technology plays a new role in transforming the manager's job.

These developments transformed the nature of management in the federal government and change the nature of the job for federal executives. The new role of federal executives is reflected by the following characteristics: they develop a clear and more shared vision; a team environment is created; employees are empowered; customers come first; communication with employees is emphasized; red tape is cut; and clear accountability is created.

In order to adjust optimally to these changes and to internalize the new culture that emphasizes quality and innovation, a couple of major hurdles were overcome (Gore, 1994). First, it was necessary for federal executives to realize that the government was being reinvented and that the world of the past is gone. Moving proactively into the reinvented paradigm set forth in the National Performance Review optimized the entrepreneurially based adjustments and helped to minimize the pain and costs inherent in the transition itself.

The second major hurdle was culture. So, efforts were made to develop a work environment that promoted and rewarded innovation, preserved accountability, maintained respect for law, and puts customers first. The work environment also needed to provide employees with a feeling of security, recognition, and personal accomplishment.

State Entrepreneurial Developments

There are increasing numbers of meaningful examples of public-sector organizations moving towards more efficiency and entrepreneurial management as they pursue enhanced quality and productivity. A variety of approaches are available for public-sector managers to examine these days, including reengineering, reinventing, privatization, contracting, and innovative combinations of models and methods.

When California was having trouble paying employee checks in the 1990's, California's Governor Pete Wilson was quoted from his inaugural address in Osborne and Gaebler's *Reinventing Government: How the Entrepreneurial Spirit is Transforming the Public Sector*. He stated:

> We will not suffer the future. We will shape it. We will not simply grow. We will manage our growth. We will not passively experience change. We will make change. But to shape our future, we need a new vision of government (Osborne & Gaebler, 1992, pp. 330–331).

Colorado's University Hospital (UH) decided to do precisely what California's Governor Pete Wilson was talking about. It wanted to become world-class, cutting-edge in teaching and research. It was a large, state organization with schools of medicine, dentistry, nursing, and pharmacy. A school of chiropractic medicine was added later. It also has over 850 research laboratories. In the way of this vision, were the traditional state purchasing and personnel systems. University Hospital also had a multimillion-dollar financial deficit and responsibility for indigent patients.

A coalition of hospital administrators, state legislators, faculty physicians, and the University Board of Regents worked together. They got a legislative bill passed (HB 1143) that created a private-sector organization. This occurred on October 1, 1989. During the next 15 months, UH made great advances. It eliminated its deficit and installed new billing and purchasing systems. It built new and expanded programs for AIDS, sports medicine, organ transplants, bone marrow transplants, and so on. It installed a new personnel system and did outstanding recruiting.

The success of their entrepreneurial management venture with privatization seemed to be right on target. Then, 15 months later, on December 24, 1990, the Colorado Supreme Court ruled that the enabling statute violated the State Constitution and that UH could not be a private-sector organization. UH is tax-supported, responsible for indigent care, a public asset, and still controlled the personnel system.

Preliminary estimates to reconvert to a traditional, and problematic, public-sector organization ranged from $10 million to $25 million. Several interim adjustments occurred, and then a strategy was focused on that essentially would re-create UH as a public authority. Political, legal, and management adjustments were fine-tuned, and SB 225 became the mechanism for the organization's transformation to its new identity.

University Hospital did end up positioned to become world-class, cutting-edge in its field. To be successful, however, it had to reinvent itself twice. First, it became a private-sector organization. Then, after the State Supreme Court ruling, it became a public authority. Its leaders did not suffer the future, they took charge. They adopted the entrepreneurial spirit to improve their quality and productivity (Johnston, 1993a). They are an exceptionally successful example of adjusted privatization and entrepreneurial management in action. Performance and productivity at UH have improved dimensionally. As we approach the 2008 national elections, UH is completing its move to its new facilities at the former federal Fitzsimmons campus.   It is a role model for successful entrepreneurial management and public policy.

Local Entrepreneurial Adjustments

Johnston, Von Stroh, and Zaveri (1994) did some preliminary research on the implementation of various models of entrepreneurial management at the local level of government. Colorado cities were selected for review because this state passed Amendment 1, which was similar to California's precedent-setting Proposition 13 but was more restrictive in limiting tax increases to inflation and population increases. Three models were applied to determine whether entrepreneurial management was being utilized to optimize downsizing, performance, and productivity.

These models are applied analytically here to examine the adjustments made in response to Colorado's Amendment 1 in three Colorado cities: Boulder, Colorado Springs, and Westminster. The changes were primarily managerial and fiscal. It became apparent that they were impacting meaningfully the delivery of services to citizens and customers. They were changing the way the governed were represented and managed, and the way that government actually worked. Each of the primary analytical models— i.e., TQM, reinventing, and reengineering—were applied to the changes being carried out in the three cities designated for analysis, as shown in Table 1.

Table 1
TQM: Key Concepts

	Boulder	Westminster	Colorado Springs
1. Quality	+	+	+
2. Productivity	+	+	o
3. Customers	+	+	o
4. Empowerment	+	+	+
5. Top Management Support	+	+	o
6. Built-in Quality-Finding Defect	o	o	o
7. Constant Improvements	+	+	o
8. Train and Educate	+	+	+
9. Goals and Plans	+	+	o
10. Teams & Boards & Council	o	o	o
11. Communicate	+	+	+
12. Develop a Quality Culture	+	+	o
13. Employee Involvement	+	+	+
14. Performance Recognition	o	o	o
15. Document Quality	o	+	o

Note
Emphasis: + = Strong; o = Some; - = None.

The research analysis demonstrated that a quality culture was being emphasized with each of these organizations. Each city implemented quality differently, yet all were utilizing the concepts supporting enhanced organizational quality. They incorporated TQM into their organizational systems. The implementation of the TQM model no doubt was due to the financial pressures these three jurisdictions experienced. It also resulted, in part, from the managerial and leadership systems that were in existence before Amendment 1 was passed. There is a strong imperative to lower costs, while improving the quality and effectiveness of the service that is delivered.

The reinventing model was examined next. As applied in the research endeavor, the model was divided into two parts: the new paradigm, and the approaches. The results are presented in Table 2.

Table 2
Reinventing: The New Paradigm and Approaches

	Boulder	Westminster	Colorado Springs
Reinventing: The New Paradigm			
1. Decentralized	+	+	+
2. Flexible	+	+	+
3. Adaptive	o	o	+
4. Competitive	o	o	o
5. Learning	+	+	o
6. Customer-oriented	o	o	o
7. Creative	o	o	o
8. Lean	+	+	+
9. Streamlined	o	o	o
Reinventing: Approaches			
1. Contracting Out	o	o	o
2. Privatization	o	o	o
3. Public/Private Partnerships	o	o	o
4. Load Shedding	-	-	-
5. Alternative Service Delivery	-	-	o
6. Vouchers	-	-	-
7. Volunteers	-	-	o
8. Participatory Management	+	+	o
9. Empowerment	o	o	+
10. Total Quality Management	o	o	o

Note

Emphasis: + = Strong; o = Some; - = None.

This research demonstrates that there is meaningful implementation of and a genuine commitment to changing from the old administrative management paradigm of government to the new entrepreneurial one based on constant change and higher expectations in all three of our sample cities. Government units are implementing a new organizational paradigm. The adjustment in orientation is clearly observable. Not all of the approaches to reinventing organizations are employed by the sample cities. They are using a wide and increasing variety of entrepreneurial alternatives, however.

The Colorado research project also looked for evidence of implementation of the reengineering model, as shown in Table 3. It was believed that it could be helpful in creating efficiencies to provide for more control in managing budget problems.

Table 3
Reengineering

	Boulder	Westminster	Colorado Springs
1. Fit management needs/government purpose	+	+	+
2. Eliminating old/reengineer	o	o	o
3. Link engineer/organizations by information	-	-	-
4. Technology/change	+	+	o
5. Parallel processes not sequential	-	-	-
6. Emphasize empowerment/work teams	+	+	+
7. Project workers to be laid off	o	o	-
8. Clear and workable problem	o	o	o
9. Visionary leaders are an asset	+	+	+
10. Timing is critical	o	o	o
11. Retraining or early retirement	-	-	-
12. Reexamine and redetermine mission	o	o	+

Note
Emphasis: + = Strong; o = Some; - = None.

The research determined that the reengineering model was not being used as much as TQM or reinventing were in our sample cities. Reengineering has more private-sector precision. It is also oriented more to production-line processes than to the kinds of work typically done in the public sector. The underlying concepts of reengineering became part of the culture in these three local government organizations, however. The model was being tried more in the public sector, but its greatest success is likely to be realized in the private sector. Perhaps more with re-engineering than with TQM or reinventing, traditional public interest values and priorities can become endangered.

PUBLIC-SECTOR CAVEATS

As entrepreneurial management was rooted deeper into the soil of management and administration in the public sector, we needed to become increasingly aware of public values, rights, and governance concerns (Johnston, 1990). The demands for increased efficiency in both the public and private sectors have been met by implementing TQM, reinventing, reengineering, the virtual organization, privatization, and so on. Yet, by their entrepreneurial and efficiency orientations, these alternative managerial models often do not protect public-sector values such as sovereignty, equity, the public interest, legitimacy, due process, and accountability. Perhaps eventually we will develop contracting skills and a public-interest orientation that will enable us to perform more successfully in this realm. It will require vigilance, however, if we are optimally to include quality, productivity, efficiency, and an entrepreneurial orientation in our federal, state, and local government organizations in the 21st century.

Among those who caution us about the risks involved in incorporating more private-sector entrepreneurial management practices and models in the public sector are O'Brien (1989) and Palumbo and Maupin (1989). From their caveats, the following potential problems can be identified.

Skimming or creaming inordinate amounts of profit is always a concern. Fraud and corruption come up regularly, due to secret and proprietary interests that public-sector management has yet to find ways to optimize. Because of the extended nature of contracting-out, or total privatization, control over quality of services becomes more difficult. This often leads to less accountability to citizens as well.

There usually are political considerations that must be dealt with when seriously emphasizing privatization. If care is not taken, there could be service interruptions due to profit declines or labor strikes. There must be enough scale or size in the market, for instance, to have enough competitive bidders so competition for contracts will drive down the cost to the consumers, citizens, and customers. Sovereignty issues must always be guarded because they add complexity that requires public-sector contractors to develop skills in order to be able to protect citizens' rights and interests. There also is the loss of capital investments concern. A typical case here would be that of the sports team abandoning a stadium or arena for a new facility before the existing publicly-financed one is paid off.

There are those over the years who have cautioned us about losing touch with a public-sector value base. Organizations, policymakers, and administrators should be consciously sensitive to whether such guidelines, policy orientations, and managerial skills are given appropriate priority.

Nagel is one of those who has offered a set of public management priorities. He writes about needing both efficiency (cost per unit) and effectiveness. Effectiveness is defined as dealing with the issue of how well private versus public management achieves the delivery of the public service being considered. Public participation is something we expect public organizations, not private ones, to provide. Predictable rules and procedural due process are public management priorities that we typically get from agencies with constitutional duties rather than from private companies. Equity represents the question of providing a safety net for those in need but not able to compete adequately in a market-based distribution of services. The public management priorities, according to Nagel (1989), also should include political feasibility from both conservative and liberal perspectives. Interests and programs supported by both are likely to be more successful.

Among those issuing caveats regarding the adoption of strong entrepreneurial management practices is Ron Moe (1994). He points out that government's traditional administrative management paradigm is based on laws passed by the congressional representatives of the people. The president has the constitutional responsibility to implement these laws. He also notes that, as Osborne and Gaebler set forth their reinventing model, this traditional administrative management model is identified as bureaucratic government. In order to adopt the more entrepreneurial reinventing model urged by the NPR, there must be a cultural and behavioral shift. In such a transition, accountability, legitimacy, and due process can be lost as customer satisfaction and economically based values supplant political and legally based values. We also find a certain amount of increasing complexity and confusion as the sectors become more blended and blurred.

The National Performance Review cited four bedrock principles of entrepreneurial management for the executive branch. (1) Red tape is removed by effective, entrepreneurial governments. Systems become accountable for achieving results rather than following rules. (2) Customer satisfaction comes next. Organizations develop focus groups and use surveys so they can listen to their customers. (3) Empowerment follows, and authority is decentralized as the culture is transformed. (4) Finally, entrepreneurial governments find ways to work better and cost less. They even reengineer how they do work. They reexamine all their processes and programs (Gore, 1993).

From these bedrock principles, Moe (1994) argued that customer satisfaction replaces political accountability for the delivery of services to the citizens. The action terms become empowering, reinventing, and reengineering. There is a reduction of the managerial role of the president. This leads to a shift from accountability to the president, to accountability to the customer.

Moe (1994) argued that the Gore report represented a genuine attack on the administrative management paradigm, which was based on the President as Chief Manager. Public law is the foundation of the traditional paradigm. Congress begins to be viewed more as a nuisance, and agency managers need to become more entrepreneurial. Congressional concerns become afterthoughts in the new mission-oriented system.

The management of the citizen's organizations, then, can be seen as being quite different than the profit-producing model being adapted from the private sector. In an attempt to highlight such differences, Charles Goodsell (1993) developed what he calls "Goodsell's Ten Principles of Rediscovering Government," shown in Figure 10. He was not bashful about sounding an alarm that citizens could become seriously disadvantaged as customers become more valued.

As midlevel managers increasingly disappear from the new entrepreneurial management systems, contractors and consultants gain enhanced position and leverage as they assume greater managerial control in the new entrepreneurial paradigm. Unpleasant and unprofitable activities could be neglected seriously as traditional lines of authority and accountability dissolve. The entrepreneurs focus on capturing the spoils. Who, under the reinventing model, is guarding the citizen's governance concerns?

Figure 10
Goodsell's Ten Principles of Rediscovering Government

1. Through their elected representatives, the people are in charge of American governance, not the entrepreneurs.
2. Government is intended to serve the public interest, not create unspent reserves or feed entrepreneurial egos.
3. Government must operate according to the Constitution and laws of the land, not niche mission statements.
4. Government can enter into partnerships with private entities as long as it is the senior partner.
5. Government should be flexible and innovative, but also publicly accountable.
6. Performance results must be demanded in government, but there must also be respect for the public employees who make them happen.
7. In government, private managerial conduct must comply to such nonprivate ideals as equal opportunity and open scrutiny.
8. Simplification of rules is fine, but no dilution of the principles of comparable treatment and due process.
9. Reduction of fiscal constraints is acceptable, but not a lessening of requirements for stewardship over the public's money.
10. Public problems should be dealt with creatively, but not so as to give away the store to those who will benefit.

ENDANGERED GOVERNANCE PRIORITIES

Among the governance priorities that increasingly need to be given attention as the entrepreneurial management model unfolds are the following developed by Johnston, as shown in Figure 11. These values and priorities are becoming increasingly endangered.

Figure 11
Endangered Public Organization Governance Priorities

1. Sovereignty
2. Legitimacy
3. The Public Interest
4. Due Process
5. Authority and Responsibility Linkages
6. Equity
7. Participation
8. Accountability
9. Governance Priorities
10. Constitutional Guarantees
11. Legal Rights
12. Stewardship

In order to give these increasingly endangered governance priorities the emphasis needed, as the entrepreneurial management model becomes more predominant, those responsible for developing strategy and policy will have to become more diligent in translating these values into managerial practices. Although the state of the field of strategic management is in some disarray (Mintzberg, 1994), it still is incumbent upon those steering us in a more entrepreneurial direction to plan and strategize for optimal levels of both efficiency and effectiveness. As the Entrepreneurial Management Productivity Optimization Model (Figure 12) suggests, optimizing efficiency and effectiveness for "your" organization really involves matching appropriate contributions from the various management strategy and planning model alternatives (arrayed across the top) to the values and conditions you must deal with (arrayed at the left side of the model) (Johnston, 1995b). The model assists managerial and policy level decision makers to be more disciplined and sensitive in designing or redesigning their own organizations when optimizing performance and productivity.

As privatization and entrepreneurial management unfold and manifest themselves in programs, contracts, and administration at different levels of government, policymakers, strategists, and managers will need to utilize all of their skills and resources. By doing so diligently, we will be able to ensure more optimally that we are guarding our increasingly endangered governance priorities, as well as delivering services to our citizens/customers as efficiently and effectively as possible (Johnston, 1995a). The world of the 21st century in America is clearly that of entrepreneurial management. The governance priorities noted in Figure 11 are of the center of the debates leading up to the 2008 national elections.

Figure 12
Entrepreneurial Management Productivity Optimization Model

Model Contributions / Values and conditions	Optimizing Efficiency + Effectiveness = Productivity: Management Strategy & Planning Model Alternatives						
	TQM	Reengineering Organizations	Reinventing Government	Rediscovering Government	The Virtual Organization	Privatization	"Your" Organization
Efficiency							
Effectiveness							
Productivity							
Quality							
Performance							
Competitiveness							
Employment							
Full vs. Part-time Jobs							
Medical Benefits							
Pensions							
Vacations							
Stress & Related Illness & Organizational Dysfunctions							
Bias for Age/Other Discrimination							
Multi-Iterative Careers							
Economic Adjustments							
Market Niches, Goals							
Political Realities & Change							
Industrial Transformation							
Business Growth/Decline							
Government Fiscal Viability							
The Public Interest							
Privatization Efforts							

REFERENCES

Byrne, J. (1993, February). The futurists who father ideas. *Business Week*, p. 103.

Byrne, J., Brandt, R., & Post, O. (1993, February). *Business Week*, pp. 98–102.

Crosby, P. (1984). *Quality without tears*. New York, NY: McGraw Hill.

Davidson, W., & Malone, M. (1992). *The virtual corporation*. New York, NY: HarperCollins.

Donahue, J. (1989). *The privatization decision: Public ends, private means*. New York, NY: Basic Books.

Ehrbar, A. (1993, March 16). Re-engineering gives firms new efficiency, workers the pink slip: One company after another redesigns tasks to curb its need for employment. *The Wall Street Journal*, pp. A1, A11.

Elling, R. (1994). The line in winter: An academic assessment of the first report of the national commission on state and local public service. *Public Administration Review, 54*(2), 107–108.

Fierman, J. (1994). The contingency workforce. *Fortune, 129*(2), 30–36.

Garvin, D. (1991). How the Baldrige award really works. *Harvard Business Review, 69*(6), 80–95.

Goodsell, C. T. (1993). Reinvent government or rediscover it. *Public Administration Review, 53*(1), 85–87.

Gore, A., Jr. (1993). *From red tape to results: Creating a government that works better and costs less*. Washington, DC: United States Government Printing Office.

Gore, A., Jr. (1994). The new job of the federal executive. *Public Administration Review, 54*(4), 317–321.

Gregory, W. H. (1994, April). Buyers beware—As the rules of federal procurement change, acquisition managers must learn a lesson from the private sector: Time is money. *Government Executive*, pp. 32–39.

Halachmi, A. (1994). The challenge of a competitive sector. In A. Halachmi & G. Bouckaert (Eds.), *The enduring challenges in public management: Surviving and excelling in a changing world* (pp. 220–246). San Francisco, CA: Josey Bass.

Halachmi, A., & Boydston, R. (1994). The political economy of outsourcing. In A. Kahn & B. Hildroth (Eds.), *Public Budgeting and Financial Management* (pp. 3–13). Dubuque, IA: Kendall Hunt Publishing.

Johnston, V. R. (1990). Privatization of prisons: Management, productivity and governance concerns. *Public Productivity and Management Review, 14*(2), 189–201.

Johnston, V. R. (1993a). *Entrepreneurial government: Privatization's contributions towards reinventing partnerships for progress*. San Francisco, CA: National American Society for Public Administration.

Johnston, V. R. (1993b). *Privatization lessons from hospital and prison experiences*. Maui, HI: Western Regional Science Association.

Johnston, V. R. (1995a). Caveat emptor: Customers vs. citizens. *The Public Manager— The New Bureaucrat, 24*(3), 11–14.

Johnston, V. R. (1995b). Increasing quality and productivity: Strategic planning, TQM, and beyond. In A. Halachmi & G. Bouckaert (Eds.), *Public productivity through quality and strategic management* (pp. 83–97). Washington, DC: IOS Press.

Johnston, V. R. (1999). Privatization lessons for hospitals and prisons. In P. Seidenstat (Ed.), *Privatizing state and local government services* (pp. 128–148). Westport, CT: Praeger.

Johnston, V.R. (2002). Competition, Conflict, and Entrepreneurial Public Managers: The Legacy of Reinventing Government. *Public Administration Quarterly. 26*(1), 9-34.

Johnston, V. R., & D'Amico, R. J. (1992). *Total quality management and the reorganization of the air force.* Chicago, IL: National American Society for Public Administration.

Johnston, V. R., & D'Amico, R. J. (1993). Integrating innovative entrepreneurship, optimal privatization, and total quality management into our defense acquisition system. In *Acquisition for the future: Imagination, innovation and implementation* (pp. 327–339). Washington, DC: Defense Systems Management College and National Contract Management Association.

Johnston, V.R., Von Stroh, G., and Zaveri, R. (1994). *Downsizing, performance and Productivity.* San Francisco, CA: Western Governmental Research Association

Johnston, V.R., Haynes, W., and Schulz, C.L. (Summer, 2006). The T-REX Megaproject: Denver's Showcase for Innovation and Creativity. *The Public Manager, 35*(2), 3-8.

Johnston, V.R., and Seidenstat, P. (2007). Contracting Out Government Services: Privatization at the Millennium. *International Journal of Public Policy. 30*(5), 231-247.

Juran, J. (1988). *Juran on planning for quality.* New York, NY: Collier Macmillan.

Kuhn, T. S. (1970). *The structure of scientific revolutions.* Chicago, IL: University of Chicago Press.

Linowes, D. F. (1988). *Privatization: Toward more effective government.* Washington, DC: United States Government Printing Office.

Martin, J. (1993). The impulse to reengineer. *Governing, 6*(6) 26–30.

Mintzberg, H. (1994). *The rise and fall of strategic planning.* New York, NY: Free Press.

Moe, R. C. (1994). The reinventing government exercise: Misinterpreting the problem, misjudging the consequences. *Public Administration Review, 54*(2), 111–122.

Nagel, S. (1989). *Higher goals for America.* Lanham, MD: University Press of America.

O'Brien, T. M. (1989). *Privatization in Colorado state government.* Denver: Colorado Office of the State Auditor.

Osborne, D., & Gaebler, T. (1992). *Reinventing government: How the entrepreneurial spirit is transforming the public sector.* New York, NY: Addison Wesley.

Palumbo, D. J. (1986). Privatization and corrections policy. *Policy Studies Review, 5*(3), 598–605.

Palumbo, D. J., & Maupin, J. (1989). The political side of privatization. *Journal of Management Science and Policy Analysis, 6*(2), 25–40.

President's Council on Management Improvement. (1991). *Federal total quality management.* Washington, DC: United States Government Printing Office.

Public Law 103-62. (1993, August 3). *Government performance and results act of 1993.*

Savas, E. (1993). Privatization in post-socialist countries. *Public Administration Review, 52*(6), 573–581.

Smith, L. (1994). Burned-out bosses. *Fortune, 130*(2), 44–55.

Walsh, B. (1994, January). National performance review—procurement team studies ways to reinvent federal acquisition. *Contract Management*, pp. 19–23.

Walton, M. (1990). *Deming management at work*. New York, NY: Putnam.

Chapter 2

PRIVATIZATION: TRENDS, INTERPLAY OF FORCES, AND LESSONS LEARNED

Paul Seidenstat

The privatization of government services, especially by utilizing the contracting-out mode, has accelerated in recent years in the United States, particularly at the state and local level. Shifts in the relative strength of forces in a political coalition model underlay the trend. There have been several benefits of privatization, especially cost containment and quality enhancement. The recent history of privatization provides a number of lessons to guide future privatization policy.

Over the last few decades, the abandonment of the communist system with its basic ideas of central planning and government production was reflective of a worldwide trend of less dependence on government and more reliance on the private sector of the economy. The application of this trend in the United States was a lot less dramatic, since, although government has become an increasingly powerful force in attempting to affect the distribution of income through transfer payments, this country had relied upon government production to a relatively modest degree compared to many other countries. The major thrust of our privatization efforts was in the accelerated movement to privatize operations at the state and local levels.

The growing recognition of the limitations of government production was undeniable. In speaking of the largest domestic nondefense government operation, Albert Shanker, President of the American Federation of Teachers, observed, "It is time to admit that public education operates like a planned economy, a bureaucratic system in which everybody's role is spelled out in advance and there are few incentives for innovation and productivity. It's no surprise that the school system doesn't improve: It more resembles the communist economy than our own market economy" (*Wall Street Journal*, 1989, p. 21).

Privatization—the transfer of ownership, control, or operation of an enterprise or function from the government/public sector to the private sector—is not a particularly new concept in the United States. Governments have long used the private sector. However, the use of private operators was very restricted. Private producers were used for only a few in-house activities and for a very limited number of direct services. The word "privatization" did not make the dictionary until the early 1980s.

Even as recently as 1980, the use of the private sector by governments was modest. In the last few decades, the range and depth of privatization efforts were enlarged substantially. Privatization became much more widespread. The extent of the effort differed by level of government, type of service, and the category of privatization. Surveys of states, counties, and cities show a significant movement towards use of the privatization option (Boycko, Shleifer, & Vishny, 1996; Chi, 1993; Council of State Governments, 1993; Eggers, 1995). After classifying the range of privatization options, this chapter will develop a model of privatization that will contribute to explaining the privatization trend. Using the model and the record of our experience, the chapter will identify some lessons that have been learned.

CLASSIFICATION OF PRIVATIZATION OPTIONS

A fundamental distinction can be made concerning the government's role in rendering services to its citizens. Government can make provision for output, and also can produce the output. Making provision basically involves financing the output, but does not necessarily require actual production. Road construction is an example of this distinction. The government can pay to have a road built and maintained (make provision), but it has a choice as to construction and maintenance (e.g., produce in-house, or hire a private contractor).

Table 1 shows a classification system for privatization options.

Table 1
Privatization Options

Who Produces	Who Makes Provision	
	Private Firm	Government Agency
	Options	
Private Firm	Load Shed	Contract Out
	Franchise	Vouchers
		Subsidies
Government Agency	Contract In	No Privatization

The most extreme form of privatization occurs when the government simply disassociates itself from providing the service and turns its financing and production entirely over to the private sector—i.e., load shedding—or simply allows the service to disappear. The government can sell an existing facility to a private bidder, who then would operate it strictly as a private business, or a direct service such as trash collection and disposal can be turned over to private vendors.

A modified form of load shedding involves franchising—i.e., a special privilege granted to a private operator. There are at least two variants of franchising: build-transfer-operate (BTO), and build-operate-transfer (BOT). In the BTO case, the government agency can utilize a turnkey model, in which the private operator designs, constructs, and transfers ownership to the government, but operates the facility. This model has been used in waste water treatment. BOT is a more complete form of privatization, since the private sector may continue to own the facility, often subject to government regulation, on a long-term basis, with transfer of ownership to the public sector after a period of years. This model has been used for toll roads, solid waste facilities, and water systems (Lick, 1995). Many of these arrangements involve a public/private partnership.

The most market-oriented mode of privatization, in which the public sector continues to make provision (i.e., pays), is the use of vouchers or subsidies. In the voucher form of this mode, the public sector provides a voucher to the user of the service which the user can use to pay the private producer's bill. If there are competing suppliers, the user is afforded choice. At the federal level, food stamps, Medicare, and housing vouchers typify this option. At the state and local levels, Medicaid, mental health, job training, and other social services can employ vouchers.

The subsidy arrangement does not afford the same degree of choice to the user as vouchers offer. Usually, the public sector restricts itself to a financing role. Government subsidies have been given to universities, hospitals, other health-related facilities, art museums, and other organizations that offer cultural services, and to a wide variety of community service organizations. For the citizen to partake of the publicly funded service in the subsidy case, he or she would have to use the subsidized private supplier, often rendering its services in a monopolized or highly concentrated market situation.

Rather than employing some form of load shedding, most governments have preferred contracting out as the method to shift operations to the private sector. In this model, the government entity retains ownership and overall control, but employs the private vendor to render the actual service. Except for activities involving infrastructure or voucher/subsidy systems, contracting out is the way that practically all privatization now is being implemented. Everything from government in-house support services to direct taxpayer services falls under the contracting-out umbrella. In rare instances, this process may work in reverse (contracting-in), as a private-sector provider hires a government producer, such as the case of an entertainment company hiring police.

A PRIVATIZATION MODEL

What happened in the United States in the 1980s and 1990s to push the public sector to accelerate the shift towards the private sector? The answer to that question requires an understanding of the theory and dynamics of the privatization process. A struggle developed between forces supporting change and those resisting change. Table 2 lists the forces supporting privatization, and those that favor the status quo.

Table 2
Contending Groups Involved in the Privatization Process

Supporters of Privatization	Defenders of Government
Private-sector owners	Elected officials
Private-sector managers	Public managers
Private-sector workers	Public workers/unions
Prospective private vendors	Present private vendors
Taxpayers	Service recipients
Antigovernment ideologues	Pro-government ideologues

Of course, these groups can be classified as the "haves" (those benefiting by government operations), and the "have-nots" (those who potentially would benefit from privatization). The two sets of groups are contending for the right to participate in the production process or to receive the benefits of the output. However, the basis of vigorous contention among these groups is rooted in monopoly theory.

The vast majority of government services are provided by a public-sector operator who is the sole producer. Like all monopolies, a typical government producer can generate monopoly rents, while a competitive market would not allow more than minimal returns to resource owners. The battle over these monopoly rents from government operations is at the core of the privatization struggle.

Elected officials can offer benefits to government stakeholders, and those stakeholders can reciprocate by supplying votes for incumbent or for aspiring officeholders. Since most public services are financed by taxes, and not user charges, the elected official has considerable discretion in the use of tax dollars, involving such decisions as what services to provide, the quantity and quality of those services, wage rates, staffing levels, work rules, input prices, input suppliers, etc. Public stakeholders can receive substantial benefits from the status quo.

The near-monopoly of the public school illustrates the benefit flow. A school system can provide benefits to input suppliers like school administrators, school teachers, and book publishers, and other nonlabor input providers in the form of above-market labor compensation and input prices. Teacher unions are strengthened in a monopoly-monopsony market structure. Parents of special student populations (e.g., mentally retarded, physically handicapped) can receive expanded (and very expensive) services. Particular firms can be granted lucrative contracts to construct school buildings or to make major repairs. Legislators and/or school board members who appropriate the funds and determine the level and mix of services can count on a significant number of votes from these beneficiaries.

The private-sector counterparts of the resource owners benefiting from public-sector operations can visualize the benefits to them from privatization. Taxpayers can benefit if privatization reduces the quantity of public services, or produces the present quantity and quality of services in a more cost-effective way.

Ideologues on both sides of the privatization issue see intangible benefits or costs of privatization. The pro-public sector advocates often see the government as a more humane and understanding provider, whereas pro-private proponents see a large public sector as a threat to a democratic eco-political system.

Changes in the socioeconomic environment can strengthen some groups and weaken the power of other groups. The pre-1980 equilibrium found groups favoring the status quo in a dominant position. However, the environment began to change in the 1980s, and through the 1990s, and into the 21st century, strengthening the forces favoring privatization.

The fiscal position of the public sector began to weaken, and there were changes in the political climate that required a public review of the size and role of government. A number of factors energized the effort to restrain the growth of government expenditures and to force governments to become more cost-effective in their operations. These factors included: the serious recession of the early 1980s, the growing concern about the federal government's budget deficit, the weakening of the economies of some large states including California and the Midwest "rust belt" states, and the continuing long-term fiscal crisis in many large cities. As a consequence of these changes, there was a stirring among voters at the state level to quash proposed tax increases, to restrain the growth of tax revenue (e.g., Proposition 13 in California, Pro-position 2.5 in Massachusetts, and Amendment 1 in Colorado), and to limit government spending.

Overall, the political environment was growing more hostile to the expansion of government budgets and to the increases in tax rates. The growing power of this message was reflected in the elections of Ronald Reagan in 1980 and 1984, and of George Bush in 1988, and was reinforced by the victory of advocates of smaller government to the Congress in 1994, accompanied by the decade-long political success of many like-minded candidates in governorships and state legislatures. The voters then elected a fiscal conservative in Bill Clinton in 1992 and 1996, and maintained their conservative fiscal orientation by electing George W. Bush in 2000 and 2004.

The coalition of stakeholders of government, who were the chief beneficiaries and supporters of a growing government, found their position to be weakened by fiscal pressures. The growing pressure on elected officials to cut budget growth—or even downsize government—forced consideration of methods to restrain government spending without substantial reduction in services. Once the government agenda focused on this issue of restructuring, or rightsizing, then privatization became a major policy option as part of a restructuring program. The political clout of the coalition supporting an expanding public sector now was challenged by another coalition that stressed lower taxes and privatization. The political weakening of the pro-government coalition was substantial in some cases (such as in trash collection or street repairing), but was not as weighty in others (e.g., education and corrections). In those states and cities where the fiscal pressures were the greatest, and the weakening of the power of the major monopoly rent recipients was the most pronounced, major privatization efforts were initiated.

OBSERVATIONS AND LESSONS LEARNED

Based upon the model of competing forces and the recent record of privatization efforts, some preliminary observations can be made; or, lessons learned. We shall review the objectives of privatization, examine the conditions essential for success, investigate preliminary results of privatized operations, and deduce some basic principles concerning designing and implementing privatization systems, while pointing to some basic lessons learned.

Objectives of Privatization

Privatization has been utilized as a management tool, a method of financing capital improvements, and a technique to realign the public/private-sector mix. The managerial objectives include cutting costs, improving the quality of services produced, or both. Most frequently, the primary aim has been to cut costs, to relieve budgetary pressures, especially since assessing the quality of output of many government services can be a complex and time-consuming activity. Privatizing also was aimed at increasing the flexibility of government operations, such that expansion, contraction, or complete elimination of specific services could be accomplished with fewer obstacles and with greater speed.

In the area of infrastructure, and in the acquisition of expensive capital equipment, privatization was aimed at relieving the government of the necessity of funding capital investment for new assets. Indeed, the sale of public enterprises to the private sector also could offer a significant revenue source.

Although the major thrust toward privatization in the United States seems to be motivated by practical managerial considerations, still the movement toward the greater use of the private sector taps into the philosophical point of view of less government, or at least a reduced role for government as a producer in a market system.

Conditions Required for Success

To achieve the objectives set forth in a privatization initiative, certain environmental factors must be present. These factors include political support, managerial/political leadership, and a supportive private market structure. Overcoming the bias towards the status quo protected by the stakeholders who receive monopoly rents is essential. A strong case must be made for change; the case must speak to the benefits to be received with a provision/production arrangement, in comparison to the costs that may have to be incurred. Legislative and voter support offers the opportunity to move in the privatization direction and to allow the new structure a fair chance to demonstrate its advantages.

The full support of political leaders, especially in the executive branch, greatly enhances the chances of success. Not only is this support required for approval of change, but enthusiastic and careful backing of the effort often is compelled to sustain it. Well-prepared and ardent political leaders often are needed to overcome the inertia of the status quo.

To achieve the required objectives usually requires more than political support and strong leadership. To achieve the maximum benefits of privatization, the private sector should be structured such that alternative suppliers exist to compete in providing the service in the case of load shedding, can compete for contracts in the case of contracting out or franchising, or can supply services in the case of vouchers. Without competition, privatization might consist simply of a private monopoly substituting for a government monopoly. (For a broader discussion, see Hakim, Seidenstat, & Bowman, 1996.)

Results: Cost Containment

The primary aim of privatization in most cases was to reduce operating costs without sacrificing the quality of the service. It follows from the monopoly model that a movement to a more competitive market would lead to more efficient operations and lower costs of production. In the vast majority of cases, the results appear to support this prediction. As one of the chief researchers of privatization has put it, "Savings from competitive contracting of public services—the most thoroughly studied form of privatization—average roughly 25 to 30 percent" (Savas, 1995, p. 16).

An array of studies supports the contention that privatization generally leads to lower costs. A study by Los Angeles County, California, covering 1979–1989, showed that the 812 contracts awarded to private suppliers for various support services saved the county $193 million, a 28% savings over the estimated original in-house costs (Goodman, 1990). The United States General Accounting Office (GAO) examined 1,661 cost-comparison studies conducted between 1978 and 1986 involving 25 major types of commercial functions performed by the United States Department of Defense, comparing the government's costs to the outside contractor's winning bid. The GAO found that the original government cost was 37% higher than the winning private-sector bid (United States General Accounting Office, 1988).

Additional supporting evidence for the lower cost hypothesis comes from examining randomly selected cases of local government privatization. These sample cases showed that government in-house costs, on average, were one-third more than the competitive bid from outside contractors (Savas, 1987). The Reason Foundation reported that mayors in major cities that engaged in privatization activities confirmed significant savings in contracting or franchising city services. Stephen Goldsmith, Mayor of Indianapolis, who had introduced competition into 50 city services, reported savings of $28 million annually. Mayor Edward Rendell, of Philadelphia, privatized 19 services since 1992, with annual savings of $21.5 million. Mayor Rendell's office estimated that costs were reduced 40% to 50%. Mayor Richard Daley, of Chicago, privatized 35 services, with significant savings (Eggers, 1995).

Franchising efforts frequently led to reduced capital and operating costs. In a notable example, Mt. Vernon, Illinois, was required by federal authorities to design, construct, and put into operation quickly an upgraded and expanded waste water treatment plant. A private contractor completed the project well before deadline and saved the city $3 million, or 32% (United States Environmental Protection Agency, 1989).

Significant cost savings in privatizing solid waste collection were found in the Canadian experience. The examination of data from British Columbia, where extensive privatization was undertaken, revealed that private producers were more efficient than public producers (McDavid, 1985; McDavid & Schick, 1987). An update of these studies showed that the costs of private-firm, compared to municipal, producers were 20% lower per household, and 28% lower per ton of solid waste collected (Adie, McDavid, & Clemens, in press).

Privatizing bus systems generated significant costs savings. Overall, the savings ranged from 10% to 50% (Hakim, Seidenstat, & Bowman, 1996). Preliminary evidence also suggests that prison privatization leads to modest cost savings. One study concluded that the private operator saved government in the range of 4% to 15% (Logan & McGriff, 1989).

Results: Quality Enhancement

Although cost restraint or reduction (without compromising quality) is a major objective of privatization, and although the record suggests impressive results, achieving high quality is an important objective in producing some services. These services often are classified as "soft services," since they are involved with helping consumers (or "clients") directly. Such services can include education, job training, drug rehabilitation, prisoner services, etc. Assessing the performance of these services is very difficult, since defining and measuring "output" is an imprecise art.

Although the privatization model suggests that the private producer would be more likely to produce a better quality output than its public-sector counterpart, the evidence of performance in the "soft services" is not clear-cut, since output is difficult to measure. In the few documented studies, the quality of service either was improved or not significantly different than when produced publicly. The Urban Institute's comparison of private and public correctional institutions in Kentucky and Massachusetts found, in applying various measures of quality, that the private institutions had a small edge (Hatry, Brounstein, & Levinson, 1993). In the operation of airports, transit systems, and ports, the private sector often improves the level of service (Hakim, Seidenstat, &

Bowman, 1996). Since school privatization ventures have started up more recently, little definitive analysis is available to make a careful judgment.

In the social service area, where nonprofit suppliers are relied upon to produce most of the contracted-for services, the performance record appears to be slightly better or the same as the public sector's record. In a study of employee assistance programs, employees gave high marks for greater accessibility, a higher degree of confidentiality, more expertise, and greater choice of referrals. At the same time, public managers preferred in-house operations, and staff personnel were ambivalent (Straussner, 1988). A study of day care programs showed no difference in quality between public and private production (Mulka, 1990).

Bases for Improved Performance

Why can private operators produce with lower costs at a given level of service, or higher quality at the same cost, or both lower cost and higher quality? The answer seems to lie in the superior performance potential of competitive markets driven by the profit motive. Most government service producers, as monopolists, may not be very sensitive to user demand. Moreover, the political process may insulate the government producer from the consequences of its poor performance and encourage the establishment of monopsony arrangements with input suppliers that result in inflexible union and/or civil service rules, elevated wage rates, and higher prices for vendor supplies and services.

Managers can have the same isolation from market forces. Except for the very top level, manager civil service protection may dull incentives for managers to innovate and improve the product in the public sector. On the other hand, managers for private producers can be induced to overcome the owner/agent tension by incorporating profit-based compensation arrangements.

Privatization in a competitive market framework will drive unit cost to the minimum level. One way the private producer accomplishes cost minimization is by limiting labor costs in such ways as using more part-time and lower-skilled workers, paying for less time off (vacation time and paid absences), using less overtime, establishing clearer job definitions and greater worker accountability, and having more workers per supervisor. Other input costs can be reduced by holding first-line managers more responsible for equipment maintenance and giving them more authority to hire and fire, shifting toward a higher capital-to-labor ratio, and utilizing more effective purchasing methods.

Relating manager pay to profitability can lead to more emphasis on innovative ways to produce, by incorporating new technology, dispensing with "red tape," and making timely decisions. On the other hand, in a private organization, removing poorly performing managers typically can be accomplished with greater speed and with less disruption than in the public sector.

Lessons Learned

After a few decades of extensive use of privatization in the United States, some preliminary observations can be made about what steps or techniques work, and what environmental elements are important. A general consensus seems to revolve around the following points:

1. Strong public support is essential for the move to a privatized operation and its successful implementation.

To gain this support typically requires enthusiastic backing by the government's chief executive, the public management group, and legislative leaders. Forceful promotion of the effort is especially important when the pro-status quo coalition of stakeholders is large and effective, and/or when the privatization move represents a major departure from past practice (e.g., privatizing secure prisons, contracting out the management of public schools, or building a private toll road).

2. Politically, privatization efforts are most likely to proceed in an *ad hoc*, piecemeal, opportunistic fashion (Windsor, 1995).

In the pragmatic American environment, rapid, comprehensive, wholesale efforts to privatize are not likely to be embraced by elected officials or by masses of voters. Where substantial benefits in the form of cost containment or improved services seem clear, where the pro-government stakeholders are not powerful politically or strongly entrenched, or where a major crisis erupts concerning uncontrolled costs or woeful service performance, opportunities will arise for privatization. The confluence of opportunity and a skilled political leadership eager for change can tilt the scale towards the new organizational arrangement.

3. To make better-informed judgments regarding the feasibility of privatization, an accurate costing system should be developed.

Besides whipping up political support, the government executive can establish some benchmarks. The major items to be benchmarked are the present cost of service and the quality of output. Output must be distinguished and measured clearly. All costs, direct and indirect, then are identified and linked to output. This accounting technique usually is called "activity-based costing" (Eggers, 1994, pp. 6–8). As a "before-and-after" measure of the performance of privatization, or as the basis for making a "buy-or-make" decision, accurate cost measurement allows for a more meaningful public/private comparison.

4. Any privatization initiative is more likely to attain its objectives if workable competition exists on the supply side of the market.

As mentioned above, the existence of competition is an important environmental factor favoring a successful privatization effort. Careful selection of the service to privatize and the mode and technique of privatization can increase the chances of success. Choosing service sectors where multiple producers, competitive bidding, multivendor contracts, and public/private competition are feasible are ways to ensure or enhance competition.

For example, in contracting out refuse collection, the local government could divide the city into several districts and award multiple contracts. The next time contracts were bid, the city then would have a better feel for minimum average cost. Beyond the stage of utilizing multiple private contractors, the city could reserve a district for city operations, and the city department then could bid for other districts in the rebidding process. Indianapolis and Phoenix, among other cities, have made effective use of city/private competition.

5. Privatization's impact on public employees can be mitigated. Treating potentially displaced workers with consideration and compassion can reduce opposition, especially from unions, to change.

A range of options is open to public officials to assist displaced public employees. Finding employment with the private contractor might be achieved by requiring or recommending the hiring of displaced workers or by encouraging those workers to form their own company for the purposes of bidding for work. The government itself can attempt to find positions for the displaced by transfer to other jobs, including a possible freeze on new hiring until that is accomplished. At the least, a generous severance or early retirement package may be offered. To garner worker support further, bonuses might be paid to the public labor force out of the savings from privatization.

6. Certain functional areas of government operations lend themselves more readily to privatization than to other areas. Generally, the activities that are most feasible both politically and economically are those that have the inherent characteristics of private goods. Pure public goods' production is better left to the government producer.

Among the private-type business-oriented services are state gaming, trash collection and disposal, lottery operations, airports, public transit, auditing, tax collection, toll roads, wastewater plants, water and gas utilities, ports, waste-to-energy plants, and college dormitories. These services fit into the business profile: potential profitmaking, financed by user charges, and devoid of significant external effects. These services also are the easiest to load shed.

7. Infrastructure projects require special consideration, owing to the size of the private investment required and the duration of a typical contract.

One key rule is to allow the private sector maximum discretion in project selection. Another important rule is to select projects of modest size in the early stage of a public/private partnership (Williams, 1996). It is a lot easier to generate support for projects that develop new capacity, rather than to repair or maintain existing capacity.

The private sector is more sensitive to business opportunities and focuses upon profitability criteria that usually are neglected by public authorities. "In the case of California's toll road program, three of the four projects selected by the private sector were not part of even the state's long range plans for transportation facilities" (Williams, 1996, p. 253).

In the beginning of a big-ticket, extensive construction project involving a public/private partnership, it is useful to minimize risks to both parties by starting small. Thus, it may be desirable to break up a large project into several phases. Additionally, voters are more willing to accept a user charge financing system for new infrastructure, rather than to pay for the use of existing capacity being rehabilitated for which they feel that their taxes already have financed.

8. Several cautions must be exercised when privatizing, particularly in contracting out, which is the predominant mode of privatization.

Where there is little competition in the private sector prior to privatization, a viable bidding process may not take place, such that the savings anticipated or the quality improvement desired may not develop; private monopoly simply may replace public monopoly. Even where there is competition and bidding is spirited, the contract must be drafted carefully and monitored. Especially in service categories where output is ill-defined and relevant costs are hard to measure, vague contracts may lead to less than optimal results and enforcement may not be practiced effectively. Also, a reasonable contract period may be required for the vendor to demonstrate results, especially for social services, where desirable outcomes may take years to achieve. During the length of this long contract, the government may not be able to rebid if performance is marginal.

Undesirable outcomes also could occur during the contract period or at the time of rebidding. The private supplier may not perform according to the contract, owing to strikes, other work stoppages, and business cessation or bankruptcy. The contracting government agency must be prepared to be able to find an alternative supplier or to resume operations itself. Where large capital investments in plant and equipment are necessary for operations, the government must be wary of disinvesting itself of backup equipment or standby private sources of capital, in case it has to resume operations.

Maintaining operations is a particularly vital issue when infrastructure is involved. Even when complete load shedding is involved, the public sector must have contingency plans to take over essential services such as waste water treatment, airport operations, and water treatment.

In monitoring, and at the rebidding phase, there also is a danger that the provider and beneficiary coalition may co-opt public decision makers. The experience of contracting out social services in Michigan illustrates the problem. In quick order, the evaluation of services and the interpretation of the "needs" of client beneficiaries became influenced heavily by providers. "For their part, self-interested bureaucrats and legislators cannot fail to see the opportunities for developing mutually beneficial relationships with contractors" (DeHoog, 1984, p. 247).

Reliance on bidder competition and aggressive public watchdog activities is essential to avoid the undue influence of suppliers on the contracting process. "Sweetheart" contracts, guaranteed contract renewal, and collusion among bidders always are a threat to undermine the potential advantages of privatization.

9. The use of voucher systems can maximize the net social benefits of privatization. Vouchers are particularly effective in the production of social and human services.

Where public provision is desired but public production has many disadvantages, using the private sector is advised. In the area of "soft" services, output is hard to measure, contracts are difficult to write, monitoring may not be an effective tool to achieve maximum results, and co-optation by suppliers is a continuing threat. The voucher mode of production possesses several important advantages. Vouchers can maximize user choice, give beneficiaries more influence over supply, enhance competition among vendors, simplify monitoring, and encourage producers to customize their product (Hall & Eggers, 1995).

Vouchers are an effective choice mechanism for consumers. Each user can specify his/her individual preference for the quality, price, and location of the service. Recipients can change suppliers at their discretion, and thus give suppliers direct feedback. This customer choice mechanism forces suppliers to cater to the diverse wants of users and, if properly designed, to contain costs and price at the marginal cost level. Since customers monitor producers, the government's monitoring activities are simplified and minimized.

Where the market structure is not likely to be competitive, where there are substantial external costs, or where consumer choice is not necessarily desirable (e.g., juvenile criminal rehabilitation programs), a voucher system may not be a viable alternative. However, for many government services vouchers may be the mode of choice.

CONCLUSION: THE FUTURE PATH OF PRIVATIZATION

The recent spurt of privatization by nonfederal governments either could represent a trend that will stretch well into the twenty-first century, or simply could be a temporary acceleration in the moderate application of a promising public management technique. The course that is followed will be a function of the relative strength of forces pushing for rapid change compared to the strength of elements moderating movement. The basic forces are threefold: efficiency factors, distributional consequences, and philosophical influences.

In the past few decades, the confluence of fiscal constraints on governments, stagnant or falling real incomes for the bottom three quintiles of households, and the growing popularity of the "smaller government" philosophy weakened opposition to privatization and encouraged use of the privatizing option. Efficiency considerations moved to a position of greater prominence in the privatization debate, especially since the preponderance of evidence suggests that competently designed privatizing almost always leads to lower unit cost, improved product quality, or both. The ability of private developers to raise funds and to take risks more efficiently than the public sector in the case of infrastructural projects also seems clear. In the face of the twin forces of budget pressure and the unpopularity of service cuts, public decision makers became more sympathetic towards experimenting with privatization initiatives.

Supplementing the efficiency forces is the "anti-big government" point of view of voting groups. These groups may take this philosophical position because of the expected favorable distributional consequences of change for them, or they simply may be altruistic in their concern about the long-run effects on political/economic freedom of a large public sector.

Countering the forces that push elected officials to move more rapidly towards privatization is the status quo coalition. Existing stakeholders attempt to hold onto their share of monopoly rents, and attempt to erect obstacles to change. Change almost always threatens to cause redistribution of the benefits and/or costs of government action.

Which set of forces is stronger will determine the particular course that privatization will follow for state and local governments. Of course, in our highly decentralized federal system, particular states or local governments may deviate from the trend, and can influence other governments, even having an impact on the trend itself by engaging in innovative experimentation.

The intensity of efforts by either opponents or proponents of privatization may depend upon whether privatization involves provision or production. Shifting responsibility for the provision of service that involves some form of load shedding is potentially the most disruptive. Load shedding may engender significant uncertainties about the future supply of the service. Issues of both quantity and quality may be raised.

Moreover, government managers and workers see the loss of the service as a permanent cost to them, with little chance of reversal. There is even a chance that the private sector may not be interested in providing the service, or may abandon it once started in the face of an unacceptable level of profitability. Only where there is strictly a private-type good involved, where government may continue to exercise some control (e.g., requiring trash pickup from voters' abodes or regulating the rates of a waste treatment plant), is there some likelihood for load shedding.

Contracting out production is a less threatening option and has a greater probability of being used. The best chance of privatizing arises when the number of public employees affected is small, specialized services are involved, output can be defined and measured clearly, several potential private suppliers exist or the entry of others is easy, and the service beneficiaries are numerous.

Vouchers, potentially the most cost-effective option, are likely to be used more widely in a number of social and human service areas. Efficiency considerations will be an important stimulus, since the costs of rendering such services have been escalating. Moreover, the use of nonprofit suppliers with many ties to the community minimizes opposition to change.

However, where there is a large and entrenched pro-status quo group of stakeholders, where the outcomes of privatization are not measured easily, and where significant externalities in providing the service are believed to exist, breaking the mold will be very difficult. Privatizing education and criminal justice functions fall within this hard-to-do category.

Theoretically, government could transfer the production of all but a handful of services that are pure public goods (e.g., some elements of law enforcement and a limited number of regulatory activities) to the private sector. The public sector could emerge as the director, rather than the producer. The interplay of many factors will determine the ultimate reach of the privatization movement. Although not a panacea for the fiscal problems facing our country, if managed properly, privatization should prove to be a strong force for delivering greater efficiency and effectiveness to the American economy as the 21st century moves beyond its first decade.

REFERENCES

Adie, D. K., McDavid, J. C., & Clemens, E. (In press). The costs of production of waste disposal service. In P. Seidenstat (Ed.), *The economics of contracting out public services*. Westport, CT: Praeger Publishers.

Boycko, M., Shleifer, A., & Vishny, R. (1996, March). A theory of privatization. *Economic Journal, 106*, 309–313.

Chi, K. (1993). *Policy options for privatization in state and local government*. Unpublished manuscript.

Council of State Governments. (1993, June/July). *Privatization in state government survey*. Lexington, KY: Council of State Governments.

DeHoog, R. H. (1984). Theoretical perspectives on contracting out for services. In G. C. Edwards, III (Ed.), *Public policy implementation* (pp. 227–259). Greenwich, CT: JAI Press.

Eggers, W. D. (1994). *Rightsizing government: Lessons from America's public sector innovators*. Los Angeles, CA: Reason Foundation.

Eggers, W. D. (1995). *Revitalizing our cities: Perspectives from America's new breed of mayors*. Los Angeles, CA: Reason Foundation.

Goodman, J. C. (1990, June 11). Address at the Third National Conference, Privatization Council. Washington, DC.

Hakim, S., Seidenstat, P., & Bowman, G. W. (Eds.). (1996). *Privatizing transportation systems*. Westport, CT: Praeger Publishers.

Hall, J., & Eggers, W. D. (1995). *Health and social services in the post-welfare state: Are vouchers the answer?* Los Angeles, CA: Reason Foundation.

Hatry, H. P., Brounstein, P. J., & Levinson, R. B. (1993). Comparison of privately and publicly operated corrections facilities in Kentucky and Massachusetts. In G. W. Bowman, S. Hakim, & P. Seidenstat (Eds.), *Privatizing correctional institutions* (pp. 193–212). New Brunswick, NJ: Transaction Publishers.

Lick, D. M. (1995, February 10). *Public franchising renaissance*. Paper presented at the meeting of the American Bar Association, Section of Public Contract Law, Miami, FL.

Logan, C. H., & McGriff, B. W. (1989, September/October). Comparing costs of public and private prisons: A case study. *NIJ Reports*. Washington, DC: National Institute of Justice, United States Department of Justice.

McDavid, J. C. (1985, September/October). The Canadian experience with privatizing residential solid waste collection service. *Public Administration Review, 45*, 602–608.

McDavid, J. C., & Schick, G. K. (1987). Privatization versus union-management cooperation: The effects of competition on service efficiency in municipalities. *Canadian Public Administration, 30*(3), 472–488.

Mulka, S. (1990). Contracting for human services: The case of Pennsylvania's subsidized child care program: Policy limitations and prospects. *Administration in Social Work, 14*, 31–46.

Savas. E. S. (1987). *Privatization: The key to better government*. Chatham, NJ: Chatham House.

Savas, E. S. (1995). *Privatization in state and local government*. Unpublished manuscript.

Straussner, S. L. A. (1988, January/February). Comparison of in-house and contracted-out employee programs. *Social Work, 33*, 53–55.

United States Environmental Protection Agency. (1989). *Profiles of success in providing environmental services: Public-private partnership case studies*. Washington, DC: United States Government Printing Office.

United States General Accounting Office. (1988). *Federal productivity: DOD functions with savings potential from private sector cost comparisons*. Washington, DC: United States Government Printing Office.

Wall Street Journal. (1989, August 5), p. 21.

Williams, C. (1996). Lessons from experience—State route 91. In S. Hakim, P. Seidenstat, & G. W. Bowman (Eds.), *Privatizing transportation systems* (pp. 249–256). Westport, CT: Praeger Publishers.

Windsor, D. (1995, February 23). *Piecemeal privatization: The United States domestic transportation example*. Paper presented at the meeting of the Western Regional Science Association. San Diego, CA.

Chapter 3

PRIVATIZING GOVERNMENT SERVICES AS A REINVENTION TOOL; ADDITIONS INTO THE 21ST CENTURY

Paul Seidenstat

Privatization became a valuable tool in the process of "reinventing government", especially for state and local governments, from the early and mid-1980s on. Among various privatization devices, contracting out has become the most widely used for practical and political reasons in the context of a "force field" model. Cost saving has become the most notable accomplishment. A variety of factors affect management's use of privatization, and the preponderance of these factors now suggests the attainment of a permanent role as we move towards the second decade of the 21st century. Other likely dimensions of future use of privatization are also discussed.

PRIVATIZING GOVERNMENT SERVICES AS A REINVENTION TOOL

Beginning in the 1980s, the pressure of slowing revenue growth and the rising cost of producing services spurred American state and local governments to seek more effective methods to control costs. The urgency to find cost containment measures was prodded by the growing resistance to tax rate hikes and the imposition of new taxes at the same time that making major cuts in services was considered to be politically unwise.

A variety of government management experiments or innovations were initiated with the objectives of increasing productivity and containing costs. These efforts, that could be termed "restructuring government", constituted a nationwide movement for government reform that was evident by the late 1980s and continued through the 1990s. Some of these efforts were acclaimed in the popular book, *Reinventing Government* (Osborne and

Gaebler, 1992). One of the key methods of reform was the privatization of government services.

Privatization, "any process aimed at shifting functions and responsibilities, in whole or in part, from the government to the private sector" (General Accounting Office, 1997: 46), is not a new concept in the United States. Governments have long used the private sector. However, the use of private operators in supplying services was very restricted. Their role was limited to providing a few in-house functions and a very limited number of direct services (Chi, 1983; and Council of State Governments, 1985). The minor use by governments of private producers was evidenced by the fact that the word, "privatization," did not make the dictionary until the early 1980s.

Spurred by the "reinventing" effort, the acceleration of privatization efforts began in the mid-1980s as shown in Table 1. Using county data as representative of local governments, the table shows that 34 percent of all counties contracted out services in 1992 compared to 24 percent of counties in 1987. In looking at specific service areas, we see a growth in privatization in every single area. Especially noticeable is that by 1992, almost all counties contracted out electric and gas utility services and almost half of all counties contracted out hospital and transit operations.

Table 1
Privatization in U.S. Counties (Percentage of services contracted out)

Type of Service	1987	1992
Airports	30%	36%
Electric utility	74	96
Fire protection	22	37
Gas utility	78	89
Hospitals	34	48
Landfills	20	26
Libraries	14	23
Nursing homes	24	28
Public transit	37	48
Sewerage	18	30
Stadiums	21	29
Water supply	21	35
TOTAL	24%	34%

Source: U.S. Bureau of Census, *Census of Government*, 1987 and 1992.

The forces behind this acceleration of privatization are discussed below. However, it should be noted that privatization can take various forms even though, as we shall see, contracting out is the dominant form. A classification of those techniques provides some prospective for examining the nature of the privatization movement.

CLASSIFICATION OF PRIVATIZATION OPTIONS

Two functions are involved in rendering services to citizens: making provision for output and producing the service. Making provision basically involves the financing of the output. Road construction is an example of this distinction as the government can pay to have a road built and maintained (make provision) but has a choice as to the construction and maintenance of the roadway (e.g., produce in-house or hire a private contractor).

Using these two variables: making provision and production, Table 2 shows a classification system for privatization processes. These processes are as follows:

Table 2
Classification System for Privatization Processes

		Sector making provision	
		Private	*Public*
Sector producing	*Private*	Asset sales Service shedding Franchising	Contracting Out Managed Competition Public-Private Partnership Volunteerism Subsidies/Grants *Vouchers*
	Public	Contracting In	No Privatization

1. Service Shedding

The most complete form of privatization occurs where the government simply disassociates itself from providing the service and turns financing and production entirely over to the private sector; i.e., service shedding (or simply allowing the service to disappear). Examples would be the government eliminating existing recreation programs, or not building a new sports stadium.

Even if the current government operation involves public ownership of buildings or equipment, those assets may be retained in the government inventory or converted to other uses. An example would be a trash collection service that is eliminated but the trash trucks are kept in the government inventory, often to be held in reserve in case the privatization effort is aborted and public trash collection is resumed in the future.

2. Asset Sales

In many cases where there are existing assets owned by government, those assets may be sold to private buyers. The assets may be sold to a bidder who would then use them to operate the previously publicly operated service such as trash collection or a golf course. In other cases, the government may just sell the assets to any buyer with no restrictions on their use. The assets may have other uses, in the case of an office-type building, or there may be no bidder who intends to continue the discontinued service. In the case where there may be a private provider, the private firm may use its own assets.

3. Franchising

A modified form of load shedding involves franchising; i.e., a special privilege granted to a private operator. The service is turned over to the private sector but the government chooses the private operator or operators. For example, a local government may decide to load shed trash collection but chooses to franchise the existing trash collection routes to one or more private collectors. The government also may exercise some operational control over the franchisee such as setting quality standards for effluent discharges in the case of waste treatment plants.

Where infrastructure-type operations are involved, especially in the case of new (highway) or expanded (waste treatment) operations, there are at least two variants of franchising: build-transfer-operate (BTO) and build-operate-transfer (BOT). In the BTO case, the government agency can utilize a turnkey model in which the private operator designs, constructs, and transfers ownership upon completion to the government but then continues to operate the facility. This model has been used in wastewater treatment.

BOT is a more complete form of privatization since the private sector may continue to own the facility, often subject to government regulation, on a long-term basis. After a number of years, however, the private firm may transfer ownership to the public sector. This model has been used for toll roads, solid waste facilities, and water systems (Lick, 1995).

4. Vouchers, Grants and Subsidies

The most market-oriented mode of privatization in which the public sector continues to make provision (i.e., pays) is the use of vouchers or grants/subsidies. In the voucher form, the government provides the user a check to pay the bill for the privately produced service. If there are competing suppliers, the user is afforded choice. Examples include: food stamps, Medicare, and housing vouchers, at the federal level; and Medicaid, mental health, job training, and other social services, at the state and local level.

Instead of allowing the consumer to pay for the service from a producer of his or her choice with a government check, the government may directly provide a grant or subsidy to a private producer. In this case, the user may have less choice as the subsidy or grant may go to one, or only a handful of producers. Government subsidies have been given to universities, hospitals, other health-related facilities, art museums and other organizations that offer cultural services, and to a wide variety of community service organizations.

5. Public-Private Partnerships

A mixed technique of service provision/production is that of a public-private partnership. Under this relationship, the government fashions a contractual arrangement with its private-sector partners. Infrastructure projects illustrate this approach such as in the BTO model where each partner has carefully defined responsibilities. Also, a government agency may work with a private social service organization to address a particular social problem. Examples would be needle exchanges or publicity efforts to reduce the incidence of HIV infection in which the government's role is to furnish the needles and provide educational materials while the private organization operates the program.

6. Volunteer Activities

Under the umbrella of government provision and/or operation of some programs, citizen volunteers may be utilized. A service may be organized and funded by a government agency that enlists volunteers to provide all or a part of the services offered, either directly under government supervision or through a non-profit service group. Examples of programs utilizing volunteers include neighborhood crime watches, tutoring programs in schools, and delivery of food in a "Meals on Wheels"-type operation.

7. Contracting-In

Although some of the above techniques are not widely used, contracting-in is an even rarer option. In this case, the private sector is the provider but the government is the producer. An example is where a private group or company hires, at its own expense, public police personnel to secure a sporting event or patrol a shopping mall. In most cases, however, the public operation was established under public provision and these additional services rendered to the private sector are incidental to the primary mission.

8. Contracting-Out

Rather than employing some form of load shedding, most governments have preferred contracting as the method to shift operations to the private sector. In this model, the government entity retains ownership and overall control but employs the private vendor to actually render the service. Except for activities involving infrastructure or voucher/subsidy systems, contracting out is the way practically all privatization is now being implemented. Everything from in-house support services to direct taxpayer services falls under the contracting out umbrella. Much of the analysis of this chapter is in the context of utilizing contracting out as the mode of privatization.

9. Managed Competition / Competitive Contracting

One variant of contracting out is that of managed competition or competitive contracting. Government departments or agencies currently producing the service (or capable of producing the service) can bid on contracts. The entire service may be contracted out to private vendors or kept in-house if the agency bid is superior to the best bid of the private competitors. Where feasible, part of the service may be outsourced and the remainder of the service may be retained in-house. An example of the splitting technique is in trash collection or in bus transport where there is a geographical dimension to service, or in solid waste operations where there are vertical processing steps such as collection and disposal.

DOMINANCE OF CONTRACTING OUT

Tables 3 and 4 show the dominance of contracting out as the preferred method of privatization at the state level. Overall, in 1993 78% of state agencies used contracting out as the primary privatization device. The pattern at the local level also reflects this pattern.

As seen in Table 3, contracting out is used exclusively for some services. These services include administrative and general services and corrections. Excluding grants or vouchers, practically all privatization in education, health, mental health, social services, and transportation relies almost entirely on contracting out.

Table 4 also demonstrates the importance of contracting out in several key government services. There is extensive use of contract workers in waste collection, street repair, building maintenance and data processing. Between 1987 and 1995, there has been a doubling of the use of contracted workers for many services.

If a government agency chooses to privatize, why would it most likely use the contracting out option? The answer appears to be that the choice of contracting out reflects a variety of practical and political considerations.

Table 3
Forms of Privatization and Frequency of Use

Forms of Privatization	Agencies frequency of Use							
	Admin/Gen Services	Corrections	Education	Health	Mental Health	Social Services	Transport	Average
	(in percentage of total)							
Contracting Out	91.7	92.1	81.3	69.6	64.7	71.3	83.5	78.1
Grants	0.6	1.1	8.6	14.1	15.6	12.5	4.5	8.5
Vouchers	3.1	0.4	0.7	4.9	5.4	9.3	0.4	4.1
Volunteerism	1.4	3.6	1.4	3.3	3.6	3.0	5.4	3.3
Public-private partnership	1.7	2.4	5.0	5.4	3.9	2.2	2.6	3.0
Private donation	0.6	0.4	0.7	0.0	2.6	0.2	1.6	1.0
Franchise	0.3	0.0	1.4	1.1	1.7	0.4	1.5	0.9
Service Shedding	0.3	0.0	0.7	1.1	0.9	0.7	0.4	0.6
Deregulation	0.0	0.0	0.0	0.5	1.5	0.4	0.2	0.5
Asset Sales	0.6	0.0	0.0	0.2	0.2	0.0	0.2	0.2

Source: Council of State Governments. 1993. *State Trends and Forecasts: Privatization.*

Table 4
Share of Public Services Handled by Contract Workers (% of Total)

Activity	1995	1987
Waste Collection	50	30
Building maintenance	42	32
Street repair	37	19
Data processing	31	16
Health/medical	27	15
Bill collection	20	10
Street cleaning	18	9

Source: *Wall Street Journal*, August 5, 1996, pp. A-5 and A-6

Practical Factors

Often, government officials wish to retain substantial control over service production while seeking the lower costs or improved performance promised by private sector producers. The major alternative to contracting out a service is to allow the private sector to have complete, or almost complete, control over the service. In the extreme case of load shedding, the public agency relinquishes provision as well as production. In the case of vouchers, subsidies, and even franchises, the degree of public control is much less as funding is the principal function of the government. By comparison, contracting out typically allows much greater involvement in the design and oversight of production by the public agency.

In the case of poor performance by the private producer, contracting out offers a degree of reversibility not available with other forms of privatization. Especially if the public agency retains some equipment and management expertise in the service area, it is not too difficult to resume public production if the private operation proves to be unsatisfactory or if the private operator goes out of business. This option to resume public operations is especially important if there are no other private producers on the horizon.

Political Factors

The loss of control over the nature and level of service (or no service at all) with load shedding, encourages public officials to rely upon contracting out to privatize services. Politically, a major loss of control opens elected officials to criticism by disgruntled citizen-consumers. The blame cannot easily be deflected, nor is it easy to make changes.

Moreover, the economic rent that often entices public provision, if not production, of services slips away with load shedding. Even with contracting out, favors for constituents are still possible to garner. Contract features may be designed to give substantial benefits to selected consumers. Even after the contract is let, public officials may be able to gain concessions for certain voters since contract renewal is on the horizon.

Contractors themselves may be encouraged to share some contract benefits with elected officials, even barring illegal forms of favors. Campaign contributions and the aforementioned favors for selected constituents may not be uncommon events.

The use of competitive contracting by some cities has also softened the political resistance to change. Offering the public agency and its workers a chance to compete for the contract to supply services is a way to show effort to contain costs while retaining the possibility of public production. Some critics of competitive contracting argue that by clever manipulation of costs, especially misallocation of overhead costs, the public agency can be given an edge and thus can win the contract. Additionally, checking the public bid winner for subsequent cost overruns can be ignored or downplayed since sanctions might be difficult to impose and the exposure of the higher costs could be politically damaging to elected officials.

RESULTS OF PRIVATIZATION EFFORTS

The primary aim of the movement toward using the private sector was to effect cost savings without reducing the quality of services. Direct contracting out or competitive contracting with government workers are both aimed at containing costs. In the case of some services, more emphasis was placed on improving the quality of service without escalating costs. The latter examples often involved producing human services such as job training or drug rehabilitation, or infrastructure operations such as water and waste treatment in the face of tightening federal environmental quality regulations.

Cost Containment

The primary aim of contracting out was to reduce operating costs without sacrificing the quality of the service. In the vast majority of cases the results appear to be favorable. As one of the chief researchers of privatization has put it: "Savings from competitive contracting of public services—the most thoroughly studied form of privatization—average roughly 25 to 30 percent" (Savas, 1995: 16).

Public-Private Competition

Cutting costs is also the purpose of outsourcing such services as solid waste collection, road maintenance, and park maintenance. The idea is to inject competition for the government agency producing the service. Where used, contracting out here usually takes the form of bidding for work that was previously the sole responsibility of a public agency producer.

The resultant competition is typically followed by lower costs and more efficient service. When spurred by outside competition, the public agency often reduces its costs and gains a share of the work. Phoenix, Indianapolis, and Charlotte have made extensive use of managed competition.

Contracting out, or its threat, also can have the effect of weakening the power of public unions. Governor Whitman of New Jersey and Mayor Giuliani of New York City have used the threat of privatization in negotiating with turnpike workers, sanitation workers, school custodians and school bus drivers, all of whom "agreed to major modifications in their work rules to stave off private competition" (Palley, 1995: 21).

Results: Quality Enhancement

Although cost restraint or reduction (without compromising quality) is a major objective of contracting and the record suggests impressive results, achieving high quality is an important objective in producing some services. These services often are classified as "soft services" since they are involved with helping consumers (or "clients") directly. Such services include education, job training, drug rehabilitation, and prisoner services. Assessing the performance of these services is very difficult since defining and measuring "output" is an imprecise art.

The evidence of performance in the "soft services" is not clear-cut. In the few documented studies available, the quality of service was either improved or not significantly different than when publicly produced. For example, in the social service area where non-profit suppliers are relied upon to produce most of the contracted for services, the performance record appears to be slightly better or the same as the public sector's record (Straussner, 1988; Mulka, 1990).

THE BASES FOR IMPROVED PERFORMANCE

Why can private operators produce with lower costs, at a given level of service? Better performance flows from the role of competition in a market system and the existence of the profit motive. Most governments producing services are monopolies that may not be sensitive to user demand. The political process may insulate producers. Moreover, monopsony arrangements for input suppliers may be imposed with resultant inflexible union and/or civil service rules and elevated wage rates.

Managers can have the same insulation from user wants. Civil service protection may dull incentives for managers to innovate and improve the product in the public sector. On the other hand, managers for private producers can be induced to overcome the owner/agent tension by incorporating profit based compensation arrangements.

It has been argued that public enterprises are inefficient because they are interested in high employment to placate their public union supporters rather than to maximize efficiency. By contrast, a private firm would seek the most profitable level of employment. Privatization is cost effective because it controls political discretion that otherwise would work in the direction of lower efficiency (Boycko, Shleifer, and Vishny, 1996).

Privatization in a competitive market framework will drive unit cost to the minimum level. One way the private producer accomplishes cost minimization is by limiting labor costs in such ways as using more part-time and lower-skilled workers, paying for less time off (vacation time and paid absences), using less overtime, establishing clearer job definitions and greater worker accountability, and having more workers per supervisor. Other input costs can be reduced by holding first-line managers more responsible for equipment maintenance and giving them more authority to hire and fire, shifting toward a higher capital to labor ratio, and utilizing more effective purchasing methods.

Relating manager pay to profitability can lead to more emphasis on innovative ways to produce, incorporating new technology, dispensing with "red tape," and making timely decisions. On the other hand, changing managers in light of poor performance in a private organization typically can be accomplished with greater speed and with less disruption.

Contractual operation of airports demonstrates some of the advantages of multi-unit private operations. The U.S. government's General Accounting Office lists 20 airports, primarily general aviation, as under private management with several of the airports operated by one company (United States General Accounting Office, 1988).

Chains in highly complex businesses such as airports have several advantages over a single-unit operator. Economies of scale are important in the procurement and personnel areas. Chains have one purchasing system that specializes in the particular items required for airports. Personnel operations, not constrained by civil service, can promote from within to develop senior managers, can offer advancement by moving to another airport, and can use specialists to troubleshoot where necessary.

ECONOMIC RENTS AND THE FORCE FIELD MODEL OF CHANGE

Given the limited use of privatization by all levels of government in the U.S. prior to the 1980s, what forces were at work to accelerate privatization by the mid-1980s? The answer to that question is best answered by developing an analytical model of privatization using a "force field" framework.

How a change in a fundamental government policy comes about requires an understanding of the forces for changes and their strength compared to the forces operating to maintain the status quo. For a change in policy to occur, the forces for change must grow in strength to the point where they can break through the resistance to change.

What happened in the United States by the late 1980s to propel the public sector to greatly accelerate the movement toward privatizing? The answer to this question lies in the weakening fiscal position of the public sector and changes in the political climate regarding the size and role of government in the society. In the wake of the serious recession of the early 1980s, the growing concern about the federal government's budget deficit, and the continuing long-term fiscal crisis in the large cities, there was a serious effort to restrain the growth of government expenditures and make government operations more cost effective. At the same time, there was a stirring among the voters at the state level to quash proposed tax increases, to restrain the growth of tax revenue (e.g., Proposition 13 in California, Proposition 2.5 in Massachusetts, and Amendment 1 in Colorado), and to limit government spending.

Overall, the political environment was growing more hostile to the expansion of government budgets and increases in tax rates. The growing power of this message was reflected in the elections of Ronald Reagan in 1980 and 1984 and the slowing of the federal government's growth in both the Bush 41 and Clinton administrations. With the election of George W. Bush in 2000 and 2004, it became clear that fiscal conservatism was a genuine asset which could be leveraged towards political office. It was also apparent that political success was more likely for candidates running for major state offices or for the state legislature who espoused smaller government and restraint on the taxing power of government.

The coalition of stakeholders of government who were the chief beneficiaries and supporters of a growing government found their position to be weakened by the aforementioned fiscal pressures. The fact that monopolistic government can generate economic rents explains the strongly held position of the status quo coalition. Using these rents, elected officials and program administrators can offer benefits to stakeholders. For example, public school monopolies can provide benefits to input suppliers like school administrators, schoolteachers, and book publishers in the form of above market average labor compensation and input prices. Parents of special student populations (e.g., mentally retarded, physically handicapped, etc.) could receive expanded (and very expensive) services. Particular firms could receive lucrative contracts to construct school buildings or make major repairs.

The growing pressure on elected officials to cut budget growth or even downsize government operations forced consideration of methods to restrain government spending without substantial reduction in services. Once the government agenda focused on this issue of restructuring or "rightsizing", then privatization became a major policy option as part of a restructuring program.

The political clout of the coalition supporting government operations now was challenged by the growing coalition that stressed lower taxes and privatization. The political weakening of the pro-government coalition was pronounced in service operations such as trash collection or street repairing but was not as strong in others such as education and corrections. In those states and cities where the fiscal pressures were the greatest and the weakening of the power of the major monopoly rent recipients was the most pronounced, major contracting out efforts were initiated.

An illustration of the force field model is the case of trash collection. Because of its inherent characteristics, trash collection is one of the public sector's services easiest to privatize. The collection activity is not a pure public good and is often performed by private companies in many suburban and small local urban government locations. Typically, there are many possible suppliers who can bid on a government contract.

Given the largely unskilled nature of the work, a private labor force is easy to assemble. Contracts are easy to monitor and enforce, as the output is well defined.

Since many studies show that public trash collection is much more expensive than its privately operated counterpart, why have some cities been slow in contracting out this service? The answer may lie in the opposition of public unions, especially in large urban areas where they are strong. A study of the 1973-88 period in municipalities with more than 10,000 people documents this union effect (Chandler and Feuille, 1991).

DETERMINANTS OF CONTRACTING OUT

The force field model of privatization suggests that certain factors would affect the relative strength of the pro-change and status quo forces. These factors include: the relative cost of providing services, the policy influence of public employees and their unions, the strength of anti-taxation forces, competition among local governments, the scope of government services, and some non-quantifiable factors.

In developing a model of privatization, Kodrycki (1994 & 1997) theorized that several factors would influence the degree of privatization as follows:

Cost of Providing Services

The extent to which private contractors can reduce the cost of services, without diminishing quality, would push the public/private line in the private direction. Several factors would affect the potential cost differential:

1. the differential between public employee earnings and private employee compensation.
2. the extent of competition among potential private vendors; competition would be more likely in a metropolitan area rather than a non-metropolitan area.
3. the extent to which economies of scale are important; smaller governments are less likely to be able to take advantage of these economies.

Unionization of Public Employees and the Effect of Community Growth

Often the major opposition to contracting out is the public employee union. Consequently, the higher the percentage of unionized workers in a government agency, the stronger would be the resistance to change. However, in communities with faster growth rates and with larger populations and income, employee and/or union opposition might be less aggressive since privatization can be accomplished without displacing existing public jobs.

Opposition to Higher Taxes

The attractiveness of cost savings that would be reflected in a stronger force field for privatization is directly related to the affluence of the average citizen. Lower than average income (using a national or regional benchmark) that usually is correlated with lower property values triggers greater support for government cost saving measures.

Competition among Local Governments

As local governments aggressively compete for businesses and affluent taxpayers, considerable effort may be exerted to minimize the cost of services in order to keep tax rates competitive. In more densely populated areas with more local governments, more inter-governmental competition can lead to greater use of the private sector in connection with the production of public services. In addition, the greater array of services offered, the greater the chance that some will be privatized.

Proportion of Government Services that are Considered Core Services

If local governments provide only essential services (e.g., courts, police, and sewage treatment), then the opposition to minimizing the public labor force by contracting out would be weak. On the other hand, if a wide range of public sector services and income redistribution activities were provided, opposition to privatization would be stiffer.

Subjective Factors

Strong political leadership can enhance support or opposition to privatization, especially if driven by ideological preferences regarding the role of government. Strong political leadership can alter the position of the public/private line. In fact to move from government to private production typically requires a strong effort by the executive to push for the change in operations.

TESTING THE MODEL

Kodrzycki (1994) tested these hypotheses by performing a cross sectional multiple regression analysis of 655 municipalities and townships with at least a population of 25,000 based on 1987 US Census data. The result of the regression analysis suggests that several of the objective factors suggested by Kodrzycki are statistically significant in explaining the extent of privatization.

Contracting out to the private sector is more likely if public sector wages are high relative to the private sector, if there is a greater degree of public employee unionization, if there is rapid population growth, if government services are highly concentrated on health and human services, and if a variety of functions or services are provided by local government. To a lesser extent, in communities where the local governments concentrate on providing core services, a more pronounced degree of privatization is found.

Other factors appear to have explanatory value as well. Possibly counted among these factors are strong political leaders who support or oppose contracting out, the reputation of local potential contractors, and differences in fringe benefits or productivity between the public and private sectors.

REGARDING SLOWDOWN OF PRIVATIZATION EFFORTS: APPLICATION OF THE FORCE FIELD MODEL

The rapid movement toward privatization in the 1985-1992 period could be explained by the relative shift in the strength of the forces for change compared to the status-quo forces. In particular, the growing fiscal difficulties of state and local governments and the increasing opposition to tax increases pushed in the direction of contracting out services to allow the cutting of costs so as to avoid raising taxes or drastically cutting the level of services.

Table 5 offers some evidence that a slowdown in the rate of privatization may have occurred starting in the early 1990s. One explanation of this slowing rate of new privatization efforts that included outsourcing or load shedding is that the state and local government economies began to recover from recession, thus easing the fiscal pressure to cut costs (Kodrzycki, 1998).

Table 5
Privatization trends, 1987 to 1992
(Municipalities and townships with a 1986 population of 25,000 or more)

Action of Government	Percent of Governments	
switching to contracting for at least one service	16.0	
switching to contracting for more than one service	3.3	19.3
dropping provision of at least one service	31.8	
dropping provision of more than one service	9.6	41.4

Source: U.S. Bureau of Census, 1987, 1992

PRIVATIZATION IN OPERATION

As indicated above, in the vast majority of privatization cases, contracting the operation of the service to a private supplier (or suppliers) has been the preferred method. The government provider typically solicits bids from private suppliers and awards the contract or contracts based on price and/or quality of service to be supplied. Occasionally contract awards are made without bids, usually in the case of professional services such as engineers, lawyers, architects, and social service organizations. In most instances the contractor is a for profit enterprise but, in some cases, non-profit agencies are used, especially in the human or social service area.

Objectives of Privatization

Privatization, especially the predominant contracting out option, has been utilized as a management tool as well as a device to realign the public-private sector mix. The managerial objectives include cutting costs, improving the quality of services produced, or both. Most frequently, the primary aim has been to cut costs in order to relieve budgetary pressures rather than to improve services, especially since assessing the quality of output of many government services can be a complex and time consuming activity. Privatizing was aimed also at increasing the flexibility of government operations such that expansion, contraction, or complete elimination of specific services could be accomplished with fewer obstacles and with greater speed.

Although the major thrust toward privatization in the U.S. seems to be motivated by practical managerial considerations, nevertheless the movement towards the greater use of the private sector taps into the philosophical point of view of a reduced role for government in a market system.

Conditions Required for Success

In order to achieve the objectives set forth in a privatization initiative, certain environmental factors must be present. These factors include political support, managerial/political leadership and a supportive private market structure. Overcoming the bias towards the status quo protected by the stakeholders who receive monopoly rent is essential. A strong case must be made for change; the case must speak to the benefits to be received with a provision/production arrangement in comparison to the costs that may have to be incurred. Legislative and voter support offers the opportunity to move in the privatization direction and to allow the new structure a fair chance to demonstrate its advantages.

The full support of political leaders, especially in the executive branch, greatly enhances the chances of success. Not only is this support required for approval of change, but also enthusiastic and careful backing of the effort often is compelled to sustain it.

Well-prepared and ardent political leaders often are needed to overcome the inertia of the status quo.

To achieve the required objectives requires more than political support and strong leadership. To achieve the maximum benefits of privatization, the private sector should be structured such that alternative suppliers exist to compete in providing the service in the case of load shedding, can compete for contracts in the case of contracting out or franchising, or can supply services in the case of vouchers. Without competition, privatization might simply consist of a private monopoly substituting for a government monopoly.

Cautions and Pitfalls

Several cautions must be exercised and pitfalls protected against when contracting out. Where there is little competition in the private sector prior to privatization, a viable bidding process may not take place such that the savings anticipated or the quality improvement desired may not take place; private monopoly may simply replace public monopoly. Even where there is competition and the bidding is spirited, the contract must be carefully drafted and monitored. Especially in service categories where output is ill-defined and relevant costs are hard to measure, vague contracts may lead to less than optimal results and enforcement may not be effectively practiced.

Also, a reasonable contract period may be required for the vendor to demonstrate results, especially for social services where desirable outcomes may take years to achieve. During the length of this long contract, the government may not be able to rebid even if performance is marginal.

Undesirable outcomes could also occur during the contract period or at the time of rebidding. The private supplier may not perform according to the contract owing to strikes, other work stoppages, and business cessation or bankruptcy. The contracting government agency must be prepared to find an alternative supplier or to resume operations itself. Where large capital investments in plant and equipment are necessary for operations, the government must be wary of disinvesting itself of back up equipment in case it has to resume operations.

Maintaining operations is a particularly vital issue when infrastructure is involved; the public sector must have contingency plans to take over. Essential services such as waste water treatment, airport operations, and water treatment must not be interrupted.

In monitoring and at the rebidding phase there is also the danger that the provider and beneficiary coalition may subvert the public interest. The experience of contracting out social services in Michigan illustrates the problem. In quick order, the evaluation of services and the interpretation of the "needs" of client beneficiaries became heavily influenced by providers. "For their part, self-interested bureaucrats and legislators cannot fail to see the opportunities for developing mutually beneficial relationships with contractors" (DeHoog, 1984:247).

Abuse of the public trust and favoritism in awarding contracts to political friends is always a possibility. Public officials who let contracts may wind up working for the contractor. A case in point was the recent Fairfax County, Virginia episode where the Fairfax County Park Authority selected a company to build golf facilities at two parks. Shortly after the contract was let, a board member of the Authority quit and went to work for the contractor as a "$500 per day consultant" (Lipton, 1996). Large contracts may even be let without competitive bidding. For example, the Washington, DC school board hired a firm to handle a $ 21 million contract to operate school cafeterias without competitive bids (Vise, 1996).

Reliance on bidder competition and aggressive public watchdog activities are essential to avoid the undue influence of suppliers on the contracting process. "Sweetheart" contracts, guaranteed contract renewal, and collusion among bidders are always a threat to undermine the potential advantages of privatization.

Several critics of contracting out point to the history of widespread corruption when several large cities undertook contracting in the 19th century. Political favoritism, bribery, and the toleration of poor contractor performance were documented in New York City, Chicago, and Detroit. Adler traces the problem to that of the existence of personal incentives for the public servant who does the hiring. "The (private) entrepreneur is interested in performance and nothing else. The public servant may trade performance for a personal gain" (Adler, 1996: DF9).

ANALYSIS AND OBSERVATIONS
ABOUT THE FUTURE

After decades of a rising tide of privatization initiatives in the U.S., several trends can be noticed. Based on these tendencies, some observations about the near-term future may be made.

1. The privatization option as a major tool of restructuring government is here to stay. Overall, the privatization experience has been positive. Costs have been cut and the quality of service has not been diminished; and, in some cases, has been improved. It would be difficult for the forces opposing the use of the private sector to reverse existing privatization efforts and to defeat promising new initiatives.
2. Contracting-out will continue to be the major mode of privatization. The more radical steps of load shedding or long-term franchising suggest a non-reversible decision and, thus, strengthen the intensity of opposition. Moreover, until the results of the privatization effort can be evaluated fully, government decision-makers desire to retain some flexibility in making provision for services.
3. Privatization will move forward unevenly across the spectrum of services. The growth areas will be those in which potential cost savings are substantial, strong pressures are being exerted to upgrade service, and the effect on public employment will be small. Infrastructure construction and operations, especially in water and

wastewater services, electric and gas utilities, and hospital and healthcare operations, will see an especially powerful privatization thrust.

At the same time, privatization will far less likely be applied where sensitive activities are involved, where cost savings are more uncertain, and where a significant number of public employees would be affected. These areas include public safety services such as prisons and police functions, and regulatory services.

4. Managed competition will be more widely employed. The threat of privatization has proven to be an effective device to improve public operations and restrain costs. Indianapolis, Philadelphia, and other cities have demonstrated the advantages of injecting competitive pressure on internal operations.

5. Local and state governments will continue to take the lead in undertaking privatization efforts as the federal government moves more cautiously. Non-federal governments face greater cost pressure as they are constrained in the framework of a balanced budget. Traditionally, there is more diversity in local governments and local officials have been at the forefront of innovation in recent times. At the federal level, there is a complex set of forces at work, slowing the process of fundamental change.

6. More relevant and accurate cost systems and evaluation models will be developed, as privatization decision making requires better data and analytical devices. The introduction of activity-based costing systems and cost-benefit analysis was accelerated by the analysis requirements of privatization proposals.

Additional Lessons and Insights

Service provision at the state and local level has stayed relatively constant over the last few decades, with privatization accounting for about 20% of services (Warner and Hefetz, 2001). Contracting has remained the major privatization technique.

The experience gained has clarified the benefits and costs of the privatization model. In many cases, either cost savings or improvements in service quality were achieved compared to the government operation. At the state level a survey found that a half of states contracting out acknowledged service quality improvements but only one-third reported cost savings (Brudney, Fernandez, Ryn, and Wright, 2005). Benefits were particularly observed in infrastructure projects such as water and wastewater systems and transportation systems. The advantages of flexibility, speed of adjustment, access to expertise, and innovation surfaced in various privatization initiatives.

As contracting out efforts were increased in selected states and cities, however, those who would incur the negative fallout associated with the loss of jobs and benefits related to government operations became more forceful opponents. Unions representing government workers stepped up efforts to block the privatization thrust. Also, those who were opposed on philosophical or ideological grounds became more vocal. Offsetting these efforts, however, government managers and elected officials recognized contracting out as a useful management option. The willingness to consider contracting out, moreover, often contributed to improving government service efficiency. In a few cities and counties, a managed competition technique was used in which the government department would compete with outside firms for the contract.

The opposition's position was strengthened by some highly publicized contract difficulties. In the case of the largest privatized water system contract in the United States, Atlanta, contract problems led to the city dismissing the contractor and retaking the operation of the water system. In the case of privatized correctional institutions, legal challenges have been raised as complaints of institutional problems were charged. Headlines were evident also when the federal government took over airport security from the airlines after 9/11.

EXOGENOUS AND MANAGEMENT FACTORS

The relatively slow growth of contracting out by state and local governments, however, is mainly the product of exogenous factors and internal management considerations. The changing fiscal environment and the varied geographical structural attributes of the private markets vying for contracts impacted the decision to turn to the private sector. The buoyant economy in the second half of the 1990's reduced the pressure to seek potential cost savings from operations and to invite project capital funding from the private sector. To optimize contracting out to improve performance also requires competitive markets for contracting. In some areas of the country for some services markets may not be competitive. For example, in rural areas it is less likely that acceptable competition among contractors is in place (Warner and Hefetz, 2003).

As a result of decades of experience, government decision makers are more fully cognizant of the management challenges that privatization can present. Contracting out can be a complex and difficult process from weighing benefits and costs, to preparing the bidding documents, and to awarding the contract. Thereupon monitoring the contract for many services can be a challenging exercise. In fact, the costs of contracting and monitoring can average 20% of total project costs (Pack, 1989).

Also concern arose as to the loss of intangible aspects of government services, especially social services. Legal rights of recipients, redress of citizen complaints, and public access to operational information became items of concern.

EXPERIMENTATION IN CHOOSING SERVICE DELIVERY OPTIONS

Although privatization became accepted as an important tool in the government manager's toolbox, a wider array of service delivery options were utilized. In particular, inter-municipal cooperation, particularly in the difficult health, human services, and culture and the arts areas was pursued. Smaller governments could achieve economies of scale while maintaining the more familiar government model. In fact, around 15% of service provision uses this mode (Warner and Hefetz, 2003).

Producing services is a dynamic process. Local governments were willing to make changes where appropriate. In the 1992-97 period, for example, for U.S. cities and counties 53% of services were produced in-house on a regular basis. (See Table 6). At the same time government took on new services but shed existing ones. Contracting out was widely used but some previous contracts were brought back in-house.

Table 6. Stability of Service Provision (1992-97)

Characteristic of Service	Percent
Stable in-house	53
New service	5
Reverse contracting out	13
New contracting out	23
Service shedding	6
	100

Warner, M.B., and Hefetz, A. (2001). Privatization and the Market Role of Local Government. Economic Policy Institute, Briefing Paper. Washington.

CONCLUSIONS

Privatization, with its multiple forms, has become an important tool in the toolbox of government managers. Under budget pressure, local, and then state, managers turned to various forms of privatization to allow them to achieve higher levels of production efficiency and service quality.

Since the mid-1980s, contracting-out and public-private partnerships became the favored privatization devices as many managers sought the least risky way to move production to the private sector. Load shedding, asset sales, franchising, and vouchers played a minor role in the management effort to achieve a higher production possibilities curve.

As expectations of lower costs and equal or higher quality output were realized, the use of privatization spread. Opposing forces found their position to be weakening. Public opinion has become increasingly benign or indifferent to the concerns about the consequences of moving toward the use of the private sector.

The management tool of privatization is in the tradition of the pragmatic American approach to public management. As such, the privatization tool is here to stay and is likely to be called upon more aggressively when public fiscal conditions require. As we experiment with this tool, more creative and imaginative applications are likely to emerge.

ANTICIPATED FUTURE DEVELOPMENTS

Large federal government deficits now may alter the environment. In the next two decades, state and local government decision makers may place renewed emphasis on privatization in the face of significant federal government budget cuts, especially grants to other governments. The focus may be not only to engage the private sector to perform government functions and or assume more capital project financing but also to generate competition as part of a managed competition scheme. Privatization, shed of much of its strong ideological flavor, is now an accepted management tool that is an available major option in producing specific government services, as we move into the second decade of the 21st century.

REFERENCES

Adler, M. (1996). "In city services, privatize and beware." *New York Times* V. 145, p. DF9, April 7.

Boycko, M., A. Shlleifer, and R. W. Vishny (1996). "A theory of privatization." *The Economic Journal* 106, March: 309-319.

Brudney, J., Fernandez, S., Ryu, J.E., and Wright, D.S. (2005). Exploring and Explaining Contracting Out: Patterns among the American States. *Journal of Public Administration Research and Theory*, *15*(3), 393-419.

Chandler, T. and P. Feuille (1991). "Municipal unions and privatization." *Public Administration Review* Vol. 51, No. 1, January/February: 15-21.

Chi, K. (1993). *Policy Options for Privatization in State and Local Government.* Unpublished manuscript.

Council of State Governments (1993). *Privatization in State Government Survey.* June and July.

DeHoog, R. H. (1984). "Theoretical perspectives on contracting out for services." In Edwards, G. C. III (Ed.). *Public Policy Implementation..* Greenwich, CT: JAI Press: 227-259.

Eggers, W. D. (1994). *Rightsizing Government: Lessons from America's Public Sector Innovators.* Los Angeles, CA: Reason Foundation.

Goodman, J. C. (1990). *Address at the Third National Conference, Privatization Council.* Washington, DC, June 11.

Kodryzcki, Y. (1998). "Fiscal pressures and the privatization of local services." *New England Economic Review*, January-February: 39-50.

Kodrzycki, Y. (1994). "Privatization of local public services: Lessons for New England." *New England Economic Review.* 010, May-June: 31-46.

Lick, D. M. (1995). *Public Franchising Renaissance.* At meeting of American Bar Association, Section of Public Contract Law. Miami, FL., Feb. 10.

Lipton, E. (1996). "Fairfax investigates ex-park authority official's work for bidder." *Washington Post*, July 26: B01.

Martin, L. (1994). "How to compare costs between in-house contracted services." *Public Private Cooperation*. Denver: Colorado Municipal League, 24-37.

Mulka, S. (1990). "Contracting for human services: the case of Pennsylvania's subsidized child care program; policy limitations and prospects." *Administration in Social Work* 14, 31-46.

Pack, J.R. (1989). Privatization and cost reduction. *Policy Sciences*, *22*, 1-25.

Palley, B. (1995). "Threat of privatization is robbing public employees of clout," *Wall Street Journal* V. 144, September 4: 21.

Reason Foundation. (1994). *Eighth Annual Report on Privatization: Privatization 1994*. Los Angeles, CA).

Savas, E. S. (1995). *Privatization in State and Local Government*. unpublished manuscript.

Straussner, S.L.A. (1988.). "Comparison of in-house and contracted out employee programs." *Social Work* 33, Jan./Feb.: 53-55.

United States General Accounting Office. (1997). *Privatization Lessons Learned by State and Local Governments*. GAO/GGD-97-48. Washington, DC: U.S. Government Printing Office.

United States General Accounting Office. (1988). *Federal Productivity: DOD Functions with Savings Potential from Private Sector Cost Comparisons*. Washington, DC: U.S. Government Printing Office.

Vise, D. (1996). "Dispute Over Food Service Bid Could Imperil Effort to Cut Jobs, Costs." *Washington Post*, July 25: A01.

Warner, M.B., and Hefetz, A. (2001). Privatization and the Market Role of Local Government. Economic Policy Institute, Briefing Paper. Washington.

Warner, M.B. and Hefetz, A. (2003). Rural-Urban Differences in Privatization: Limits to the Competitive State. *Environment and Planning C: Government and Policy*, *21*(5), 703-718.

Windsor, D. (1995). *Piecemeal Privatization: The U.S. Domestic Transportation Example*. Paper presented at Western Regional Science Association, San Diego, CA., February 23.

Chapter 4

DEREGULATION, PRIVATIZATION AND COMPETITION IN TELECOMMUNICATIONS

*J. Roberto Evaristo**

Telecommunication deregulation is happening worldwide with far reaching implications for business, government and society. The increasing connection between information systems and telecommunications brings this issue into the direct area of interest of Information Systems Professionals. In this chapter, a model of telecom deregulation trajectory and correspondingly changing information and intelligence needs is developed. The objective of such a model is to provide guidance to those being impacted by increasing entrepreneurial policy and administration as competition forces change on the stakeholders.

Telecommunication deregulation, privatization and competition continue to gain momentum not only in the United States, but around the world as well. For instance, the European Union, the largest common market in the world, deregulated telecommunications on January 1, 1998. Most South American countries are also rapidly deregulating or privatizing their telecommunications monopoly, with a few having already completed the process. The winds of change are also blowing in Asia. This response to the increasing competition has important implications for the software and telecommunications industry organizations dealing with large domestic and foreign telecommunications service providers, even after the turn of the century.

First, it is likely that there will be a dramatic increase in the number of international companies in the telecommunications industry well into the 21st century. These companies will be falling over backwards to provide differentiated service in a highly competitive environment. With the increasing connection between telecommunications

---

* The author acknowledges the support of Prof. Kuldeep Kumar and the Rotterdam School of Management.

and software, this is likely to imply a bonanza of new contracts for software manufacturers worldwide. Software needs will range from traditional customer and billing services to enhanced products being offered to customers.

Second, this heightened activity will surely create a need for tracking information on the status and situation of these companies and their rapidly changing needs and competitive environments. Here is where the concept of competitive intelligence becomes relevant. Competitive Intelligence (CI) or Environmental Scanning has been experiencing a rapid increase in popularity in the last decade (e.g., Yasai-Ardekani & Nystrom, 1996). CI is the gathering, analysis and dissemination of information about suppliers, customers and competitors with the purpose of improving one's own competitive position vis-à-vis others in the industry. This is the sort of dimensional adjustment which becomes necessary in deregulated, or privatized environments where competition not only determines winners, but often survivors as well.

The objective of this chapter is to provide stakeholders involved in the telecommunication deregulation process a model to help guide them through changes in information and intelligence needs during different deregulation phases. We will start by discussing the typical structure of a "natural" monopoly, and then move on to how most PTTs (Postal Telephone and Telegraph Monopolies) are organized. A framework describing deregulation trajectories is then developed. The structure of the framework is helpful for understanding the industry changes for the PTTs as well as for the competing client and supply organizations that interact with them.

MONOPOLIES AND DEREGULATION

Scherer states that: "The most traditional economic case for regulation assumes the existence of natural monopoly – that is – where economies of scale are so persistent that a single firm can serve the market at a lower unit cost than two or more firms. Reasonably clear examples include electric power and gas distribution, local telephone service..." (Scherer, 1980).

Conspicuously absent from this list of natural monopolies are telecommunications (other than local services), typically a government owned monopoly. This is the case with PTTs in most countries. The key reasoning to protect these monopolies has been the concept of "universal service," or (1) giving network access to everyone and (2) charging reasonable – and many times similar – prices to everyone regardless of the cost of providing this service. In return for the occasional letter shipped to the Amazon or call made to a mountainous village in the Alps, monopolies have enjoyed the absence of competition in lucrative areas. According to Mueller, (1997a) although the Telecommunication Act of 1996 was supposed to bring the U.S. into a new era of competition and deregulation, section 254 kept calling for universal service, potentially creating the need for cross-subsidies and therefore for more future regulation and/or less competition. In the remainder of this section, we will analyze the traditional PTT structure and give examples of how different governments have dealt with this problem.

The typical structure of PTTs until recently was a monopoly on all telecommunication, postal and related services countrywide. In some countries this monopoly was exercised by the same organizations, but in most others two organizations were formed. One would be in charge of postal services. The other would provide telecommunication services. Overlap between services was typically very low. In this analysis, we will focus on Telecommunications Providers. This structure is somewhat similar to the one prevailing in the U.S. until the AT&T divestiture, with the exception that telecommunications providers abroad were government owned.

Key stakeholders have disagreed about the role of government in monopolies and, therefore, the extent of ensuing deregulation, as exemplified in a 1985 OECD meeting. The U.S., Japan and the United Kingdom agreed that only a competitive market would move swiftly to incorporate new technologies and services, and that government planning is too slow or ponderous to be timely. The contrasting position, taken by several European countries, was the belief that the free market alone would not necessarily produce the ideal telecommunication system (OECD, 1987). This position has changed over the last ten years, as demonstrated by the EU deregulation of telecommunication services on January 1, 1998.

These arguments can be explained in two ways. The first is ideology. The free market perspective is that prices should be a function of market conditions. If a particular area is more expensive to service, then prices should reflect that. The opposite argument tends to be more socially oriented. It supports cross-subsidies for the sake of universal service. However, there are cases where the free market created only marginally higher priced services yet with better quality. This brings into question the assumption that prices would skyrocket under such conditions. For instance, when U.S. West sold its rights to provide local service to some sparsely inhabited rural communities of the American West to local telecommunications concerns, not only did they improve services, but they were also able to maintain prices. A different purpose of the "socially oriented" argument may be to protect a highly inefficient domestic telecommunications monopoly.

A second important explanation is that the rate of technological advances keeps unfolding. A consequence is the creation of new services, mostly not covered by old laws regulating the industry. The regulatory body may take the perspective that whatever has not been legislated upon is totally regulated, and therefore a monopoly concern; or, taking the law literally, that it is not regulated at all. Therefore, introduction of new technology typically outpaces regulatory efforts. Another consequence of technological advances is experimentation with pricing. Currently the most common pricing model depends on distance and time of day. New trends may include charges based on actual congestion of circuits and not on a surrogate such as time of the day. Distance may become a moot point in pricing.

So, how have telecommunications monopolies been deregulated worldwide? In South America, and organizations from Europe, the Far East, or North America have stepped in to fully acquire or just to compete with the local PTTs when deregulation legislation was enacted. This situation contrasts with deregulation in more developed countries. The AT&T divestiture in the U.S. separated local from long distance phone service and therefore allowed competition by other U.S. long distance companies such as MCI, Sprint and many others (Brock, 1994). In Britain, British Telecom's (BT) monopoly was liberalized and eventually partially deregulated in stages. First the equipment began to be offered by other organizations, and eventually telecommunications services were also liberalized via concession to Mercury Telecom, a consortium formed by Cable and Wireless, Barclays Bank and British Petroleum (Hulsink, 1996). BT was also privatized via stock market offerings. A similar situation occurred in Japan. The telecom monopoly (NTT) was privatized, and to a large extent, also liberalized (Sueyoshi, 1996). These examples stress the point that there have been different types of deregulation. The basic structural differences among them will be the topic of the next section.

TYPES OF DEREGULATION AND RESPECTIVE INFORMATION NEEDS

A simplified view of monopoly deregulation alternatives is presented in Table 1. It only includes state owned monopolies, and suggests two alternatives: partial or full deregulation. For the purposes of this manuscript, "partial" deregulation – or liberalization – means that some of the services previously offered by the monopoly holder have been opened to competition, whereas in "full" deregulation[1] all services are now open to competition, even if still regulated as to implementation details.

Table 1 – State Owned Telecom Monopoly Deregulation Alternatives

	Partial (some services)	**Full** (all services)
With ownership transfer	(A) Selective Privatization – Focused competition possible	(B) Complete Privatization – No concerns about competitors
Without ownership transfer	(C) Focused competition guaranteed	(D) Competition in all segments between ex-monopoly and new entrants

In either case, transfer of ownership or asset divestiture is possible but not required. Ownership transfer typically implies a privatization of assets. Reasons for selling assets by governments vary, but may include the need to raise funds to reduce the deficit or to pay loans previously taken. A desire for "smaller" government, or simply recognition of the lack of resources to support large capital outlays needed in some highly capital intensive industries, are also possibilities.

Each quadrant has an inherently different situation regarding the information needs and perspectives of the various stakeholders involved in the process. Typical stakeholders include: the government as the regulator and monopoly owner, foreign and local concerns

---

[1] This is the case in England, for instance, where OFTEL (The Office of Telecommunications) oversees the telecommunication market. FCC uses this rule in the U.S. long distance, and increasingly in the local, telephone market (Telecommunications Act of 1996). The Ministry of Post and Telecommunications (MPT) also regulates the telecommunication market in "fully" deregulated Japan.

that intend to buy or compete in the telecommunication sector as allowed by deregulation overtures, suppliers to the rest of the stakeholders, and the users themselves.

In this analysis we will examine the information needs of the organizations that intend to compete with the incumbent, or with new entrants (henceforth called "competing organizations"). This is not only the most general perspective, but as will be shown, it is also the one that the others default to. One of the reasons is that in this case both the incumbent and the new competitors need to have in depth knowledge of the market and of the possible strategies that others may choose to apply. This is where a tool like competitive intelligence can create value.

Competitive Intelligence (CI) is the collection, analysis and internal dissemination of information about the suppliers, customers and competitors with the objective of creating competitive advantage. Examples of CI abound in many industries: Banking (Landau, 1995), trucking (Kahaner, 1996), electric utilities (Mann, 1995), and R&D (Ojala, 1993). Information can be collected from sources ranging from primary research to newspapers, trade unions or computerized databanks. Typically the problem is not too little information, but too much. Therefore, part of the value added of this approach is to organize the information acquired for easier analysis using one or more techniques from a CI toolkit (Prescott & Grant, 1988). The resulting report or analysis has to be disseminated to the appropriate information users, which can be challenging.

FULL DEREGULATION

Full deregulation is an attractive option when government either wants to raise higher amounts of money, e.g., in situations involving ownership transfer (quadrant "B"), or when it would like to encourage competition from diverse private enterprises with the previous monopoly still fully governmentally owned (quadrant "D"). The second alternative is the least interesting for the government and therefore rarely used. In the quadrant "B" option, there is a concentrated need for information "before deregulation implementation" regarding the sale of the monopoly. These information needs center on valuation of assets and debits of the monopoly, as well as policy decisions regarding the format of the resulting enterprise. For instance, will it be sold to only one concern or to a consortium? And, will this concern be allowed to still run it as a monopoly, or be forced to divest assets to potential competitors? Or, will it be sold in the form of a stock offering with or without controlling votes to buyers? Although these questions are interesting, this chapter will concentrate on issues of partial deregulation. Once the sale in the full deregulation scenario is concluded, the "ex-monopoly" organization ceases to exist as a government owned enterprise and therefore requires no further information for its operation. In other words, the management of this sector of the economy will have been completely outsourced by the government. Of course, in those situations like British Telecom, where the sale happens via a stock offering to the public, the company still exists with the same name. The owners are different, and the information needs now default to "A," as discussed below. This is so for all services of the organization, instead of selected ones. This perspective holds for competing organizations as well.

PARTIAL DEREGULATION

In cases of partial deregulation, the analysis is more complex. Several telecommunication services are natural candidates for partial deregulation, including long distance telephone services, the path adopted by the U.S. when AT&T was divested. In particular, the advent of wireless telephone services changed the "natural monopoly" character of local telephone service. The infrastructure installation costs of a wired telephone may be as high as $2,000, whereas cellular phones can be as little as $800. In addition, cellular networks can be easily and rapidly installed, given enough capital. Due to higher per minute tariffs, return on investment is also much faster. This also increases the interest of potential new entrants.

Without Ownership Transfer

Let us first examine quadrant ("C"), the one without ownership transfer. In this case, the incumbent organization will face competition in the deregulated areas. For instance, the Telecommunications Act of 1996 forced telecommunication companies providing local service in the U.S. to give access to part of their infrastructure to qualified competitors. In practice, it became very expensive to create and improve interfaces between the incumbent's system and the systems of potential competitors. This was expensive in terms of process, too. For instance, there were a lot of details, which have been difficult and slow to implement. One of the "self-regulation" outcomes is "skimming" by competitors. For example, in 1980 long distance bus service in England was deregulated (Foster, 1992). The original company, National Express, was not owned by the government in this particular case, but the issues are basically similar. Immediately, ten independents grouped together to compete on the key inter-city routes. The result was halved fares, with a corresponding increase in supply frequencies and demand. It should be noted, however, that by 1983 most of these independents had left the market, defeated by National Express' better marketing, exclusive access to transfer stations and deep pockets that match competitors lower prices. There was still a net gain for the public, since the quality of service was at least as high afterwards. Prices, although generally increasing to levels similar to pre-deregulation, entered a self-policing zone where any unusually high priced connection ("monopoly profits") could be skimmed by competitors deciding to enter only in these high profit potential routes.

An example of quadrant "C" was the cellular operation of Telebrás S.A., the Brazilian Telecommunication Monopoly (Evaristo, 1998). Telebrás was created in 1972 as a holding company that included the local providers in most of the Brazilian States plus Embratel, the long distance operator. In the early 1990's, legislation was proposed to allow most Brazilian monopolies to go through a period of liberalization, and eventually privatization. Cellular service liberalization did not include ownership transfer, only sales of concessions to new operators in the B-Band digital frequency spectrum. Current monopoly operators planned to still be in the cellular telephone market in the A-Band analog frequency spectrum.

One of the key issues for the monopoly holder prior to deregulation, as in the case described above, is getting ready for the competition. In some cases, monopoly input in the form of lobbying may help define which areas will be, or not be, deregulated. In this way, the monopoly could try to influence the opening of the market in an area where it is particularly strong or, conversely, does not have strong interests. This presupposes strong situation analyses using CI techniques; for instance, scenario analysis based on industry analysis, crossed with SWOT (Strengths, Weaknesses, Opportunities and Threats) analysis and appropriate decision-making as a result. Another concern is to avoid blind spots or situations that have not been clearly analyzed (Zahra & Chaples, 1993).

A good example of the pre-deregulation competitive intelligence effort occurred in Brazil in April, 1997. Fifteen consortia submitted their proposals for B-Band cellular telephone concessions amidst extreme secrecy and some paranoia. Some proposals came in lead lined metal boxes to foil CI efforts by the competition (Rocha, 1997). Others brought their proposals in armored trucks. Others yet had specialists in electronic bugging sweeping the premises where the proposals were being prepared. Proposals were submitted separately for each of 10 regions. One could argue that the information so strongly sought after by the competitors was the proposal price to the Brazilian government. Small differences could imply loss of large future profits. This is a significant example of active CI, and also of extraordinary efforts in counterintelligence. On the other hand, as predicted by the framework presented in Table 1, the information needed by the monopoly to decide the geographical areas, and the minimum price required for each region, was the expected investment in that area as well as the GDP, population, percent of population with telephone, and area size. The original objective was to create similarly sized markets with respect to these criteria. One of the Competitive Intelligence tools used was demand forecast, based on the variety, quantity and quality of information kept and utilized by the monopoly.

Concurrently, Embratel was making efforts to improve quality to meet competition in a partially deregulated environment. It hired consultants and embarked on a restructuring effort, eliminating regional management, offering employees early retirement packages, and embracing a Total Quality Program. This behavior is typical of companies on the verge of open competition. Embratel was eventually sold in mid 1998. The information Embratel was seeking at the time involved, for instance, good knowledge of the B Band consortia quality and how Embratel and the local telephone providers may still have been able to compete with successful bidders using the previous monopoly allocated A Band cellular spectrum. It is interesting to note the asymmetry of intelligence acquired and needed both by the incumbent and by the potential new entrants. The new entrants have been involved in this business elsewhere previously, and have data from their efforts in other countries. Therefore, they understand each other's capabilities pretty well. On the other hand, the incumbent has to learn about its own capabilities in a deregulated market.

And, it needs a crash course on what competitors are doing abroad as well as the significance of those efforts.

Another financially painful example in quadrant "C" is the creation of callback services, a de facto competitor to PTTs even before deregulation became an issue. Single handedly, call back services were responsible for one of the first long distance call price reduction waves in localized markets such as Europe and South America. Although there was no ownership transfer, its existence forced the monopolies to alter their strategy.[2] This is clearly a one-time only event, but competitive intelligence tools may help decrease the importance of future "surprises" by offering longer forewarning periods as well as potential counterstrategies.

With Ownership Transfer

Partial deregulation with ownership transfer ("A") is typically more complex than "C," depending on which assets are being sold. If all assets relative to a segment of the telecommunication market (say, telegraphy) were sold, we fall back into quadrant "B," already discussed. However, if there is a partial sale of assets, but the monopoly keeps the ability to compete in this particular segment, then the needs for information are similar to quadrant "C."

In Italy, Telecom Italia SpA is moving from quadrant "C" to "A" and then to "B." The first move from "C" to "A" happened in a similar way to Telebrás, with partial sale of the cellular frequency spectrum. The current move is from "A" to "B," although it is not clear at this point that full scale privatization will ever be reached.

Let us analyze the presence of AT&T in Italy, which started over ten years ago with a small two-person shop in Rome. Its objectives were always very clear: (1) to identify its competitive advantages and select specific areas in which to compete; (2) to fully understand the local market; (3) to lobby with the Italian government for telecom liberalization; and (4) to develop local partnerships (Mueller, 1997b). First, AT&T Italia started by servicing U.S. military personnel stationed at several NATO bases. Concurrently, it was increasing its intelligence base by learning more about the Italian market. In an intensive market research program, it was able to segment Italian consumers by residential and commercial users, and then analyze the needs of each.

Several interesting findings ensued. Because the Italian commercial market is more fragmented than in other countries in Europe; and because it is dominated by small and medium size businesses, it became clear that a successful telecommunications strategy should involve geographical presence in a larger number of areas, as compared to one hub close to a major capital. Lobbying also had special characteristics. Since there was not an independent regulatory body for telecommunications, it became important to have

---

[2] We are considering more than just pricing strategy here. In a typical battle against this kind of problem, a South American PTT tried to stop callback services by blocking calls to the area code in the U.S. where callbacks originated, a remote place in the Midwest. The Callback Company responded by changing their switch to a Washington, D.C. area code. End of argument.

closer contact with legislators and the national operator. Another use of competitive intelligence at this point is the analysis of potential partners as the liberalization of the market progresses. One obvious partner may be Telecom Italia itself; but the state power company ENEL, the energy and gas group ENI, and the Ferrovia dello Stato train company all could make interesting partners as well. They have either right-of-way ownership needed for optical fiber network laying (when not already installed for private communication) or deep penetration in the local market with their monthly energy billing. Finally, Berlusconi's media conglomerate combines a television network and advanced technological know-how with good marketing skills. And naturally, potential competitors in Italy, such as BT, MCI, and Sprint are also looking for partners themselves.

In Italy, privatization efforts are underway as part of deregulation. Telecom Italia's success has more than tripled its stock valuation in the last year. Therefore, to acquire a board seat one would have to give $1.04 billion. That would return a 1.5% stake in the company. This is a good example of governments raising money, but by widely dispersing ownership, not giving away too much control. Telecom Italia is planning to make one of the largest ever equity offerings in Europe, potentially raising more than $15 billion.

Something similar happened with France Telecom (FT). As much as 49% of the company was expected to be sold on the open market starting in October of 1997. A further 7.5 % share swap with Deutsche Telekom is expected, increasing regional ties and stabilizing the market under the perspective of the incumbents. Even before there was increased competition in the French market, FT had already reduced its inflated long distance and international tariffs and concurrently increased local service connection charges. One of the consequences, as in situation "C" above, is that cherry picking becomes more difficult for new entrants. In practice, this has moved the battle into an area where FT enjoys considerable advantage, the home connection service. At the current level of technology, this includes millions of miles of lines in the ground. This could change, if enough radio spectrum was made available to create fixed wireless service at reasonable prices. This is another example of where CI tools could be helpful in predicting and analyzing various scenarios.

In the case of the liberalization of British Telecom, the situation moved from quadrant "C" to "B." It provides evidence of an interesting behavior change. One of the earlier steps in liberalization of the monopoly involved only equipment sales liberalization, which would be characteristic of quadrant "C". In fact, most deregulation efforts started this way. The proposed timetable was that telephones and modems should be liberalized first (November, 1981), ending with PABX by July of 1983. The ordering of liberalization, according to Hulsink (1996) was such that the market in which BT would be most susceptible to external competition, namely the small PABX market, was also the one kept under BT's strict control for the longest period. This is a typical example of behavior from quadrant "C." When the company's shares were sold to the public, the only interest from the government through their regulatory arm was to ensure some degree of fairness of competition between the duopoly players (quadrant "B"), quite a difference from the earlier effort to improve BT's position before divestiture.

Another interesting example is the possibility of strategic alliances, mergers or buyouts which can happen in any of the quadrants, but are more likely to occur when there has been at least some history of deregulation (quadrants "A" and "B"). One of the reasons for such alliances is the large corporations' need for worldwide services in the form of a seamless communication network with large contracts providing economies of scale to all participants. One of the largest alliances including BT, MCI and Telefonica of Spain – Concert – may fall through because of a $32 billion hostile takeover bid of MCI by Worldcom. Anticipating such moves, as well as analyzing their consequences, is one of the prime areas of competitive intelligence use.

IMPLICATIONS

Practice

The data analyzed in this chapter suggests that most telecommunication monopolies, attempting to deregulate, move from quadrant "C" into "A" and then into "B." Fewer move directly from "C" to "B." The first path is more common because of the existence of increasing deregulation. That path also exhibits fewer sudden discontinuities regarding the status quo of the primary organization involved.

Telecommunications equipment deregulation, which has already happened almost everywhere, is characteristic in quadrant "C." The sale of an asset that did not belong to the monopoly holder, such as a limited frequency spectrum accompanied by cellular operating licenses, is another possibility as seen in the case of Telebrás. Callback companies also started operating worldwide recently. They also had their share of deregulation activities. Therefore, one could start in quadrant "C" with an intelligence analysis of the new entrants still competing with the incumbent. In this case, all players need to know about everybody else. It also permits a glimpse of the natural path that events may take. One may anticipate that "C" will evolve into "A." Quadrant "A" is characterized by even smaller incumbent presence. The earlier new entrants may want to entrench themselves for the possibility that other competitors may decide to enter the market when the incumbent fully divests itself of the specific market segment, or sell at least part of the segment. In the latter case, the competition among new entrants with the incumbent is the keenest, and there is much space for intelligence efforts.

Finally, there is a move to "B." This quadrant is characterized by complete divestiture of the government telecommunications monopoly. As seen above, the government did not own the telecommunications monopoly in the U.S., so this was not an issue. England has done so already. Some countries such as Italy and Japan are unlikely to move into this quadrant in the short run because of union agreements and remnant laws, respectively. Others yet, such as Brazil, just recently got there. The larger the competitive space left by this divestiture, the more likely the appearance of new entrants, or alternatively market share acquisition by earlier entrants.

What does the future hold for the deregulated telecommunication markets? For how long will long distance call pricing be based on distance as opposed to congestion or the market's ability to bear it? Such a solution has long been adopted by airlines. What will the new telecommunication provider structure look like, both individually and as a network/industry? These and many other questions are unanswered at the moment, but competitive intelligence will be one of the tools that will help guide stakeholders in telecommunications to make sense out of this complex situation and to strategize for different future scenarios.

Research

There is increasing research on the impact of innovations regarding technology diffusion in societies. Telecommunications has changed modern society forever. Adoption patterns can be quite different in regulated, deregulated, or "in-flux" telecommunications environments. This current analysis offers the possibility of studying the effect of this third possibility on societal patterns, such as telecommuting, virtual organizations, work habits, and many others.

A limitation of this research is that it only analyzes government-owned monopolies. A more general analysis could also include privately owned monopolies and go further in explaining the types of ownership transfer that are possible. The relationship between regulating bodies and ownership transfer, in particular, seems to be a fertile ground for more research.

This chapter focuses on telecommunications monopolies, which are strongly technologically dependent. Other types of monopolies may have different characteristics and therefore different deregulation and privatization trajectories, a potentially interesting question to be empirically analyzed.

CONCLUSIONS

This chapter started with a description of monopolies and their overriding characteristics. A framework that analyzed possible deregulation and/or privatization alternatives was developed. The data analyzed suggested that not only were there numerous deregulation possibilities, but also that there was a most likely trajectory among them. The resulting deregulation model is dynamic, since it takes into consideration the value of time in the deregulation progression. This framework was used to show that in each phase the information and intelligence needs of the organizations are different. In particular, it was suggested that competitive intelligence, as a tool, might help guide PTTs in the maze that characterizes the deregulation process as well as in the analysis of future possibilities in what promises to be an even more turbulent and competitive environment.

REFERENCES

Brock, G. (1994). *Telecommunication policy for the information age.* Cambridge: Harvard University Press.

Evaristo, J. R. (1998). The impact of privatization on organizational information needs: Lessons from the Brazilian Telecommunications Holding Company. *Information technology and people,* 11(3), forthcoming.

Foster, C. D. (1992). *Privatization, public ownership and the regulation of natural monopoly.* Oxford: Blackwell.

Hulsink, W. (1996). *Do nations matter in a globalising industry?* Delft, The Netherlands: Eburon Publishers.

Kahaner, L. (1996). Who's watching you? *Fleet Owner,* 91(10), 12.

Landau, N. (1995). Managing Banker's Intelligence. *International Business,* 22-25.

Mann, J. K. (1995). Ask an intelligent question... *Electric perspectives,* 20(3), 82-84.

Mueller, M. (1997a). Universal service and the telecommunications act: Myth Made Law. *Communications of the ACM,* 40(3), 39-47.

Mueller, T. (1997b, August). Playing to win in a monopoly market: AT&T Italia. *Hemispheres,* 35-38.

OECD. (1987). *Trends of Change in Telecommunications Policy.* Paris: North Holland Publishing Co. on behalf of the OECD.

Ojala, M. (1993). The patent and the trademark database: What can they do for you? *Link-Up,* 10(5).

Prescott, J., & Grant, J. (1988). A manager's guide for evaluating competitive analysis techniques. *Interfaces,* 18(3), 10-22.

Rocha, L. (1997, April 16). Uma virada na telefonia Brasileira. *Veja,* 118-121.

Scherer, F. M. (1980). *Industrial market structure and economic performance.* Chicago: Rand McNally.

Sueyoshi, T. (1996). Divestiture of Nippon telegraph and telephone. *Management Science,* 42(9), 1326-1351.

Yasai-Ardekani, M., & Nystrom, P. (1996). Design for environmental scanning systems: Tests of a contingency theory. *Management Science,* 42(2), 187-204.

Zahra, S., & Chaples, S. (1993). Blind spots in competitive analysis. *Academy of Management Executive,* 7(2), 7-28.

Chapter 5

PRIVATIZATION, COMPETITION, AND ORGANIZING THE ECONOMY

Stuart S. Nagel

Probably the two most important issues in organizing the economy of a nation are: (1) the relationship between the public and private sectors of the nation, and (2) within each sector, to what extent should multiple firms or agencies be encouraged, rather than a single large-scale firm or agency.

On the division of labor between the public and private sectors, one could have: (1) variations on capitalism (or private ownership and operation), (2) variations on socialism (or governmental ownership or operation), (3) something in between (such as a mixed economy), or (4) something that emphasizes the advantages of both (such as contracting out with liberal requirements in the contract to protect workers, consumers, and the environment).

On the matter of a single, or multiple firms or agencies, one could have: (1) monopoly under socialism or capitalism, (2) competition under socialism or capitalism, (3) a compromise such as an oligopoly of a few firms generally working together, or (4) the benefits of competition, including having lower prices and higher quality, while making provision for relocating displaced workers through retraining and job facilitators.

The first part of this chapter discusses privatization issues especially in the context of converting communism in East Europe. The second half of this chapter discusses competition, especially in the context of newly bringing it to (1) the private sector in electricity and telephone services and, (2) the public sector in public education, the post office, and other public services.

I. PRIVATIZATION, INFLATION, AND SUPER-OPTIMUM SOLUTIONS

The changes that have occurred in Eastern Europe and in many other regions and nations of the world provide an excellent opportunity to apply systematic policy analysis to determine such basic matters as how to organize the economy, the government, and other social institutions. Super-optimum solutions refer to public policy alternatives that can enable conservatives, liberals, and other major viewpoints to all come out ahead of their best initial expectations simultaneously. The problems of privatization and inflation can illustrate what is involved in super-optimum solutions.

A. Privatization

1. Alternatives

Table 1 analyzes the fundamental issue of "socialism versus capitalism" in the context of government versus private ownership and operation of the basic means of producing industrial and agricultural products. The essence of socialism in this context is government ownership and operation of factories and farms, or at least those larger than the handicraft or garden-size, as in the Soviet Union of 1960. The essence of capitalism is private ownership and operation of both factories and farms, as in the United States of 1960. The neutral position or middle way is to have some government and some private ownership-operation, as in Sweden of 1960. The year 1960 is used because that is approximately when the Soviet Union began to change with the advent of Nikita Khruschev. The United States also underwent big changes in the 1960s with the advent of John F. Kennedy's administration.

Table 1 refers to government ownership-operation as the liberal or left-wing alternative, as it is in the United States and in world history at least since the time of Karl Marx. The table refers to private ownership-operation as the conservative or right-wing alternative, as it is in the U.S. and elsewhere, at least since the time of Adam Smith. In recent years in the Soviet Union and in China, those favoring privatization have been referred to as liberals, and those favoring retention of government ownership-operation have been referred to as conservatives. The "labels" make no difference in this context. The object of Table 1 is to find a super-optimum solution that more than satisfies the goals of both ideologies or groups, regardless of their labels.

Table 1
Government Versus Private Ownership and Operation

Criteria Alternatives	C Goal High Productivity C=3 L=1	L Goal Equity C=1 L=3	L Goal Workplace Quality C=1 L=3	L Goal Environmental Protection C=1 L=3	L Goal Consumer Protection C=1 L=3	N Total (Neutral Weights)	L Total (Liberal or Socialistic Weights)	C Total (Conservative or Capitalistic Weights)
L Alternative Government Ownership & Operation (Socialism)	2	4	2	2	2	24	32*	16
C Alternative Private Ownership & Operation (Capitalism)	4	2	2	2	2	24	28	20*
N Alternative Some Gov't & Some Private	3	3	2	2	2	18	24	18
S Alternative 100% Gov't Own & 100% Private Operation	>3	>3	>3	>3	>3	>30	39**	>21**

2. Goals and Relations

The key capitalistic "goal" is high productivity in terms of income-producing goods, substantially above what it costs to produce them. The key socialistic goal is equity in terms of the sharing of ownership, operation, wealth, and income. Other goals that tend to be more socialistic than capitalistic, but are less fundamental consist of: (1) workplace quality, including wages, hours, safety, hiring by merit, and worker input; (2) environmental protection, including reduction of air, water, radiation, noise, and other forms of pollution; and (3) consumer protection, including low prices and goods that are durable, safe, and high quality.

The "relations" between each alternative and each goal is shown on a 1-5 scale where 5 means highly conducive to the goal, 4 means mildly conducive, 3 means neither conducive nor adverse, 2 means mildly adverse, and 1 means highly adverse to the goal. We have here a classic tradeoff.

Going down the "productivity" column, the liberal socialistic alternative does not score so high on productivity for a lack of profit-making incentives and a surplus of bureaucratic interference in comparison to the capitalistic alternative, assuming the level of technology is held constant. The empirical validity of that statement is at least partially confirmed by noting that the capitalistic countries of Japan and West Germany are more productive than their socialistic counterparts of East Germany and China, although they began at approximately the same level as of 1945 at the end of World War II. Going down the "equity" column, the liberal socialistic alternative does score relatively high. By definition, it involves at least a nominal collective sharing in the ownership and operation of industry and agriculture, which generally leads to less inequality in wealth and income than capitalism does.

On the goals that relate to the "workplace, the environment, and consumers," the socialists traditionally argue that government ownership-operation is more sensitive to those matters because it is less profit oriented. The capitalists traditionally argue that private ownership-operation is more sensitive in competitive marketplaces in order to find quality workers and to increase the quantity of one's consumers. The reality (as contrasted to the theory) is that without alternative incentives or regulations, both government managers and private managers of factories and farms are motivated towards high production at low cost. That kind of motivation leads to cutting back on the expenses of providing workplace quality, environmental protection, and consumer protection. The government factory manager of the Polish steelworks may be just as abusive of labor as the private factory manager for the U.S. Steel Company. Likewise, the government factory managers in the state factories of China may be just as insensitive to consumer safety and durability as their monopolistic counterparts in the American automobile industry.

3. A Super-Optimum Solution

As for how the super-optimum solution operates, it involves government ownership, but all the factories and farms are rented to private entrepreneurs to develop productive and profitable manufacturing and farming. Each lease is renewable every year, or longer if necessary, to get productive tenants. A renewal can be refused if the factory or farm is not being productively developed, or if the entrepreneur is not showing adequate sensitivity to workers, the environment, and consumers.

As for some of the "advantages" of such an SOS system, it is easier to not renew a lease than it is to issue injunctions, fines, jail sentences, or other negative sanctions. It is also much less expensive than subsidies. The money received for rent can be an important source of tax revenue for the government to provide productive subsidies elsewhere in the economy. Those subsidies can be especially used for encouraging technological innovation; diffusion, the upgrading of skills, and stimulating competition for market share which can be so much more beneficial to society than either socialistic or capitalistic monopolies. The government can more easily demand sensitivity to workers, the environment, and consumers from its renters of factories and farms than it can from itself. There is a conflict of interest in regulating oneself.

This SOS alternative "is only available to socialistic countries" like the USSR, China, Cuba, North Korea, and others since they already own the factories and land. It would not be economically or politically feasible for capitalistic countries to move from the conservative capitalistic alternative to the SOS solution by acquiring ownership through payment or confiscation. This is an example where socialistic countries are in a position to decide between socialism and capitalism by compromising and winding up with the worst of both possible worlds. That means the relative unproductivity of socialism and the relative inequity of capitalism. The socialistic countries are also in a position to decide between the two basic alternatives by winding up with the best of both possible worlds. That means retaining the equities and social sensitivities of government ownership, while having the high productivity that is associated with profit-seeking entrepreneurial capitalism. It would be difficult to find a better example of compromising versus super-optimizing than the current debate over socialism versus capitalism.

B. Inflation

As part of the transition from a communist economy to a free marketplace, a key problem is the inflation which is likely to occur. It occurs for a number of "reasons", such as: (1) The lifting of price controls which provide for artificially low prices on essentials like food, shelter, and clothing. The better approach is food stamps, rent supplements, or subsidies rather than price controls. (2) The shortages of goods at least until the private sector can replace the production of the public sector. This may require subsidies to enable would-be entrepreneurs to get started, especially if competition among producers is desired. (3)The tendency on the part of the government to print money in order to meet government payrolls and other expenditures. That tendency is stimulated by the loss of income due to the government turning over income-producing activities to the private sector. In theory, the remedy is to establish new taxes and raise old ones. In practice, one of the prices of democracy is effective public resistance to being taxed. The long run solution is to increase the gross national product through well-placed subsidies. Doing so increases the tax base so that relatively low tax rates can bring in more revenue.

1. Alternatives and Goals

Some of these ideas are incorporated into Table 2 on "Inflation and Russia, Starting 1992." The conservative alternative in Russia would have been to maintain the command economy of price control as much as possible. The liberal position would have been to establish a free marketplace with a hands-off policy by the government. The compromise position was indexing of wages to cushion the effects of inflation, manipulating interest rates as with the American Federal Reserve system, and decreasing government spending while increasing taxes in accordance with Keynesian theory. Indexing is objected to in Russia on the grounds that it encourages inflation. Raising interest rates does not mean much for reducing inflation in Russia if people are not driving up prices with borrowed money. Reducing government spending and increasing taxes may be even more difficult in Russia than it is in the United States. This is so because of the need for well-placed government spending as part of the transition and because the people may be more resistant to being burdened with new taxes than having old taxes raised.

The key "conservative goal" is to put a fast stop to inflation. The key "liberal goal" is to facilitate a fast move to free enterprise. On stopping inflation, price controls in a command economy can do that better in the short run than a free marketplace, especially one that has both a shortage of goods and a shortage of competitive producers and sellers. On a fast move to free enterprise, a hands-off policy by the government does that almost by definition, although not necessarily competitive free enterprise. A command economy interferes with free enterprise almost by definition, but that partly depends on what the economy commands.

2. A Three-Part SOS

A super-optimum solution involves raising the GNP fast by well-placed incentives. That means incentives that relate to better marketing, more competition, and more equitable distribution. On the matter of "marketing" relative to production, the Russian economy is not doing so badly in producing food, housing, clothing, and other essentials, but the products are not getting to the consumers the way they should be. Food is rotting in the fields for lack of adequate storage and transportation facilities. A key reason in the past for spoilage was low controlled prices. Food that is getting out of the fields to the cities may then rot in warehouses for lack of a well-organized retailing system. Communist Russia drove out a high percentage of its retail businessmen in the early years and drove out their sons and daughters in more recent years. Communist Russia as of 1917 was comparable to medieval Spain in 1492 in driving out the Arab, Jewish, and other merchants. Both places went downhill thereafter. Russia, however, is in a position through well-placed subsidies (including training subsidies) to stimulate a new entrepreneurial class.

Table 2
Inflation and Russia, Starting 1992

Criteria / Alternatives	C Goal Fast Stop to Inflation C=3	N=2	L=1	L Goal Fast Move to Free Enterprise C=1	N=2	L=3	N Total (Neutral Weights)	L Total (Liberal Weights)	C Total (Conservative Weights)
C Alternative Command Economy (Price Control)		4			2		12	10	14*
L Alternative Free Marketplace (Hands-Off)		2			4		12	14*	10
N Alternative Indexing, Interest Rates, Spending-Taxing		-			3		12	12	12
S Alternative Raise GNP Fast by Well-Placed Incentives	≥ 3.5			≥ 3.5			≥ 12	≥ 14**	≥ 14**

NOTE:

The SOS incentives are designed to stimulate:

(1) Better marketing

(2) More competition

(3) More equitable distribution through vouchers for food, clothes, and housing.

On the matter of more "competition", it was an enriching experience to hear one of the leaders of the Communist Party of the Soviet Union speak at a conference at the Russian Academy of Sciences on the need for a competitive free market. His position was that the Communist Party had no objection as of 1990 to private ownership and operation of the means of production and distribution. They did, however, object to putting those facilities into the hands of national, regional, and local monopolists. In that sense, the Communist Party was preaching a doctrine of competitive capitalism more akin to Adam Smith than either Marxist-Leninists or American conservatives. Both Marx and Lenin objected to monopolies, but thought that government ownership would show sensitivity to workers and consumers that private monopolies do not. That was a bit naive in view of the abuse of workers by such government-owned entities as the Polish steel mills, or the abuse of consumers by such government-owned entities as public power companies. Likewise, American conservatives tend to be quite supportive of monopolistic power companies, as opposed to the competitive system of the New Deal whereby the Tennessee Valley Authority and other publicly-owned power companies would serve as competitive yardsticks.

It is one thing to say that competition is desirable. It is another thing to bring it about. It does not occur through natural forces or invisible hands, as indicated by the increasing monopolization of the American economy through business mergers. It also does not occur through anti-trust penalties since both conservative and liberal governments are reluctant to break up what they consider to be efficient big businesses using economies of scale. The Japanese Ministry of International Trade and Industry may have an ideal modern approach of combining privatization with competition. The MITI gives subsidies to Japanese firms in such industries as automobiles, electronics, and computers. It does so in such a way as to guarantee multiple Japanese firms in all those industries, rather than a single monopolistic giant, or two or three oligopolistic giants. Well-placed subsidies in Russia could deliberately encourage the development of competing firms. Such competition results in lower prices, better quality goods, and better workplaces to attract workers.

The third area for well-placed subsidies is to guarantee more "equitable distribution". Private enterprise is not likely to want to provide unprofitable mail service to isolated rural families. The publicly owned post office is willing to do so. A private enterprise, though, would also be willing to do so with a well-placed equity subsidy, assuming society feels that there should be rural mail service. That is more efficient than forcing the price of postage below a profitable level across the country causing private mail delivery and other enterprises to want to sell out to the government. It makes more sense in terms of prices that operate within the laws of supply and demand to let the price of food and housing rise or fall in accordance with those forces. Food stamps and rent vouchers can be provided to those who otherwise would not eat or go homeless.

C. Tabular or Spreadsheet Analysis

Thus with a system of well-placed incentives to improve marketing, competition, and equitable distribution, the Russian economy could reduce inflation, especially inflation that is due to shortages of goods and monopolistic pricing. The effect may not be as great in the short run as price control, but it avoids black markets and is better in the long run. Likewise, such a system of incentives can move the economy fast toward free enterprise, especially competitive free enterprise that the public will accept and even welcome. The effect on free enterprise may not be as great in the short run as a total hands-off policy, but the incentives system avoids the unfree system in the long run of monopolistic control with inflated prices.

Tables 1 and 2 both illustrate how the super-optimum alternative can be a loser on every goal and still be an overall winner. Being that kind of a loser means not coming out in first place on any of the goals, but generally running contrary to the tradeoff idea that if an alternative does well on some goals, then it must not do so well on other goals. All we need are alternatives that are generally on the positive side on a 1-5 scale, which means doing better than a 3. Such an alternative is then likely to score higher on the liberal totals than the liberal alternative, which does poorly on the conservative goals. The SOS alternative is also likely to score higher on the conservative totals than the conservative alternative, which does poorly on the liberal goals.

D. Progressive versus Reactionary Privatization

Privatization does not mean an inherent conflict between government ownership and operation, and private ownership and operation. It can mean government ownership and private operation through a progressive system of contracting out as contrasted to a reactionary system.

A progressive system involves contracting out with contract provisions requiring environmental protection, workplace safety, and consumer protection. It also involves contracting out to more than one supplier of the service in order to provide competition. It also involves relatively short-term contracts that come up for renewal and do not get renewed if they are not being complied with . . . as well as provisions in the contract for terminating the contract before the term is up if violations are severe enough.

A reactionary system involves contracting out, leaving the private entrepreneur free to do about anything with regard to the environment, workplace, or consumers. Worse, the entrepreneur is given a monopolistic franchise that leads to even more abuses than simply not having any contract provisions against the firm. Also highly undesirable is that the contract is for an indefinite time, or a definite time that is so long that the idea of nonrenewal gets lost in inertia. Or, the contract provides for a relatively short time, but there is no monitoring of the contract to see if it is being well complied with; and renewal tends to be automatic.

The concept of contracting out normally refers to the reactionary version, and therefore it tends to be opposed by liberals. A progressive version of contracting out, though, can be even better for promoting liberal values than government ownership and operation. The progressive version is also politically and administratively feasible. It is politically feasible because it represents a move away from government ownership and operation, which conservatives should endorse. It is politically feasible for liberals, given the liberal provisions.

It is administratively feasible because there will be entrepreneurs who will be pleased to accept those contracting provisions, if what they are supplying in the way of services or other activities involves substantially less expense on their part than what they are being paid to do. If the contract is highly profitable, they can easily absorb the environmental, workplace, and consumer provisions.

Even though they are making a profit, the government and taxpayer may also be coming out well ahead. That is so because the private entrepreneur may be getting expenses way down through the incentive of competition and the private profit motive. Those incentives may also be substantially improving the quality of what is being provided, better than a monopolistic government agency could provide.

E. Some Conclusions

Overall conclusions can be derived from this analysis in terms of the substance of what is involved in the transition from socialism to capitalism in Russia and Eastern Europe.

1. Avoid Extreme Capitalism
Do not go to the opposite extreme of adopting a form of capitalism that capitalistic United States would consider to be too far in a right-wing conservative direction. The American federal government owns lots of land, especially in the western United States. It would be virtually unthinkable in American politics for the federal government to give the land away to private business, or even to sell a place like Yosemite National Park for private commercial development. It is not unthinkable, though, for the federal government to lease federal land for grazing, farming, or other development. It is likewise not unthinkable to award franchises to private entrepreneurs to sell products in Yosemite National Park.

The American federal government, even (and maybe especially) during the conservative Reagan administration, did not have a hands-off policy regarding the American economy. Reagan sought to make use of "well-placed subsidies" in the form of enterprise zones to attract business firms to the inner cities, and housing vouchers as a way of providing equity in the housing market.

2. Avoid the Middle Way and the Mixed-Up Economy

Do not go to the so-called middle way that is associated with places like Sweden, or the mixed economies of Western Europe. It may provide the worst of both possible worlds, rather than the best. This shows up in government versus private ownership and operation. The middle way of the mixed economy provides lots of production and distribution exclusively by the private sector and other production and distribution exclusively by the public sector. Each sector may operate "monopolistically" with insensitivity to workers, consumers, and the environment. This is contrasted with the super-optimum system of having title to the property in the government, with a renewable lease for private development; subject to non-renewal for violating the rights of workers, consumers, or the environment.

This also shows up in the command economy versus the laissez-faire marketplace. The mixed economy involves some products that are subject to price control; like rents in New York City, or the price of food in Africa. The prices of other products are allowed to rise and fall in accordance with the market. The controlled prices result in "shortages". The market prices result in "exploitation". Both undesirable occurrences can be avoided by: (1) letting all prices rise and fall in accordance with the market, and (2) having well-placed subsidies to provide for: (a) a more efficient market and marketing, (b) plus competition, and (c) plus equity for those who cannot meet the market prices.[1]

II. COMPETITION IN THE PUBLIC AND PRIVATE SECTORS

The purpose of this section of the chapter is to discuss ideas relating to such matters in the private sector as: (1) competition and cooperation occurring simultaneously, (2) competition versus monopoly, (3) encouraging competition and cooperation in the workplace, marketplace, academia, and the world, and (4) innovative ideas about competition. Ideas discussed relevant to the public sector include: (1) consolidation versus competition among agencies, and (2) competition within public schools, police departments, and political parties.

---

[1] On privatization in the Soviet Union and Eastern Europe, see Jan Prybyla (Ed.), *Privatizing and Marketizing Socialism* (Annals of the American Academy of Political and Social Science, 1990); and Richard Noyes (Ed.), *Now the Synthesis: Capitalism, Socialism and the New Social Contract* (Holmes & Meier, 1991). This book contains, in an appendix, an open letter to Mikhail Gorbachev advocating retention of title to collective farms while renting the land for entrepreneurial development. The open letter is signed by Nobel prizewinners Modigliani, Tobin, and Solow, as well as leading economists from throughout the world.

A. Competition in the Private Sector

1. Competition and Cooperation Simultaneously

A. In the Workplace

Some people make the wrong dichotomy between competition and cooperation as if they are in conflict with each other. Some Japanese assembly plants emphasize cooperation and competition simultaneously. Competition occurs partly by teams working against each other, but each person on the team is expected to cooperate almost to the point of giving one's life for the team. The teams are both highly competitive and cooperative with each other. They are fighting to see which team will do the best, but at the same time seeking to advance the well-being of the assembly plant. Also, within each team there is competition between the individual team members, with those falling behind subjected to severe rebuke. There are thus two levels of competition among team members on the same team and among teams. There are also two levels of cooperation by people working together within each team to make their team win, and the teams working together to boost the overall productivity of the assembly plant. Both kinds of activity are desirable. They can and should operate simultaneously.

B. The Academic World of Nobel Prizes

In the academic world, many of the Nobel prizes (maybe 90 percent of those won recently) have been won by people who are part of teams. They are not working alone. They have a number of assistants and colleagues and associates, although one person may be the acknowledged leader who gets the prize but who cannot do it by himself or herself. The competition between those teams trying to crack the genetic code was ferocious, as indicated by the double helix discovery. It is not so ferocious as trying to assassinate each other. It is ferocious with the separate teams working around the clock in order to find the solution before the other team does. There is actually cooperation among those academic teams, although it is not explicit. They are all working towards a common goal of cracking the genetic code, finding a cure for cancer, or whatever it is. Whatever one team discovers gets known by other teams, given the propensity of academics to publish what they learn, as contrasted to private companies. Academics not only publish, but also present at conferences even before publication can occur.

C. Public-Private Orientation

This does tie in a bit with the private-public orientation, not because private is competition and public is cooperative. It ties in since the solution to the private-public problem is to do both public and private. Likewise the solution to the competitive-cooperation problem is to do both competition and cooperation. That is not having much in common though. There are numerous dilemmas in which the solution is to do both.

2. Competition Contrasted with Monopoly, Rather than with Cooperation

A. Post Office as a Government Monopoly

There is a need to talk about encouraging competition, even among government owned entities. That could include thinking about breaking up the post office so people could have a choice as to what post office they are going to send their mail out of. As of now, they only have a choice with regard to Express mail. Such mail is very important to people who send it, and does amount to a lot of dollars, especially on a per letter basis, but it is a relatively trivial aspect of the total quantity of mail carried. One could have competition more easily between private post offices and the government post office.

One big problem there is artificial rules on both sides. The government post office has its hands tied by rules that are totally arbitrary, such as being prohibited from using FAX mail. Private carriers have their hands tied as well by such rules as saying they cannot put private mail into mail boxes. That is highly arbitrary. The person who has a mail box in his hallway or in front of his house should be able to allow people other than the post office to put things in it. The post office argues that it is protecting the private mailbox owner from having a lot of junk thrown in his mailbox. Maybe it should be up to the private mailbox owner to decide whether it wants junk put in it by the local pizza store or whoever is distributing circulars. The circular distributors would find it easier to put their circulars in the mailbox at the curb than have to put them in the doors. Likewise with the private mail distributor. The rule should be that, so long as the distributor is not creating a nuisance by way of littering, they should be able to put things in mailboxes that are not locked unless the owner objects.

B. Typical Private Monopolies are Electricity and Telephoning

We need not get into every kind of monopoly, and what should be done about them individually. The typical monopolies are electricity and telephone service. The answers to what should be done about them are fairly simple. There is no reason why MCI and other such companies could not service local telephones as well as long distance telephone. The answer, though, is that they are basically just WATS resellers. They have no equipment of their own. There are no WATS discounts to be bought locally. The telephone company allows people in Champaign to make all the phone calls they want within the Champaign area at a flat fee. There is no discount available for making a trillion calls versus ten calls. Thus there would be no advantage from buying local telephone service from a middleman like MCI since the middleman gets no break by organizing a lot of people together. The local telephone service competition would have to come from real telephone companies, not just resellers.

There are enough other real telephone companies in the world besides Illinois Bell or the other Bells to provide competition if telephone service, like television and radio, could be handled without wires. Long distance telephone service is handled without wires. Therefore, it seems technically possible for a person to be able to phone down the block by way of a satellite, although that might be highly inefficient. If the call can go through an overhead wire or underground wire for 3 cents, it might cost 30 cents for the variable cost alone; forgetting for the moment about the fixed cost, to bounce the call off a satellite system. The bouncing of electricity rather than telephoning, though, could be highly profitable. It would not take much for a firm in St. Louis to be able to compete with the Illinois Power Company, charging lower rates, especially if the St. Louis firm does not have the burden of having to pay off an outrageously expensive and wasteful Clinton Power Plant. This is a public policy problem in that the Illinois Public Utilities Commission will not allow the St. Louis firm to compete in this Illinois area. Illinois Power will complain that it has invested a lot of dollars in the Clinton Power Plant, and that it is entitled to have a monopoly so it can pay off what it has invested.

The answer to that might be that, unless there is a binding legal contract guaranteeing a monopoly, the legislature is free to change its mind in passing a new statute that authorizes out of state electric companies, or even upstate or downstate electrical companies to come into the Champaign-Urbana area. In fact, the legislature could even subsidize them to do so in order to provide desirable competition. If Illinois Power goes bankrupt, the consumers will probably be better off because its facilities will be bought up by a more efficient company. It would be hard to ever find another company less efficient.

C. Competition in Place of Government and Private Monopolies

From the point of view of the consumer, the consumer is better off having two electrical companies to buy from, whether they are both government owned, both privately owned, or one government owned and one privately owned. So long as the companies know that they could lose their consumers to their competition, they provide much better service at lower costs than if they feel they have a captive set of consumers who have no place else to go.

3. Encouraging Competition and Cooperation in the Workplace, Marketplace, Academia, and the World

A. Workplace

There is also a lot of relevant literature in public and private administration and management textbooks dealing with human resources, organization behavior, personnel, management, and so on.

B. Marketplace

With regard to the marketplace, there are chapters in the economic regulation textbooks. They are nearly all obsolete though. They still talk about natural monopolies, and they talk about regulation for encouraging socially desired behavior, rather than well-placed subsidies and tax breaks. Some of the more modern literature, though, that deals with industrial policy and supply-side economics is relevant. The discussion of monopoly and competition in mail service, electricity, and telephoning (above) is also significant.

C. Academic Competition

Little has been written on academic competition. There are books, though, that deal with intellectual innovation. They are typically with the productivity and creativity books. They may contain some good ideas on how to stimulate inventions and discoveries. The phenomenon tends to be almost totally haphazard. Public policy does a lot more with regard to worker productivity and business firm productivity than it does with regard to stimulating the winning of Nobel Prizes. The prevailing attitude seems to be that it is a mysterious process that public policy cannot do anything about, that it just sort of happens. Public policy could definitely provide subsidies for academics to do more innovative things than is currently the case.

The NSF, for example, may almost have more of a stultifying influence on innovation than a stimulating influence. One of its key principles is peer review, which means that new ideas are much less likely to be supported than ideas that people on peer review committees already have. They tend to endorse ideas like they themselves support. That means they tend to support people who are like themselves, as contrasted to people with new ideas who may pose a threat. There is a real need for requiring a version of affirmative action in NSF programs whereby approximately 20% of the funding in each unit should go for stimulating new ideas. In the political science unit, for example, there ought to be 20% of the budget for a program called "innovative Ideas in Political Science." The applicants would be required to show that there is nothing they could cite that would be very relevant to what they are proposing to do. They would be required to show that none of the previous literature is especially relevant, although it may have some connection. It may be better to encourage crackpot ideas than to fund nothing but redundant mainstream material that adds nothing new.

That, however, sounds like it is getting away from the competition versus cooperation idea. It sounds like it is just a concern for public policy designed to stimulate innovation. The competition comes in offering prizes for certain kinds of new ideas on a highly competitive basis. An example would be the federal government's offering to buy, or totally replace, its automotive fleet with electric cars for anybody who can develop an electric car that meets certain specifications. This has caused some competition among innovative car developers. None of them so far has been able to meet the specifications, partly because of the need for more research funds rather than emphasizing a prize for a developed product.

It is harder to have competition like that in political science. The analogy would be like having a contest to see who could develop the best set of ideas for improving the efficiency of the Office of Personnel Management regarding its hiring guidelines, or improving the Office of Management and Budget regarding its budgeting guidelines. Political scientists would object to a contest like that as being too practical, and not sufficiently theoretical.

One thing that needs to be made clear is that we are not talking about competition to see who can do the most useless things, but competition to see who can do the most useful things. Competition is of no value if it has to do with people competing for some new kind of correlation coefficient that meets some kind of abstract math criteria. That is the statistical equivalent of squaring the circle, trisecting an angle without a protractor, or getting decimal roots of four-digit numbers in one's head without using a calculator. Those are all problems that pure mathematicians have been trying to solve for centuries that would serve no useful purpose if they ever solved them. That kind of competition should not be encouraged, although it should not be discouraged in the sense of prohibiting anybody from doing it. Trying to find a perpetual motion machine may be impossible; but if it is ever done, it would be highly useful. Trying to trisect an angle without a protractor may also be impossible, but even if it is someday done, it would be useless. Even third or fourth grade children know how to use a protractor to trisect an angle, and they do it with great accuracy. One could divide an angle into any number of parts with a protractor. Why play games pretending protractors do not exist, or pretending that calculators do not exist in order to play games seeing what kind of impressive calculations one can make in one's head.

D. International Realm

In the international realm, the best material dealing with competition is in the international economics textbooks or in the international trade chapter in more elementary economic textbooks. The best material dealing with cooperation is in the international organizations textbooks or in the international organizations chapter in more elementary international relations textbooks.

4. Other and General Aspects

A. Material Dealing with Competition and Cooperation in the Abstract

There is a lot of textbook material on all of these realms; the workplace, the marketplace, the international realm, and to a less extent the academic and innovative realm. There is also material dealing with competition and cooperation in the abstract in the social psychology literature. There are chapters, or at least a chapter on the subject in Kimble Young's sociology textbook (pp. 67-73, *Sociology: A Study of Society and Culture*, American Book company, 1949), and in the social psychology textbooks.

B. Innovative Ideas about Competition

The key question is: what is there that can be said on the subject that goes beyond the textbook literature. Some of the innovative ideas include the following.

(1) The idea of competition within so-called natural monopolies in the private sector.
(2) The idea of competition where a government-owned operation is involved.
(3) The idea of competition among workers to the point of what may to outsiders look like extreme stress. The kind of competition that is sometimes looked upon with favor among workers is piecework, which is not necessarily competition since a worker can be paid on a piecework basis who is the only worker working for the firm. It does not require any kind of competitive interaction. It is just a different kind of incentive system as contrasted to being paid by the hour. What is interesting is the idea of workers being more

productive in spite of the fact that, at least to outsiders, it looks like they are under extreme stress even to the point of looking like they would be likely to have a nervous breakdown when in reality the stress is comparable to that of playing on a football team or basketball team; and for many, it becomes almost fun.

(4) The idea of extreme competition among academics as being socially desirable. Normally competition is thought of as being desirable primarily among business firms and is frowned upon in the academic world.

(5) The idea of extreme competition among countries being good, as long as it is not violent. Violent competition is not desirable whether it is among countries, businesses, workers, or academics.

(6) The idea of combining extreme cooperation with extreme competition has some innovative aspects to it whereby workers can be extremely competitive within a team to see who can do the best job, but at the same time they recognize that they have to work together in order for their team to win over the competing team.

A good example is a relay race with four people on each relay team. Each tries to outrun other members of the team. They do not do so in a destructive way whereby they put thumbtacks in each other's shoes. They do so in a positive competitive way where each member of the relay team wants desperately to do better than everybody else on the relay team, but at the same time recognizing that the big honors or additional honors are from having the team win over other teams. That means cheering the other members of one's own team, although partly to provide stiff competition for one's self. That is in recognition that one will be better running against good players than having the competition be weak.

A good example is also in table tennis, where good players refuse to play with people that they can beat by more than a certain number of points. It hurts their game, it wastes their time. They only want to play against people who have a reasonably good chance of beating them because they recognize that improves their own playing. They may even welcome players who will beat them in order to improve their game. It is that kind of competitive attitude that needs to be encouraged. The table tennis analogy could be extended by talking in terms of playing doubles. A good table tennis player in a doubles match wants to excel as an individual. At the same time, he wants his team to win. It is a good combination of competition between two people on the same side, along with cooperation. Each player wants to be a separate hero while at the same time having the sum of the two heroes add up to being an unbeatable team.

Any team that does not have people striving to be individual heroes, and only thinking in terms of sacrificing for the good of the team, will not do as well as a team that combines both a highly competitive internal spirit and enough cooperation to enable the sum of the parts to outdo the sum of the parts on the opposing teams. There has been no sports hero in any field of sports such as baseball, basketball, or football who ever won much recognition by being great on assisting others. The all-time most valuable player awards (and those are team awards not individual awards) go to leading pitchers, hitters, quarterbacks, and basketball scorers. They do not go to the person who feeds off to the leading basketball scorer or to the person who is great on lateral passes to the runners in football.

C. Liberals and Conservatives to Still Fight

The material ties in with SOS analysis in trying to bring out the fact that even though an SOS solution enables liberals and conservatives to come out ahead of their best expectations, that does not mean that they submerge their identities in some kind of cooperative effort which loses their individual contributions. Many would say free speech is the most important public policy, because that is where public policy ideas get generated. Its essence is to encourage individuality, and not to encourage people to become part of some kind of cooperative effort where one does not deviate from the mainstream. We want some kind of cooperative effort where one does not deviate from the mainstream. We want super-optimum solutions where everybody comes out ahead, but everybody still preserves their separate competitive existence. We want liberals and conservatives to still fight, not in the sense of doing anything violent towards each other, but in the sense of competing to see who can come up with the best solutions for social problems and public policy problems. SOS analysis is a brining together to resolve disputes on a high level of super satisfaction, but not a brining together to wipe out individuality and competition. We want simultaneously to have vigorous competition partly because it leads to super-optimum solutions.

Someone might say that after achieving the super-optimum solution, then the vigorous competition is no longer needed. The answer to that is that there are always new problems to be resolved because it is impossible to achieve a state of being where there are no scarce resources, where everybody says that they have all they want in terms of : health, job opportunities, housing, environmental protection, compliance with the law, and everything else regarding public policy problems.

We know well from previous experience that the more people get, the more their appetites frequently get whetted for wanting more. People who have virtually nothing in pre-literate societies frequently have very little ambition to improve, partly because they are so much in a rut that they find it difficult to conceive that anything could make life better. People who are on the rise, though, get rising expectations and the satisfying of their previous goals causes them to raise their expectations and their future goals. Thus, society can always benefit from competition as to how those goals can be best satisfied at any given point in time with super-optimum solutions.

B. Competition in the Public Sector

1. Consolidation versus Competition among Agencies

A good example would be in the environmental field where policy analysis people in the early 70's pushed for the establishment of an environmental protection agency at the federal level and in all 50 states, arguing that having environmental responsibilities dispersed in so many separate agencies made for a lack of coordination. Now having them all concentrated in a single agency, though, would lead to a lack of competition. We could have an SOS in that context by giving the EPA all kinds of coordinating and generalized planning authority without taking away any of the responsibilities from the other agencies. It does not have to be a tradeoff. The other agencies can even increase their responsibility. The Department of Agriculture, for example, could increase its responsibility for seeing to it that environmentally harmful pesticides are not used more so than prior to 1970, while at the same time having the EPA look into the subject as well. Or the degradation of forests through clear cutting, and other anti-conservation activities, can be strengthened in the forest service which is in another agency, e.g., Interior or Agriculture. At the same time, the EPA can also be concerned with protecting the forest environment, including cross-national coordination that might relate to the harm that acid rain, global warming, or ozone depletion does to forests in other countries. The key point is that competition is meaningful between government agencies just as it is meaningful between political parties and intelligent ideas and business firms, industries, and nations. It is applicable to stimulating "doing a better job" regardless what the job is, even if it is contrary to traditional administration and organization ideas about pyramidal structures and centralization of authority.

The environmental field has been used to talk about branches of government, levels of government and incentives. It can also be used to talk about the consolidation of agencies versus competition among agencies. We should add a SOS table on that important cross-cutting subject. It happens to apply to the environmental field more clearly than elsewhere because the environmental field is relatively new. Every other problem already has a government agency dealing with it prior to 1970. The environmental field acquired its key governmental agency in about 1970. So did the energy field. There was no Department of Energy prior to the 1970's. There was not even a subunit on energy in some other department or some unit on environment in some other department, unlike the Department of Education which was formerly part of HEW. And before that there was an Office of Education, before HEW was established. Thus the environment and energy fields presented recent opportunities to decide the question of consolidation versus competition. The feeling was almost unanimously in favor of consolidation. In fact, the concept of competition was not even mentioned as a consideration. It was just considered an obvious conclusion that one did not have ten different agencies all operating in the same area with duplication and conflict and gaps. The tradeoff thinking led to taking power away from those agencies and giving it to the EPA. SOS thinking would have resulted in strengthening their power while simultaneously creating an Environmental Protection Agency.

If we think in terms of a liberal approach towards the consolidation versus competition issue, or consolidation versus nonconsolidation in the environmental field, the liberal approach was definitely pro-EPA on grounds that this would more effectively deal with pollution problems. The conservative approach was not so pro, but no so clearly anti-EPA either, but more in that direction. Some conservatives were explicitly anti-EPA, like Herman Kahn and Julian Simon. The neutral approach would be a weak EPA. Reagan could be considered anti-EPA. He appointed Anne Gorsuch-Burford to head the agency. She immediately asked to have the budget cut to almost nothing, which was the equivalent of dissolving the agency. The super-optimum solution, on the question of consolidation versus nonconsolidation was to both consolidate and strengthen the components. That would not necessarily please conservatives since they really not only wanted a weak EPA, they also wanted weak components too. The farmers did not want the power of the Department of Agriculture to increasingly clamp down on bad pesticides. For them, arguing in favor of the Department of Agriculture retaining pesticide control, versus the EPA getting it, was viewed in light of the fact that they could control the United States of America more than they could control EPA. If USDA, though, was going to be given a congressional mandate to crack down on harmful pesticides, the farmers might prefer a weak EPA in that area rather than a strong USDA.

There are four possibilities. Weak both, strong both, strong EPA with weak USDA, or weak EPA and strong USDA. The liberals were in favor of the third. The conservatives really wanted the first, but argued in favor of the fourth in order to keep the EPA weak. The liberals really should have argued in favor of the second, but wrongly perceived that somehow a strong USDA would get in the way of a strong EPA rather than supplement a strong EPA.

If one goal is to protect the environment, then clearly that is better done by having both a strong EPA and a strong USDA on the matter of environmental protection. One, though, has to recognize that protecting business interests is also a goal in this context, and strong on both does not do that. The conservative position does not really have a goal of protecting the USDA or the Interior, or any other government agency that was involved with environmental matters; which actually includes almost all of them. Clearly, the State Department is very much involved in anything that is international, not just matters involving Canada or Mexico. The United States is capable of wrecking the environment of every country in the world by shipping them harmful pesticides or other harmful products. That particularly gets into the jurisdiction of the Commerce Department with regard to international trade agreements, and can relate to American automobiles not complying with the exhaust requirements of other countries; either explicit requirements or matters regarding the public interest of other countries.

This is not an SOS situation where both environmental interests and business interests come out ahead of their best expectations. It applies only where the pro-consolidation and the pro-decentralization both come out ahead of their best expectations. Centralization, though, and decentralization are often just camouflage for some other economic interests. Business may greatly favor decentralization of the states when it comes to environmental protection since the states are easier to manipulate by business boosters. They do not favor decentralization of the states, though, when it comes to regulating interstate transportation, especially trucking where, different and possibly conflicting state rules can make the trucking of goods needlessly expensive, as contrasted to a uniform national system.

This is a subject that is actually more worth discussing in terms of competition than in terms of the environment. What it mainly contributes is a broadening of the usefulness of the concept of competition to include competition among government agencies which, carried to its logical extreme, might involve competing police departments, fire departments, and public schools.

(1) The public school idea, and the fire and police ideas, are already almost old hat. All three have to compete with various forms of private alternatives. The public schools compete with private schools. The public schools compete with each other in the sense that people are somewhat free to move from Chicago to another school district outside of Chicago if the Chicago schools are not performing to a minimum level. They can also change police departments and fire departments by moving to another location too. That is a form of geographical competition. It does not work so well with cable TV or electric power companies, because they are almost 100% uniformly inefficient; or with electric power companies, because they are almost 100% uniformly inefficient, and arrogant. Some police forces, however, are much better than others, as are some public school systems and some fire departments. It is interesting to note that the city of Chicago seriously contemplated throwing out Commonwealth Edison as intolerable and inviting bids from all electric companies anywhere in the world to supply electricity to the city of Chicago. That would be actively encouraged by free market conservatives as well as anti-big business liberals. It could establish a wonderful new precedent that could lead to the same kind of breakup of monopoly, replacing it with competition, as occurred in long-distance telephone service. Airline passenger activity benefited similarly.

(2) Within the same city one can do some choosing between public and private schools, and also private police protection. There is not that much of a market for private fire protection. Fire departments seem to be almost the opposite of electricity companies in that they tend to be almost uniformly above an acceptable level of competence, with the electric companies being almost uniformly below an acceptable level of competence; and the police departments and schools varying, with some above and some below, and some in the middle.

(3) It does not seem so likely that within the same city one would have two units of each: state police, city police, and federal police. All three levels of government compete in some areas, especially in the more major crimes. The FBI is not going to arrest somebody for overtime parking, but all three levels of police might be interested in a kidnapping case that cuts across numerous states, as most are likely to do, involving competition for which they can most effectively stop the abuse of consumers that may be occurring. The former Illinois Attorney General, before he went to prison for income tax evasion, won many votes by suing General Motors or other big businesses for various kinds of consumer fraud that was occurring in states other than Illinois, just as much as in Illinois.

2. Competition among Public Schools, Police Departments, and Political Parties

A. Public School Education can be made More Competitive in the Following Ways.

(1) More competition among teachers; with salary rewards for quality work, or for working in neighborhoods where teachers are reluctant to work.

(2) More competition among students for academic honors, and less competition for sports honors.

(3) More competition among school districts by publicizing how well school districts are doing on SAT scores, college entrance percentages, and other variables; including publicity over time so that they are in effect competing with their past.

(4) Rent supplements and anti-snob zoning laws in order to facilitate people voting with their feet by moving to better school districts more easily.

(5) Conservatives talk about vouchers that would enable public school children to go to private schools. That is not necessarily an example of competition to improve quality. It is frequently motivated by racism and economic class bias.

(6) A voucher system could be meaningful to enable public school children to pay transportation costs and school lunch costs to attend a public school in the middle class neighborhoods of their district, or even outside their district. That is an example of a use of vouchers to promote integration.

(7) We could also talk about competition at the higher education level, which gets into regional and international competition. One of the best ways the government can promote competition among universities or among business firms is to publicize how well each producer is doing on various objective criteria so as to embarrass many universities in the United States.

B. Competition with Regard to Police Protection:

(1) The first thing that comes to mind is hiring private police. That is all right for rich business firms. A ghetto dweller is not going to hire a private police company to protect his family from being burglarized and mugged.

(2) As mentioned above, publicizing quality indicators for different police departments across the country, or different police stations within a given city, stimulates better output, including quality indicators over time, so that one competes with oneself the way a jogger tries to improve.

(3) The rent supplement idea enables people who live in neighborhoods with bad police protection to move elsewhere more easily, just as it enables people to move who live in neighborhoods with bad schools. Most of what is said above about competition among schools can also apply to police protection and other government services.

(4) More competition among police officers for internal police department rewards such as salary increases, promotions, and honors.

(5) In dealing with competition at the governmental service level, some of the methods that apply in the private sector may not be so applicable; but thinking about them might stimulate some applicable ideas such as contracting out to domestic or internal business firms. This is not the same as a business firm hiring a private detective agency. What it means is that the city of Chicago would have the responsibility for providing good police protection throughout the city. Instead of doing it through Chicago employees, however, it might hire a professional agency, if the agency or business firm can meet the specifications with regard to personnel and equipment. There would then be competition among such business firms to get the contracts. All contracts would be subject to renewal every year or so, in order to make it clear that the contracts do not last forever, regardless of a drop in the quality of service. It is quite possible that such a contracting out could lead to a more sensitive police operation in the inner city than is currently provided by a police force that in effect does have a contract forever.

C. One-Party Non-Competition

(1) This is a totally different area in which to encourage competition. Here it definitely does not make sense to say we will contract out to business firms to set up political parties.

(2) The device that is sometimes advocated for getting more competition among parties is proportional representation rather than single-member districts, where only a major or dominant political party can win. Proportional representation provides too much diffusion and gives too much power to small swing parties in forming a ruling condition.

(3) Free speech is very important in developing opposition, which develops opposition political parties. That means no restrictions on political communication with regard to content.

(4) There may have to be restrictions on spending, so as to prevent one party from spending itself into a monopolistic position. The best way to deal with that is through government financing of elections, which pays the costs of both the incumbent party and the opposition, as well as other major parties if there are any.

(5) The government can provide facilities for political parties that are capable of getting at least ten percent or so of the vote. The facilities can include a speaking hall, radio time, TV time. The object is to subsidize the low-income parties that are not minor splinter parties, but which include major viewpoints as indicated by the percentage of votes they are capable of getting. Such parties would not be very competitive without a subsidy, which the dominant party does not need. This would not run contrary to majority rule. The minority party would still have to convince voters that it is the better or best party in order to get elected.

(6) Redistricting so as to give opposition parties a fair chance of getting represented in the legislature. That is the proportionate representation that goes with geography, not with saying that a party that gets one percent of the votes is entitled to one percent of the legislators.

(7) Anything that increases registration and turnout is likely to increase political action and a diversity of major viewpoints. If only a relatively small portion of the population is registered and votes, that segment of the population in effect has a monopoly on running the government, even though within that segment there may be more than one.

C. The Public and the Private Sectors

The East German economy was a relative failure compared to the West German economy since World War II. This was used as a factor to show the superiority of capitalism over socialism. Some contrary evidence was the fact that the Swedish socialistic economy flourished since World War II in spite of relatively few people and resources. The Spanish capitalistic economy was a much greater failure than the East German socialistic economy after World War II. One can get much greater predictability out of knowing whether a society has a competitive economy and political system (versus a monopolistic one) than out of knowing whether it is a capitalistic private-ownership economy (or a socialistic government-ownership economy).

Both East Germany and Spain were failures in terms of providing high standards of living for their people. They both demonstrated one-party monopolistic political systems, although one was communist and the other was fascist. They both had monopolistic economic systems which tried to keep out foreign goods through high tariffs, with government-favored business firms; although one had government-owned firms and the other had privately-owned firms.

Both West Germany and Sweden have been successes in terms of providing high standards of living for their people. They both have competitive political systems, with strong two-party competition, whereby the out-party is constantly trying to offer better ideas than the in-party. They both encourage competition among business firms and allow foreign competition. Thus comparing East Germany and West Germany does point to ways in which public policy can improve the quality of life, but it is a public policy that encourages competition over monopoly, not necessarily one that encourages capitalism over socialism.

Table 3 shows that political and economic competition relate to a high degree of prosperity. Both kinds of competition have been present in prosperous West Germany and Sweden. Until relatively recently, both kinds of competition have been absent in relatively impoverished East Germany and Spain. Table 3 analyzes competition as an SOS economic solution. In this table, the conservative alternative is the unregulated marketplace, which may lead to privatized monopolies. The liberal alternative is public ownership, which leads to a government form of compromise. The SOS alternative is stimulating competition through well-placed seed money to facilitate the establishment of competing business firms. Also see Table 4 for a reinforcing perspective.[2]

Table 3
Political and Economic Competition as Key Causes of Prosperity

		COMPETITION (Casual Variable) (In Politics and Economics)	
		No	Yes
PROSPERITY OR HIGH STANDARD OF LIVING (Effect Variable)	Yes		West Germany (Capitalism) Sweden (Socialism)
	No	East Germany Pre-1990 (Socialism) Spain Pre-1980 (Capitalism)	

NOTES

1. The table only includes industrial nations. A separate table could be made for developing nations.

2. Among industrialized nations, those that provide for competition in politics and economics have more prosperity than those which do not provide for competition in both activities. Industrialized nations that provide for competition in only one of the two activities are likely to have middling prosperity, although competition in politics may be more important to prosperity than competition in economics.

3. The table is mainly designed to relate political and economic competition as key causes in prosperity. One could also interpret the table as tending to show that countries that have economic competition are more likely to have political competition and vice versa.

4. One could also interpret the table as tending to show that industrialized nations are more likely to have a higher standard of living than non-industrialized nations regardless of political and economic competition. Another conclusion which the table generates is that whether a country has capitalistic private ownership or socialistic government ownership is virtually irrelevant to prosperity in comparison to political-economic competition and industrialization.

---

[2] The classic socialist literature includes Karl Marx, *Capital* (Kerr, 1906-1909) (originally published between 1865 and 1896); and Vladimir Lenin, *The State and Revolution* (International, 1932) (originally published in 1917). The classic capitalist literature includes Adam Smith, *The Wealth of Nations* (Methuen, 1930) (originally published in 1776); Alfred Marshall, *Principles of Economics* (Cambridge University Press, 1890). By "classic," in this context, is meant highly influential works that were originally published between the late 1700s and the early 1900s up until about 1945. On the history of capitalism-socialism in theory and practice, see Edward Burns, *Ideas in Conflict: The Political Theories of the Contemporary World* (Norton, 1960); Harry Laidler, *Social-Economic Movements* (Crowell, 1946); and George Soule, *Ideas of the Great Economists* (Viking, 1952).

Table 4
Competition as an SOS Economic Solution

Alternatives	C Goal Business Profits	L Goal Low Prices	N Total (Neutral Weights)	C Total (Conservative Weights)	L Total (Liberal Weights)
C Alternative Marketplace (Monopoly)	4	2	12	14*	10
L Alternative Gov't Ownership or Tight Regulation	2	4	12	10	14*
N Alternative Some of Both (Mixed Economy)	3	3	12	12	12
S Alternative Stimulate Competition Through Well-Placed Subsidies	≥ 3.5	≥ 3.5	≥ 14	$\geq 14**$	$\geq 14**$

NOTES

1. The conservative alternative of an unregulated marketplace may lead to only one or a few firms dominating most industries. That arrangement may be profitable in the short run, although contrary to low prices.

2. The liberal alternative of government ownership or tight regulation tends to mean a government monopoly or stifled private enterprise. That means reduced business profits, although it might mean artificially low prices to satisfy consumers as voters.

3. The mixed economy scores in the middle on both business profits and low prices.

4. The SOS alternative may draw upon the stimulus to innovation and efficiency of private profit making. The SOS alternative may encourage competition through well-placed seed money. Doing so results in lower prices through a competitive marketplace, rather than through a monopolistic one or through artificial price constraints.

REFERENCES

On privatization in general, see John Donahue, *The Privatization Decision: Public Ends, Private Means* (Basic Books, 1989); and Randy Ross, *Government and the Private Sector: Who Should Do What* (Crane Russak, 1988).

For books specifically on inflation reduction without increasing unemployment especially in the context of Eastern Europe, see Paul Peretz, *The Political Economy of Inflation in the United States* (University of Chicago Press, 1083); Kreisky Commission on Employment Issues in Europe, *A Programme for Full Employment in the 1990s*

(Pergamon Press, 1981); and Laszlo Cwaba (ed.), *Systemic Change and Stabilization in Eastern Europe* (Dartmouth, 1991).

On increasing productivity in the public and private sectors, see Marc Holzer and S. Nagel (eds.), *Productivity and Public Policy* (Sage, 1984); Rita Mae Kelly (ed.), *Promoting Productivity in the Public Sector: Problems, Strategies, and Prospects* (St. Martin's, 1988); Marc Holzer and Arie Halachmi, *Public Sector Productivity: A Resource Guide* (Garland, 1988); Michael LeBoeuf, *The Productivity Challenge: How to Make it Work for America and You* (McGraw Hill, 1982); and Ryuzo Sato and Gilbert Suzawa, *Research and Productivity: Endogenous Technical Change* (Auburn House, 1983). These books are relevant to inflation-reduction in general since they emphasize the idea of giving consumers more for their money, rather than reducing prices. This includes employers who are consumers of labor.

On the general aspects of socialism versus capitalism, see Ralph Blodgett, *Comparative Economic Systems* (Macmillan, 1956); William Ebenstein, *Modern Political Thought: The Great Issues* (Rinehart, 1954); William Loucks and William Whitney, *Comparative Economic Systems* (Harper & Row, 1973); Joseph Schumpeter, *Capitalism, Socialism, and Democracy* (Harper, 1942); and Earl Shaw (Ed.), *Modern Competing Ideologies* (Heath, 1973). Modern defenses of socialism include Michael Harrington, *Why We Need Socialism in America* (Dissent, 1971); Robert Heilbroner, *Marxism: For and Against* (Norton, 1980); John Putnam, *The Modern Case for Socialism* (Meador, 1946); and Paul Sweezy, *Socialism* (McGraw-Hill, 1949). Modern defenses of capitalism include Milton Friedman, *Capitalism and Freedom* (University of Chicago Press, 1963); George Gilder, *Wealth and Poverty* (Basic Books, 1980); Frederick Hayck, *The Road to Serfdom* (University of Chicago Press, 1945); and Irving Kristol, *Two Cheers for Capitalism* (Basic Books, 1978). On regulated capitalism as a system between pure socialism and pure capitalism, see James Anderson (Ed.), *Economic Regulatory Policies* (Lexington-Heath, 1976); Barry Mitnick, *The Political Economy of Regulation* (Columbia University Press, 1980); and James Q. Wilson, *The Politics of Regulation* (Basic Books, 1980).

For further details on the public-private controversy in a contemporary context, see E.S. Savas, *Privatization: The Key to Better Government* (Chatham, N.J.: Chatham House, 1987); Martin Rein and Lee Rainwater (eds.), *Public/Private Interplay in Social Protection: A Comparative Study* (Armonk, N.Y.: M.E. Sharpe, 1986); Dennis Thompson (ed.), *The Private Exercise of Public Functions* (Port Washington, N.Y.: Associated Faculty Press, 1985), and Richard Hula (ed.), *Market Based Public Policy* (London: Macmillan, 1987). Also see the symposium issues on privatization and reinventing government in: the *Journal of Policy Analysis and Management* (Summer 1987), *Public Administration Review* (November/December 1987), the *Proceedings of the Academy of Political Science* (1987), and *Policy Studies Journal* (Autumn, 1996).

PART II

ENTREPRENEURSHIP, REINVENTING GOVERNMENT, FRANCHISING AND CONTRACTING OUT

Part II is about entrepreneurship and government, and how government has become increasingly entrepreneurial over the last few decades. It explores the roots of change from budgeting and information systems, towards efficiency based politics, and the more market and private sector oriented emphases we now experience. Reinventing government represents a substantial thrust of the surge towards entrepreneurship and it is another significant entrepreneurial development. Franchising is another critical entrepreneurial development. It is analyzed later in Part II, along with contracting principal agent theory.

In Chapter 6 of Part II, Thomas Lynch, Cynthia Lynch and Peter Cruise develop *The Road to Entrepreneurship in the Public Sector*. They begin by exploring the development of the forces for change that have led to reinventing government, or REGO. The authors discuss that the traditional "command and control" model of management in business and government is no longer appropriate for our needs as organizational conditions and needs have greatly changed because of information technology. They analyze how the changes and adjustments experienced in budgeting and information technology link up with political, economic, and managerial forces, and thus became a movement that ended up transforming the world of work as we have known it.

The authors review the functions of budgeting and relate them to reform objectives. An analysis of Schick's functions of budgeting is presented to demonstrate how different budgeting formats achieve various reform objectives. They then explain the impact of budget function revisions and the REGO implications involved as we have moved from one era to another. There is then an analysis of the fundamental shift from the progressive/liberal era to the information era and the general budgeting implications resulting from the REGO reforms. They also analyze resistance to REGO and entrepreneurial budgeting from external and internal forces, focusing on ways to overcome such resistance. The authors end with their conclusions regarding REGO innovations and the entrepreneurial transformation, noting that these reforms should continue to yield positive improvements in public services.

Chapter 7 of Part II, by Burt Useem, is *Reinventing FEMA: Gains and Limits of the Newest "New Federalism."* Early in the National Performance Review Process, former Vice President Gore announced that the Federal Emergency Management Agency would be used as a laboratory to study and assess government wide changes. A basic premise was that government is broken and that it should work better and cost less. In this chapter, the author analyzes this agency that had operated poorly and was facing extinction. A reinventing government model is used to analyze the agency's turnaround. The author ends with the implications to be derived form this exceptional reinventing government experience.

In Chapter 8, *The Federal Emergency Management Agency (FEMA) and Hurricane Katrina*, Van Johnston and Claire-Lauren Schulz analyze FEMA and the catastrophic effects of its consolidation into the Department of Homeland Security. The authors explain how placing FEMA within the Department of Homeland Security added to the bureaucratic structure of federal emergency management. Johnston and Schulz specifically focus on the impact that the changes in the control of the agency had on the management structure and employees of the agency, and how this ultimately hindered FEMA from functioning as an effective federal agency.

The authors use the 2005 Hurricane Katrina disaster to discuss how the absorption of FEMA into the Department of Homeland Security severed FEMA from its core functions, shattered agency morale, and broke relationships with stakeholders. This disaster began to force changes in FEMA, and the authors present an analytical overview of the FEMA investigations and reports following Hurricane Katrina. The authors then study the current changes with FEMA with a discussion of the strengths and weaknesses of those changes. Johnston and Schulz end with a recommendation that FEMA clarify its core functions and objectives and strengthen its abilities to execute. Further, the authors recommend that FEMA focus on managing federal emergencies, and leave other responsibilities to appropriate agencies.

Chapter 9 of Part II is entitled *Franchising in Government: Can a Principal-Agent Perspective Be a First Step Towards the Development of a Theory?* In this chapter, Arie Halachmi studies a number of franchise funds to determine their feasibility for improving productivity by introducing competition and capitalizing on specialization and size economies. The author goes on to explain and develop principal-agent relations from economic theory. He proposes that an agency theory could be developed to assist in optimally utilizing franchising in government.

In Chapter 10 of Part II, *Agency Theory, Competition and Transaction Analysis in the Public Sector*, Arie Halachmi begins by noting that government organization products and services are not subject to direct market competition. He finds that in this increasingly entrepreneurial environment that managers are increasingly asked to replace their traditional production and service models with new models that utilize contracts. He discusses that these arrangements are problematic because this market competition has not yet been tested within the theoretical frameworks of neo-institutional economics. With transactional costs and economic reality thus neglected, he raises questions regarding efficiency, economy, and motivation to control costs. The author moves on to an analysis of the increased significance of contracts in the new entrepreneurial environment. Contracts lead to agency theory and to franchising and transaction costs; specifically, the principal-agent perspective can help reduce the dysfunctions often linked with performance measurement, incentives, and hiring.

Halachmi integrates his theory with an applied analysis of contracting out Davidson County, Tennessee's Medical Examiner's Office. This factual case study demonstrates the significant and serious managerial implications associated with contracting. He concludes with a review of best practices, and fickle ones, as they relate to outsourcing. The author's final analysis is thoughtful and provides readers with takeaway lessons regarding contracting out, or outsourcing.

Chapter 11 is the final chapter of Part II. In *The Increasingly Complex Policy Field of Multiple Principals and Agents: Effective Aid in Problematic Personal Debt Situations*, Peter Boorsma and Judith Tijdink apply their evolving principal agent theory to deal with an increasingly complex and serious problem in the multi disciplinary world of debt management. Their models and theories are at the threshold of our abilities to understand the complexities of the world of contracts that we entered when entrepreneurship, reinventing and franchising emerged. Boorsma is a professional colleague of Arie Halachmi. Their combined efforts in Part II of this book will provide readers with a wealth of information on the principal agent focus that is emerging in the contracting and franchising literature.

Chapter 6

THE ROAD TO ENTREPRENEURSHIP IN THE PUBLIC SECTOR

Thomas D. Lynch
Cynthia E. Lynch
Peter L. Cruise

INTRODUCTION

The twenty-first century is upon us. For several decades, futurists like Naisbitt (1994), Drucker (1989a, 1989b), and Reich (1992) have told us that information technology (IT) is transforming our society. They predicted that the more successful organizations among us will alter themselves to take advantage of new technology and we will change in the process. The writing teams of Hammer and Champy (1992) and Osborne and Gaebler (1993) echoed the thoughts of the futurist in their calls for the re-engineering and reinvention of not only private organizations but also government.

Since the publication of Reinventing Government (Osborne and Gaebler, 1993) reengineering and reinvention, once a revolutionary school of thought regarding bureaucratic development and performance in America, is now conventional wisdom for many. Once dismissed as a "passing fad," the literature now uses the acronym REGO to designate it (Wolf, 1997). As Laudicina (1995) noted the REGO reform movement first caught the academic community by surprise. Once caught, then that community viewed it with considerable skepticism and even alarm. Reengineering, entrepreneurial management, empowerment, and privatization, according to the skeptics, were, at best, simplistic, and, at worst, doomed to failure. Even the noted management writer Peter Drucker once dismissed many REGO pronouncements as "empty slogans." (The Economist, 1996, p. 67). Today, the public sector accepts many REGO prescriptions uncritically.

REGO has influence for several reasons. First, the REGO movement has the double-barreled stimuli of the Osborne and Gaebler book as well as the concurrent publication of the *Report of the National Performance Review* (1993). The latter work was the result of the national committee chaired by Vice President Al Gore. Both of these publications received wide national and international press attention. Second, local, state and national governments adopted quickly many REGO principles, especially privatization of services. For example, previously thought of as government-only services shifted either to the private sector or to the new public-private partnerships.

Third, a growing anti-big government movement swept the U.S. and the world. Although scholars can dispute the exact date of the beginning of the current movement, a reasonable beginning date is the late 1970s with the California Proposition 13 anti-tax initiative. The movement picked up steam in the 1980s with the New Federalism approach adopted by Ronald Reagan and the election of Margaret Thatcher as Prime Minister in Great Britain. More recently, we see it as the backlash against the U.S. Health Care Reform Task Force chaired by Hilary Rodham Clinton in 1994. Now, the phrase "The best government is the least government" is especially significant with "least" often meaning not small government but the least expensive government in terms of taxation. Also the public and many successfully elected officials saw reengineering and right-sizing of government as needed reform but often those terms did not mean reorganization but cutting the total number of government employees (*The Economist*, 1996).

Because of IT, reforms are changing society including the role of government, which changed fundamentally as more organizations adapted. The old command and control model of doing business and government of the past century is no longer adequate for our needs. As we move further into the information age, we experience polar opposite organizational conditions from the command and control management approach of the progressive/liberal era. As shown in Table 1, the speed of technological advance is faster in the information era than in the progressive/liberal era earlier in this century. The major source of new jobs in society shifted from manufacturing to service and knowledge industries. Organizations are changing their structures from top down hierarchical configurations to networks and webs working in coordinated partnerships. In the past the key to economic success was mass marketing and now it is specialty niches found in the global market. Finally, even our social structures are shifting from strong neighborhood and family units to isolated individuals and fragmented communities often with dysfunctional family units.

Yet, despite the advancing IT and REGO movements, reformers of the public sector organizations have not reengineered or right-sized to the extent possible or even desirable compared to their counterparts in the private sector. IT helped to continue the major transformation that actually began in the 1980s with waves of private sector mergers and consolidation. During the last decade, reformers threw out traditional bureaucratic structures in favor of flattened organizations with fewer workers and even fewer managers. The reforms eliminated established lines of authority and rewarded empowered workers to take risks. Now into the twenty-first century, the rapid growth of

IT is creating virtual organizations across department and even corporate lines (*Healthcare Financial Management*, 1997).

Table 1. Progressive/liberal versus information age characteristic

CHARACTERISTICS	PROGRESSIVE/ LIBERAL ERA	INFORMATION ERA
Speed of Technological Advances	Evolved Slowly	Breathtaking Speed
Source of New Employment	Mainly Manufacturing	Service and Knowledge Industries
Organizational Structure	Top Down, Hierarchical	Networks, Webs, Partnerships, Coordinated Teams
Key to Economic Success	Mass Marketing	Global Marketing Targeted at Specific Niches
Social Structure	Strong Associations, Communities, Neighborhoods, and Family Units	Isolated Individuals, Fragmented Communities, Dysfunctional Family Units

Source: David Osborne and Ted Gaebler. *Reinventing Government*. New York: Plume, 1993, p. 15.

Although the REGO movement and the IT revolution created sometimes rapid and radical change in the private sector, the public sector has not achieved a parallel development. Thus, the desire for reform and radical right sizing in the public sector continues while reformers are only accomplishing limited success. For example, the Clinton Administration cut over 244,000 positions from the federal government after 1992 but delayed addressing right sizing conceptually (*The Economist*, 1996).

This chapter explains that reformers can only achieve true public sector change with a comprehensive approach keyed to implementing IT. In particular, this chapter examines the shifting role of budgeting functions caused by the change from one era to another. The first section of the chapter reviews Schick's functions of budgeting in terms of reform objectives and how different formats achieve various reform objectives. The second section explains the revised functions of budgeting in the information era and the implications in terms of REGO reforms. The third section explains the fundamental shift from the progressive/liberal to the information era with its REGO reforms implications in general and budgeting in particular. The fourth section discusses sources of resistance to REGO and Entrepreneurial Budgeting (EB) reforms both from inside and outside of government, and possible ways to overcome the resistance. The final section presents the conclusions of the chapter.

SCHICK'S FUNCTIONS OF BUDGETING

In an often cited article—"The Road to PPB: The Stages of Budget Reform"— Allen Schick (1966: pp. 243-258) refers to the budget innovation Planning Programming Budgeting System (PPB) as a "revolutionary development in the history of government management." He pointed out that the "radical" PPB is "anchored in a half century of tradition and evolution" (Schick, 1966: p.250). Forty years later students of budgeting could well apply his comments to the emerging Entrepreneurial Budgeting (EB) as the current shift portends an equally "radical change in the central function of budgeting" (Schick, 1966: p.250). However, in the 1990s, a *full* century of tradition and evolution, which includes the earlier PPB reform, now anchors this transformation. EB is consistent with Schick's (1966: p. 250) prediction that "the budget systems of the future will be a product of past and emerging developments."

Built on Robert Anthony's definitions of budgeting processes, Schick argued that the budget cycle consisted of strategic planning, management, and control. He is quite consistent with the command and control concepts of the progressive/liberal era. Planning is "the determination of objectives, the evaluation of alternative courses of action, and the authorization of select programs." Planning is particularly prevalent in the early budget preparation phase of the budget cycle. Management is "the programming of approved goals into specific projects and activities, the design of organizational units to carry out approved programs, the staffing of these units, and the procurement of the necessary resources." The management phase exists throughout the budget cycle but it is particularly important in the budget execution period. Control is "the process of binding operating officials to the policies and plans" set by policy makers or managers. According to Schick, control is most dominant during the budget execution and audit phases of the budget cycle. However, like the other functions it is present in all phases of the cycle (Schick, 1966: p. 251).

Regardless of the era, reforms, including budget reforms, take place when the results of the existing process do not please key leaders in society. Normally this occurs when society is undergoing rapid change and the current practices are neither adequate nor adapting fast enough. Within any era and between eras, budget reforms occur when those key leaders feel that reform is essential. In the 1960s, President Johnson's felt that the budget process was inadequate in terms of setting policy objectives in his desired command and control approach to government reform. In the 1990s, President Clinton and Vice President Gore felt that the budget process was not innovative enough in terms of cutting costs and seeking out new ways of efficiently managing the tasks of government.

As pointed out by Pettijohn and Grizzle (1997), budget format and process are not neutral factors as such adjustments do influence the outcome of the process. Budget formats define the readers' reality and channel the readers' attention and thought processes. Edward Lehan (1981: p. 3) says, "People tend to think in terms of what is put in front of them. This axiom of human behavior plays a heavy role in the budgetary process." For example, line item budget takes decision-makers attention away from policy issues and forces them to consider expenditure items. Thus, most people think about the correctness of the size of the various expenditure items rather than the larger issues of the correctness of the programs and policies associated with those items.

For exercising control, the line item budget is very useful, especially if one wants to tightly control employees in an agency. The line item format stresses accountability in terms of what the units spends by object classification but it does not inform decision-makers in terms of the larger impacts the unit has on society. When decision-makers control for object of expense only, they achieve a type of accountability but their approach shows little faith in the managers' ability to direct and ultimately achieve impacts on society. By adding the auditing process to the line item budget, decision-makers focus on expenditure spending. Thus, they increase their ability to achieve accountability in terms of confronting corruption, discouraging public employees from deviating from strict instructions, and enhancing their tight control over the employees' behavior. However, they also discourage initiative and foster costly red tape within the organization.

The reality of line item budgeting is that this form of accountability obscures meeting the purpose for which policy makers created government programs. Thus, in the progressive/liberal era, there was frustration with government bureaucracy in general and budgeting in particular. Reformers created program budgeting to help address this problem. Program budgeting groups planned spending not by expenditures but by activities, which reflect the purpose for which policy makers wish the money spent. For example, instead of budgeting by salaries one budgets by activities such as code enforcement and housing inspection. This approach allows decision-makers to focus their policy debates among themselves on policy differences and choices among alternative selections of programs and program levels of spending. Program budgeting is therefore a useful tool for strategic planning as it focuses the human mind on policy issues with analysis of programs used to inform the policy resolution process.

Program budgeting assumes the modernist approach of philosophers like Jeremy Bentham (Martin, 1998) that rationality is not only possible in human decision making but it is desirable. A counter position of the 19th century conservatives like Edmund Burke (Haque, 1998) maintained that such an assumption is foolishness and the best that human decision making can do is reason from existing precedent. In the late 20th century public budgeting literature, Aaron Wildavsky articulated that position best (Jones, 1997).

Built on the program budgeting tradition, performance budgeting takes the programs in program budgeting and adds the use of specific performance measures reflecting either program outputs or outcomes. Budget experts define the former as the products and services produced by the programs and the latter as the impacts of those outputs on individuals served by the program and the larger society. The PPB budget reform was a version of performance budgeting. With performance budgeting, analysts and decision-makers can focus on questions of efficiency and effectiveness. Analytical techniques such as benefit-cost and productivity studies become quite relevant. Another reality is that all the arguments about the impossibility of rational analysis apply even more specifically to performance budgeting. The history of budget reform is a quest to achieve greater rationality in public policy decision making. These attempts lead to frustrations, partial abandonment, and then yet another cycle of attempts. There are some success stories but there are failures as well (Lynch, 1975).

A NEW PROCESS MATRIX

Brokering, Monitoring, Steering

In the information era, EB is only beginning to appear but we can make some observations as it emerges. As pointed out in Illustration 2, the very purpose of budgeting appears to be shifting. In the information era, budgeting takes its direction not from planning but from strategic brokering. It is a process of continuously scanning the entire environment for options and possibilities that better fit the organization's objectives. This holistic approach means that decision-makers are always searching for better partnerships and relationships to better service the objectives of the whole. This approach brings the problem identifiers and problem solvers together with a continuing concern for any negative ethical connotations that might exist. As noted by Reich (1992: p. 88), "mutual learning and discovery occurs within the team as insights, experiences, puzzles and solutions are shared."

PURPOSE OF BUDGETING	PROGRESSIVE/ LIBERAL ERA	INFORMATION ERA
Source of Direction	Planning	Strategic Brokering
Method of Direction	Management	Steering
Purpose of Direction	Control	Monitoring

Illustration 2. Progressive/liberal versus information era purposes of budgeting

The method of giving direction also shifts from management in the progressive / liberal era to steering in the information era. Now organizations are increasingly not vertical but horizontal with much greater decentralization. To be successful, adapting to swift changes in direction, which are so common in the information age, require agile organizations. Policy makers steer organizations by setting output and outcome objectives and parameters for managers and other employees. This tells them what policy makers expect from them but this guidance does not tell them exactly what process they must follow or what object expenditures they must spend to reach those objectives.

With EB, the steering comes from four directions. First, it comes from the direct language of the appropriation acts and other legislation that policy makers tie to specific measurable performance indicators of desired program outputs and outcomes. Second, it is from the direct orders of the elected and properly appointed leaders of the government, which are essential but also consistent with the laws of the nation. Third, it is in the deep roots of the nation's culture. For example, in the United States democracy is important and accountability runs ultimately to the people. There is a desired and actual linkage of accountability between elected and appointed officials and the public. According to the Government Accounting Standards Board (GASB, 1995), government agencies entrusted with resources and authority for applying them have a responsible to render a full accounting of their activities. This accountability means that public managers should identify not only the objects for which they devoted public resources but also the manner and effect of their application.

Lastly, steering comes from the absolute values and ethics of the public managers and decision-makers. One place to look for these ethical standards is in the code of ethics of such groups as the Government Finance Officers Association (GFOA), the American Society for Public Administration (ASPA), and other professional organizations. Another place to look is in the religious communities and their primary literature. Entrepreneurial government will have its greatest difficulty facing up to the challenge of values and ethics because society will need to use a much higher standard due to the information age requirement of greater individual initiative and professional empowerment. Hopefully, extensive and continuing training on those subjects can significantly help individuals meet those challenges.

In the information age, the purpose of direction in budgeting shifts to monitoring rather than control. Accurate feedback is essential in the information age and given the advances in both hard and software, remarkable feedback arrangements are now possible. The information age requires workers to self adjust; and throughout the organization, decision-makers including public managers use information to see if the parts and the whole organization are adjusting correctly. We need not base our information selection on the rational model of decision making as we can base our selection of data on the concerns of the major program stakeholders. We can use those concerns to help define program outcomes and output information needs.

In the information age, monitoring is the process of providing accurate, reliable, and timely feedback to all appropriate parties. Illustration 3 is the Heuristic System Approach (HSA) model, which provides an explanation of the feedback monitoring system. Budgeting is conceptualized as a system with a cause and effect relationship running from input, to process, to output, and finally to outcome. Analysts select performance measures for each element of the government program. They define input as the resources used to fuel the program including workforce time, money, and leadership direction. Process is the daily work activities of the program. Outputs are the products and services of the program. Outcomes are the impacts of the program output on individuals and society (Lynch, 1989: pp. 321 - 341).

The model has three interrelated feedback loops, which all return to input. The outer loop is program evaluation. It looks at desired program outcomes or outcome benchmarks and compares them with actual accomplished outcomes and sometimes presents the information as a program effective ratio of input to outcome. The middle loop is progress reporting. It looks at desired operational outputs or output benchmarks and compares them with actual outputs. Sometimes, the model presents the information as an efficiency or productivity ratio of input to output. The inner most loop is process reporting. For example, in this model managers can monitor process by comparing their desired and targeted line item amounts to the actual amounts spent. Using this model allows all necessary parties to know that each unit spends its current year money at the desired rate during the fiscal year (Lynch, 1995: p. 128).

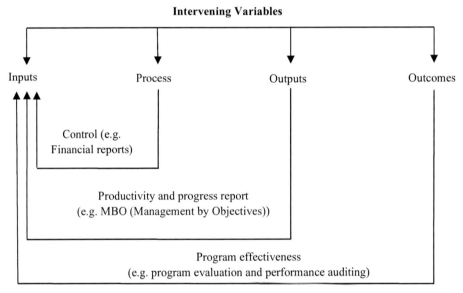

Illustration 3. The Budget System Approach

Source: Thomas D. Lynch. "The Budget System Approach." *Public Administration Quarterly*. 13,3 (Fall, 1989), p. 327.

Each feedback loop provides specific data to each stage of the budget cycle often in the form of a report. For example, financial monthly reports inform the agency exactly how close they are to the spending plan for the year. Progress reports, including management by objective reports, tell key people if various units are on their targeted output objectives during the year. Evaluation reports inform leadership and interested persons of the program impact on individuals and society. For example, is the crime rate going down? Are we living longer? Is pollution going down?

The monitoring function embraces all of the functions that Schick (1966) describes as essential to all budgets. In addition, they help encourage self-accountability and provide the whole system with information necessary for readjusting strategic brokering decisions. The monitoring systems insure that all interested parties know what actually is happening in each program in terms of their inputs, process, outputs, and outcomes. Voters and policy makers can hold elected officials and managers accountable for the results of their decisions and performance. This approach to feedback can use the best practices of the program based on historical information to establish a standard or use bench marking of the current best practices. Either or both can help program teams with the data needed to inspire an attitude striving for organizational excellence (Lynch, 1995: p. 128).

THE NEW ENTREPRENEURIAL CONTEXT OF BUDGETING

A Different Age -- A Different Mindset

The French economist J. B. Say around 1800 coined the term entrepreneur. He said, "the entrepreneur shifts economic resources out of an area of lower and into an area of higher productivity and greater yield" (Drucker, 1989a : p. 21 and Osborne and Gaebler, 1993: p. xix). In other words, the entrepreneur uses resources in new ways to maximize productivity and effectiveness. Increasingly, public leaders begin to ask civil servants to operate governmental programs as entrepreneurs including generating reasonable revenue for their programs (Geri, 1997). The U.S. tax revolts of the 1970s came in the reforms called Proposition 13 in California and 2 1/2 in Massachusetts. In the 1980s, there was a general downturn in the economy, an increased demand for public services, and a cumulative questioning of government's ability to perform. Public administrators can no longer be fixated only on spending. They are now being asked to think also about the revenue side of the budget. With EB, public managers develop new revenue sources for their activities.

An entrepreneurial spirit in budgeting means changing the management and policy approach used in the public sector to get those institutions to think in entrepreneurial ways. In other words, public institutions must use their resources in new ways to heighten both their efficiency and their effectiveness (Osborne and Gaebler, 1993: xix). This is not saying the public sector should be run like a business, as there are fundamental differences between the public and the private sector. Rather, the focus should be on governing and delivering public services in a significantly more entrepreneurial manner (Osborne and Gaebler, 1993: p. 22).

The practice of EB is in its early development stage but we can describe its elements. Merrill Stephen King (1995: p. 1) defines it as, "a method of budgeting whereby policy and chief executives establish the total spending limits and policy priorities, then provide flexibility and private sector-like incentives for program managers to determine how best to specifically spend their budgets and determine the means to accomplish the priorities."

In exchange for the increased spending authority, policy makers hold managers accountable for results. The procedure seeks to create an organizational environment that is, "lean, decentralized, innovative, flexible, adaptive, quick to learn new ways when conditions change.... and able to get things done as effectively and creatively as possible" (Osborne and Gaebler, 1993: p. 2).

In traditional command and control budgeting, policy makers wait for department heads and program managers to submit requests to them. In EB, much greater delegation occurs. Expenditure limits and performance measures are often benchmarked against the previous year expenditures and measures to provide a point of departure for steering decisions. Sometimes policy makers express expenditures in a formula that holds over all spending to a percent increase or decrease determined by the policy makers. The EB budgets are quite brief --- sometimes only a few pages long and in sharp contrast to the progressive era control oriented line item budget that is commonly hundreds of pages. This approach focuses policy makers on the big policy issues instead of the line items where there is a tendency on the part of policy makers to use those items to micro manage agencies' activities (Cothran, 1992: p. 446).

The agency heads and program managers are at liberty to allocate and expend their money in the best possible way to achieve the policy mission mandates. In exchange for this liberty, however, each program must have clear mission statements and measurable goals using specific performance measures in order to hold agency heads and program managers accountable to policy makers. One of the most distinguishing features of the Entrepreneurial Budget is the ability of the agency and in some cases even the program to keep a portion of both their unspent money and earned income. The success of the Entrepreneurial Budget is built upon its predecessor --- performance budgeting. The latter requires mission statements, measurable goals and objectives, performance measures for both efficiency and effectiveness, and feedback loops for both including the use of citizen satisfaction surveys and focus groups. Performance budgeting assigns responsibility and achieves accountability from agency heads and program managers (Cothran, 1992: pp. 446 - 448).

EB is a fundamental, radical departure from the older command and control approach to budgeting (Hammer and Champy, 1992: p. 32). EB is part of a larger mind-set change that requires focused attention on transforming the bureaucratic behavior of agency heads or program directors into thinking about revenue generation and efficiency oriented management. EB requires these administrators to focus on the program's bottom line performance rather than just spending the appropriated moneys before the end of the fiscal year. EB focuses them to ask, "How can one insert competitiveness into an essentially monopolistic activity we call government service?"

Policy makers can successfully using market mechanisms and competition within government. In the progressive era, budgeting used monopolistic public agencies to manage public functions. EB adopts a competitive approach and abandons to the extent possible the monopolistic approach. With few exceptions, there is no service or government function that policy makers and managers cannot subject to a true competitive process or arrangement. For example, Phoenix, Arizona, provides an often cited example of this kind of competitive process (Osborne and Gaebler, 1993: p. 88). The city decided to privatize their solid waste collection. Greater Phoenix divided itself into five zones. Over a five-year period, managers offered publicly multiple year contracts for each zone. By ensuring that there was a minimum of three contractors providing the service, the City of Phoenix safeguarded a true competitive process. The result was better service at a lower cost to the public.

Policy makers anywhere can build on the same EB approach used by the City of Phoenix and applied it to almost all government services and functions. As noted by Lawrence Martin (1993), there are many public services that lend themselves easily to privatization or contracting out including garbage collection, snow removal, food services, and vehicle towing. Other functions like prisons, school systems, and homeless shelters have joined the ranks of the newly privatized. The concept of privatization is normally to select and contract with a single provider thus merely switching from a public to a private monopoly situation. If that occurs, one simply substitutes a private for a public monopoly. Policy makers should use competition in the selection process of the service provider as well as to renew the contract (Osborne and Gaebler, 1993: pp. 19 - 20). An alternative to privatization, which still achieves competition, is to divide the function into competitive public employee teams.

Ideally the key to the successful competitive process is to always have at least three service providers for the same service. Policy makers can apply such competition to most services or functions, which they can divide into reasonable proportions by areas, time periods, function, or activities. For example, policy makers can contract out the audit function to accounting firms and data collection companies. The city prosecutor's office work can contract out to law firms on a geographical basis or a type of legal case such as contracts and torts. The number of public employees can diminish radically or stay the same depending on the entrepreneurial approach taken. Savings and costs avoidance in personnel benefits, fiscal office space, office supplies and equipment, support services can be enormous. By maintaining a minimum of three service providers for every service, the competitive market forces ensures the best service for the best price (Lynch, 1989). Where service areas are too small to divide, policy makers can partner or create service coalitions among several governments or agencies (e.g., city, county, state, and federal) to give the necessary economy of scale.

Illustration 4 presents an EB format that explains how the concept can be implemented.

CODE ENFORCEMENT

REVENUE SUMMARY	Past Year	Current Year	Budget Year	BY - CY
Total Revenue Needed	**$55,576**	**$59,100**	**$68,196**	**$9,096**
Less				
Plan Examination Fees	10,000	11,888	12,331	998
Inspection Fees	30,000	30,000	40,000	10,000
Tuition	11,000	2,879	15,526	2,647
Total	51,000	54,767	67,857	13,645
Subsidy From the General Fund	$4,576	$4,333	$339	($4,549)

PROGRAM SUMMARY	PAST YEAR			CURRENT YEAR		
	OUTPUT	INPUT	UNIT COST	OUTPUT	INPUT	UNIT COST
Plan Exams (Average)	111	$2,000.00	$18.02	132	$2,377.60	$15.01
Contractor One	110	2,000.00	18.18	134	2,377.60	17.74
Contractor Two	109	2,000.00	18.35	129	2,377.60	18.43
Contractor Three	107	2,000.00	18.59	132	2,377.60	18.01
Contractor Four	114	2,000.00	17.54	131	2,377.60	18.15
Contractor Five	115	2,000.00	17.39	134	2,377.60	17.74
Total Plan Exams	**555**	**10,000.00**	**$18.02**	**660**	**$11,888.00**	**$17.17**
Inspections (Average)	2,000	6,915.20	3.46	3,753	6,866.60	1.83
Contractor One	2,050	6,915.20	3.37	3,750	6,866.60	1.83
Contractor Two	2,140	6,915.20	3.23	3,690	6,866.60	1.86
Contractor Three	1,930	6,915.20	3.46	3,860	6,866.60	1.78
Contractor Four	1,830	6,915.20	3.49	3,770	6,866.60	1.82
Contractor Five	2,000	6,915.20	3.78	3,695	6,866.60	1.86
Total inspections	**10,000**	**34,576.00**	**3.46**	**18,765**	**34,933.00**	**1.86**
Education (Average)	1,176	2,200	1.89	2,260	2,575.80	1.14
Contractor One	1,100	2,200	2.00	2,250	2,575.80	1.14
Contractor Two	1,180	2,200	1.86	2,210	2,575.80	1.12
Contractor Three	1,200	2,200	1.83	2,100	2,575.80	1.23
Contractor Four	1,400	2,200	1.57	2,235	2,575.80	1.10
Contractor Five	1,000	2,200	2.20	2,290	2,575.80	1.12
Total Education	**5,880**	**11,000**	**1.89**	**11,300**	**12,879.00**	**1.14**
Total Code Enforcement	**16,435**	55,576	3.38	30,725	59,100.00	1.92

Illustration 4: Performance, Entrepreneurial and Competitive Budgeting Format

PROGRAM SUMMARY	BUDGET YEAR			BY - CY		
	Output	Input	Unit Cost	Output	Input	Unit Cost
Plan Exams (Average)	149	$2,466.20	16.55	17	$199.60	$11.74
Contractor One	147	2,466.20	16.78	18	199.60	11.09
Contractor Two	150	2,466.20	16.44	16	199.60	12.47
Contractor Three	149	2,466.20	16.55	17	199.60	11.74
Contractor Four	151	2,466.20	16.33	18	199.60	11.09
Contractor Five	148	2,466.20	16.66	16	199.60	12.47
Total Plan Exams	**745**	**12,331.00**	**16.55**	**85**	**$998.00**	**11.74**
Inspections (Average)	3,874	8,067.80	2.08	121	1,090.20	9.01
Contractor One	3,870	8,067.80	2.08	121	1,090.20	9.01
Contractor Two	3,850	8,067.8	2.09	123	1,090.20	8.86
Contractor Three	3,900	8,067.8	2.07	125	1,090.20	8.72
Contractor Four	3,810	8,067.80	2.12	119	1,090.20	9.16
Contractor Five	3,990	8,067.80	2.06	117	1,090.20	9.32
Total Inspections	**19,370**	**$40,339.00**	**2.08**	**605**	**5,451.00**	**9.01**
Education(Average)	2,465	3,105.20	1.26	343	529.40	1.54
Contractor One	2,465	3,105.20	1.26	345	529.40	1.58
Contractor Two	2,520	3,105.20	1.23	347	529.40	1.52
Contractor Three	2,410	3,105.20	1.29	338	529.40	1.57
Contractor Four	2,400	3,105.20	1.29	340	529.40	1.56
Contractor Five	2,530	3,105.20	1.23	345	529.40	1.53
Total Education	**12,325**	**15,526.00**	**1.26**	**1,715**	**2,647.00**	**1.54**
Total Code Enforcement	**32,440**	**68,196.00**	**2.10**	**2,405**	**9,096.00**	**3.78**

Illustration 4: Performance, Entrepreneurial and Competitive Budgeting Format (continued)

Source: Lynch, Thomas D.,Yen Won Hang and Cynthia E. Lynch. "Cycle of History and Twenty-First Century Budget Reform: Performance, Entrepreneurial, and Competitive Budgeting?" paper presented to International Spryer Workshop on "Assessing and Evaluating Public Management Reform" held at Speyer, Germany, November 1996

BARRIERS TO ENTREPRENEURIAL BUDGETING AND REGO SUCCESS

Although, as noted at the beginning of this chapter, the will exists to implement EB and REGO reforms, barriers are in place that frustrates the desired changes. The bureaucratic command and control systems developed at a time when:

- society evolved much slower,
- manufacturing creating the new jobs,

- large corporations and governments used hierarchy to control their organizations,
- mass markets were the key to economic success, and
- society often associated together with strong family units

As we near the next century and as noted earlier, we are experiencing almost the polar opposite conditions. We live in a time of:

- breathtaking change,
- service and knowledge industries creating the new jobs,
- organizations using networks and webs,
- global markets with market niches being critical, and
- people living in more isolated communities with fragmented family units (Osborne and Gaebler, 1993).

As explained earlier, futurists continue to tell us that technology changed our society and we change our organizations to accommodate the new technology. The rapid evolution of the computer and related software makes using information in daily work activities radically different. The very nature of how we can and do accomplish our work shifted dramatically. New jobs are increasingly information dependent and organizations can work better as decentralized units that connect together not by hierarchies but by webs (e.g., Naisbitt, 1984; Reich, 1992; Hammer and Champty, 1992). However, we need to identify and address barriers inside and outside of government before the public sector can fully take advantage of IT and what the Information Age offers. For REGO and EB to be optimally successful, we must continue to overcome important barriers including job protectionism, the technical expertise barrier, the need for a higher ethical plateau, and the lack of an entrepreneurial attitude in government.

JOB PROTECTIONISM

Nearly 17 percent of all union members in America are public sector employees with more than six percent of all union members working in the federal government, and more than ten percent have jobs in state and local governments. About 37 percent of all government workers belong to unions. Of this number, about 60 percent are federal employees and 43 percent are state and local government employees (Henry, 1995). U.S. federal, state and local governments must deal with many different unions as well as a plethora of individual bargaining units (Gray and Johnson, 1997).

Although public sector employee organization efforts go back to the early nineteenth century, a major landmark occurred with the passage of the Lloyd-LaFollette Act in 1912, which first allowed the federal government employees to organize. Even with this and other new rights to organize and collectively bargain on issues such as salaries, hours and working conditions, governments on all levels continued to resist the rights of their employees to use the ultimate weapon at their disposal: the right to strike (Henry, 1995).

In the late nineteenth and early twentieth centuries the lives of many American workers, both in and out of government, were not very pleasant. Until the union movement began to take hold in the early twentieth century, common problems included work weeks of eighty or more hours; child labor abuses; monitoring worker's tasks with minute detail; and providing little latitude including asking permission even to go to the bathroom. For example, Henry Ford carried such practices one step further: he even had a company police force whose job was to monitor the private lives of employees (Buell, 1997).

The union movement, formed to address these and other important problems of a previous era, now finds itself (sometimes unwittingly) serving as a barrier to many of the necessary REGO reforms in the public sector. For example, as noted earlier, IT ends the days of assembly lines and many kinds of rote, tedious jobs. Modern IT changed the face of the public sector workplace. Today, activities in the public sector need more thoughtful and flexible workers who both use the new technologies and can fashion continuously improving public services.

The information age breaks down traditional boundaries between production and management. Because unions assume a permanent division of interest between managers and owners on the one hand and the work force on the other, they too often hinder flexible adaptation to the IT twenty-first century workplace (Buell, 1997, p. 41). Moreover, the union movement, for the first time in a generation, successfully mobilized members to vote and to volunteer in campaigns for major political offices at all levels.

According to AFL-CIO President John Sweeney, the hoped for result of this involvement is to preserve past union gains and slow or reverse many of the REGO inspired reforms (Gray and Johnson, 1997). Exit polls indicated that voters from union households made up 23 percent of the total vote for U.S. House of Representative seats, up from 14 percent in 1994 and 19 percent in 1992 (Candaele and Dreier, 1996). In a recent election in California, the Los Angeles County Federation of Labor targeted three state legislative seats in suburban Burbank, Glendale, and Pasadena that Republicans held for half a century. The unions used computerized lists to identify households with union members and organized a political education and voter registration effort among their members. All three union candidates won, regaining a Democrat majority in the State Assembly and preserving a narrow Democrat majority in the Senate (Candaele and Dreier, 1996, pp. 9-10).

Finally, in the health and human service sector, union activity attacked the very premises of work redesign. For example, the California Nurses Association (CNA) and the local 250 make no secret of the fact that they intend to attack the very premises on which policy makers founded the market-based healthcare (Gray and Johnson, 1997). In particular, they warn their members of the dangers of workplace restructuring and downsizing, promoting studies that indicate that increased illnesses and injuries befall nurses who work in organizations that managers reengineered (Shogren, 1996).

TECHNICAL EXPERTISE BARRIER

Advancing IT and the Information Age requires a new type of public sector employee: the "knowledge worker" with an entrepreneurial spirit. In the public sector of the past and even now, the tight command and control system restricted managers and workers to such an extent that the process itself encouraged individuals not to work "outside of the box" or act in an entrepreneurial manner. REGO reforms require workers and managers to have this expertise because thinking creatively and in an entrepreneurial manner are essential. However, one of the most difficult barriers to implementing REGO reforms is the lack of such expertise in the public sector.

REGO involves the processing of large amounts of data, which will require higher levels of computer skills, as well as greater analytical and behavioral talent and skills (Lynch and Lynch, 1998). The command and control environment of the public sector does not attract knowledge workers, who can accomplish these tasks. We can overcome this barrier using a two level strategy. First, the public sector must compete for the best talent, as does the private sector. The fact that the public sector does not react quickly to changing external market forces makes this more difficult. Second, we must reduce and even overcome the public sector organizational resistance to employing entrepreneurial, "out of the box" knowledge workers and managers. If we can not accomplish this, then the internal organizational environment will be dysfunctional and even hostile to the needed change.

HIGHER ETHICAL PLATEAU NEEDED

A basic tenet of democracy is that governments elected by the people are responsible and accountable to the people. Therefore achieving a responsible and accountable government is critical to the success of REGO reforms in democracies. Although citizen empowerment and customer satisfaction determine the parameters of the entrepreneurial spirit in government, the larger ethical issue of accountability for spending the people's money (in the case of budgeting) and redesigning and right sizing remain a central concern. If the public and policy makers are to entrust public managers to perform tasks without the traditional command and control micro management, then some means of accountability must exist if we are to maintain our democracies. With REGO comes the need to more independently decide issues of what is right and wrong and the potential of loss of accountability and responsibility to the whole society.

Examples of REGO-based accountability mechanisms that confront this challenge are many. Governments on all levels are already implementing performance measures based on outcomes. Such measures create managerial accountability and often policy makers establish them with memoranda of understandings, performance contract agreements using incentives, and work plans with targeted revenues and expenditures. Management can easily extend performance contracts to public/private ventures, as well as contracted service providers, licensees, and franchisees in almost all areas of service (Lynch, Hwang, and Lynch, 1996, pp. 22-23).

The challenges for implementing these accountability mechanisms are many, especially in a rapidly transforming environment. For example, Joseph Rost in *Leadership for the Twenty-First Century* (1991) argued that the world experience of a radical transformation is due to the changing basic values from the industrial era. Following this theme, others predicted that the "rational, male, technocrat, quantitative, goal-dominated, cost-benefit driven, hierarchical, short-term, pragmatic, materialistic model must give way to a new kind of leadership based on different assumptions and values" (Garafalo,1995). Our fundamental perspectives on life are changing radically and any new values or perspectives built on the industrial paradigm are not adequate for the next century.

Unfortunately at a time when the public sector manager should look to academia and its study of public policy and administration for assistance in working within this new entrepreneurial environment, the field itself is in turmoil. As Lynch, Omdal, and Cruise (1997) noted, we have allowed the public service to become secularized and we have lost our links to a greater wisdom. In the past, public policy and administration focused on objectivity, detachment and the logical positivist legacy promoted in mid-century by Herbert Simon. Now, postmodernism supplants even this approach by rejecting all objectivity and replaces it with nothing (e.g., Cruise, 1999). Without a viable link to ethics, public sector managers working within networks and web environments are faced with moral dilemmas that can, among other things, threaten democratic governance and reduce political responsiveness (e.g., O'Toole, 1997; Cope, 1997). If REGO reforms are to prosper in the twenty-first century in a networked environment, public sector managers will need to develop a much better basis to make ethical decisions. As Lynch, Omdal, and Cruise (1997) suggest, a source for such a value base should include the spiritual wisdom of the ages (p. 484) and might easily be built on Aristotle's value ethics (Lynch and Lynch, 1998).

ENTREPRENEURIAL ATTITUDES

Giving citizens input into determining their services empowers them and makes the organization more customer-driven. Such reforms help distinguish entrepreneurial from command and control government. Empowering citizens helps define the quality of service parameters and equity issues within which the entrepreneurial spirit can work. They help define the possibilities of strategic brokering. Citizens are a familiar part of the budget process as they propose and press measures, which effect the collection and disbursement of public funds. California's Proposition 13 was a citizen led initiative. Citizens can petition, demonstrate, agitate, sue, advertise, speak, write, publish, and vote. However, longtime observers of citizen action and interest groups' note that key to their success is access to information and knowledge. For proper strategic brokering to occur, all parties must access accurate and unbiased information. Lehan (1981: p. 75) notes that "regardless of other factors, group representatives who seek to influence official conduct must be well informed." Therefore, in Entrepreneurial Budgeting citizens have as great, if not greater stake than other decision makers in the quality and accuracy of budget related documentation and data.

Energizing earning potential, creating competition between and among service providers, and allowing market mechanisms to work to determine unit costs liberates the program managers and agency heads to discover endless possibilities. However, it also creates potential public interest problems. Radical changes in organizations and management patterns may be necessary to achieve the organizational mission. They may decide to turn a profit in one program to fund a "loss leader" in another as an entrepreneurial strategy. Using user fees in new forms like franchising, licensing and increasing investment return are but a few ways information age managers can become entrepreneurs. However, each of these situations can raise equity questions, which could easily become the largest problems in the information age. Answers to equity of distribution issues will not be easy in EB as procedural responses to disparities are often difficult to identify and manage. Empowered agencies can become non-responsive to the overall public good in their quest to satisfy *their* customers rather than the larger public interest. The whole must be the orientation but pressures to serve the parts over the whole will make servicing the whole quite difficult.

An underlying concern for entrepreneurial innovations is that policy makers must determine the true cost of the public service in order to know the break-even point. Analysis must answer, "How can an analyst determine the rate of return on an investment if the true cost of the investment is unknown? How can managers seek profits if the true spending is unknown? How can policy makers determine an appropriate subsidy for a given government program if the true cost of the service is a mystery including the hard to operate support services and leadership costs?" Analysts must use analytical techniques to answer the above questions and EB is one such technique. The EB exposes general fund subsidies to the program, relies on public pressure to do away with them where they can, and thus encourages managers to search for new ways to make money from profitable services to finance essential non-profitable ones. With EB, policy makers are likely to expand greatly the use of enterprise funds in government accounting.

CONCLUSION

As Peter Drucker (1985: p. 17) stated, "That the time has now come to do for entrepreneurship and innovation what we did first for management in general thirty years ago: to develop the principles, the practice and the discipline." If the futurists are correct, then we are well into a new age and we must recognize that fundamental changes are occurring in government including public budgeting. If the previous hundred years are suggestive, we can anticipate that there will be waves of budget reform that address the three purposes of budgeting but within the context of REGO and advancing IT. Our challenge is recognize the changes that are upon us and use our abilities to help develop continuing improvements in government activities.

We need to innovate. According to Drucker (1985: p. 19), "Innovation is the specific tool of entrepreneurs, the means by which they exploit change as an opportunity. . . It is capable of being presented as a discipline, capable of being learned and capable of being practiced." Our challenge is to build always on the best of the past and improve ourselves for the future. We must innovate and accept change as our friend. Every practice rests on theory and we need to improve that theory as conditions such as the information age forces us to see the wisdom of changing our practices. Our challenge is to recognize we are in an era where we must search for change, respond to it, and exploit its opportunities rather than resist it. We need to develop our public organizations as agents of change and we need to develop theories on how we can best do that.

Although there are negative and uncomfortable aspects to REGO and the entrepreneurial approach to budgeting, these reforms should lead to improved public services and we should accept those improvements. The price for not accepting the change is great, but one consequence will mean an increasing inability for government on all levels to address even the most basic needs of its citizens at a tax level people are willing to pay. Moreover, if recent history is a gauge, citizens will demand even lower tax levels at the cost of rapidly diminishing public sector services in spite of negative consequences to society.

Like the Progressive Era early in this century, the Information Era is now and will continue to have profound effects on all aspects of society. The Progressive Era reforms in budgeting addressed the practices brought about by the spoils system in an earlier time. The Information Age, advancing IT, REGO reforms and Entrepreneurial Budgeting confront and are antithetical to Progressive Era centralized command and control structures and practices. If twenty-first century reform is to be successful, then we cannot let them be sustained.

REFERENCES

Brier, S. (Ed.). (1992). *Who Built America?* New York: Pantheon Books.

Buell, J. (1997). The Future of Unions. *Humanist, 57*(5), 41-42.

Candaele, K., & Dreier, P. (1996). Labor's Growing Pains. *Commonweal, 123*(22), 9-10.

Cope, G. (1997). Bureaucratic Reform and Issues of Political Responsiveness. *Journal of Public Administration Research and Theory, 7*(3), 461-471.

Cothran, D. A. (1993). Entrepreneurial Budgeting: An Emerging Form. *Public Administration Review, 53*(5), 445–454.

Cruise, P. (1999). Values, Program Evaluation and the New Public Management. *International Journal of Organization Theory and Behavior, 2*(3-4), 383-412.

Drucker, P. F. (1985). *Innovation and entrepreneurship practice and principles.* New York: Harper & Row.

Drucker, P. F. (1989). *Managing for the future the 1990s and beyond*. New York: Truman Talley Books/Plume.

Drucker, P. F. (1989). *The new realities in government and politics, in economics and business, in society and world view*. New York: Harper & Row.

Gaebler, T., & Osborne, A. (1992). Entrepreneurial Government Makes Good Sense. *The Public Manager*, 4-6.

Garafalo, C. (1995) "Leadership, Ethics and Change." Paper presented at the American Society for Public Administration (ASPA) 1995 Annual Conference. San Antonio, Texas, 1995.

Geri, L. R. (1997). Federal User Fees and Entrepreneurial Budgeting. *Journal of Public Budgeting, Accounting and Financial Management*, 9(1), 127-142.

Gore, A. (September 7, 1993). *From Red Tape to Results: Creating a Government That Works Better and Costs Less. A Report of the National Performance Review*. Washington, DC: U.S. Government Printing Office.

Government Accounting Standards Board (GASB). (1995). *Government Accounting Series Concept Statement Number 2 on Concepts Related to Service Efforts and Accomplishments Reporting*, Norwalk, CT.

Gray, R., & Johnson, J. (1997). *Health Care Labor-Management Relations*. Kansas City, MO: Woods and Waters.

Hammer, M., & Champy, J. (1992). *Reengineering the corporation a manifesto for business revolution*. New York, NY: Harper Business.

Haque, A. (1998). Edmund Burke: The Role of Public Administration in a Constitutional Order. In T. D. Lynch, & T. J. Dicker (Eds.), *Handbook of organization theory and management the philosophical approach*. New York: M. Dekker.

Henry, N. (1995). *Public administration and public affairs* (6th ed.). Englewood Cliffs, N.J: Prentice Hall.

Jones, L. R. (1995). Aaron Wildavsky: A Man and Scholar for All Seasons. *Public Administration Review*, 55(1), 3-16.

Laudicina, E. (1995). Rethinking the Agenda for Reinvention. *Journal of Public Administration Education*, 1(2), 154-157.

Lehan, E. A. (1981). *Simplified governmental budgeting*. New York: Longman, Inc.

Leviathan Re-engineered. (1996). *The Economist, 341*, 67.

Lynch, T. D. (1975). *Policy analysis in public policymaking*. Lexington, Mass: Lexington Books.

Lynch, T. D. (1989). Budget System Approach. *Public Administration Quarterly, 13*(3), 321-341.

Lynch, T. D. (1995). *Public budgeting in America* (5th ed.). Englewood Cliffs, N.J: Prentice Hall.

Lynch, T.D., Hwang, Y., and Lynch, C. (1996). "Cycle of History and Budget Reform: The Next Stage Entrepreneurial Budgeting?" Paper presented at the 1996 International Speyer Workshop on Assessing and Evaluating Public Management Reform, Speyer, Germany.

Lynch, T.D., and Lynch, C. (1998). "Global Ethics for Public Administration: Possible or Foolish." Paper presented at the American Society for Public Administration 1998 Annual Conference, Seattle, Washington.

Lynch, T. D., Omdal, R., & Cruise, P. (1997). Secularization of Public Administration. *Journal of Public Administration Research and Theory, 7*(3), 473-487.

Lynch, T. D., Omdal, R., & Cruise, P. (1997). Secularization of Public Administration. *Journal of Public Administration Research and Theory, 7*(3), 473-487.

Martin, L. (1998). Jeremy Bentham: Utilitarianism, Public Policy and the Administrative State. In T. D. Lynch, & T. J. Dicker (Eds.), *Handbook of organization theory and management the philosophical approach*. New York: M. Dekker.

Martin, L. L. (1993). Contracting Out: A Comparative Analysis of Local Government Practices. In T. D. Lynch, & L. L. Martni (Eds.), *Handbook of comparative public budgeting and financial management* (pp. 225-239). New York: Marcel Dekker.

Martin, L. (1998). Jeremy Bentham: Utilitarianism, Public Policy and the Administrative State. In T. D. Lynch, & T. J. Dicker (Eds.), *Handbook of organization theory and management the philosophical approach*. New York: Dekker, Inc.

Naisbitt, J. (1984). *Megatrends: ten new directions transforming our lives*. New York, N.Y: Warner Books.

Naisbitt, J. (1994). *Global paradox the bigger the world economy, the more powerful its smallest players*. New York: Avon Books.

O'Toole, L. (1997). The Implications for Democracy in a Networked Bureaucratic World. *Journal of Public Administration Research and Theory, 7*, 443-459.

Osborne, D., & Gaebler, T. (1993). *Reinventing government how the entrepreneurial spirit is transforming the public sector*. New York, N.Y: Plume.

Pettijohn, C. D., & Grizzle, G. A. (1997). "Structural Budget Reform: Does It Affect Budget Deliberations?". *Journal of Public Budgeting, Accounting and Financial Management, 9*(1), 26-45.

Q & A Realizing the Promise of Reengineering. (1997). *Healthcare Financial Management, 51*(4), 24.

Reich, R. B. (1992). *The work of nations: preparing ourselves for 21st century capitalism*. New York: Vintage Books.

Rost, J. C. (1991). *Leadership for the twenty-first century*. New York: Praeger.

Schick, A. (1978). "The Road to PPB: The Stages of Budget Reform. Public Administration Review 26 (December 1966): 243-258. Reprinted in Jay M. Shafritz and Albert C. Hyde, *Classics of Public Administration*, Moore Publishing Company, Inc., Oak Park, Illinois, pp. 249-267.

Shogren, E. (1996). Restructuring May Be Hazardous to Your Health. *American Journal of Nursing, 96*(11), 64.

Stephen King, M. (1995). "The Entrepreneurial Budgeting System of Texas Parks and Wildlife Department." A paper presented at the American Society for Public Administration, San Antonio, Texas.

Wolf, P. (1997). Why Must We Reinvent the Federal Government? Putting Historical Developmental Claims to the Test. *Journal of Public Administration Research and Theory, 7*(3), 353-388.

Chapter 7

REINVENTING FEDERAL EMERGENCY MANAGEMENT AGENCY: GAINS AND LIMITS OF THE NEWEST "NEW FEDERALISM"

Bert Useem

The Federal Emergency Management Agency, facing possible extinction for its poor performance, achieved a remarkable turnaround. This chapter examines how this turnaround was achieved, considering the independent effects of new leadership and the National Performance Review's reinvention initiative. The empirical focus is the response by FEMA to the January, 1994 Northridge, Los Angeles earthquake. The implications for a "new federalism" are discussed.

Despite its modest size of 2,700 employees, or perhaps because of it, the Federal Emergency Management Agency (FEMA) has played a key role in the effort to "reinvent" the federal government. At a press conference early in the National Performance Review (NPR) process, Vice President Gore announced that his staff would use FEMA as a laboratory to assess possible government-wide changes. He stated that FEMA's "size is not unmanageable. It has a clearly understood mission, and. . . the people here [at FEMA] want it [reinvention]" (Gannett News Service, 10/10/93). When NPR was initiated in September 1993, a handful of agencies were singled out for agency-focused supplemental reports. FEMA was one of them (NPR, 1993b).

A premise of NPR is that the "government is broken," meaning that it ought to "work better and cost less." FEMA was more than "broken" in that sense. It was in crisis. Any effort to appraise FEMA's reinvention must do so in terms of the agency's effort to pull itself out of that crisis.

The Federal Emergency Management Agency (FEMA) was established in 1979 by President Jimmy Carter to improve the federal government's response to disasters (O'Bryant and Bea, 1995). FEMA has responsibility for administering federal policies related to civil defense, disaster relief, reduction of earthquake hazards, flood-plain insurance, disaster mitigation programs, and dam safety.

The agency's operating organization included: five "directorates" (divisions), two administrations (sub-agencies), and ten regional offices. Each of the ten regions has its own area headquarters. Region 9, for example, is headquartered in San Francisco.

Government agencies are mortal; and Hurricane Andrew brought FEMA near the brink of extinction. Reaching shore in August, 1992, this third most-powerful hurricane in U.S. history destroyed 80,000 homes, left 160,000 homeless, and caused $30 billion in damage (U.S. Senate, Committee on Governmental Affairs, 1993; Portes and Stepick, 1993). By virtually all accounts, the governmental response was inept. A Government Accounting Office (GAO) investigation, for example, reported that disaster victims were forced to loot grocery stores for food, consume potentially contaminated water, and stave off looters by setting up makeshift huts in front of their homes. Not until the fifth day were feeding operations established in the hardest hit areas (GAO, 1993a; GAO, 1993b).

In the aftermath, both state and federal officials came under criticism. Florida officials stated that they had initially been under the impression, mistakenly, that the network of state, local, and volunteer personnel was handling the situation adequately. Efforts to arrive at an accurate assessment were delayed by closed airfields and debris blocking ground transportation. As a result, Florida failed to request federal assistance in a timely manner (U.S. Senate, Committee on Governmental Affairs, 1993).

FEMA officials stated that they believed that the agency had no authority (under the Stafford Act[1]) to act, or ask other federal agencies to act, until a governor requested and obtained a presidential declaration that a major disaster or emergency exists. The root of the problem was Florida's delinquent request for assistance. Yet, even granting this, observers pointed out that FEMA should have conducted its own assessment of the situation, especially since it had access to satellite and other technology that could have been used for that purpose (U.S. Senate, Committee on Governmental Affairs, 1993, p. 84). At a minimum, FEMA should have mobilized its resources so that when a request did come, the agency could be on the scene quickly.

The criticism of FEMA, though, went deeper. A U.S. Senator complained that the agency seemed to have a "Holiday Inn mentality," by which he meant that FEMA officials were more concerned about: staying in a nice hotel, getting a nice rental car, and returning home as soon as possible rather than committing themselves fully to helping disaster victims (U.S. Senate, Committee on Governmental Affairs, 1993, p. 38).

Another Senator accused FEMA of being a "dumping ground for retread military career officers" or other patronage appointees (U.S. Senate, Committee on Governmental Affairs, 1993, p. 15). In short, Andrew seemed to reveal that FEMA lacked administrative competence, energy, and commitment.

---

[1]The Robert T. Stafford Relief and Emergency Assistance Act (as amended) specifies the terms under which the federal government may assist disaster-stricken areas.

In this context, "many in Congress began to call for the abolition of FEMA," observed a member of that body (U.S. Senate, Committee on Governmental Affairs, 1993, p. 89). An academic observer told a Senate hearing on FEMA that the agency is ". . .like a patient in triage. The President and Congress must decide whether to treat it or let it die" (U.S. Senate, Committee on Governmental Affairs, 1993, p. 55). Several reorganization plans were floated, including turning responsibility for disaster management over to another Cabinet-level department or to some other major agency. On February 4, 1993, a bill was introduced in the House of Representatives that, if passed, would have abolished FEMA and transferred all of its powers, functions, and duties to the Department of Defense. While the bill died in committee, Congressional anger at FEMA did not.

FEMA's response to another disaster cast additional doubt on the agency's future. On March 13-14, 1993, a snowstorm blanketed the East Coast. At FEMA's recommendation, 17 states and the District of Columbia were declared to be eligible for $30 million in disaster relief. The disbursements occurred before current-director James Lee Witt took office, but it was under his watch that FEMA's response was subjected to Congressional scrutiny. In a Senate hearing, Senator Glenn complained that FEMA seemed to have strayed from its mission

> Now that was hardly what we envisioned . . . when FEMA was established. . . . Was there some inconvenience to people in communities during that time period? Yes, there certainly was. Is that a function [of FEMA] to step in and spend some $30-some million to assist in snow removal? (U.S. Senate, Committee on Governmental Affairs, 1993, p. 2).

The NPR supplementary report on FEMA did not hide its sarcasm: "Snow is a regular, recurring event in many of the affected areas" (NPR, 1993b, p. 5).

In fact, the issues were more complex. Responding to questions from a Senate Committee, Director Witt made the following points: (1) more people died as a result of this winter storm (200) than had been killed by Hurricane Andrew; (2) millions of citizens were stranded or immobilized, requiring in some areas air drops of food, water, and medicine; (3) the storm had a measurable, negative impact on the nation's economy. Indeed, the snowstorm turned out to be the fourth most costly disaster in U.S. history, at $1.75 billion in estimated losses (U.S Senate, Committee on Commerce, Science, and Transportation, 1994, p. 75).

The problem was that this "regular recurring event" was, in fact, a constituent element of a historically unprecedented upsurge in the cost of disasters. Before 1989, no U.S. disaster had resulted in more than $1 billion in insured losses. After 1989, that threshold was exceeded six times. Hurricane Andrew alone caused an estimated $25 billion in losses. This is more than the three next most costly hurricanes combined (U.S. Senate, Committee on Governmental Affairs, 1993, p. 94). The demands on the federal treasury escalated accordingly. Between 1984 and 1988, the annual appropriations for FEMA, here to include disaster supplementals, hovered around $500 million. Then, between 1989 and 1995, the average per year appropriations for disasters more than tripled.

Table 1. FEMA Funding, FY 1984-1995
Fiscal Years 1970-1994
(Dollars in millions)

FEMA

Fiscal year	Appropriations[a]
1984	$658
1985	480
1986	493
1987	644
1988	644
1989	1,757
1990	1,810
1991	579
1992	4,783
1993	2,575
1994	5,926
1995	7,539

[a] Includes all appropriations, including emergency supplementals.

Sources: CRS Report for Congress, *FEMA and Disaster Relief*, Congressional Research Service, The Library of Congress, March 6, 1995; U.S. Senate, Bipartisan Task Force on Funding Disaster Relief, *Federal Disaster Assistance, Report of the Senate Task Force on Funding Disaster Relief*. March 15, 1995; JoAnne O'Bryant and Keith Bea, *FEMA and Disaster Relief*. (Washington, D.C., Congressional Research Service, Library of Congress, March 6, 1995.)

Moreover, there was a growing concern within the polity that the costs of disasters to the federal government had become unacceptably high, especially in a period of mounting pressure to reduce the deficit. A member of the House observed,

> Events of the last several years helped teach us what is wrong with our current disaster policies: . . the federal government cannot continue to be a bottomless pit of disaster relief (U.S. House, Committee on Public Works and Transportation, 1994a, p. 13).

A final turn of events would help set the stage for FEMA's reinvention initiative. Since its inception, FEMA had two primary missions. One was to prepare for and respond to natural hazards; the other was to ensure that U.S. government would be able to operate in the event of a massive nuclear attack. An administrative wall separated the staff assigned to each function, which created a tension (NAPA 1993:52). For example, in the aftermath of Hurricane Andrew, FEMA staff assigned to the "continuity of government" program were criticized by other FEMA staff for doing little to help. Their response was that they were never asked (NPR 1993b, p. 5). In any case, with the end of the Cold War, the U.S. security strategy shifted from a concern over a major nuclear attack to smaller-scale attacks by foreign terrorists. From an emergency management point of view, planning for a small-scale foreign attack is similar to planning for a natural hazard. In 1993, the "National Preparedness Directorate" was abolished, and its resources and staff were redistributed within FEMA (Sylves 1994:304). The agency, as a whole, could focus on a single mission of preparedness for all hazards.

In sum, the historical context presented FEMA reinventors with two problems, one organizational and the other strategic. The organizational problem was to improve the performance of the agency. The strategic one was to rethink the agency's mission, so as to somehow reduce the costs of disasters to the nation.

The National Performance Review would have two formally-designated stages. NPR, Phase-I was initiated on March 3, 1993 by President Clinton and put under the direction of Vice President Gore. NPR, Phase-II was announced by President Clinton in December, 1994 and formally launched in a January 3, 1995 memo from the Vice President to agency heads. At FEMA, NPR-I efforts focused primarily on the organizational challenge, while NPR-II efforts focused on the strategic.

NATIONAL PERFORMANCE REVIEW I: THE APPOINTMENT OF JAMES LEE WITT

Soon after taking office, President Clinton appointed James Lee Witt as director of FEMA. Witt breathed new life into the agency. Soft-spoken yet articulate, personable, and hard-working, Witt conveyed in words, manner, and action that his primary commitment was to the agency and its mission of helping disaster victims, not to his own career advancement. He quickly became very popular among FEMA employees, and engendered a strong sense of connectedness to them. This built organizational solidarity among them. Agency morale improved sharply. Few, inside or outside FEMA, would challenge President Clinton's assessment, to be made several years later, that "Under the leadership of James Lee Witt" FEMA has been transformed "from being a disaster into being a model disaster relief agency" (*Federal News Service*, 4/27/95). This assessment is supported below.

Witt's leadership may have been the primary force behind the FEMA turnaround. If so, this would not be the first time a transformative leader would have a deep impact on a public agency (Hargrove and Glidewell, 1990). Still, one can also reasonably argue that Witt's leadership took root because it was planted in ground tilled by NPR. Witt may have been effective because of NPR, not the other way around. If, as the reinventers argued at the outset, FEMA would be used as a NPR test-case, it is important to distinguish the independent effects of Witt's leadership versus those of the NPR strategy.

One way to gain leverage on the issue is to focus on what might be called "implementation integrity." The key question is the extent to which FEMA reformers actually adhered to NPR principles. To the extent that they did not, then greater weight would have to be given to Witt's leadership (or other factors) than to the NPR itself. In attempting to determine this, speeches and testimony are less revealing than the actual behavior of FEMA in the first major disaster handled by Witt under NPR, the January, 1994 Northridge (Los Angeles) earthquake.

A REINVENTED FEMA AND THE NORTHRIDGE EARTHQUAKE

The January 14, 1994, Northridge earthquake caused severe ground shaking for ten minutes and resulted in 61 deaths, 8,700 injuries, and over $20 billion in property damage. The evidence from in-depth interviews with members of FEMA's Region 9 office (San Francisco), FEMA officials in Washington headquarters, and state of California officials suggests that FEMA had become a well-managed, well-led agency. Director Witt later told Congress in a self-congratulatory yet probably accurate summary:

> The State of California and hundreds of local governments, FEMA and the Federal Departments and Agencies formed a very strong working partnership as a team, a team that delivered one of the most rapid and effective response operations (U.S. House of Representatives, Committee on Armed Services, 1994, p. 9).

FEMA's multifaceted response to Northridge can be briefly summarized. Useful here is Grodzins' distinction between "marble-cake" federalism (the three levels of government are intertwined, working to assist one another) and "layer-cake" federalism (each layer of government is neatly separated and performs only those functions appropriate to it) (Grodzins and Elazar, 1974). The evidence suggests that a marble-cake federalism was quickly and efficiently achieved at Northridge. The marbling took place at both the operational and administrative levels.

A. Operational Marbling. If the problem at Andrew had been that FEMA officials were slow to assess the situation, this was not to occur at Northridge. The FEMA Regional Operations Center was activated within 90 minutes of the earthquake (U.S. Senate, Committee on Appropriations, 1994a, p. 59). Working out of this center, the agency actively collected, collated, and assessed information on the location and extent of the damage. The agency collected data from aerial reconnaissance photographs and geographic information systems (GIS). It also drew heavily from information provided by the state, in sharp contrast to FEMA's work at Andrew.

Disaster Application Centers were opened three days after Northridge, compared to six days at Andrew. Teleregistration centers were opened 12 hours after Northridge, compared to six days in the wake of Andrew. Traditionally, according to a FEMA official, the agency had tended to "regulate and administer as opposed to actually do things." However, after Andrew and especially at Northridge, the agency: "actually got out and started doing a lot of things that historically had been a state and local government responsibility and capability."[2]

Almost immediately, FEMA mobilized its Urban Search and Rescue teams, Disaster Medical Assistance Teams, and Mobile Emergency Response System. One Region 9 official commented that, much more so than in previous disasters, "We put up tents and brought in generators." Other resources provided by the federal government included: bulk water distribution, bulk food distribution to shelters and other points of distribution; foreign language translators to assist applicants in Disaster Assistance Centers; military personnel to assist in the construction of temporary rail stations; structural engineers to help inspect buildings; and grants to individuals to make repairs to damaged residences.

B. Administrative Marbling. At least during the first several days after the disaster, the relationship between Region 9 and state officials was that of an integrated team. The experience of a Region 9 staff member seems representative. Two hours after the earthquake, he arrived at the state's emergency operations center in Sacramento, where he would serve for four days as the FEMA-liaison officer. He later reported:

> I found myself helping [state officials] get their job done, having a lot of contact with both county and city governments. . . . [as well as] some special districts. . . I was asked by the people in the state operations center to respond to inquiries that they had received from local jurisdictions. So I was in effect making a call back on their behalf, as part of an **integrated state-federal team**. (emphasis added).

Over the course of the first several days, some tension emerged between FEMA and state officials but, ironically, this tension seems to support claims of FEMA's reinvention. Richard Andrews, Director of California's Office of Emergency Services testified to Congress that:

> In the days following the Northridge earthquake, it was very difficult to manage the level of Federal response. Earlier agreements that the Federal emergency support functions would be activated only on the request of the State of California. . . . were not followed. . . . It is essential that Federal response be to specific needs identified and resources requested by the states and local governments (U.S. House of Representatives, Committee on Public Works and Transportation, 1994b, p. 66).

From FEMA's point of view, the conflict was a product of the magnitude of the federal government's presence. One Region 9 member explained, there were: ... up to at one point 5,000 [FEMA] responders ... [T]hat clearly is very overwhelming to a small state agency like OES, and I think that's where some of the resentment comes in. We're sort of caught between a rock and a hard place, because we get criticized for not being proactive, but if we start being too proactive, then we get criticized because we're essentially infringing on the state's area of operation.

---

[2] All interviews not otherwise cited are with FEMA officials, either in Washington FEMA headquarters or at FEMA 9 Regional headquarters in San Francisco. The interviews were conducted by the author. Respondents were pledged anonymity.

In sum, the organizational conflict between OES and FEMA in the first several days reflected the presence of two relatively strong organizations which, from time to time, stepped on each other's toes. From the point of view of disaster victims, the conflict seems to have had few negative consequences.

NORTHRIDGE RESPONSE AS EVIDENCE OF FEMA REINVENTION

Returning to the issue of implementation integrity, FEMA's response at Northridge suggests that many of the NPR-I mandated changes were achieved. FEMA had transformed itself from a passive agency to a hard-driving, problem-solving organization with a much deeper commitment to "serve its customers." Perhaps most importantly, the agency developed a national and regional cadre of skilled, dedicated emergency management specialists.

At a more general level, FEMA itself has catalogued more than two dozen specific changes either directly mandated by NPR or inspired by its philosophy (FEMA, n.d.) They include:

- a greater reliance on teleregistration to receive application for disaster assistance.
- greater public outreach efforts, including the use of surveys and focus groups to determine customer satisfaction, establishing an Internet site to release emergency information, and the creation of a television broadcasting capability.
- establishing at FEMA's Washington headquarters three National Emergency Response Teams (ERTs), one of which is always on standby-by so that it can be immediately dispatched to help manage the initial response to a disaster.

Although a full listing of these changes is not provided here, this is not meant to diminish their significance. It is unassailable that: "Californians got the help they needed more quickly and efficiently than ever before," (FEMA, 1995a, p. 7) in large measure because of these NPR-based reforms.

Still, one suspects that many of these gains could have been secured simply through effective leadership, as Witt provided. There is, though, one fundamental issue that does distinguish the NPR philosophy. NPR reformers argue against "top-down, centralized bureaucracies" as the "root problem" of American government. These "industrial-era" organizations "don't work very well . . . in today's world of rapid change, lightening-quick information technologies, tough global competition, and demanding customers" (NPR, 1993a, p. 3). The solution, according to NPR, is to decentralize federal agencies, so as to "empower" government workers to make better decisions and cut through red tape (NPR, 1993a, p. 6-8).

The theory at work here is that, as power within public organizations shifts from the top levels to the mid- and bottom-levels, their culture changes. Given greater responsibility and armed with knowledge of specific problems their clientele face, government workers will become more energetic, creative, and focused on meeting real needs. This is NPR's distinctive, and most contested, claim.

The argument against this approach was that the NPR-vision was all sail and no anchor (Moe, 1994; Wilson, 1994; Garvey, 1995). One of the most enduring dilemmas of government in democratic societies is to improve government agency performance without jeopardizing agency accountability to elected officials and, ultimately, to the people. NPR focused almost exclusively on agency performance, saying little or nothing about the value of democratic accountability. If government employees are empowered to make decisions on their own authority, they could easily substitute their policy preferences for those to whom they are responsible or simply make poor decisions with little accountability to anyone. Under NPR, democratic control of the federal agencies would be put at risk.

Yet on the key issue of agency decentralization, reinvention at FEMA was never pushed very far. First, although the *reinvention process* at FEMA has involved employee "input," there has been no devolution of power to those on the lower rungs. Most FEMA employees, at least those in Region 9, reported some vague recollection of being asked to send in comments to the agency's NPR steering committee, but the level of participation never went beyond that. The process had a "suggestion box" quality to it.

Second, again in Region 9, FEMA employees generally dismissed the idea that they have been empowered to make decisions while they disregarded "red tape." From their point of view, the organization is no less hierarchical than it ever was. Some of the superficial trappings of hierarchy have been removed, but little more than that.

Third, as Kettl (1995, p. 13) notes, "the NPR seeks to shift power from Congress to the bureaucracy and, within the bureaucracy, from top to bottom levels." Here the evidence suggests FEMA moved in the opposite direction. According one FEMA official, historically, the regions exercised considerable autonomy. For example, in a disaster's aftermath, a regional disaster coordinator (called a "Federal Coordinating Officer" or "FCO") would be charged with "getting it done." Once so charged, the FCO: . . . had great latitude in how to interpret the regulation. But that great latitude meant that disaster A was interpreted one way, disaster C was another. Disaster E comes along and they . . . say which of those interpretations do I like.

Under NPR, FEMA became increasingly centralized at the expense of autonomy and authority of the regions. A Region 9 employee observed:

> Two years ago our new director . . . came out here and said "We're going to give the regional directors all the authority they need to do their jobs and then we're going to hold them accountable." That is exactly the opposite of what is happening. Everything is centralized in D.C.

As evidence for this, it was pointed out that Director Witt arrived in Los Angeles shortly after the earthquake and, by the second day, headquarters staff began to arrive en masse. By about the fourth day, headquarters staff took over the operation of the disaster field office (DFO). Regional FEMA staff were located elsewhere in the Los Angeles County area. The theoretical significance of this is that it challenges the NPR ideas. For instance, agency reinvention mandates agency decentralization and the devolution of power to lower parts of the organization.

NATIONAL PERFORMANCE REVIEW II AND PERFORMANCE PARTNERSHIPS

The NPR-I report stated that: "Today, the central issue we face is not *what* government does, but *how* it works" (1993a, p. 2. emphasis in original). Phase II of the NPR, launched in late 1994, exactly reverses that. The key question under NPR-II, as Alice Rivlin (Director of President Clinton's the Office of Management and Budget) put it, is "What should the federal government be doing?" (Rivlin, 1995).

FEMA gave two broad answers to this: one substantive, the other procedural. The substantive answer was advanced in two key strategic planning documents, one issued in September, 1993 and the other in October, 1995. Both proposed an expanded role for the agency, based on three premises.

Premise 1: The costs of disasters to the nation, in terms of lost lives, property damage, demands on the federal treasury, and disruption of the economy, had become unacceptably high. Through most of its history, FEMA had focused on post-disaster relief and recovery. Now the agency would expand its role to include lowering those costs through a greater emphasis on pre-disaster mitigation. FEMA's mission was formally redefined according to the following:

To reduce the loss of life and property and to protect our institutions from all hazards by leading and supporting the Nation in a comprehensive, risk based emergency management program of mitigation, preparedness, response, and recovery (FEMA, 1993, p. 2).

In short, FEMA's NPR-I plan had stated that mitigation should be the cornerstone of federal disaster policy. NPR II began to build an edifice around that cornerstone.

Premise 2: No additional revenues. There can be little doubt that had the October, 1995 *National Mitigation Strategy* (FEMA, 1995b) been issued a decade earlier, it would have called for a major new funding initiative. Yet a quarter century of annual and increasing deficits, accumulating to a debt in excess of $4.5 trillion, would kill any initiative that would require new federal funds. The *Strategy* does, in fact, suggest the need for a major funding initiative, but there is no call to action. FEMA is to: ". . .within 5 years determine the most effective means for providing increased resources for pre-disaster mitigation." But it is probably fair to say that the shelf-life of such a report is less than five years.

Premise 3: Accommodation to the devolution revolution. In this period, central to the conservative agenda is a belief that decisionmaking authority should be shifted from Washington to the states. Liberals, as well, came to accept key elements of the devolution revolution, such as a willingness to give states greater latitude to experiment in welfare reform. Common to both conservative and liberal devolution philosophy is that the state governments might actually do it better than the federal government. At minimum, they should be allowed to try.

The commitment to devolution underlies the Republican efforts to make greater use of block grants (direct cash payments to states in the form of lump sum payments with few strings attached). Yet in a Senate hearing, Director Witt stated, although somewhat obliquely, that he opposed greater use of block grants in disaster policy.

Senator Mikulski: Would you support a block grant approach?

Mr. Witt: If we can be sure that it would be spent toward meeting those risks, then I
    would be willing to look at that, yes (U.S. Senate. Committee on
    Appropriations, 1994b, p. 368).

Of course, the whole idea of block grants is that the federal government cannot "be sure" how federal funds will be expended. Moreover, Hurricane Andrew exposed gaping holes not only in FEMA's response capability but in those of the state and local authorities. A "block grant approach" would not ensure that the states, left to their own devices, would use federal funds in a way that would fill those holes.

In sum, the three premises put FEMA in the difficult position of simultaneously having to: a) advance new national disaster policy goals, especially mitigation; b) operate with no additional funds; and c) devolve authority to state and local government. Probably "a and "b", and certainly "a" and "c," pulled federal disaster policy in opposite directions. This was a genuine dilemma. FEMA attempted to resolve it through an arrangement called "Performance Partnerships Agreements" (NPR Phase II Federalism Team, 1995).

PERFORMANCE PARTNERSHIPS AGREEMENTS (PPA)

PPAs are formally signed, five-year agreements between the federal government and each state government. With regard to FEMA, the intent is to: (a) consolidate many federal programs for disaster assistance into one or two funding streams; (b) eliminate "micro-management" by FEMA of state and local programs; (c) reduce paperwork; (d) insist on broader federal goals and priorities, and, at the same time; (e) permit state and local government to determine how to achieve those goals and priorities given the hazards that affect them. Performance Partnership Agreements replaced "Cooperative Community Agreements," which had provided federal funds primarily for emergency preparedness and response planning.

In signing the agreement, the federal government (through FEMA) obligates itself to provide financial and technical assistance to a state at an agreed upon level over a five year period. A year-by-year "Cooperative Agreement" between the federal and state government provides the actual funds, and requires the state to report to FEMA the progress being made toward the five year goals established in the PPA. Criteria for measuring the states' performance is to be negotiated as part of the PPA itself.

Three points can be made about PPAs. First, it is hard to imagine that the PPA/NPR II process could work absent the success of FEMA's reforms under NPR I. Implicitly, the PPA process requires state disaster agencies to raise their standards of operations to the level of quality established by FEMA. FEMA is both stimulus for state reform and the model for that reform.

Second, Mark Moore (1995), Peter Drucker (1995), and others have argued that governments at all levels would benefit from the greater use of "strategic management." For Moore, strategic management entails defining a mission, summoning political support and legitimacy for that mission, and developing the operational capability to achieve the mission. The NPR II/PPA process, not only embraces the idea of strategic management for the federal agencies, but has encouraged it for state government as well. One FEMA region, for example, held a workshop that trained state officials in the strategic planning process. Other states' disaster agencies reported that, because of the PPA process, they had engaged in a strategic planning process for the first time.

Third, if there is an Achilles' heel to the PPA process, it would be the problem of measuring "outcome results." Students of public policy and administration have long noted the difficulty of measuring the outcomes of public agencies. Business firms have a bottom line. Government agencies often do not. For example, for an earthquake of a given magnitude and location, what is a tolerable number of injuries and deaths? How does one measure the value of citizens' interest in building beach front homes that are vulnerable to hurricanes? And perhaps most importantly, performance measures are often based on what can be most easily and accurately measured rather than focusing on contributions to the agency's statutory purposes, mission statement, or strategic plans.

FEMA's solution is to negotiate performance measures state-by-state (and territory-by-territory) based on local standards rather than national norms, and then incorporate those performance measures in each state's PPA. Yet some of the currently negotiated measures seem to remain only distantly related to actual outcomes. These measures include, for example, the number of town meetings held, efforts to pass more responsible building codes, and the number of reports produced in efforts to get state legislation passed.

CONCLUSION

NPR I succeeded at FEMA in transforming the agency's culture and enhancing its performance. Still, it is not clear how much credit should be given to NPR itself versus the leadership of James Lee Witt. The easy answer is both, although a fairer one would probably give greater weight to leadership than to NPR ideas. A key element of the NPR model, devolution of power within the organization, was never really attempted. Still, some of the NPR tenets were implemented. At a minimum, NPR provided Witt a useful platform to launch FEMA's revival.

NPR II at FEMA is a search for a deeper reform. Driven by an unprecedented rise in the costs of disasters, NPR II attempts to expand FEMA's mission, primarily by lowering the national costs of disasters through mitigation. Yet it is one thing to argue that mitigation is in the national interest, and quite another to show politically and administratively how the federal government can promote that interest. Disaster planning and response have traditionally been primarily the responsibility of state and local governments. The Stafford Act explicitly states that the federal government's role is to assist state and local efforts.[3] Further, with the Republican assumption of majority status in the 104th Congress, any effort to federalize disaster policy runs against the political tide of the devolution revolution.

NPR II navigates cleverly through these tumultuous waters. On the one hand, PPAs maintain the federal government's role in establishing broad national goals. On the other hand, states retain considerable autonomy in figuring out how to achieve the nationally established goals. The two sides meet in a process, not of regulation nor unrestricted funding pass-downs, but rather interest-based negotiation. The idea behind interest-based negotiation is the search for a solution that optimizes joint gains and satisfies the legitimate interests of both parties.

Do PPAs offer a new model of federalism? John Kincaid (1995) has recently observed that over the last 30 years *every* presidential administration has proposed a "new federalism": Lyndon Johnson's Creative Federalism, Richard Nixon's New Federalism, Jimmy Carter's New Partnership, Ronald Reagan's New Federalism, and George Bush's "Sununu Federalism." Thus, any claim that NPR II represents a new chapter in federalism must be met with skepticism. Yet, in my judgment, current efforts to transform FEMA and the FEMA-state collaboration at least offer the possibility of significant change in how federal-state relations work. If the PPAs can be used successfully to coordinate federal emergency response while advancing state autonomy, and if the risk of this strategy can be kept in check by a clear commitment to a shared mission, an energizing "new federalism" might really be on the horizon. The record has not yet unfolded sufficiently that we can make such an assessment.

---

[3]The Act's preamble states: "It is the intent of the Congress, by this chapter, to provide an orderly and continuing means of assistance by the Federal Government to State and local governments in carrying out their responsibilities to alleviate the suffering and damage which result from . . disasters." The Robert T. Stafford Assistance and Emergency Relief Act, As Amended, 42 U.S.C., 5121, et seq., p. 6 [page number per Internet version]. Indeed, under current law, FEMA has no authority over building codes; has no authority to direct state and local governments in disaster training, plans, response and recovery; no authority to directly respond to disasters; and no authority to sanctions states, communities, or citizens who fail to take reasonable precautions against disasters.

NOTES

This chapter benefited from the helpful comments of Professors Van Johnston, Joanne Nigg, Kathleen Tierney, and Richard Wood, and FEMA's Calvin Byrd and David O'Keeffe. In addition, I appreciate a large group of FEMA's officials who consented to be interviewed but to whom I promised confidentiality. The interpretation is my own.

The research was supported by a grant from the National Science Foundation, Earthquake Systems Integration System Division to the Disaster Research Center, the University of Delaware, and a Research Allocation Grant from the University of New Mexico to the author.

REFERENCES

Drucker, P. (1995). *Managing in a Time of Great Change.* New York: Dutton.

Federal Emergency Management Agency [FEMA]. (1993). *FEMA Renewal: Federal Emergency Management Agency National Performance Review Report*, Washington, DC: FEMA.

Federal Emergency Management Agency [FEMA]. (1995a). *The Northridge Earthquake: One Year Later.* Washington, DC: FEMA.

Federal Emergency Management Agency [FEMA]. (1995b). *National Mitigation Strategy: Partnership for Building Safer Communities.* Washington, DC: FEMA.

Federal Emergency Management Agency [FEMA] (n.d.). "Improvement in Disaster Management Since Hurricane Andrew," Washington, DC: FEMA, Mimeograph.

Federal News Service. (4/27/95). "Remarks by President Bill Clinton and Vice President Al Gore at Reinventing Government Event Federal Communications Commission Auction Room Washington, DC." (Westlaw).

Gannett News Service. (10/10/93). "Disaster Agency to Lead Government Reform Drive." (Westlaw).

Garvey, G. (1995). "False Promises: The NPR in Historical Perspective." In D. F. Kettl and J.J. DiIulio (Eds.), *Inside the Reinvention Machine: Appraising Governmental Reform* (pp. 87-106). Washington, DC: Brookings Institution.

General Accounting Office [GAO]. (1993a). *Disaster Management: Recent Disasters Demonstrate the Need to Improve the Nation's Response Strategy*, (GAO/T-RCED-93-4). Washington, DC: GAO.

General Accounting Office [GAO]. (1993b). *Disaster Management: Improving the Nation's Response to Catastrophic Disasters Strategy*, (GAO/T-RCED-186). Washington, DC: GAO.

General Accounting Office [GAO]. (1994). *Los Angeles Earthquake: Opinions of Officials on Federal Impediments to Rebuilding; Report to Congress.* Washington, DC: GAO.

Grodzins, M. & Elazar, D.(1974). "Centralization and Decentralization in the U.S. Federal System." In R.A. Goldwin (Ed.), *A Nation of States: Essays on the American Federal System, 2nd ed.* (pp.). Chicago: Rand McNally.

Hargrove, E.C.& Glidewell, JC (Eds.). (1990). *Impossible Jobs in Public Management.* Lawrence: University of Kansas Press.

Kettl, D. F. (1995). "Building Lasting Reform: Enduring Questions, Missing Answers." In D.F. Kettl and J.J. DiIulio (Eds.) *Inside the Reinvention Machine: Appraising Governmental Reform* (pp. 9-83), Washington, DC: Brookings Institution.

Kincaid, J.. (1995). "The New Federalism Context of the New Judicial Federalism." *Rutgers Law Journal.* 26(4): 913-18.

Moe, R.C. (1994). "The 'Reinventing Government' Exercise: Misinterpreting the Problem, Misjudging the Consequences." *Public Administration Review.* 54(2):111-122.

Moore, M. H. (1995). *Creating Public Value: Strategic Management in Government.* Cambridge: Harvard University Press.

National Academy of Public Administration [NAPA]. (1993). *Coping with Catastrophe: Building an Emergency Management System to Meet People's Needs in Natural and Manmade Disasters.* Washington, DC: National Academy of Pubic Administration.

National Performance Review [NPR]. (1993a). *From Red Tape to Results: Creating a Government that Works Better and Costs Less.* Washington, DC: Government Printing Office.

National Performance Review [NPR]. (1993b). *Federal Emergency Management Agency, Accompanying Report of the National Performance Review.* Washington, DC: Government Printing Office.

NPR Phase II Federalism Team. (1995). "Performance Partnerships: Summary and Guiding Principles. Working Draft." Washington, DC, NPR, mimeograph.

O'Bryant, J. & Bea K.. (1995). *FEMA and Disaster Relief.* Washington, DC: Congressional Research Service, Library of Congress.

Portes, A. and Stepick A.. (1993). *City on the Edge: The Transformation of Miami.* Berkeley, University of California Press.

Rivlin, A. (1995 August 21). "Comments." In *Industry Week*, 244(15) (Westlaw).

Sylves, R.T. (1994). "Ferment at FEMA: Reforming Emergency Management." *Public Administration Review*, 54(3):303-307.

U.S. House, Committees on Armed Services and Public Works and Transportation, (1993, February 4). "H.R. 867, Federal Emergency Management Agency Sunset Act of 1993." Bill, 103rd Congress, 1st Session. Washington, DC: Government Printing Office.

U.S. House, Committee on Armed Services. (1994). *National Defense Authorization Act for Fiscal Year 1995--S. 2182 (H.R. 4301), Hearing, 103rd Cong., 2nd ses., April 21, 1994.* U.S. House, Committee on Public Works and Transportation. p. 9. Washington, DC: Government Printing Office.

U.S. House, Committee on Public Works and Transportation. (1994a). *Report together with Additional Views, Natural Disaster Protection Partnership Act of 1994. October*

7, 1994, U.S. House, Committee on Public Works and Transportation. Washington, DC: Government Printing Office.

U.S. House, Committee on Public Works and Transportation. (1994b). *The Northridge Earthquake: Extent of Damage and Federal Response. Hearing, 103rd Cong., 2nd. ses.* Washington, DC: Government Printing Office.

U.S. Senate, Committee on Appropriations. (1994a). *Earthquake Supplemental. Hearing, 103 Cong., 2nd Ses., February 3, 1994*, p. 59. Washington, DC: Government Printing Office.

U.S. Senate, Committee on Appropriations. (1994b). *Department of Veterans Affairs and Housing and Urban Development and Independent Agencies Appropriations for Fiscal Year 1995. Hearing, 103rd Cong., 2nd ses., March 4, 1994*, Washington, DC: Government Printing Office.

U.S Senate, Committee on Commerce, Science, and Transportation, *The Natural Disaster Protection Act. Hearing, 103 Cong., 2nd ses., May 26, 1994*, Washington, DC: Government Printing Office.

U.S. Senate, Committee on Governmental Affairs. (1993. *Rebuilding FEMA: Preparing for the Next Disaster. Hearing, 103rd Cong., 1st ses., May 18, 1993*, Washington, DC: Government Printing Office

Wilson, J.Q. (1994). "The 1994 John Gaus Lecture: Reinventing Public Administration." *PS, Political Science and Politics.*27: 667-73.

Chapter 8

THE FEDERAL EMERGENCY MANAGEMENT AGENCY (FEMA) AND HURRICANE KATRINA

Van R. Johnston
Claire-Lauren Schulz

The General Accounting Office released a report in the early nineties that summarized the findings of several expert reports. The common conclusion among these reports stated: "The response to Hurricane Andrew raised doubts about whether FEMA is capable of responding to catastrophic disasters" (Roberts, 2006b). Following this, the agency was given an ultimatum to make changes or to face eradication. The agency made changes, had a remarkable turnaround, and became well-respected by the government and citizens due to its professional level management of the Northridge Earthquake in California in 1994. In 2001, the Federal Emergency Management Agency was taken in a new direction in light of the 9/11 terrorist attacks. It was forced to merge into the new Department of Homeland Security, along with over 20 other agencies. By 2005, Hurricane Katrina struck the Gulf Coast, and it became evident that the once strong Federal Emergency Management Agency had deteriorated. A catalytic event has, once again, forced the Federal Emergency Management Agency to deal with criticism and to make changes.

BACKGROUND

After the 9/11 terrorist attacks, President George W. Bush established the Department of Homeland Security. The Department of Homeland Security was formed with the intent to better coordinate efforts among the different federal agencies that deal with disaster, law enforcement, disaster preparedness and recovery, border protection, and civil defense. The Federal Emergency Management Agency began to coordinate its activities related to national preparedness and homeland security with the Department of Homeland Security.

In March 2003, the Federal Emergency Management Agency was consolidated into the Department of Homeland Security—along with over 20 other federal agencies, programs, and offices—with the task to plan for, respond to, recover from, and to mitigate against disasters (Federal Emergency Management Agency, 2006). This major reorganization left different stakeholders concerned as to whether this would actually improve responses to terrorist attacks and natural disasters (Morris, 2006).

Placing the Federal Emergency Management Agency within the Department of Homeland Security added to the bureaucratic structure of federal emergency management. In 2005, Hurricane Katrina showed that the absorption of the Federal Emergency Management Agency into the Department of Homeland Security severed the Federal Emergency Management Agency from its core functions, shattered agency morale, and broke established, effective relationships with states and first responder stakeholders (Grunwald and Glasser, 2005). There were publicly expressed fears by numerous stakeholders, including the director of the agency Michael Brown (Grunwald and Glasser, 2005). This change resulted in an inefficient, ineffective, and disorganized response to Hurricane Katrina. The warnings that the absorption of the Federal Emergency Management Agency into the Department of Homeland Security would result in a mockery of the Federal Emergency Management Agency's motto of "A Nation Prepared" ultimately—and unfortunately—came true (Grunwald and Glasser, 2005).

Following Hurricane Katrina, the Federal Emergency Management Agency has been the subject of an enormous amount of criticism due to its mismanagement of the Hurricane Katrina natural disaster. This catastrophe resulting from mismanagement demands change. Congressional inquires have been launched, panels have been formed, and investigations have continued to be pursued in an attempt to determine how to address the problems of the agency. The United States Senate Homeland Security and Governmental Affairs Committee—a bipartisan committee—has 86 recommendations after finding that the United States remains unprepared for disaster and that changes to the Federal Emergency Management Agency must occur in order to better prepare and respond to disaster (U.S. Senate Committee on Homeland Security and Governmental Affairs, 2006).

Since Hurricane Katrina, the Federal Emergency Management Agency has attempted to regroup. FEMA has spent billions of dollars on improved technology, workforce expansions, and engineering contracts in attempts to better prepare for handling future disasters (Block, 2006a). These efforts have not restored confidence among stakeholders of the agency's capability to handle a major disaster, though. In analyzing the limitations and shortcomings of the Federal Emergency Management Agency, it seems evident that the agency needs significant reorganization in order to be able to effectively manage future disasters.

CONTROL OF THE AGENCY

Before joining the Department of Homeland Security in 2001, the Federal Emergency Management Agency was known as an organization that effectively prepared for, responded to, recovered from, and mitigated against significant hazards (Roberts, 2006b). As an independent agency, the Federal Emergency Management Agency had more flexibility in responding to disasters. The agency was streamlined and focused on disaster management, known as the "all hazards" approach. It had "patience and support" from Congress and the President (Roberts, 2006b).

When the Federal Emergency Management Agency joined the Department of Homeland Security, the Department of Homeland Security got control over the budget, people, and programs of the Federal Emergency Management Agency and the other agencies in the department. Acting on this began to appear a form of micromanagement. The Department of Homeland Security believed that this provided it with flexibility in responding to the ever-changing terrorist threats. However, micromanagement can prevent high performance. By not having control over their "resources," the Federal Emergency Management Agency was unable to effectively respond to Hurricane Katrina.

When the Federal Emergency Management Agency joined the Department of Homeland Security, the direct report hierarchy changed. The director of the agency reported to the Department of Homeland Security and did not have direct access to the President. In times of national disaster, contact with the President is critical. When there is no direct line of communication from one party to another, the quality of communication is weakened. A "middleman" cannot often clearly convey the desired message as well as the actual "sender" of the message. Many argue that the FEMA director should always directly report to the President, at least during times of emergency. This would give the FEMA director more credibility and control. During disasters, quick, decisive actions must be taken. By having a direct line of communication with the Federal Emergency Management Agency Director, the President can have a more accurate picture of what is occurring. A more accurate picture with details can provide for a better, more appropriate response.

Following Hurricane Katrina, there has been a debate as to whether the Federal Emergency Management Agency should remain under the control of the Department of Homeland Security, or if it should revert to operating as its own federal agency. The Federal Emergency Management Agency has clearly struggled with being integrated into the Department of Homeland Security. Some argue that returning the Federal Emergency Management Agency to an independent agency would eliminate red tape and improve the agency's ability to respond before, during, and after disasters. Others defend the Federal Emergency Management Agency's inclusion within the Department of Homeland Security, citing that the agency benefits from being part of the department by being able to draw on the resources and expertise of other agencies, such as the United States Coast Guard.

PEOPLE

Many management and policy professionals argue that people are the most important resource of any organization, and this has been a significant weakness for the Federal Emergency Management Agency in recent years. Inexperience among employees and the basic lack of employees has hindered the agency significantly.

When the agency became part of the Department of Homeland Security, this fueled an "exodus" of experienced employees who did not support the reshuffling. As a result, people without backgrounds in emergency management were appointed as leaders for the agency. Lack of experienced employees has been problematic for the Federal Emergency Management Agency. Michael Brown, former director of the agency, had no experience in disaster and emergency management when Hurricane Katrina struck the Gulf Coast. "Hands-on" experience allows for a more comprehensive, accurate understanding of a situation, thereby helping to provide a more effective and appropriate response. In Hurricane Katrina, the lack of experience of the top agency officials prevented an effective response. Experience with disaster management would allow for more appropriate responses following a disaster.

Job dissatisfaction continued to increase at FEMA, resulting in lower morale and more frequent employee exits. The agency received a ranking of "next to last" among agencies in a list of "best places to work in government" (U.S. General Accounting Office, 2001; Barr, 2005). The Federal Emergency Management Agency could not recruit top talent with its ranking of "next to last" in best agencies. The agency's regional officers were put under a hiring freeze once that agency was moved under DHS, leaving staff shortages (Kitfield, 2006).

Many of the errors of the agency can be attributed to the inexperience of its employees. Leaders must have experience in disaster management in order to be more optimally effective. More appropriate training programs should be implemented for all employees. The Federal Emergency Management Agency failed to complete the Hurricane Pam disaster simulation. The Hurricane Pam simulation foretold catastrophic events like Hurricane Katrina, and if completed, the simulation would have allowed agency individuals to develop better disaster management strategies and to learn how to allocate resources more effectively (Morris, 2006). Nor did the Purple Crescent exercise to examine infrastructure interdependencies happen. It was scheduled for October, 2005, shortly after Katrina (Leavitt and Kiefer, 2006). Investments in workforce development clearly would benefit and strengthen the performance of the agency.

FEMA AND KATRINA

In late August, 2005, the Gulf Coast became increasingly aware of a potentially catastrophic storm approaching the mainland. The news media and weather services let us know that this could be "the big one" all had feared for decades. Then, on the morning of August 29, 2005, Hurricane Katrina surged on land near Pass Christian, Mississippi.

Devastation occurred from Baton Rouge, Louisiana to Mobile, Alabama (Morris, 2006). New Orleans suffered the greatest impact, but communities across the Gulf Coast were devastated. The "big one" had indeed arrived (Leavitt and Kiefer, 2006).

Immediately clear to television viewers across the nation was that the damage was extreme. Buildings collapsed, or were blown away, or were under water. People were injured, or trying to survive flooding, or were seen confused and in pain, or were starving or thirsty, or were dead or dying. There were rescue attempts with boats and helicopters; but, there were also over a hundred buses in New Orleans that were unused because the drivers did not show up.

Whatever the perceived condition of emergency response systems and mechanisms was before Katrina, that all changed with Katrina. On the local and state levels for the most part, there was concern and frustration that emergency management officials seemed to be missing. Because of the severity of the catastrophe, there was general confusion and serious concern that the Federal Emergency Management Agency was not even arriving on the scene to do its job. After a couple of days, it became obvious that the situation was manifesting a virtual total collapse of whatever positive emergency management support that anyone had perceived and expected. The question that percolated to the surface regularly was: "Where is FEMA?" (Morris, 2006).

In spite of having worked on several natural disasters in the past, from Hurricane Andrew to the Northridge Earthquake, it appeared that FEMA did not have a clue. It not only was not out in front, leading the emergency management efforts as expected in a natural disaster of this magnitude; it seemed not even to be able to show up in a timely way... as days went by, and as the damage continued to occur, and the morbidity and mortality statistics continued to increase.

Eventually, more than 1,300 people lost their lives. Estimates have been made that between $200 billion and $300 billion in economic losses were sustained (Waugh, and Smith, 2006; Berman, Lynch, Lynch, and Berman, 2005). This makes Katrina the new benchmark for economic damage due to a natural disaster (Waugh and Smith, 2006).

The City of New Orleans suffered the greatest quantifiable impact. It had the largest population. It had more business than other communities. It was geographically insecure, due to its below sea level location, which was only marginally secured by fragile levees. And, it had a large indigent population. The city lost approximately 40 percent of its homes. It could lose half of its businesses. Restaurant, tourism and convention impacts were catastrophic. School and government activities were crippled. Current assessments include forecasts of a much smaller New Orleans in the future (Waugh and Smith, 2006).

The scale of the Hurricane completely overwhelmed the existing infrastructure. 172 sewage treatment plants across the impacted area failed. Over 1,000 drinking water systems were affected. The levee failures also caused flood waters to be contaminated. This caused concern about chemical and petroleum leaks, industrial wastes, and raw sewage. Besides the health concerns arising from the situation, there were also serious electrical shortages that impacted the community in a wide variety of ways (Leavitt and Kiefer, 2006).

The enormous scale of the disaster overwhelmed the communications infrastructure. Katrina's impact made it impossible to manage the critical communications infrastructure. Emergency managers were unable to adequately respond in the short term with first responders, public works managers, or public officials. Coordination of an effective interorganizational infrastructure, therefore, collapsed. Physical communication infrastructures were destroyed, and critical personnel in the communications system were uninformed, disconnected, and even missing (Comfort and Haase, 2006).

When analyzing vulnerabilities for emergency management disasters, infrastructure interdependencies can quickly become critical. Infrastructure normally refers to physical systems which provide public services or public works such as utilities, transportation, telecommunications, and waste disposal. Human resources and management systems are considered part of the infrastructure which can be based either in the public or the private sector.

Critical infrastructure is typically considered to be: systems, assets, and facilities important enough that if destroyed could critically impact the safety, health, security, welfare, or economy of the community (Leavitt and Kiefer, 2006). Hurricane Katrina devastated the critical infrastructure in its path.

Interdependency indicates two or more infrastructures are linked in complexity and scale so that if one infrastructure is severely enough impacted that it fails, at least one other infrastructure will be significantly affected enough that it will not be able to perform adequately either. There are four major classes of interdependencies: geographic, physical, cyber, and logical (Leavitt and Kiefer, 2006). Hurricane Katrina was of such an enormous scale that all of these were negatively impacted. The infrastructure failures cascaded until there was a collapse of the system.

In order to study such interdependencies, private sector organizations and public sector agencies at the federal, state, and local levels collaborated to develop an exercise series named the Purple Crescent exercises. Lessons were learned from the first two exercises about the importance of infrastructure interdependence and the significance of developing collaborative networks of stakeholders to increase effective responses to emergency management situations. Unfortunately, Katrina struck before the third Purple Crescent exercise scheduled for October, 2005, and before the analysis of the exercise series yielded lessons and results that when implemented, could have mitigated the impact of a major hurricane like Katrina (Leavitt and Kiefer, 2006). Lessons on the positive effects of professional collaborative efforts are increasingly being researched and studied in business and public policy. Recognizing the importance of implementing collaborative efforts can improve both efficiency and effectiveness significantly (Johnston, Haynes, and Schulz, 2006).

Emergency management relative to natural disasters has been set up in accordance with a federalism model. In brief, when local emergency response systems find a disaster beyond their capacity to manage, they then go to the state level, and likewise from the state to the federal level. Hurricane Katrina was so enormous and developed and unfolded so quickly that both local and state level emergency management officials were overwhelmed virtually immediately. When these intergovernmental relationships function adequately, an effective emergency response can be implemented.

The speed and scale of Katrina collapsed the available resources and infrastructures so quickly and so thoroughly that it appeared that almost no professional emergency management responder, and almost no emergency management agency, with a few exceptions, even showed up. Since this catastrophic event covered several states and numerous communities, and had such a great impact on: the health and safety of the population, the economy, and both the private sector and the public sector, and was broadcast around the country and the world ... it is really quite natural that FEMA (the Federal Emergency Management Agency) became the target of multiple investigations for failing to meet expectations (Morris, 2006; Leavitt and Kiefer, 2006).

THE INVESTIGATIONS AND PRIMARY REPORTS

There were numerous investigations after Katrina. There were also reports and other documents that followed. Two reports stand out above the others. One is the House Select Bipartisan Committee Report: *A Failure of Initiative.* The other is: *The Federal Response to Hurricane Katrina: Lessons Learned* by Frances Fragos Townsend, Assistant to the President for Homeland Security and Counterterrorism.

The House Select Bipartisan Committee Report was harsh. It spared no one. Noting a failure of leadership and initiative, it directly identified the following: FEMA Director Michael Brown, Secretary of Homeland Security Michael Chertoff, Louisiana Governor Kathleen Babineaux Blanko, New Orleans Mayor Ray Nagin, and though not mentioned by name, President George W. Bush.

Agencies were not spared either. The Department of Homeland Security was faulted for being unfamiliar with its various responsibilities and duties in its various roles, including those relative to the National Incident Management System and the National Response Plan. New Orleans emergency response actions were especially criticized, as well.

The House Committee Report was particularly harsh when focusing on FEMA. It noted that FEMA was unprepared and seriously troubled. It pointed out the problems emanating from its merger into the Department of Homeland Security and the struggles between Brown and Chertoff. The report identified the FEMA brain drain, highlighting that eight of the 10 FEMA regional directors were working in an acting capacity. And, the report pointed out that 500 of FEMA's 2,500 positions were not filled at the time Katrina impacted the Gulf Coast (Menzel, 2006).

The language of the House Committee Report is clear. It notes the response to Katrina was: "...a litany of mistakes, misjudgments, lapses, and absurdities all cascading together, blinding us to what was coming and hobbling any collective effort to respond" (U.S. House Select Bipartisan Committee to Investigate the Preparation for and the Response to Hurricane Katrina, 2006; Ink, 2006).

Importantly, the report identified the primary failures as being the result not of lack of plans, but more directly as a lack of performance. It lauded the National Weather Service and the National Hurricane Center, noting the military did a good job too but could have had better coordination. It was especially critical, however, of the Department of Homeland Security, FEMA, the Louisiana Governor's office, and the New Orleans Mayor's office.

Among the major problem areas, the following were identified in the House Report: Warnings were not heeded; Levee failures; Lack of coordination; Inadequate training; Information gaps; Communication failures; Lack of shelter; Medical shortcomings; and the role of the Private Sector. Perhaps most importantly, there was a failure to act (Ink, 2006). Fixes focused on making adjustments in these significant problem areas and providing more coordination and control.

The House Report also identified the failure of imagination, flexibility, adaptability, and agility as well as initiative. It also noted the National Response Plan was implemented late, ineffectively, or not at all (U.S. House Select Bipartisan Committee to Investigate the Preparation for and the Response to Hurricane Katrina, 2006).

The White House Report by Frances Fragos Townsend, *The Federal Response to Hurricane Katrina: Lessons Learned*, highlights the lessons that: all federal officials need to know their roles and responsibilities. They must be aware of the situation at hand, and have a common operating picture when an incident unfolds. Because there were significant problem areas during Katrina, a National Operations Center is recommended as a mechanism to deal with such critical emergency response situations.

The White House Report also identified federal government interaction with other government jurisdictions and the private sector and recommends that this problem area be focused on in developing, promoting, and strengthening community and citizen preparedness. The National Response Plan also needs to be improved. And, the Department of Homeland Security needs to make changes to promote emergency preparedness.

A common theme throughout this report identifies the disconnect between planning and implementation. So, the recommendations include more significant emphasis on planning and coordination. It also calls for more involvement by other agencies including the following departments, among others: Defense, Transportation, Health and Human Services, Justice, State, and Housing and Urban Development (Townsend, 2006).

This White House Report characterized the response to Hurricane Katrina as a systemic failure. It contains 34 lessons and 17 critical challenges. This report calls for a national preparedness transformation and points out we need to be more proactive and less reactive. It also makes 125 recommendations for improvement in the emergency management arena (Menzel, 2006).

MAKING CHANGES

Since Hurricane Katrina, many changes to the Federal Emergency Management Agency have been made. More staff has been hired, new technology has been employed, and the logistics department has been upgraded. These changes, albeit appearing "good on paper," are far from a solution.

In September 2006, Congress reached a tentative deal regarding Federal Emergency Management Agency modifications and reorganization (Block, 2006b). This proposed deal allows for the Federal Emergency Management Agency to:

- Remain an independent entity that would be expanded within the Department of Homeland Security
- Retain control over its own budget, personnel, and structure (similar provisions granted to the Secret Service and United States Coast Guard)
- Directly access the President during a crisis, and
- Expand the Federal Emergency Management Agency regional offices and reconnect the Federal Emergency Management Agency's preparedness and response functions that were lost when the Department of Homeland Security was created.

Additionally, the deal would also increase the Federal Emergency Management Agency's $2.4 billion budget by 10 percent annually for three years. It would provide increases for emergency planning grants, emergency medical teams, and emergency search-and-rescue teams (Block, 2006b). Yet, after the pulling and hauling of the budgeting process, there is no guarantee that the budget will include these increases. No specific allocation has been designated in this proposal to help facilitate communication among the Federal Emergency Management Agency and local police and fire stations in emergencies (Block, 2006b).

This deal would also incorporate the new Department of Homeland Security "Second Stage Review" units into the Federal Emergency Management Agency. The Directorate for Preparedness, which handles all first-responder and homeland-security grant programs and coordinates threat and vulnerability analysis with state, local, and private sector officials, would be absorbed directly into the Federal Emergency Management Agency. There is concern that this deal would dissolve this directorate and weaken the relationships with state, local, and private sector officials. The remaining directorate programs, with the exception of the Office of Infrastructure Protection, the National Communications System and the National Cyber Security Division, would be integrated into the Federal Emergency Management Agency (Block, 2006b).

CONCLUSION

Managers consolidate to streamline. Consolidations suggest more efficiency by eliminating existing overlaps. However, consolidation is not always the right answer, as evidenced by the case of the Department of Homeland Security and the Federal Emergency Management Agency. This consolidation created a larger, more inefficient bureaucracy—a megabureacracy. When a bureaucracy is enlarged, more complications arise because there are often too many "chains of command." Consequently, it is more difficult to effectively manage, make decisions, and communicate. Larger scale systems are in fact different. More complexities demand appropriate managerial adjustments.

The creation of the Department of Homeland Security combined federal agencies with different goals and missions. In both the private and public sectors, organizations with multiple complex missions typically do not achieve higher levels of performance. Without a clear, focused mission, organizations tend to run in multiple directions and often perform sub optimally. Organizations do not reach high performance without management clarity. In this case, the new Department of Homeland Security's primary focus on terrorism trumped FEMA's significant focus on hurricanes and other natural disasters.

The Federal Emergency Management Agency needs to change in order to more effectively prepare the United States for hurricane disaster responses. The bureaucratic red tape needs to be cut. The agency needs to clarify its core functions and strengthen its abilities to execute those functions. The Federal Emergency Management Agency should be focused on managing federal emergencies and leave other responsibilities to the appropriate agencies (Roberts, 2006b).

If the agency is to have control over disasters, like major hurricanes, then the agency needs to regain this control. The Department of Homeland Security must reexamine and change its existing "micromanagement style." The Federal Emergency Management Agency needs the responsibility to both prepare and respond to incidents of disasters. The agency leaders need much more flexibility in managing their agencies so that they can change strategies and funding levels as circumstances demand. The director of the agency needs both authority and support to be able to respond to and manage disasters.

The Federal Emergency Management Agency needs significant reform. The agency is once again lacking clear objectives, adequate resources, and government commitments. In 1993, it was said that, "FEMA is like a patient in triage. The President and Congress must decide whether to treat it or to let it die" (National Academy of Public Administration, 1993; Roberts, 2006a). This statement appears to be applicable again after Katrina, given the recent inadequate performance of FEMA.

Note: See also Waugh, Chapter 15 on Katrina analysis; ...and Haynes and Wright, Chapter 17; and Johnston, Chapter 18, for analytical applications of Johnston's Entrepreneurial Management and Public Policy Model to FEMA and Katrina.

REFERENCES

Barr, S. (September 14, 2005). Morale Among FEMA Workers, on the Decline for Years, Hits Nadir. *Washington Post*, B2.

Berman, E.M., Lynch, T.D., Lynch, C.E., and Berman, M.D. (October, 2005). There was no plan- A Louisiana perspective. *P A Times*, 3-5.

Block, R. (August 7, 2006a). FEMA Regroups After Katrina, But Some Questions Its Readiness. *Wall Street Journal*, A1.

Block, R. (September 19, 2006b). Politics & Economics: FEMA Revamp Snubs Homeland Security Chief; Congressional Negotiators Unraveled Some Changes

Chertoff Had Supported. *Wall Street Journal*, A8.

Comfort, L.K., and Haase, T.W. (April, 2006). Communication, Coherence, and Collective Action: The Impact of Hurricane Katrina on Communications Infrastructure. *Public Works Management and Policy, 10*(4), 328-343.

Federal Emergency Management Agency (March 21, 2006). *FEMA History.* Retrieved September 28, 2006, from http://www.fema.gov/about/history.shtm

Grunwald, M., and Glasser, S.B. (December 23, 2005). Brown's Turf Wars Sapped FEMA's Strength. *Washington Post*, A1.

Ink, D., (November/December, 2006). An Analysis of the House Select Committee and White House Reports on Hurricane Katrina. *Public Administration Review, 66*(6), 800-807.

Johnston, V.R., Haynes, W., and Schulz, C.L. (Summer, 2006). The T-REX Megaproject: Denver's Showcase for Innovation and Creativity. *The Public Manager, 35*(2), 3-8.

Kitfield, J. (2006, June 2). *New Coast Guard Chief Discusses Lessons Learned from Katrina.* Retrieved September 20, 2006, from http://www.govexec.com/story_page.cfm? articleid=34234&dcn=todaysnews

Leavitt, W.M., and Kiefer, J.J. (April, 2006). Infrastructure Interdependence and the Creation of a Normal Disaster: The Case of Hurricane Katrina and the City of New Orleans. *Public Works Management and Policy, 10*(4), 306-314.

Menzel, D.C., (November/December, 2006). The Katrina Aftermath: A Failure of Federalism or Leadership? *Public Administration Review, 66*(6), 808-812.

Morris, J.C. (April, 2006). Whither FEMA? Hurricane Katrina and FEMA's Response to the Gulf Coast. *Public Works Management and Policy, 10*(4), 284-294.

National Academy of Public Administration. (February, 1993). *Coping with Catastrophe – Building an Emergency Management System to Meet People's Needs in Natural and Manmade Disasters.* Washington, D.C.: NAPA.

Roberts, P.S. (Spring, 2006a). FEMA and the Prospects for Reputation-Based Autonomy. *Studies in American Political Development, 20*(1), 57-87.

Roberts, P.S. (June/July, 2006b). FEMA After Katrina. *Policy Review*, (137), 15-33.

Townsend, F.F., (2006). *The Federal Response to Hurricane Katrina: Lessons Learned.* Washington, DC: Office of the Assistant to the President for Homeland Security and Counterterrorism. Retrieved December 15, 2006, from http://www.whitehouse.gov/reports/Katrina/Lessons/learned/

U.S. General Accounting Office. (July, 2001). *Federal Emergency Management Agency: Status of Achieving Key Outcomes and Addressing Major Management Challenges (Publication No. GAO-01-832).* Retrieved September 25, 2006, from General Accounting Reports Online: http://www.gao.gov/new.items/d01832.pdf

U.S. House Select Bipartisan Committee to Investigate the Preparation for and the Response to Hurricane Katrina. (2006). *A Failure of Initiative.* Washington, DC.

U.S. Government Printing Office. *U.S. House Katrina Report.* Retrieved December, 15, 2006, from http://katrina.house.gov/full_katrina_report.html

U.S. Senate Committee on Homeland Security and Governmental Affairs. (May, 2006). *Hurricane Katrina: A Nation Still Unprepared.* Retrieved November 20, 2006, from HSGAC Web Site: http://hsgac.senate.gov/_files/Katrina/FullReport.pdf

Waugh, W.L., and Smith, R.R. (August 2006). Economic Development and Reconstruction on the Gulf After Katrina. *Economic Development Quarterly: The Journal of American Economic Revitalization,* 20(3), 211-218.

Chapter 9

Franchising in Government: Can a Principal-Agent Perspective be the First Step toward the Development of a Theory?

Arie Halachmi

In 1995, the federal government started five pilot Franchise Funds (FF), to study their feasibility for improving productivity through the introduction of competition, and capitalizing on specialization and economy of size. This chapter describes the current approach to the use of FF. It suggests that the relationship between the FF and those that contract them for service resemble what economists call "principal-agent relations" and what they study as "agency theory." The chapter concludes that the vast research on agency relations may help the development of a theory or a conceptual framework for studying and managing FF and contracts with them.

According to M. D. Serlin (1996, p. 29), "The bracing breeze of competition is about to begin blowing through the halls of the U.S. government, pitting agencies against one another in a race to sell their services." NASA, for example, is entering this race not to offer its expertise in space-related activities to other agencies, but rather to offer its slack capacity of conference management. The United States Department of Agriculture, through its National Finance Center, is offering its expertise for processing payrolls and other financial activities, rather than its expertise in agronomy. Other agencies offer services in areas such as data processing, travel, occupational health, telecommunication, or simple office services. The deputy director for management of the United States Office of Management and Budget (Koskinen, 1996) offers the following commentary to explain this new development:

Like the private sector, the Federal Government is reevaluating the way it operates. All organizations perform basic administrative support activities: buying equipment and supplies, paying and training employees, managing budgets and information technology, and much more. While some perform these activities superbly, others would just as soon have someone else handle the administrative support work, freeing their personnel to concentrate on other organizational missions.

Many of the products and services of government organizations are not subject to direct market competition. Noting that no competition exits for the market share of a ministry of foreign affairs or for a nation's customs service, we ask, "What is the motivation to keep overhead costs down? Why should a government producer of goods or services strive to be efficient or effective?" (Halachmi, 1996, p. 1). These questions resonate with the repeated arguments of those who, like Niskanen (1971), are critical of government operations from the point of view of efficiency and economy. According to Savas (1987, 1992), public managers must address the claim that competition is a key to efficient and effective government. By making available for cross-service purposes the special competencies of various services within government, it is possible to introduce some measure of competition.

Let us overlook for a moment the wasteful aspects of competition, and agree that it is a necessary condition for efficiency. However, can we go on to conclude that the introduction of competition is also a certain method of improvement of efficiency in government? There is no simple answer to this question. As will be pointed out in this chapter, it is hard to resist the pragmatic elegance of introducing competition by making cross-servicing subject to competitive bids. However, the need to introduce competition has become the rationale for justifying the current experiment (Serlin & Bruce, 1996), rather than such a need being a product of rationale based on competition's proposed outcomes. The establishment of Franchising Funds (FF), as will be explained below, involves the creation of new administrative arrangements. On their face, these arrangements seem to comply with assertions offered by Savas (1987, 1992) (e.g., about the functional role of competition) and Niskanen (1971) (e.g., about the budget-maximizing bureaucrat). Yet, because the use of franchise funds and competitive cross-services involves an extensive use of contractual relations, the idea behind FF could benefit, before the launching of costly experiments, from testing within the theoretical frameworks offered by neoinstitutional economics and the principal-agent perspective.

These theoretical frameworks address the issues of transaction cost, property rights, and economic rationality. They must play a part when assessing a new production model that makes extensive use of contractual relationships for replacing the traditional production model of public goods and services, in whole or in part. The importance of such an assessment becomes obvious when we are asked to determine whether these new contractual agreements are beneficial under all circumstances. To illustrate the difficulty involved in answering this question, one only has to examine the implications of either of the following two scenarios. The first scenario starts with one of the common premises of the principal-agent perspective, namely, that the two governmental parties to the contract have different utility functions. Accordingly, maximization of each utility function contributes to overall government performance. However, if the parties to the contract find themselves involved in a zero-sum game, greater efficiency may not be realized because the gains of one party may be offset by the losses to the other.

The second scenario involves the high likelihood that for at least one of the actors the contract in question may be only one of several contracts with other governmental or nongovernmental entities. This contract may include obligations to public entities from other levels of government or other jurisdictions (e.g., other states, or other countries in the case of the European Union). Thus, a principal (e.g., a government agency in the market for copying or security services in various parts of the country or even in the same area) may have contracts with multiple agents (that may or may not have inconsistent interests among themselves). In a mirror image, an agent (i.e., the agency providing cross-services) may have simultaneous contracts with multiple principals. These multiple principals also may have interests that are inconsistent, or mutually exclusive, with respect to the agent's performance.

The purpose of this chapter is to make the case for the need to develop a theoretical framework for examining contractual relationships where at least one of the parties is a governmental agency. As a first step in that direction, the chapter suggests that examining such contracts from a principal-agent perspective can be helpful to both administrators and students of outsourcing. Such an approach involves the mobilization and utilization of a vast body of theoretical and empirical knowledge. It can save unnecessary experimentation, on the one hand; and, on the other, augment our ability to draw better lessons from the pilot projects that are under way to test the merit of franchise funds.

The chapter starts by describing the background and the concept of "franchising in government." The chapter continues by examining some of the possible liabilities of buying rather than producing. It poses the question: "Why, or in what way, can contracting-out within government be superior to contracting-out with private providers?" The chapter moves on to describe the theoretical framework that uses a principal-agent perspective for studying the behavior of the parties and the issues involved in contractual relations. It points out that there is a need for a theory or model to guide managers in establishing franchise funds and for contracting with them before the pilot phase of the project is over. It concludes by suggesting that a principal-agent perspective may be a promising starting point for developing such a theory or model, especially if agency relations can be studied within their environmental context.

A SIMPLE BACKGROUND OF FRANCHISE FUNDS AND CONTRACTING-IN

According to Koskinen (1995), every U.S. administration since 1955 has endorsed the principles of competition and general reliance on the private sector for provision of commercial activities. In 1979, during the Carter administration, the Office of Management and Budget (OMB) issued Circular A-76, instructing agencies to pursue a specified process of comparison to assure that "agency 'make/buy' decisions were cost effective and that cost-based decisions to perform in-house or by contract reflected 'a level playing field'" (Koskinen, 1995, p. 2). The Reagan and Bush administrations also supported the circular's cost-comparison process. However, the circular's handbook describes the specific cost elements of a cost comparison, but it also postulates that at least 10% savings must be expected before a function can be converted from in-house to contract performance (Koskinen, 1995, p. 4). The concept of "franchising in government" goes one step further, to address all cases where it is not necessarily cost-effective nor efficient to contract-out the provision of a support service to a nongovernmental provider.

The working teams of the National Performance Review (NPR), under Vice President Al Gore, addressed the need to motivate public managers and government agencies to make real efforts to improve effectiveness and efficiency. Borrowing the idea of "reinventing government" from Osborne and Gaebler (1992), the first NPR Report (Gore, 1993) proposed to combine the effort to improve customer service with efforts to enhance effectiveness and efficiency. This double goal should be served, according to the authors of the report, by introducing competition within government for providing common support services. The NPR people (Serlin, 1996) named this approach "franchising," to highlight its three key characteristics:

- Reimbursable services: support services are not free,
- Competitive procurement: users of services have a choice of providers,
- Conformity to standards: providers must meet pre-established levels of service.

Not long ago, all support services in all federal agencies were monopolies. If an agency manager involved in making products or providing services wanted to hire personnel, pay them, buy a desk, or even sign a contract with a private company—e.g., for an employee training program—standard procedures required that the agency's own staff-support office arrange for any such provision. If managers received timely and high-quality service, they were pleased. However, when the service was slow and poor, they had virtually no recourse. The problem was exacerbated when poor support services undermined the delivery of the agency's programs, i.e., its effectiveness in selected areas or even across the board.

The U.S. federal budget traditionally has listed funds for offices that provide support services as part of each agency's general appropriations. As a result, internal customers—subunits of the agency which took advantage of agency resources—did not know, or, in many cases, did not care to know, anything about the cost of the support service they were using. As a matter of fact, little accounting was done, even by the providers of services within the agency, to allocate operational costs by users. In service areas that involved the consumption of tangible assets, automatic budget transfers from designated line items, e.g., for printing, were the standard operating procedures. Even in such cases, when public managers knew how much they were charged for the service, e.g., cost per printed page, they could not tell whether they were getting the best value for their resources. Managers could not determine how efficient their departments were, e.g., in meeting their printing needs, nor were they able to influence their efficiency in that respect. The initiative of the NPR team was meant to reintroduce the desire to improve efficiency and effectiveness by bringing the dynamics of the market to influence production and procurement decisions.

FRANCHISING IN GOVERNMENT:
FROM A CONCEPT TO A PLAN OF ACTION

The enabling legislation for the Franchise Fund Pilot Program was established under Title IV of GMRA—the Government Management Reform Act (Public Law 103-356, Section 403), enacted in October, 1994. The legislation encourages the use of various approaches by administrative units of the federal government to provide common administrative services to other administrative entities on a cost-reimbursable, competitive basis. The GMRA legislation applies to administrative entities operating under statutes that provide for working-capital funds, revolving accounts, or business-operations funds. It also applies to those agencies empowered under the Economy Act (31 USC, Section 1535) or the Training Act (41 USC, Title IV of PL 85-07) to provide cost-reimbursable services on an ad hoc basis or to require annual recertification. In addition, the legislation applies to those agencies created through the Franchise Fund Pilot Program.

Support services that may be offered by one administrative unit to other units for fees include accounting and financial management, security, employee health care, wellness, facilities management, mail management, alternate dispute resolution, procurement (acquisition, contracting, purchasing), travel, property (real, personal), telecommuting, and data processing. Though the list was tentative in nature, it reflected the positive experience of government agencies that have agreed to cooperate with each other for "cooperative provision of services," which is known by the acronym CASU—for Cooperative Administrative Support Unit.

As pointed out by Master (1996), the CASU program is a nationwide network of locally based, interagency consortia for providing administrative services. The CASUs were initiated by the President's Council on Management Improvement in 1986 and supported at the national level by the U.S. General Services Administration (GSA). In fiscal year (FY) 1995, the program reported serving over 1,800 customers from more than 50 federal departments or agencies, other branches of the federal government, and state and local governments (Cooperative Administrative Support Unit, 1994, p. 4). In addition to the Economy Act, CASUs use the Intergovernmental Cooperation Act and other agency-specific authorities to extend service agreements to state and local instrumentalities. The reimbursable service that CASUs have provided most often to state and local governments is common-needs training.

A cursory examination of the services included in the above list suggests that they are of the type that do not necessarily fall within the domain of any agency's programmatic mission. Thus, there is no reason to assume or require any special expertise in providing such services; i.e., they may be performed by any agency of the federal government when a more cost-efficient private provider cannot be used.

According to Newman (1996), provisions contained in Title IV of the Government Management Reform Act of 1994 (Section 403 of Public Law 103-356) enable the establishment of a limited number of franchise fund pilots as revolving accounts within a department or agency. This legislation permits as many as six government agencies to provide any number or type of reimbursable common administrative services, on a pilot basis, under an FF. The GMRA requires the OMB director, after the completion of an Agency Application review process, to designate the pilots, in consultation with the chairs and ranking members of the Senate and House Appropriations Committees and the Senate Governmental Affairs and the House Government Operations Committees. The head of each agency designates a pilot, in accordance with guidelines issued by the OMB director, and picks the common administrative support services (franchises) that will be provided through the franchise fund.

Each franchise under the fund must conduct business on a reimbursable basis, offering services to other agencies and/or to components of its own agency. Procedures must foster competition and meet appropriate standards and legal requirements for both the service rendered and the method for accounting for franchise expenditures and charges. The fund may acquire capital equipment, automated data processing systems, financial management, and management information systems necessary to conduct the business of the fund. An agency head may transfer to the fund existing inventories, inventories on order, equipment, and other assets or liabilities pertaining to the purposes of the fund. Fees, charged for services, are to be established by the head of the agency and can cover the total estimated costs of operating the franchise(s) under the fund. The fees will be deposited in the fund and remain available until expended, and should be expended for purposes of the fund. The franchises may use government employees to provide services to their clients, or they may "outsource" the services to contractors. However, the pilot agencies are not exempted from any duty under applicable procurement laws.

The director of OMB was required to report on the pilots by March 31, 1998. The report is to include the financial and program-performance results of the pilots, including recommendations for the composition of the funding mechanism and for the desirability of extending the application and implementation of the FF to other federal agencies.

The groundwork for the pilot FF was to be in place by October 1, 1995—the start of FY 1996—or soon thereafter, to allow it to run through FY 1997. This schedule covered two fiscal years in the report to Congress, which was due on March 31, 1998. The Franchise Fund Pilot Program's authority terminated effective October 1, 1999, unless extended (i.e., through legislation). It should be noted here that government business operations under authorities other than the Franchise Fund Pilot Program differ from one another, because separate statutes define and govern each one's charter and activities. Similarly, each fund is accountable separately within the executive branch, subject to OMB and Federal Accounting Standards Advisory Board requirements for cost-accounting procedures and financial-management reporting, and subject to congressional oversight and authorization and General Accounting Office (GAO) audits.

Many departments and agencies of the federal government already have special funds in place for this purpose. Chartered under separately enacted federal statutes, they exist under various names and titles, such as working-capital funds, business-operations funds, and revolving funds. Some agencies and departments provide services only to their own internal customers; others provide services to internal, as well as to external, customers; and the clients of some are primarily external to the host agency or department. Also, a particular fund may have been established to support more than one such business operation.

The law that authorizes FF provides that fees for services shall be established by the head of the agency at a level to cover the total estimated costs of providing the services. The fees are deposited in the agency's fund and remain available until expended. The receipts from the provision of services may be used to carry out the purpose of the fund. This means that rate-setting mechanisms must be in place before the FF starts to offer services.

A common proposal for addressing this issue is to establish an advisory board (Newman, 1996), providing service users representation and urging a fair and reasonable price schedule. In the case of the FF pilot projects, the pricing of services was to be in place by the beginning of FY 1996 to permit a true pilot test of all features. Yet, using an advisory board as part of the mechanism may be impossible. Such a board, while contributing support, efficiency, effectiveness, and customer loyalty, may turn out to be problematic in the long run. The reasons for this unattractive prospect may have to do with the differences in interests and in utility functions that are likely to arise between a service provider and service recipients, and differences within a heterogeneous group of service recipients having in common only the existence of a contract with the same provider.

PRIVATIZATION AND CONTRACTING-OUT WITH PRIVATE VENDORS: A LOOK AT SOME OF THE LIABILITIES

Halachmi (1989, p. 625) points out that "the debate about the merit of privatization has to do with ideology and political considerations as much as it has to do with questions of effectiveness, efficiency and equity in the delivery of services." The concept of "Government Franchise" offers little, if any, help to those who favor privatization and contracting-out in order to reduce the government workforce, its total outlays, or the scope of its involvement in the lives of individuals and communities. The concept may have something to offer when one approaches the study of government operations with the notion that some government services can run like their counterparts in the private sector or use the same procedures to be even more efficient or effective. To those with antigovernment sentiments, any possible liabilities or shortcomings of privatization and contracting-out may be lesser evils than those that can be associated with big government. For members of this group, this chapter cannot raise doubts about the shortcomings of outsourcing. The points I am trying to make here are meant for those who are willing to consider privatization and contracting-out in the same critical manner used to examine standard government operations.

Proponents of privatization, like Savas (1987), argue that: whenever possible, private enterprise should replace government for pragmatic considerations (e.g., privatization leads to more cost-effective public services). Many supporters of privatization embrace the position that public agencies are inherently inefficient because they face no competition—sometimes called the public-choice school of thinking (Rehfuss, 1991, p. 239). According to Savas (1992, p. 81): "Competition, achieved by prudent privatization, is the key to improving the productivity of public agencies, more broadly, of public programs and public services." Other supporters of privatization point out that there are no guards against overproduction by government, because budgets and staffing levels of agencies are used for projecting images of power and influence, rather than for satisfying consumers' demands for services (Niskanen, 1971; Wolf, 1979). Other arguments in favor of using nongovernmental providers echo ideological positions (e.g., government is too intrusive; the less government, the better; business is inherently more efficient than government) that promote the more efficient use of national resources by private agencies or urge the reform of society through volunteerism, on the level of family, church, neighborhood, and community (Savas, 1987, p. 5). According to Jennings (1991 [1986]), supporters of privatization believe that government is doing more than it should or can handle, that government cannot act effectively or efficiently, that public officials and agencies are not sufficiently responsive, and that government makes excessive resource demands that threaten economic growth and diminish individual economic well-being.

In contrast, detractors of privatization identify some specific liabilities and pitfalls. Critics of privatization point out the negative impact of privatization on the attractiveness of careers in the public sector; the undesired consequences of eroding hard-won merit systems; the harming or interrupting of service quality through work stoppages by disaffected employees of private firms; creaming practices; loss of tax revenues because of private-sector service delivery incentives; and the encouragement of bankruptcies, fraud, and corruption (Morgan & England, 1988). Others are concerned about the erosion of constitutional protections (Sullivan, 1987), the impact on local government budgets, regressive local taxes, and insufficient social services for the poor (Oates & Schwab, 1991, p. 127). This list of liabilities and shortcomings is eternally incomplete because, as times goes on and with greater experience with using private contractors, additional issues will have to be added to it. In addition, it is important to note here that many writers on privatization do not address some basic realities about government operations, namely: (a) that government often gets involved because of shortcomings in private arrangements and private markets, or because of ideological reasons that have to do with the welfare of citizens (Darr, 1987, p. 43; Graham & Hays, 1986, pp. 9–13; Naff, 1991, p. 24); (b) that privatization suggests competition, but may not facilitate or sustain it (Darr, 1987, p. 48; National Academy of Public Administration, 1989); (c) that competition may lead to waste of resources (Thayer, 1987); (d) that privatization and contracting-out may not be synonymous; or (e) that some government operations, like criminal courts, foreign affairs offices, immigration and customs, or national security, are inherently public and do not lend themselves to simple privatization or contracting-out.

From a systemic, public-welfare viewpoint (as distinct from a general-will point of view), some of the above issues manifest themselves in connection with the following three issues.

1. How Can Short-Term and Long-Term Liabilities be Balanced?

Privatization is promoted as a way to reduce the number of public employees and, thus the cost of government operations (Brudney, 1987). However, the use of a proxy does not relieve government from its responsibility under the law to assure the availability of services, such as water treatment or corrections. Thus, it is not always true that using a private contractor results in net savings to government, to service recipients, or to the taxpayer. For example, contracting-out the management of water treatment or correction facilities does not absolve state and local authorities from their responsibility or liability if something goes wrong. The direct and indirect costs for managing such contracts may deprive a local authority of some of the fiscal savings in the short run without shielding it from various legal and fiscal liabilities in the long run.

A recent evaluation of the outsourcing of garbage collection for a small city in the United States Southeast illustrates the point. The official purpose of the contract was to reduce direct costs for salaries, benefits, and the city's liability for workers' compensation claims for lower back injuries. The study computed the immediate savings to the city after the first year. However, the evaluation also pointed out that the city acquired a possible liability and had no way to estimate or plan for it in advance. The city, it was found, could not escape its workers' compensation liability if the contractor defaulted on its obligations as an employer of individuals assigned to work alongside city employees (Twilla, 1991).

2. How Can Sunk Costs be Reduced?

When a government agency stops delivering a service, it generates a sunk cost to the public. One part of the cost results from the liquidation of tangible assets such as buildings, equipment, and inventories. Another part of the sunk cost results from lost intangibles, such as special expertise and common, but valuable, know-how. Governments have several options for reducing the tangible part of the sunk cost, and these can produce a net savings to the public in the short term. Reducing the sunk cost to the public for the intangibles of a government service is not as simple. As governments divest themselves of services, they generate the conditions that allow individuals trained at public expense to offer their government experience to private industry, perhaps becoming entrepreneurs themselves. In other words, governments pursuing privatization may deprive their citizens of a fair return on their past investment in the formal or on-the-job training of employees.

A case in point is the Federal Employee Direct Ownership Opportunity Plan (FED CO-OP), as proposed by Constance Horner, a former director of the Office of Personnel Management under Ronald Reagan. The plan offered employees the partial ownership of privatized activities through an employee stock-ownership plan (ESOP). According to Naff (1991, p. 27), the vendor winning the contract to take over a government operation was required to establish the ESOP and to hire the employees who had been running the government operation previously. In the case of the FED CO-OP, the public would be deprived of some of the returns on its investment in the training of former employees, not by default (i.e., by abolishing a government service) but through a direct government intervention. The government assumes an active role in helping employees to profit, as private citizens, from the expertise and know-how that were acquired at the public's expense. The sunk cost is, in effect, nonrecoverable.

In addition to a consideration of tangible and intangible sunk costs, at least two other points should be noted about the FED CO-OP plan. First, the provision that requires a vendor to hire former government employees contradicts the position that free-market forces should determine whether government or separate private agencies should undertake the provision of services. The second point addresses popular views of employee motivation. It is untenable to argue that under a private contract FED CO-OPs are going to be more efficient than their governmental predecessors, while at the same time arguing that a poor work ethic among public employees and their agencies is responsible for the high cost of government services. That is tantamount to arguing that the only variable determining the different levels of productivity of public- and private-sector employees doing the same task is a civil service status, as distinct from tenure or seniority. By the end of 1991, the FED CO-OP plan was far from being a success story (Naff, 1991, p. 27). Its history illustrates some of the problems in conceptualizing privatization (which this chapter does not equate with contracting-out) as a coherent approach for dealing with the provision of essential public services.

The difficulty of asserting a clear-cut dichotomy between efficient and inefficient organizations (or employees) solely on the basis of ownership is illustrated in a comparative study of urban transit systems. According to Perry and Babitsky (1986), privately owned and privately managed transit systems were found to perform significantly better, as measured by output per dollar, than four other types of organizations, including contract-managed systems. However, the same study showed that the efficiency of contract-managed (but publicly owned) systems is no better than the efficiency of those owned and run by the government. Perry and Babitsky (1986, p. 61) go on to suggest that "forces in the environments of private organizations encourage efficiency, and analogous forces for public organizations discourage efficiency." They support this possible interpretation of their findings by pointing out that "costs are held down by private systems by running older, possibly more accident-prone buses for longer periods of time" (Perry & Babitsky, 1986, p. 63). Such policy decisions are more likely to be made by owners than by managers of a transportation system: This implies that ownership is a more important influence than management on efficiency.

Business practices, such as the ones used by the private transportation system in the above study, may not be a viable option for a public transportation system. Public managers cannot afford an audit finding that they take chances with the safety of the public, nor can they risk being the subject of letters to editors or of editorials on the looks or cleanliness of their aging fleet. Although private business also may want to avoid negative images, concern for sales figures and the bottom line, the overriding concern in business, is not properly relevant to or as clearly measured by the public manager. Commenting on such contrasting approaches, one observer points out that "the private sector obtains cost advantages by purchasing more effective equipment better suited to perform specific tasks. Public Agencies ... purchase equipment to match the budget" (Darr, 1987, p. 47). Thus, for example, an American private-business manager would like to select a machine that is cost-effective for the job at hand, perhaps new, perhaps used, perhaps foreign-made. His counterpart in the public sector will buy a new American-made product, as stipulated by the budget. The cost differential could be significant.

For public managers, the need to anticipate public opinion (e.g., "buy American") is a constraint as much as the politics involving the development and the execution of an agency's programs. Expressions such as "to get what you want you have to ask for more" or "use it or lose it" (what you don't spend this year will reduce your budget for next year) suggest some scenarios typical of the political implementation process in government. Both expressions sum up one of the reasons why public administrators end up making decisions on the basis of a criterion that has to do with the bureaucratic context, rather than with the substance of the issue at hand. Indeed, the findings of Perry and Babitsky (1986) support the thesis that efficiency is not solely a function of the legal provision under which an organizational entity operates or of the framework for the relationships between its managers and its employees. Efficiency, as they suggest, may have to do more with the organizational context, i.e., with the different environmental forces at work in public and private organizations. Thus, as will be pointed out later, changing the nature of those forces may affect the performance of both private and public agencies.

3. Public Accountability vs. Contractual Obligations

Privatization implies that public accountability for the quality of the service is replaced by a contractual relationship. Such relationships are established when a user becomes eligible (or pays a provider) for a service. Such a relationship moves issues of government accountability from the ballot box to the courthouse. It replaces the democratic process that implies responsiveness to emerging need with a legal competence that jealously monitors the cost of existing services. In the process, considerations of public will and public welfare may be displaced as lawyers put more emphasis on the integrity of the contract, as a legal instrument, than on the essence of the service(s) at stake. Contracts are proper for dealing with commercial transactions, but may not be the optimal instruments for dealing with issues involving the provision of vital public goods. In such cases, the public expects that the spirit, not only the letter of the "contract," be used for reference. The built-in provision for an appeal addresses this expectation in the public sector. Contractual relations with private providers, on the other hand, may serve the desire for greater managerial competence and net profit at the expense of other cherished public values (Morgan & England, 1988, p. 984), such as fairness or social justice.

The problem, as some writers see it, is not with the paring of expenses from the public budget, but with the abdication of the government's responsibility for the welfare of its citizens (Abramovitz, 1986; Darr, 1987, p. 47). To use the terminology that was offered by Brudney (1987), provision (i.e., public policymaking) can be separated from production of services. Once separated, however, the actual determination of the policy is made by the provider, and not by the official who contracted-out the service. The contractor assumes the policymaking capacity to become the real policymaker, like one of Lipsky's (1980) "street level bureaucrats." The "what, how, and when" of the service are determined by their implications for the bottom line, rather than by concern for the public welfare. We are back again to the looming specter of the "hollow state," with agencies outsourcing the provisions of the service they are expected to administer under the law.

The attractiveness of a "hollow state" should be weighed against the odds that an agency that contracts-out or provides no direct services at all, over time, may lose the expertise it once brought to policy issues (Rehfuss, 1991, p. 242). A case in point is the use of GEO Consultants, Inc., to operate a Superfund hotline. Answering questions from government agencies, industry, and the public, the contractor ends up interpreting federal statutes on behalf of the Environmental Protection Agency (EPA) (Goldstein, 1990, p. 31), thus becoming the actual policymaker. By outsourcing the service, the EPA drew a little closer to the "hollow corporation" model, but in the process gave up some of its own input into the policymaking process.

One of the questions that should be addressed here, at least from a theoretical point of view, is: Why can government franchises provide their clients with the convenience of dealing with a private vendor without the liabilities or concerns typically manifest in privatization or contracting with private providers? The answer seems to be that by contracting with another public entity, the agency that awards the contract benefits from the forces that stimulate public confidence. Unlike the occasionally unscrupulous private provider, the heads of public agencies cannot skip town overnight or rename themselves to hide irresponsible practices with impunity. Media scrutiny, audits, and oversight by legislative bodies and by boards of directors assures the contractor a better chance of getting what it contracted for from a public vendor than from a private one.

THE PRINCIPAL-AGENT PERSPECTIVE

Carr and Brower (1996, p. 1) point out that the principal-agent model was developed initially in the literature of economics and finance, but has noteworthy followings (and critics!) in political science and organization theory. Neelen (1993, p. 63) suggests that the principal-agent model, and neoclassical economics are, in fact, large families of diverse theories. Indeed, for the present purpose, it is very important to note that the various theories and models of principal-agent relations do not represent a unified body of knowledge or a consensus about their usefulness. One even can argue that the richness in the diversity of the principal-agent perspective reflects the diversity and ever-changing plausible context for the interactions and the contractual agreements between any two actors who enter willingly into a contractual relationship. Because so many of the attempts to offer a theory or a model of principal-agent relations have been challenged (Carr & Brower, 1996), it is not prudent to attempt to characterize their theoretical core. Instead, it seems more promising to refer to them by reference to their shared analytical approach to the study of contractual relations. For that reason, this chapter uses the term "principal-agent perspective," to emphasize the common analytical approach to the study of this important subject, rather than to endorse any specific set of assumptions, or any specific theory or model of agency relationships.

According to Moe (1984), the shared analytical foundations of a principal-agent perspective include a focus on the individual as the unit of analysis; the assumption of rational utility maximization behavior; a concern for efficiency, optimization, and equilibrium; and a preference for mathematical modeling. However, Jensen (1983) suggests that the literature that uses mathematical modeling is very different and was developed independently of the other body of theories which are nonmathematical and empirical in nature. According to Neelen (1993, p. 62), DeVries argues that both types also differ with respect to the question of whether property rights or transaction costs are regarded as endogenous variables in the analysis. The term "principal-agent perspective" is used in this chapter as a catchall phrase, because a complete phenomenological and epistemological discussion of the various approaches and writings on principal-agent relationships and their antecedents in the literature on the separation of ownership and control (Douma & Schreuder, 1991, p. 78; Jensen & Meckling, 1976, p. 309) is beyond the scope of this discussion.

The principal-agent perspective looks at the interaction between actors and stakeholders (i.e., individuals, groups, or institutions) who agree to cooperate with each other in a contractual relationship that requires the principal to pay the agent for actions the agent makes on behalf of the principal. Some of the differences among various theories and models that use a principal-agent perspective result from alternative assumptions about the nature of the relations between the two players. Carr and Brower (1996, p. 5) describe the three assumptions they use in the following way: (a) goal conflict exists between principal and agent, (b) agents are more risk-averse than are the principals, and (c) agent behavior is difficult to monitor.

According to Neelen (1993, p. 64), the relationship between the actors involves a longer list of assumptions, which are expressed by the articulation of the following agency-specific conditions:

- Conflict of interest or, more technically, negative externalities: The decisions of the agent affect both his own welfare and that of the principal (more on that interdependency below).
- Asymmetric information: The principal is faced with a situation of imperfect monitoring, because it is impossible to observe all the actions and decisions of the agent or to infer them by observing the outcomes of the agent's decisions. Therefore, the agent has some opportunity for discretionary behavior.
- The relationship between principal and agent is based on a contract.
- Actors maximize their utility functions subject to institutional constraints.

- Because principals and agents have different utility functions, decisions that are mostly in the interest of the agent do not necessarily serve the interest of the principal.
- Transaction costs are positive.

Neelen (1993, p. 65) notes that, with this characterization of agency relationships, the principal always faces questions of control in the context of information asymmetry and conflict of interest. Thus, Neelen (1993, p. 65) concludes that it is impossible for the principal to ensure, at zero cost, that the agent will make optimal decisions from the principal's point of view. Earlier, Jensen and Meckling (1976, p. 306) pointed out that in most agency relationships the principal and the agent will incur positive costs. The principal incurs the cost for having to monitor the agent's behavior. The agent incurs the cost of bonding, i.e., of assuring the principal that certain actions that are inconsistent with the principal's interest will not be taken. Jensen and Meckling went on to suggest that the dollar equivalent of the reduction in welfare experienced by the principal due to a divergence, i.e., between the agent's decisions and those that would maximize the principal's welfare, is also a cost of the agency relationship. Jensen and Meckling refer to this cost as the residual cost. Accordingly, they define "agency cost" as the sum of: (a) the monitoring of expenditures by the principal, (b) the bonding of expenditures by the agent, and (c) the residual cost.

Douma and Schreuder (1991, p. 77) point out that agency relations can be found both within organizations (e.g., manager and subordinate) and between organizations (e.g., licensing and franchising). Since the actual development of the agency relationships is influenced by changes in the environment, understanding the role of environmental variables (which can influence agency cost) should be of interest to practitioners and researchers alike. The problem is that most writing on the principal-agent perspective does not offer a conceptual framework for exploring the complex relationships among the principal, the agent, and the environmental context of their relationship.

A promising approach offered recently by van der Zaal (1993) incorporates the environmental dimension into the study of agency relations. Van der Zaal (1993) starts by making two important points that can be used for explaining why the principal-agent perspective may be suitable for studying and understanding the challenge of franchise funds and cross-servicing in government. First, van der Zaal (1993, p. 1) claims that using the concept of a principal-agent relationship appears to suit the required perspective for studying interorganizational strategic management issues. This claim is a direct challenge to one of Moe's (1984) above assertions, namely, that the common analytical foundation of the principal-agent perspective includes a focus on the individual as the unit of analysis. In addition, van der Zaal (1993) sees this perspective also as a promising candidate for the development of an integrative framework in which connections can be made among such environmental-dimensions as "uncertainty" and "dependency" and such intraorganizational dimensions as organizational resources, strategic assets, core capabilities, and core competencies. Such an inside/out approach would be complementary to strategic management, in which competitive analysis starts with an outside/in perspective. It should be noted here that there is a possible parallel between this assertion of van der Zaal's (1993) and the requirements of OMB (Koskinen, 1995) for competitive bidding: specifically, that, while an effort must be made to identify the best bid from outside government (an outside/in perspective), another effort should take place to identify the cost of the proposed activity if carried out by the best performer within government, which may be other than the contracting department (i.e., an inside/inside or inside/out perspective).

Van der Zaal's second claim (1993, p. 8) is that agency cost reduction is not enough to explain the cooperation between the principal and the agent. The other reason for the cooperation is the incentive to create value. Van der Zaal (1993, p. 8) calls this concept "agency benefit," and makes two propositions: (a) that by integration of the "agency benefit" concept into the principal-agent framework, it may be possible to develop "a well balanced benefit/cost framework for analyzing cooperative interorganizational relations from a principal-agent perspective;" and (b) that the principal-agent perspective deals with three levels of analysis. The first level is the focal organization. The partner in the relationship is part of the first party's environment and represents the second level of analysis. The environmental context of the agency relationship (which may or may not encourage such activities) forms the third level of analysis (van der Zaal, 1993, p. 9). In the case of franchising and cross-servicing in government, these three levels of analysis offer a very different way of studying agency relations than the common approach, which tends to overlook long-term implications due to the heavy emphasis on short-term gains, or "savings."

The conceptual framework offered by van der Zaal (1993, p. 11) is summarized in Table 1. It requires us to consider the relationships among the principal, the agent, and the environment, in two ways: first, by considering the uncertainty of the environment, i.e., by using an information perspective, as illustrated by cells 1, 2, and, 3; second, by using a resource perspective, i.e., the dependency relations, as illustrated by cells 4, 5, and 6.

Table 1
Van der Zaal's Conceptual Framework

	Principal	**Agent**
Environmental uncertainty—an information perspective	1. Uncertainty about (the relation to) the agent	2. Uncertainty about the (the relation to) principal
3. Uncertainty about the environment surrounding the principal-agent relation		
Environmental dependence—a resource perspective	4. Dependency on(the relation to) the agent	5. Dependency on(the relation to) the principal
6. Dependency on the environment surrounding the principal-agent		

This conceptual framework is an interesting option for exploring many issues and contingencies of the new effort to encourage federal entities to secure administrative support services from other federal entities. While it may need further refinement and elaboration, it illustrates how the use of the principal-agent perspective can help managers and researchers get better insights into agency relationships in government.

CONCLUDING REMARKS

This chapter explains the attempt to improve the efficiency and effectiveness of federal agencies through the use of a two-prong approach: (a) introduction of competition and (b) better utilization of resources across the board, by taking advantage of economies of size. While it is not hard to see why the idea of establishing an FF can be attractive to both would-be providers and users of services, some difficult questions remain open. These include not only issues concerning congressional oversight, but the future and proper roles of central staff units of the executive branch as well. Other concerns about the new reality that involve the future of FF can be illustrated by a question that was posed in a recent conference on that important subject, namely: "Can the manager of an FF with deep pockets use dumping strategy to undermine and eliminate a competitive FF?" The answers to such questions may depend on how we answer more basic questions about business ethics and how we reconcile possible conflicts between the public interest in the short run (general will) and societal interests in the long run (general welfare).

It was pointed out in the introduction to this chapter that the pragmatic nature of the proposed approach to fostering efficiency through the introduction of competition is very attractive to managers and legislatures. Yet, there is little to suggest that all the likely contingencies of the contractual relations between service recipients ("principals") and providers ("agents") have been sorted out. The rational behavior that is assumed by proponents of the "franchising in government" movement may prove to be wrong. A major fiasco, or any scandal, in connection with an FF may doom this innovative initiative. The side effect of such failure is the undermining of the prospect of introducing or experimenting in the future with other administrative innovations in the public sector.

Testifying before a subcommittee of the United States Congress, a representative of the United States Comptroller's Office claimed that before major changes are made, as part of NPR, "decisionmakers should assure that the capacities of both the entities receiving new responsibilities and the entities responsible for program oversight are able to perform those duties" (Bowsher, 1995, p. 6). The initiative to establish FF is a case in point. In order to be proactive in determining what those capacities are necessitates an examination of the likely contingencies that the actors, i.e., both principals and agents, may face. A prudent approach to the introduction of franchising in government requires developing a theoretical framework to assure a systematic examination, and maximizing the learning we can derive from the experiment with FF. Mobilizing the vast knowledge already developed in connection with the effort to deal with agency relations may be a promising way of developing the concept of FF. As long as we do not have a better offer, managers and researchers should consider the challenge of operationalizing van der Zaal's assertion of the need to study agency relations within the environmental context.

NOTE

The author wishes to acknowledge the important comments of Peter Boorsma and Piet de Vries on an earlier version of this chapter.

REFERENCES

Abramovitz, M. (1986, July/August). The privatization of the welfare state: A review. *Social Work, 31*, 257–264.

Bowsher, C. A. (1995). *Government reform: GAO comments on the national performance review: Testimony before the Subcommittee on Government Management, Information and Technology, Committee on Government Reform and Oversight, House of Representatives. GAO/T-GGD-95-154.* Washington, DC: United States General Accounting Office.

Brudney, J. L. (1987). Coproduction and privatization: Exploring the relationship and its implications. *Journal of Voluntary Action Research, 16*(3), 11–21.

Carr, J. B., & Brower, R. S. (1996, August). *Principal-agent as an explanation of unsanctioned managerial behavior: Is the theory useful?* A paper for the 1996 Academy of Management Meeting, Cincinnati, OH.

Cooperative Administrative Support Unit. (1994). *Annual report.* Washington, DC: United States Government Printing Office.

Darr, T. B. (1987). Pondering privatization may be good for your government. *Governing, 1*(2), 42–50.

Douma, S., & Schreuder, H. (1991). *Economic approaches to organizations.* Englewood Cliffs, NJ: Prentice-Hall.

Goldstein, M. L. (1990). The shadow government. *Government Executive, 22*(5), 30–31, 34, 36–37, 56–57.

Gore, A., Jr. (1993). *Creating government that works better and costs less: Report of the national performance review.* Washington, DC: United States Government Printing Office.

Graham, C. B., & Hays, S. W. (1986). *Managing the public organization.* Washington, DC: CQ Press.

Halachmi, A. (1989). Ad-hocracy and the future of the civil service. *International Journal of Public Administration, 12*(4), 617–650.

Halachmi, A. (1996). Entrepreneurial government in theory/in practice. In A. Halachmi & K. Nicholes (Eds.), *Enterprise government* (pp. 1–26). Burke, VA.: Chatelaine Press.

Jennings, E. T. (1991 [1986]). Public choice and the privatization of government: Implications for public administration. Reprinted in J. S. Ott, A. Hyde, & J. Shafritz (Eds.), *Public management: The essential readings* (pp. 113–129). Chicago, IL: Lyceum Books, 1991.

Jensen, M. C. (1983). Organizational theory and methodology. *The Accounting Review, 56,* 319–339.

Jensen, M. C., & Meckling, W. H. (1976). Theory of the firm: Managerial behavior, agency cost and ownership structure. *Journal of Financial Economics, 3,* 305–360.

Koskinen, J. (1995). *Federal policies related to contracting out: A testimony before the House Subcommittee on Civil Service, March 29.* //pula.financenet.gov:70/00/ happen/congress/ mica2a.

Koskinen, J. A. (1996). Foreword. In A. Halachmi & K .L. Nichols (Eds.), *Enterprise government* (pp. iii–iv). Burke, VA: Chatelaine Press.

Lipsky, M. (1980). *Street level bureaucrats.* New York, NY: Russell Sage.

Master, W. (1996). Connecting with the franchise customer. In A. Halachmi & K. Nicoles (Eds.), *Franchising in government* (pp. 191–196). Burke, VA: Chatelaine Press.

Moe, T. M. (1984). The new economics of organizations. *Journal of Political Science, 28,* 739–777.

Morgan, D. R., & England, R. E. (1988). The two faces of privatization. *Public Administration Review, 48*(6), 483–497.

Naff, K. C. (1991). Labor-management relations and privatization: A federal perspective. *Public Administration Review, 51*(1), 23–29.

National Academy of Public Administration. (1989). *Privatization: The challenge to public management.* Washington, DC: National Academy of Public Administration.

Neelen, G. H. J. M. (1993). *Principal agent relations in non-profit organizations.* Enschede, The Netherlands: University of Twente, Faculteit Bestuurskunde.

Newman, G. (1996). Financial considerations in the franchising environment: Keys to success. In A. Halachmi & K. Nicoles (Eds.), *Enterprise government* (pp. 77-93). Burke, VA: Chatelaine Press.

Niskanen, W. A. (1971). *Bureaucracy and representative government.* Chicago, IL: Aladin Atherton.

Oates, W. E., & Schwab, R. M. (1991). The allocative and distributive implications of local fiscal competition. In D. A. Kanyon & J. Kincaid (Eds.), *Competition among states and local governments* (pp. 127–145). Washington, DC: Urban Institute.

Osborne, D., & Gaebler, T. (1992). *Reinventing government.* Reading, MA: Addison-Wesley.

Perry, J. L., & Babitsky, T. T. (1986). Comparative performance in urban bus transit: Assessing privatization strategies. *Public Administration Review, 46*(1), 57–66.

Rehfuss, J. (1991). A leaner, tougher public management? Public agency competition with private contractors. *Public Administration Quarterly, 51*(2), 239–252.

Savas, E. S. (1987). *Privatization: The key to better government.* Chatham, NJ: Chatham House.

Savas, E. S. (1992). Privatization and productivity. In M. Holzer (Ed.), *Public productivity handbook* (pp. 79–98). New York, NY: Marcel Dekker.

Serlin, M. D. (1996). The competitors. *Government Executive, 28*(6), 29–33.

Serlin, M. D., & Bruce, R. R. (1996). Origins of franchising. In A. Halachmi & K. Nicols (Eds.), *Enterprise government* (pp. 27–43). Burke, VA: Chatelaine Press.

Sullivan, H. J. (1987). Privatization of public services: A growing threat to constitutional rights. *Public Administration Review, 47*(6), 461–467.

Thayer, F. C. (1987). Privatization carnage, chaos and corruption. In J. S. Ott, A. Hyde, & J. Shefritz (Eds.), *Public management: The essential readings*, (pp. 154–168). Chicago, IL: Lyceum Books.

Twilla, G. T. (1991). *Out sourcing services: An evaluation of a contract employee program.* Unpublished seminar paper, Institute of Government at Tennessee State University.

van der Zaal, G. A. W. (1993). *On cooperative organizational relations: An integrative principal agent perspective.* Management Report Series no. 164. Rotterdam, Netherlands: School of Management, Erasmus University.

Wolf, C. (1979). A theory of nonmarket failure. *Public Interest, 55*, 114-133.

Chapter 10

AGENCY THEORY AND TRANSACTION ANALYSIS IN THE INCREASINGLY COMPETITIVE PUBLIC SECTOR

Arie Halachmi

Many claim that direct market competition is the key to achieving high levels of performance in the public and private sectors. In the public sector, products and services are not subject to direct market competition. With the new entrepreneurial environment, managers in the public sector now are being asked to consider replacing their traditional production and service models with new models that make use of contracts. These arrangements—based on the claim that free competition yields optimal performance— are problematic because this market competition has not been tested yet within the theoretical frameworks of neo-institutional economics, thereby neglecting the transactional costs and economic reality. The principal-agent perspective can provide a better understanding and improved application of utilizing contracts. The insights from this perspective, used effectively, can help reduce the dysfunctions associated with performance measurement, use of incentives, and hiring. As affirmed in a factual case study, contractual relationships present significant and serious managerial implications: managers who gain the latitude to contract also acquire a new source of power and the ability to substitute their own interests for the interests of other stakeholders.

Government organizations' products and services are not subject to direct market competition. No competition exists for the market share of a Ministry of Foreign Affairs or for a nation's Customs Service, nor would the public want to see any. However, without the discipline of competition, one must ask: "What is the motivation to keep overhead costs down?" Why should a government producer of goods or services strive to be efficient or effective? As a matter of fact, under many government systems the squeaky wheel gets the grease, meaning that the inefficient and the ineffective agencies are rewarded with greater budgets and a larger work force. Niskanen (1971), and other writers who are critical of government operations, from an economic point of view, add support to proponents of privatization and contracting out. As illustrated by the various works of Savas (1987, 1992), managers of the public sector resources are asked to consider the claim that competition is a key to efficient and effective government. However, as will be pointed out in this chapter, the practical and pragmatic elegances of new administrative arrangements organized on the premise that the free market and competition can solve all problems is as problematic.   The reason is that market competition (which on its face seems to comply with assertions offered by Savas (1987, 1992), e.g., about the functional role of competition) and Niskanen (1971, e.g., about the budget-maximizing bureaucrat) have yet to be tested within the theoretical frameworks offered by neo-institutional economics, such as principal-agent theory (Neelen, 1993). These theoretical frameworks address the issues of transaction cost and economic reality. Such issues must be considered in assessing the virtues of replacing traditional production models with new ones, i.e., those that make extensive use of contractual relationships.   The complexity of such issues increases several fold when one considers the fact that those government employees dishing out the contracts and serving as "principals" are themselves in reality "agents" of their respective agencies and their selected officials, who, in turn, are "agents" themselves.

The significance of such testing will become more apparent to the reader after considering two important issues concerning these new contractual relationships.   First, the two parties to the contract have different utility functions and are likely to find themselves involved in a zero-sum game as they try to maximize these utility functions. This gaming is not without cost, and the question is: who will bear that cost?   Second, for at least one of the actors, the "agent," the contract in question may be one of several contracts the actor has with other government or non-governmental entities.   Current economic writings refer to this as multi-tasking.   Under such circumstances of multi-tasking, problems (and thus added cost) may develop when a contract(s) includes conflicting obligations, i.e., conditions that may interfere with the ability of the agent in one respect to deliver the best performance under the same or under another contract in another respect.   Thus, a principal (e.g., a government agency in the market for say copying, or security services, in various parts of the country or even in the same area) may have contracts with multiple agents (which may or may not have inconsistent interests among themselves).   In a mirror image, an agent may have simultaneous contracts with multiple principals.   These multiple principals may also have interests that are inconsistent, or mutually exclusive, with respect to the agent's performance.   Agency managers must understand the behavioral implications of the contractual relations between principals and agents for at least two reasons.   First, if they are to serve the real public interest, as different from performing a symbolic gesture that is inconsistent with the economic interest of the policy.   Second, if they intend on using performance measurement in general and linking compensation, incentives, and hiring to them in particular.

The purpose of this chapter is to highlight one contingency commonly overlooked by many scholars of entrepreneurial management and public policy as they discuss the virtues and faults of outsourcing government services. I call this contingency "principal opportunism," though, in essence, it is another case of "agent opportunism." The chapter starts with a brief review of the theoretical basis of the principal-agent perspective. To address the possible reasons why using a principal-agent perspective can be useful, the chapter does two things. First, it goes on to discuss the current thinking and writing about performance measurement, use of incentives, and hiring from the perspective of a principal-agent relationship. Second, it goes on to review a true case study that illustrates how the possible opportunism of one stakeholder leads to outsourcing where this stakeholder, who himself is an agent to others, becomes the principal. The chapter concludes with a short discussion pointing out how a subtle change in governance structure may take place during the process of contracting out, when a stakeholder who is an agent in one respect becomes the ad-hoc principal for a given contract. The chapter also asserts that by gaining the permission to outsource an essential service for a hefty price, stakeholders with the latitude to do so gain a new source of power and the ability to substitute their own interests for the interests of the public they were elected to serve.

PRINCIPAL-AGENT PERSPECTIVE AND TRANSACTION COST

The early principal-agent relationships research, such as Spence and Zeckhauser (1971), Ross (1973), and Jensen and Meckling (1976), are now part of a massive, but diverse, body of literature (Neelen, 1993). As noted elsewhere (Halachmi, 1998), the terms "agency relationships," "an agency approach," or "principal-agent relationship" are being used indiscriminately to characterize a large variety of functional and contractual relationships between two parties. A brief review of significant articles and conference papers can help illustrate this point. According to Killick (1997, p. 487), "Principal-agent issues arise when the maximization of more than one party's utility function requires some form of cooperative action and when the objective functions of the parties differ." The problem, according to Killick, is for principals to design contracts which embody rewards that make it in the interest of agents to further the principal's objectives. On the face of it, though not in reality as would be shown below, this translates into a very simple employment formula in the public sector: the government would like to have in place such employment contracts that would provide employees with incentives to meet the public policy objectives of their departments.

According to Barney and Hesterly (1996, p. 124) and others (e.g., Arrow, 1985), agency relationships develop whenever one partner in a transaction (the principal) delegates authority to another (the agent) and the welfare of the principal is affected by the choices of the agent. The agency problem, they say, arises with the "possibility of opportunistic behavior on the agent's part that works against the principal" (Barney and Hesterly, 1996, p. 125). Such behavior is possible due to the information asymmetry, which prevents the principal from perfect and costless monitoring of the agent's action or of the information which is available to the agent.

According to Arrow (1985), the two essential sources of agency problems are moral hazards and adverse selection. Moral hazard has to do with the cost of observing or uncovering secretive actions of the agent. Adverse selection has to do with the cost to the principal of the information that is available only to the agent and which prevents the principal from ascertaining that the principal's interests are being served by the agent's decisions. To protect the principal's interests, attempts must be made to reduce the possibility that the agent will undermine them.

The term used to depict the cumulative cost of such attempts to both the principal and the agent is "agency cost." Agency cost includes the principal's expenditure for monitoring the agent and the bonding expenditures of the agent. The total agency cost also includes the residual cost that results from the imperfect monitoring of the agent and from the inability of the agent to assure the principal that their mutual interests do not diverge (Jensen and Meckling, 1976). Because agency costs are not insignificant, one must ask: "What compelling reasons encourage the principal to enter into agency relationships?" For our purposes here, agency costs constitute the cost of carrying out a transaction by the use of a proxy. I will borrow the term "transaction costs" to describe the added indirect cost to the entity that contracts out. This cost comes on top of any direct expenditures for carrying out the task, i.e., the cost of entering into a contract, monitoring the implementation of the contract, added overhead due to the fact that a task is performed by other than the entity's employees, etc. It should be noted here that the term "transaction cost" is used here in a slightly different way from the way it is used by some economists, though others use it to address related situations (Williamson, 1991).

PERFORMANCE MEASUREMENT AND PRINCIPAL-AGENT PERSPECTIVES

Performance measurement has been a salient issue for all organizations for quite some time. But as noted by Courty and Marschke (2004) and others (Halachmi, 2005), different performance measures generate different responses by employees. The insights that can be obtained from the use of the Principal-Agent perspective can help prospective users of performance measurement avoid some of its possible dysfunctions (Halachmi, 1996a, Halachmi, 2002).

One common feature of all performance measurements is that they attempt to communicate the true organizational goal. However, they are imperfect proxies and their source of imperfections is likely to differ. One of the reasons for this imperfection is that employees, as agents, may be wrong in identifying who is the Principal that contracted their services. In the case of public employees in general and professionals such as social workers, auditors or teachers, is it an abstract entity like "society," "government," or "the organization" to which they belong? Or, is it the very concrete manager(s) who supervise them? Using the Principal-Agent perspective, it is not hard to see how their efforts are going to change when they aim to reach the organizational goal, or when they try to please or meet what they assume are the expectations of their flesh and blood supervisors. Since those managers are the ones who transcribe performance reports into merit pay, promotions, etc., it is not hard to see why employees, as agents, would strive to satisfy them. To maximize the returns on their efforts, employees are doing what is most likely to reward them: serving what they think are the priorities of their bosses even at the expense of what they know to be the organizational goal. Thus, as noted by Courty and Marschke (2004, 2003) after a measure is activated, the agent takes measure-specific actions that maximize the measure but that do not maximize the true effort to attain the organizational goal. These actions increase the variability of the measures and thus reduce the correlation between the measure and the true goal. Understanding this hazard should effect the design or the selection of performance measurements and how they are being used.

Performance measurements can motivate or de-motivate employees by virtue of the incentive they provide employees, or the possible direct or indirect "cost" they impose on them as agents. In addition, and as would be explained below, incentive contracts have both a selection effect and an effort effect (Milgrom and Roberts, 1992). These contracts motivate employees, as agents, to work according to the desires of the managers, as principals, by linking their compensation to measured performance (the effort effect). If structured in a way that is attractive to individuals with certain traits, but unattractive to employees without these traits, incentive contracts can be used to select appropriate people for the job (the selection effect) (Bouwens and van Lent, 2003). In other words, performance measurements effects not only the behavior of the employees as agents but also the makeup of the human resources of the organization as would be discussed below.

Bouwens and van Lent (2003) note that while the accounting literature has recognized early on that the selection and effort effects of incentive contracts are affected by the properties of the measure of performance specified in the contract (Waller and Chow, 1985; Chow, 1983), relatively little attention has to date been paid to exploring the exact nature of the relation between performance measure properties and incentive contract effects. In their study, they attempt to demonstrate the interdependence of the effort and selection effects of incentive contracts. They claim that generous incentives attract better employees, who, in turn, exert greater effort. In other words, pampered employees are more productive. Bouwens and van Lent (2003) emphasize that great incentives do not affect the work effort directly. Rather, it is through the impact of the incentives on selection that effort increases. They go on to assert, "we do find strong evidence that performance measures with desirable properties increase the effort provided under incentive contracts *and* positively affect the selection via incentive contracts" (Bouwens and van Lent, 2003). To understand this conclusion of Bouwens and van Lent (2003) one needs to consider the earlier propositions of Bonner and Sprinkle (2002) arguing that the effort effects of incentive contracts are a function of: (1) personality traits of the agent, (2) characteristics of the agent's task, (3) the context of employment (organizational structure, features of the accounting system), and (4) design choices within the incentive system. In other words, that the effort is a function of the possible set of results and their desirability which is exactly the essence of Vroom's (1964) Path or Expectancy Theory of Motivation (Halachmi, 2005a). The "path" in Vroom's theory of motivation has three elements, and the resulting strength of the motivation is a function of the synergistic relations among them. The first element is a belief that the performed effort would lead to certain results, and the second element is the belief that these results, in turn, would effect certain, but desired, outcomes. The level of desirability, or in

Vroom's terminology *valence,* would, in turn, influence the level of effort the individual exerts. For our purposes here, it is easy to see how the particulars of the measurement system, as perceived by employees (or would-be employees) can be important. These perceptions can influence not only decisions about the effort worth exerting to perform the job, but the decision whether to join, stay or leave employers.

Individuals who consider the performance measurement scheme a desired external intervention (see below) are likely to react favorably to it. They may be inclined to join or stay with the employer, the "principal," while those who see it as unfair, for any reason, may leave for a workplace where the performance measure might be more favorable to their case. Thus, for example, those who are paid by actual measurement of results or outcomes would join or stay with the organization when they expect to be able to score well, e.g., produce more items, serve more customers, get better returns on investments, etc. Those who are not so sure about the ability of the performance measurement scheme to translate their efforts, loyalty, and dedication to the tangibles that are counted by the performance measurement scheme may opt to work at a place where a flat base compensation is assured (Bonner and Sprinkle, 2002; Prendergast, 1999). In short, "the effort effect of incentive contracts depends on the incentive power specified in the contract. Stronger incentives will elicit more effort, *ceteris paribus*" Bouwens and van Lent (2003).

Yet, things are not as simple as they look. As would be illustrated below, other reported research alleges a possible dysfunctional relation between tangible, external incentives, and the more potent motivation that results from intrinsic drive. The research on this topic provides possible insights that are important for understanding and predicting the behavior of "agents." Sliwka (2003) says: "Indeed there seem to be very different views in individual firms on whether contracts based on individual performance are beneficial or not. Some see incentive contracts as an important component of their human resource management practices, whereas others take a much more skeptical (sic) view and may even consider individual extrinsic incentives as harmful."

Extrinsic incentives are forces or considerations that shape behavior because the individual is anxious to receive from the "principal" promised rewards or avoid a punishment, whether tangible or intangible. The principal can be the direct supervisor, the employing organization, or society. Intrinsic incentives, on the other hand, have to do with the individual needs for self fulfillment, accomplishment, affiliation or power as discussed by proponents of various theories of motivation (Halachmi, 2005a). In most cases, intrinsic incentives generate intangible but powerful rewards. These have merit for the individual employee but no market value.

According to Frey and Jegen (1999), the effects of external interventions on intrinsic motivation have been attributed to two psychological processes:

(a) *Impaired self-determination.* When individuals perceive an external intervention to reduce their self-determination (e.g., by forcing them to perform in a way that corresponds to a given performance measure), they substitute intrinsic motivation by extrinsic control, i.e., that performance measure. As the common saying goes, "what is being measured is being done." As the locus of control in the presence of performance measurements shifts from the inside to the outside of the affected person, it changes motivation and influences the level of the exerted effort. While this shift may be a promising strategy in a few cases of certain low level employees who perform routine and repetitive tasks, it may be a serious de-motivator. In fact, it may be a dysfunctional way of prompting professional and mid-level employees to do the right thing by innovating and thinking outside the box. Instead, such a shift may encourage employees, as contracted agents, to ignore the true interest of their organization and do things "right," i.e., by the book.

(b) *Impaired self-esteem.* When an intervention from outside, such as the use of performance measurement, is perceived as implying that the actor's motivation is not important, his or her intrinsic motivation is effectively rejected. The affected employees are likely to feel that their involvement, skill and contributions are not appreciated, which undermines their value. An intrinsically motivated person is deprived of the chance to display his or her own interest and involvement in an activity when someone else offers a reward, or commands one, to undertake it. As a result of impaired self-esteem, individuals, as agents, reduce their effort.

Frey and Jegen (1999) assert that the two processes listed above allow us to derive the *psychological conditions* under which part of the motivation may be negatively affected when a previously non-monetary relationship is transformed into a monetary one. Frey and Jegen (1999) label the said transformation "the crowding-out effect" and claim that:

(1) External interventions, such as those resulting from the introduction of performance measurements, *crowd-out* intrinsic motivation if the individuals affected perceive them to be *controlling*. In that case, both self-determination and self-esteem suffer, and the individuals react by reducing their intrinsic motivation in the activity controlled. In other words, the articulation of the contract by the use of performance measurement brings the agents to exert the minimum effort they think is required of them to meet the conditions of the contract and nothing more than that. Without performance measurement, the effort exerted would aim to meet the level of performance they set for themselves, and that level may be higher than the contract.

(2) External interventions crowd-in intrinsic motivation if the individuals concerned perceive it as *supportive,* e.g., as an opportunity to show off and articulate the "true" level of accomplishments and achievements. In that case, self-esteem is fostered, and individuals feel that they are given more freedom to act, thus enlarging self-determination. As pointed out above, employees who are happy with the performance measurement in place would stay while those who are not comfortable with it would leave.

The mounting volume of research about the possible dysfunctions of external incentives provides important insights into the nature of performance measurement, use of incentives, and change of performance. One of the most common cases cited is the case of Lincoln Electric Company, which is often held up in management education as a model for implementing high powered incentives based on a piece rate system (Courty and Marschke, 2003a). The company once tried to measure stenographer productivity by counting the number of times the keyboard keys were operated. The company soon observed that one of its workers was earning much more than the others. In investigating the cause, the company discovered that the worker "at her lunch, using one hand for eating purposes, and the other for punching the most convenient key on the typewriter as fast as she could" (Berg and Fast, 1975, as cited by Courty and Marschke, 2003). Obviously, the company then terminated this performance measure. But what happens when a performance measure is changed?

Clearly one cannot expect the principal to come up with the perfect performance measurement the first time around, or that such measure would be a valid, and a relevant, measure forever. But changes of the performance measurement scheme can: a) result in a new cost the agent may seek to avoid, and b) change the asymmetry of the information, or c) send the agent a message the principal did not intend to send. Any of these three possibilities can make agents change their behavior, i.e., their performance.

As pointed out above, the introduction of performance measures is an external intervention that may be perceived as reducing the agents' control of their own situation, reducing or replacing efforts that were based on intrinsic motives with external incentives. In terms of information asymmetry, the use of performance measurement replaces the agent's own kind of information with the principal's kind of information. A case in point was reported by Deci and Flaste (1971, 1995). They discuss the case of a perfectionist child in violin class. Once 'gold-stars' were introduced as a symbolic reward for a certain amount of time spent practicing the instrument, the girl lost all her interest in trying new, difficult pieces. Under the new system of performance measurement the girl's own standards of excellence and learning which motivated her in the past were put aside. Instead of improving her skills, the aim shifted towards spending time playing well-learned, easy pieces in order to receive the award.

In a related report, Frey and Jegen (1999) cite a three-phase experiment at a daycare center. Daycare centers are commonly confronted with the problem that some parents arrive late to pick up their children. This forces employees to stay after the official closing time. A typical principal-agent approach would suggest introducing a fine for collecting children late to address this problem. Increasing the transaction cost for the principal (the delinquent parent) might serve as a deterrent for bad practice. Assuming economic rationality, such a punishment is expected to induce parents to reduce the occurrence of belatedly picking up their children. The effect of such a policy was studied for one daycare center. According to Frey and Jegen (1999), the researchers first recorded the number of parents coming late over a particular period of time. In a second period extending over twelve weeks, a significant monetary fine for collecting children late was introduced. After an initial learning phase, the number of late-coming parents increased substantially, which is consistent with the assumption of economic rationality.

The introduction of the monetary penalty in the second phase of the experiment was perceived by tardy parents as modifying the relationship between parents and teachers rather than as an increase in the transaction cost. The fine made tardiness an economic transaction on its own merit. As a result, the parents' intrinsic motivation to be fair and adhere to the time schedules was reduced or was crowded out altogether. Due to the additional cost for being late, the feeling of tardy parents now was that the teachers are "paid" extra for extra service, i.e., for having to stay longer. In the third phase of the experiment, the monetary fine was phased out. The observation that the number of late-coming parents remained stable at the prevailing level, even after the fine was cancelled, suggests that the parents' behavior was changed for good as a result of the introduction of a penalty system in phase two. In other words, the new perception of the relationship was irreversible. If before the experiment, intrinsic motivation to be fair to the teachers was driving parents to collect their children on time, the side payment in the form of a fine crowded out that motivation.

Intrinsic motivation has been argued to be important for volunteering (Freeman, 1997). According to Frey and Jegen (1999), the use of rewards "is found to reduce volunteering. While the size of the rewards induces the individuals to provide more volunteer work, the mere fact that they receive a payment significantly reduces their work efforts by approximately four hours. The magnitude of these effects is considerable. Evaluated at the median reward paid, volunteers work indeed *less*." These findings, Frey and Jegen (1999) argue, "have important implications for policy towards volunteer work. Direct incentives may backfire, leading to less volunteering." There are several possible explanations of the possible effects of external rewards on the performance of volunteers, as agents (Sliwka, 2003). Yet, as noted by Bouwens and van Lent (2003), other studies have shown incentives to induce greater efforts by managers of charities. However, until more conclusive evidence is available, it is important to remember that the mere use of performance measures or external incentives, which at times are inseparable, can be dysfunctional in surprising ways (Halachmi, 2002).

Using a principal-agent perspective, the studies like those cited above highlight another possible serious issue with the use of performance measurement. As noted by Courty and Marschke (2003), the principal does not know when it selects a performance measure, whether it will induce the right behavior. Only over time does the principal discover the agent's responses and then uses this additional information to update and fine-tune the measure and the corresponding incentive system. These studies suggest that imperfect information about the quality of performance measures means that the mechanism for developing performance measurement systems must be evolutionary. The problem is that in this "evolutionary" process the behavior of the agent may be changing with any modification of the measures, and in ways that cannot be predicted in advance. Following each "improvement" of the performance measure, the principal may need to adapt the measurement system once more in response to new information that is revealed after a measure has been activated and so on. The reason for the need for such modifications is that the introduction (or change) of performance measures may induce gaming. The gaming results from strategic responses of the employees, the "agents" to the uncertainties or possible adverse affects that may result from the use of the "new" measure. In most cases this gaming is counter productive from the organizational point of view. For example, this gaming may include costly misallocation of resources as employees adjust their performance to score "right" on the new performance measure (Courty and Marschke, 2004). The main implication of the model proposed by Courty and Marschke (2003) for the design of performance measurement systems is that "selecting performance measures on the basis of their correlation with the organization's true objective may not always be a valid approach. In particular this selection rule will be flawed when gaming plays an important role, and in these situations the selection of performance measures has to be an experimental process."

More recent works (Courty and Marschke, 2004, 2003) in the principal-agent literature discuss the situation where performance measures communicate objectives that imperfectly correspond to the organization's true goal. This misalignment, in turn, results in a misallocation of resources. This literature identifies a trade off in the design of performance bonuses between effort, incentives and risk. Courty and Marschke (2003) note that since the seminal work of Holmstrom (1979), this trade-off has been analyzed in great detail in the literature. The basic idea is that to elicit effort, the principal must link the agent's compensation to a noisy performance outcome. The outcome is random and because, while the agent is assumed to be risk-averse, incentive-provision imposes costs.

Bouwens and van Lent (2003) assert that performance measures may impose undue risk on agents and reduce the efficacy of incentives. They go on to point out that recent research reports have drawn attention to the possibility that performance measures may be subject to distortion, i.e., are not congruent with desirable corporate goals or do not communicate strategy well enough. Bouwens and van Lent (2003) conclude that noise and distortion are disadvantageous properties of performance measures and harm the applicability of the measure in incentive contracts. Noise and distortion are separate properties; nonetheless, they have the same effect on measure applicability.

Noisy performance measures may contain observation errors with regard to the true action choice of an agent. Since the agents cannot trust the principal to be rewarded for delivered effort (because the measured performance may incorrectly reflect their true effort choice), they bear additional risk. Assuming agents are risk-averse implies that the principal has to compensate the agents for this additional risk. Although empirical studies on the relation between noisy performance measures and effort effects have been scarce, the few that exist seem to yield mixed results (Bouwens and van Lent, 2003).

One possible way to overcome distortion and noise is to use multiple measures of performance. However, this might be an expensive solution due to the mere cost of data collection analysis and reporting. This strategy is problematic for still another reason since it assumed that any given set of multiple measures is likely to include only measures that are consistent with each other. By the same token, crafting a set of performance measures that are consistent with each other may introduce the risk of an un-intended bias. In short, the problems are likely to mount as the number of performance measures in use increases. As noted by Bouwens and van Lent (2003), the use of multiple measures may reduce the employee's understanding of the overall organizational goals and cause confusion. What's more, when many measures are used to evaluate performance, top management's judgment is needed to aggregate information to one, overall conclusion. This, in turn, increases the odds that subordinates would engage in lobbying behavior or other unproductive effort, which is likely to be detrimental to performance.

The discussion offered in this section touches on some important issues that have to do with performance measurements, use of incentives, and their implications for recruitment and retention of employees. However, this brief overview barely touches on the wealth of publications and recent research addressing these important issues from a principal-agent perspective. The section that follows uses a true case study to illustrate the possible usefulness of the principal-agent perspective for better understanding of the political economy dynamics of the budgetary process in the context of local government.

CONTRACTING OUT DAVIDSON COUNTY'S MEDICAL EXAMINER'S OFFICE

The cover story of the *Nashville Scene* on March 13, 1997 (Garrigan, 1997) screamed "Insufficient funds: without revenues, what's Bredesen got left to spend?" The accompanying photo showed Nashville-Davidson County Mayor Phil Bredesen (and later on Governor Bredesen) standing near a teller machine. Reflecting on the Metro Council in the 1990s, Garrigan (1997) noted that "today's elected officials are generally more mindful of the public demand for good clean responsive government. Ironically though, today's government is much less responsive. It seems to be driven much less by constituents' service than it was in the old days of municipal micro-management." This observation was made when Metro's budget topped the 1 billion dollar mark for the first time, doubling, in the process, the debt it had just three years earlier. Nashville was emerging in 1997 as an engine of economic activity and urban development. Following the construction of a multipurpose sports arena and a face lift of most of downtown, the area of severest downtown decay was mostly removed. In its place, Metro residents saw the emergence of a new entertainment zone, known locally as "the district" with establishments such as the Hard Rock Café, Planet Hollywood, Wild-Horse Saloon, Hooters, and Market Street Micro-Brewery. Music City became in 1997 the home of the Tennessee Titans, the relocated Houston NFL team the "Oilers," a National Hockey League (NHL) expansion team called the Nashville Predators, a site of a future super speedway and the future site of a new mega-mall next to Opryland Hotel, the recently expanded 2800 room luxury hotel with indoor tropical gardens, waterfalls, and fountains of all colors and shapes.

Homicides, too, reached a historic high in 1997, prompting Mayor Bredesen to appoint a 12-member Citizen-Task-Force to come up with new ideas and ways to reduce crime. In the midst of all these varying indications of a city in progress and turmoil, the decision was made to outsource the services of a Medical Examiner. In order to evaluate the decision, it will be helpful to consider the political and demographic context in which that decision took place.

METRO NASHVILLE-DAVIDSON COUNTY

The Metropolitan Government of Nashville-Davidson County (Metro) may be the most successful metropolitan government in the United States. Metro has changed in many ways during the last 25 years. Toward the end of the millennium, Nashville was very different from what it used to be when its metropolitan form was created in the early 1960s. Metro resulted from merging the government of Davidson County, the fifth largest county in the US, with the governments of most of the local authorities within its boundary into one administrative unit. Nashville, already the second-largest city in Tennessee, became the hub of this new governing body. Some of the changes Metro experienced were the result of economic and demographic changes—mostly a population growth due to migration from the North, the "rust belt" to the "sun belt." The economic base of Middle Tennessee changed as Metro Davidson County evolved as a center for country music and the recording industry. In the last 20 years, it has also been the home for some leading corporations in the areas of health and corrections management, e.g., Columbia-HCA and Correction Corporation of America. Metro also benefited from a large and very active cluster of publishers and printing houses for several religious denominations, including the world's largest bible publisher. In the 1980s, the city and its suburbs in the adjacent counties experienced additional influx of what the locals referred to as "new money," when well paid executives and other professionals relocated to Middle Tennessee. Such moves took place in connection with the industrial growth around Metro as the new plants for Nissan and later for GM's Saturn were finished and started to produce cars. In spite of the drastic difference between the economic and demographic changes in Metro between the 1960s and the 1990s, there seems to be little change in the role of Metro's Mayor. The direction of economic development and character of governance in Davidson County had been influenced by the personality and the style of management of the individual mayors in this strong mayor-council (with a very large 40 members) form of government. The mayor is elected directly with a limit of two consecutive terms. Members of the council became subject to term limits only in recent years. They represent 35 electoral districts with five at large seats.

THE RECENT AND STORMY HISTORY OF THE MEDICAL EXAMINER OFFICE (MEO)

Dr. Charles Harlan, Chief Medical Examiner for Metro Nashville-Davidson County, resigned his position in 1993 amid allegations of mismanagement and sexual harassment. Under the four medical examiners that Metro has employed since Dr. Harlan's resignation, the medical examiner's office has been an embarrassment to the citizens of Nashville and Davidson County. In the minds of many citizens, every week brought new problems at the MEO. While such perceptions were far from being true, the smoke was not without fire. Due to the nature of its business, the MEO is always subject to special scrutiny by the media. Thus, any possible story about the MEO and its staff is likely to be exploited by the media, partly as lip service to the public and mostly for boosting ratings and sales of advertisement space. This heightened attention to the MEO is a tradition that developed with the publicity-seeking medical examiner in Los Angeles many years ago and immortalized in a popular TV series. Thus, for example, constant media reports in the last four years have dealt with various problems at the MEO ranging from allegations that accused the ME (first Dr. Harlan and later at least one of the other MEs who was recruited to replace him) of sexual harassment, excessive employee turnover, and lengthy delays in turning bodies over to funeral homes for burial. Additionally, the District Attorney's office has complained that some serious criminal cases have been delayed. In some cases it seemed there was a need for the DA to dismiss cases because the pathologist had failed to complete the autopsy reports. Recently, a state medical examiner likened the situation in Nashville to a "cesspool" and noted it would remain that way without major changes in the operation of the office ("Street Talk," WTVF 1997).

The allegations about the sexual misconduct of the ME were more than just an embarrassment to a mayor of a city whose political climate could pressure the DA to consider an indictment of a local bookstore for carrying books containing pictures of nude people. The Major still had aspirations to become Governor or a US Senator, which no doubt influenced decisions he made as a mayor. For our purposes here, it should also be noted that the Mayor was a transplant from the Northeast. This gave him an image problem in this Southern city. In his previous unsuccessful bids for office, including the position of Mayor, Bredesen had a hard time convincing the voters that he is a clean and fiscally conservative candidate, befitting the virtues of a Southern gentleman. Thus, it is easy to see why the Mayor would be anxious to rid the City of anything that smelled of scandal. The official position of the city was that a positive image of Metro and its elected officials was very conducive to economic development. The MEO was a source of too many controversial stories, an agency ripe for programmatic and financial adjustment.

It appears that for many years the MEO was never adequately funded, which resulted in the office being (1) understaffed, and (2) unable to attract or maintain qualified personnel (Bryant, Chester, and Nicolson, 1997). Being understaffed for a long time made the MEO an unattractive place to work and contributed to Metro's inability to hire a high caliber medical examiner. This, in turn, prolonged the situation in which nobody was fighting to make the staffing needs of the MEO a priority for the city. To be sure, in the last 15 years the budget proposal for the MEO has never included requests for new resources to bring the funding for personnel to a level commensurate with other similar agencies. Such requests are made on a regular basis by other city services for justifying proposals for higher levels of funding by Metro. The MEO has failed to pursue the matter partially because the agency has had little to show for itself and even less to illustrate its ability to make proper use of the resources that were available to it. For example, an audit performed in 1995 cited the office for sloppy record keeping and poor management. It stated that the ME should be concerned with medical procedures and leave office management to a professional (Moritz, 1997). And little has changed since then. The City over the past two years has continued exhaustive efforts to recruit forensic pathologists with little success. The Mayor says that "the problem is not caused by a lack of attention to management issues or by searching in too narrow an area. But it has been proven that merely adding professional personnel does not solve the problem." Further, the Mayor explains: "There were three (3) candidates in 1994 and one (1) in 1995. When contacted in April 1997, none of these individuals were interested in working for Metro." Facing such a reality, it is not hard to see why the MEO became an administrative and political liability for all elected officials, i.e., the Mayor and Metro Council.

According to (Bryant, et al., 1997), the Mayor's office has been told several times by nationally recognized forensic pathologists that no one wanted to work for Metro. Prior to her leaving, efforts by Dr. Bucholtz to recruit an assistant were equally unsuccessful. A physician research firm was used to assist in the search for qualified doctors. Letters were sent to every known forensic pathologist in the country. 65 responses were received, but at the end of the interview process no one indicated willingness to work directly for Metro. It was the belief of at least one state medical examiner and of the president of a nationally recognized physician recruiting company that if the Medical Examiner's office was not privatized, Metro would not be able to attract physicians of the quality needed to run this office (Bryant et al., 1997). The prospect of stabilizing a situation that seemed to get out of hand so often was not very attractive. Careful scrutiny of the operational details and the economics of any such arrangement became non-issues as the consensus evolved that the MEO could not continue to be managed as it was in the past. The embarrassments and the need to deal with the problems at MEO again and again made the search for a permanent solution a priority for the Mayor and the Council.

On March 10, 1997, Mayor Phil Bredesen submitted to the Metropolitan City Council, Substitute Bill No. 097-652. This bill requests:

> *A substitute ordinance approving the privatization of the Medical Examiner's Office of the Metropolitan Government of Nashville and Davidson County and approving a contract for professional services to manage the Medical Examiner's Office between the Metropolitan Government of Nashville and Davidson County and Forensic Medical Management Services, P.C.*

In a public interview Mayor Bredesen stated: "I've struggled with this. It is not pleasing to me when any branch of government is not doing its job. I sincerely hope privatizing the Medical Examiner's Office can get the job done...decrease the backlog of cases and bodies...and calm the turmoil" (WTVF News, 1997). Any member of the Council who saw it differently was put on the spot to come up with a more promising solution or join the consensus that there was a need for a radical change at the MEO.

In his move to make the privatization of the MEO a possible option for dealing with MEO problems, the Mayor was capitalizing on common assumptions in some circles (Kettl, 1993) that contracting facilitates competition among prospective private providers and is also likely to produce better quality services than government monopolies. However, in the case of the Metro Medical Examiner's Office, exploiting the merits of the competition for the contract was not an option according to Larry Brinton, a local reporter for one of the TV stations. During his regular "Street Talk" segment of the evening news on March 27, 1997, Brinton noted that:

> *Mayor Bredesen wants to privatize the Medical Examiners Office, and he's hoping the Metro Council will approve a contract with Associated Pathologists - a group based in Brentwood (TN) Approve a contract? What about bidding the service? Or asking for and evaluating other proposals from the private sector?*

According to Bryant, et al. (1997), conversations with Metropolitan government officials and available documentation indicated: "The decision with whom to contract was made as a *policy* decision rather than a management one" (emphasis added) without consideration of any alternative providers.

Not considering alternative providers may explain why the appearances of the economics and some details of the proposed contract may be questioned by those outside the Mayor's inner circle. However, these accounts do not explain what the "policy" issue was that the Mayor was addressing by the said decision. Was it a policy issue which is limited to MEO? Was it the broader issue of contracting and privatization of government services? Or, was it the beginning of a new policy of getting rid of any potential liability?

The Mayor's Office acknowledged that it selected the firm without a competitive bid because the law did not allow bidding for professional services (Moritz, 1997). This provision allows the Mayor and the Council to retain the services of individuals they trust, or for any other consideration. This practice reflected the strong political context of any decision about the daily management of the County's business affairs. The 1992 Procurement Code of the Metropolitan Government, Section 4.08.080, gives Metro the authority to contract for professional services:

> A. Contracts for legal services, medical services, accounting services, fiscal agents, financial advisors or advisory services, educational consultants, architectural services, engineering services, and similar services by professional persons or groups of high ethical standards, shall not be based on competitive sealed bids, but shall be awarded on the basis of recognized competence and integrity.

> B. Contracts for Professional Services as described above shall be awarded pursuant to regulations adopted by the Standards Board and shall be approved by the Mayor. The Board's regulations may exempt such services from the requirements of centralized purchasing.

When asked about the lack of bidding for the private management of MEO, the Mayor stated, "You don't hire doctors based on who charges the lowest price." (Moritz, 1997). If the normal bidding process is not a reasonable or a legal way as indicated by current law, what about an RFP (Request for Proposal)? This would allow for the development of a business plan detailing the needs for Metro government, allow all interested, qualified vendors to make a proposal, and allow Metro officials to then evaluate the proposals based upon cost, scope of services, and past performance, and award the contract on the basis of which vendor best addresses the requirements of that business plan.

According to Metro Council members, the Mayor's staff, and the Director of Purchasing, no other agencies or contractors were contacted. But when the Council approved privatization on second reading by a margin of one vote, an attorney representing Dr. Harlan sent a three-page letter to Council members detailing why the doctor should be returned to the job he held for 10 years. Put in a local newspaper in 1997, the attorney wrote: "If he is reinstated, you will save a million dollars a year...and repolish our tarnished image in the national community of medical examiners." The paper also noted that a spokesperson for the Mayor said that the idea of Harlan returning to the Medical Examiner's Office was never considered by Mayor Bredesen based on the allegations made against him, though most of the allegations were dismissed or not pursued (1997). At the same time the paper reported that the DA for Davidson County acknowledged that 10 homicide cases lacked final autopsy reports. At the same time, the Metro Public Defender Office filed a motion asking a judge to drop a homicide charge because of delay in getting an autopsy report.

OUTSOURCING: BEST PRACTICES AND FICKLE ONES

Ultimately, Substitute Bill No. 097-652 authorizing the privatization of the Medical Examiner's Office was approved. When all the negotiations with the contractor have been concluded, the total package for providing Nashville with forensic services amounts to $2,393,600 for the first year. This represents a 99.5 percent increase over the expenditures for the MEO in its last year under Metro's jurisdiction. Pointing out all of the above, a reporter asked on the air: "And there were no other vendors knocking down the door for a share of this pie?" The reader should add two other questions: Where was the Council? And, where was the public?

DISCUSSION

A common explanation of the need to enter into agency relations is a difficulty the principal experiences in carrying out a given task on his or her own (Neelen, 1993). The "contract" with the agent increases the involved expenditure but generates certain benefits. The theoretical difficulty is to locate the point at which the principal forfeits more by using an agent than is gained in return. Some of the difficulty results from the real difference between the expected economic value and the expected utility of the transaction with the agent from the principal point of view. Because of such differences, individuals can and do purchase insurance, i.e., when the expected economic value is negative, but to the insured individual the expected utility computes as a positive value. The problem that is illustrated in this case goes beyond a simple calculation of the expected economic value and the expected utility. The Mayor is an agent of the residents of Nashville Davidson County. The question is: "What happens when he decides to employ his own agent for carrying out the contract he signed with the residents as he took the oath of office?" While there may be no economic impact in entering the second contract to carry out the first contract, a difference does arise between the expected utilities because the utility function of the Mayor as "principal" and the utility function of the resident of Nashville, the "principal"-once-removed, are different by definition. Thus, what may constitute a wise, if not an acceptable, decision for the Mayor may be a questionable proposition from a taxpayer point of view. The problem gets even more complicated when one considers the implications that result from the fact that the Council, another agent of the taxpayers but another "principal" for the Mayor, changes roles as well. To be sure, the Mayor could have gone to the electorate to ask for a "change" in his contract, i.e., put a referendum to the voters for a proposal to contract out the MEO (or any other public service to the voters). Instead, he opted to use an agent for getting the necessary approval, i.e., the consent of the Council. By approving the initiative to contract out to the MEO, the Council not only delivered the electorate's approval to the change in the Mayor's contract with it as an agent, but also a subtle amendment of the governance structure of Metro. Instead of being responsible for delivering certain results, the Mayor now is accountable only for managing the contract. In the absence of the intended outcomes, the Mayor needs to answer only for being lax in overseeing the implementation of a written document, but not for getting the taxpayers the best value for their money. Economists are not strangers to this question. They have attempted to answer the problem by addressing the ways to protect the best interests of the stockholders when their agents, the corporate executives, can make their own salary and perks decisions, which in turn, reduces the returns on their investment (Jensen and Meckling, 1976; Douma and Schreuder, 1991).

It is impossible to fully review here the rich body of research on the principal-agent relationship. However, it seems that students of entrepreneurial management and public policy can develop a better understanding of the issues involved in contracting out by studying the insights that are offered by economists about principal-agent relations and transaction costs.

Last but not least, Miranda (1994) pointed out why Niskanen's (1971) "budget maximizing bureaucrat" does not capture the true reality expressed by the term "discretion maximizing bureaucrat." Miranda (1992, 1994) ably explained that bureaucratic power results not from the total budget the bureaucrat is allocated, but that part of it over which he or she has complete discretion. Miranda (1992, 1994) further illustrates how the ability to channel contracts to supporters provided Mayor Washington of Chicago with a power base which was independent of the control of the "party." As our case illustrates, the Mayor of Nashville has done just that. Instead of having to comply with Council oversight of the MEO, he managed to expand his ability to award a large size contract for professional services. Not only that, he can award the contract without going through a process of open bidding or having to give it to the lowest bidder.

Under these circumstances, some of the restraints the "principal," i.e., Nashville residents or the electorate, assumed they have in place to guard their interest are gone. The Council, the other agent of the same "principal," and elected to help guard that interest, ends up empowering the Mayor and allowing him to use other than pure economic considerations in producing city services. At the end, under the pretenses of efficiency and effectiveness, the best interest of the Mayor, the "agent," seems to prevail over the interest of the "principal."

REFERENCES

Arrow, K.J. (1985). The Economics of Agency. In R. Zeckhauser, & J.W. Pratt (Eds.), *Principals and Agents: The Structure of Business*. Boston: Harvard Business School Press.

Barney, J.B., & Hesterly, W. (1996). Organizational Economics: Understanding the Relationships Between Organizations and Economic Analysis. In S. Clegg, C. Hardy, & W.R. Nord (Eds.), *Handbook of Organization Studies* (pp. 115-147). Thousand Oaks: Sage Publications.

Bonner, S., & Sprinkle, G. (2002). The effects of monetary incentives on effort and task performance: theories, evidence, and a framework for research. *Accounting, Organizations and Society, 27*(4), 303-345.

Bouwens, J.F., & van Lent, L.A.G.M. (2003). *Effort and Selection Effects of Incentive Contracts* (Discussion Paper No. 2003-130; ISSN 0924-7815). Tilburg University, Center for Economic Research. Retrieved December 20, 2006, from *http://greywww.kub.nl:2080/greyfiles/center/2003/doc/130.pdf*

Bryant, J., Chester, T., & Nicolson, G. (1997). *Privatizing Local Government Services* (Unpublished Seminar Paper). Nashville.

Chow, C.W. (1983). The effects of job standard tightness and compensation scheme on performance: an exploration of linkages. *The Accounting Review, 58*(4), 667-685.

Courty, P., & Marschke, G. (2003). *Dynamics of performance measurement systems* (Working Paper). Retrieved December 20, 2006, from *http://faculty.london.edu/ pcourty/mypubfiles/orep.pdf*

Courty, P., & Marschke, G. (2004). *A general test of gaminq* (Discussion Paper No. 4514; ISSN 0265-8003). London: Centre for Economic Policy Research.

Deci, E.L., & Flaste, R. (1995). *Why we do what we do: the dynamics of personal autonomy*. New York: Putnam & Sons.

Deci, E.L. (1971). Effects of externally mediated rewards on intrinsic motivation. *Journal of Personality and Social Psychology, 18*, 105-115.

De La Cruz, B.M. (March 20, 1998). New medical examiner sets goals. *The Tennessean*, p. 2B.

Douma, S. W., & Schreuder, H. (1991). *Economic approaches to organizations* (pp. 77-101). New York: Prentice Hall.

Fredrickson, G. (1997). When politics becomes administration. *PA Times, 20*(11), 6.

Freeman, R.B. (1997). Working for nothing: The supply of volunteer labor. *Journal of Labor Economics, 15*(1), 140-166.

Freeman, R.E. (1984). *Strategic management: A stakeholder approach.* Boston: Pitman.

Frey, B.S., & Jegen, R. (1999). *Motivation Crowding Theory: A Survey of Empirical Evidence* (Working Paper No. 26, ISSN 1424-0459). Zurich: Institute for Empirical Research in Economics, University of Zurich. Retrieved December 20, 2006, from http://e-collection.ethbib.ethz.ch/ecol-pool/incoll/incoll_562.pdf

Garrigan, L.M. (1997, March 13). Insufficient funds: without more revenue what's Bredesen got left to spend? *Nashville Scene*, pp. 16-23.

Halachmi, A. (1996). Franchising in government: can a principal-agent perspective be the first step towards the development of a theory? *Policy Studies Journal, 24*, 478-494.

Halachmi, A. (1996a). Promises and pitfalls on the way to SEA. In A. Halachmi, & G. Bouckaert (Eds.), *Organizational performance and measurement in the public sector toward service, effort, and accomplishment reporting* (pp. 77-100). Westport: Quorum Books.

Halachmi, A. (1998). Franchising in government: an idea in search of a theory. In A. Halachmi, & P. B. Boorsma (Eds.), *Inter and intra government arrangements for productivity an agency approach* (pp. 45-58). Boston: Kluwer Academic Publishers.

Halachmi, A. (2002). Performance measurement: a look at some possible dysfunctions. *Work Study, 51*(5), 230-239.

Halachmi, A. (2005). Performance measurement: test the water before you dive in. *International Review of Administrative Sciences, 71*(2), 255-266.

Halachmi, A. (2005a). The role of the manager in employee motivation. In S. E. Condrey, & J. L. Perry (Eds.), *Handbook of human resource management in government* (pp. 469-498). San Francisco: Jossey-Bass.

Holzemr, & Moritz, B. (April 14, 1997). Harlan offers to again handle examiner's office. *Nashville Banner*, p. A5.

Jensen, M.C., & Meckling, W.H. (1976). Theory of the firm, managerial behavior, agency cost and ownership structure. *Journal of Financial Economics, 3*, 305-360.

Kettl, D.F. (1993). *Sharing power public governance and private markets.* Washington, D.C: The Brookings Institution.

Kettl, D.F. (1997). The global revolution in public management: driving themes, missing links. *Journal of Policy Analysis and Management, 16*(3), 446-462.

Killick, T. (1997). Principals, agents and the failings of conditionality. *Journal of International Development, 9*(4), 483-495.

Lowi, T. (1964). American business, public policy, case studies and political theory. *World Politics, 16*(3), 677-715.

Milgrom, P., & Roberts, J. (1995). Complementarities and fit: strategy, structure, and organizational change in manufacturing. *Journal of Accounting and Economics, 19*(2), 179-208.

Miranda, R.A. (1992). *Privatizing City Government: Explaining the Budgetary Consequences of Alternative Service Delivery Arrangements.* Unpublished doctoral dissertation, University of Illinois, Chicago.

Miranda, R.A. (1994). Privatization and the budget maximizing bureaucrat. *Public Productivity and Management Review, 17*(4), 355-370.

Moritz, B. (1997). Bids for private water/sewer firms on hold until council shows interest. *Nashville Banner.*

Moritz, B. (April 14, 1997a). Harlan offers to again handle examiner's office. *Nashville Banner*, p. A3.

Moritz, B. (July 25, 1997b). Medical examiner making changes. *Nashville Banner*, p. A5.

Neelen, G.H.J.M. (1993). *Principal-Agent Relations in Non-profit Organizations.* Unpublished doctoral dissertation, University of Twente, Enschede, The Netherlands.

Niskanen, W.A. (1971). *Bureaucracy and representative government.* Chicago: Aldine-Atherton.

Prager, J. (1994). Contracting out government services. *Public Administration Review, 54*(2), 176-184.

Prendergast, C. (1999). The provision of incentives in firms. *Journal of Economic Literature, 37*, 7-63.

Prendergast, C. (2002). Uncertainty and incentives. *Journal of Labor Economics, 20*(2), 115-137.

Ross, S.A. (1973). The economic theory of agency: the principal's problem. *American Economic Review, 63*, 134-139.

Salisbury, R.E., & Heinz, J. (1970). A theory of policy analysis and some preliminary applications. In I. Sharkansky (Ed.), *Policy analysis in political science* (pp. 39-60). Chicago: Markham.

Savas, E. S. (1982). *Privatizing the public sector: how to shrink government.* Chatham: Chatham House Publishers.

Savas, E.S. (1987). *Privatization the key to better government.* Chatham: Chatham House Publishers.

Sliwka, D.D. (2003). *On the Hidden Costs of Incentive Scheme* (Discussion Paper No. 844). Bonn, Germany: IZA. Retrieved December 20, 2006, from ftp://repec.iza.org/RePEc/Discussionpaper/dp844.pdf

Spence, M., & Zeckhauser, R. (1971). Insurance, information and individual action. *American Economic Review, 61*, 380-387.

Waller, W., & Chow, C. (1985). The self-selection and effort effects of standard based employment contracts: a framework and some empirical evidence. *The Accounting Review, 60*(3), 458-476.

Williamson, D.E. (1991). Comparative economic organization: the analysis of discrete structural alternatives. *Administrative Service Quarterly, 36*, 269-296.

Chapter 11

THE INCREASINGLY COMPLEX POLICY FIELD OF MULTIPLE PRINCIPALS AND AGENTS: EFFECTIVE AID IN PROBLEMATIC PERSONAL DEBT SITUATIONS

Peter B. Boorsma and
Judith L.J.L. Tijdink

Institutions which can be thought of as organizations, decision-making procedures, and legislative rules and norms have been the subject of interest to social scientists like North (1986), Williamson (1985) and Shepsle (1986) over the last decades (Powell and DiMaggio, 1991). The study of institutions has been taken up by many disciplines, such as: economics, organization theory, political science and public choice, history, and sociology. The common subject in these studies relates to a scepticism towards atomistic accounts of social processes and a conviction that institutional arrangements and processes matter (Powell & DiMaggio, 1991). However, there are various approaches to the study of institutions. The alternative definitions of the term 'institution' is a case in point. In new institutional economics, institutions are, for instance, defined as 'customs and rules that provide a set of incentives and disincentives for individuals' (North, 1986) or as 'governance structures, social arrangements geared to minimize transaction costs' (Williamson, 1985). Political scientists in the rational-choice and game-theory tradition use definitions such as 'frameworks of rules, procedures and arrangements' (Shepsle, 1986). As political scientists tend to reserve the term 'institutions' for those frameworks closely associated with organizational relations, sociologists use a broad definition of institutions in order to include symbol systems, cognitive scripts, and normative codes (Hall & Taylor, 1994). As striking as these differences in definitions may be, an important commonality is that they all connote stable designs for chronically repeated activity sequences (Jepperson in Powell and DiMaggio, 1991). This chapter addresses the role of institutions in dealing with problematic personal debts by conceptualizating institutions in two different ways: institutions as regulations; and, institutions as organizations.

The regulations definitions set refers to arrangements for overindebted consumers, viz. debt assistance out of court and legal debt settlements. In the Dutch situation, the following forms of debt assistance out of court are provided: budgetary advice, budgetary control, debt mediation and debt consolidation. The organizations refer to the various agencies that provide debt assistance. In the Dutch situation, different agencies try to solve the problem of problematic personal debts; such as the municipal loan bank (MLB), the municipal social service (MSS), welfare work, and private agencies contracted by the municipality. These agencies will be denoted as 'institutes' in the policy field of problematic debts in order to distinguish them from the arrangements for overindebted consumers (who will be denoted as 'institutions').

The policy concerning overindebted Dutch citizens is developed at the local level by each city. This may explain the existence of so many different ways of assisting individuals with personal debts. Looking at this issue from a public-policy point of view one must ask what is the most effective way of dealing with problematic personal debt situations? It seems to us that in order to answer this question one must give due consideration to the implications of neo institutional economics, especially the Principal Agent Theory. This theory offers an interesting perspective for analyzing the process of debt assistance.

The second section will begin by providing some background information on problematic personal debt situations. Next, the various forms of debt assistance (the institutions) will be discussed, as well as the effectiveness of these institutions. The fourth section will deal with the various debt assisting agencies (the institutes) as well as the findings of the Boorsma Committee which paid special attention to the attitudes and working methods of these institutes in the Netherlands. The chapter continues by focusing on the theory of neo institutional economics, particularly Principal Agent Theory. It concludes by drawing on this body of theory to formulate some hypotheses as to the most effective debt assistance constellation. These hypotheses reflect emerging lines of thought regarding the policy field discussed, which may be field tested in the early part of the new millennium.

PROBLEMATIC PERSONAL DEBT SITUATIONS

It is estimated that some 200,000 households in the Netherlands (about 3 percent of the total households) cope with problematic personal debts (Boorsma Committee-Report, 1994). According to the Dutch Ministry of Social Affairs, a problematic personal debt (PPD) is defined as a situation in which a household has debts and has problems paying the rent or mortgage; and/or problems with paying gas, water and electricity bills (Vermeulen, *et al.*, 1992). However, in the Netherlands as well as in other countries, variant definitions are also used (Haane in Huls, *et al.*, 1994). In Belgium, for example, a household is regarded as being overindebted when there is a default in repayment of more than three months (National Report on Belgium, 1994). According to this definition, between 3% and 4% of the Belgium population has problematic personal debts. In Germany, a PPD is defined as a situation in which the monthly salary is no longer sufficient to meet the payments due by law (National Report on Germany, 1994). About 4.3% of the German population is confronted with such a situation. Denmark has no record of the total number of PPD situations. Only the number of 'bad payers', i.e. the number of persons who have been in default since the first month of the agreement, are registered, some 11% of Denmark's population (National Report on Denmark, 1994).

The lack of agreement on how a PPD is defined deserves closer examination. One reason is that while the implications of PPD's on national economies, the social fabric and the political agenda may be the same, as a public policy issue, countries seem to treat it differently. Yet this diversity of perspectives and approaches in dealing with PPD's, though unintended, hampers the prospects of simple analysis and comparison of international data.

Numerous Dutch authors, e.g., (Vermeulen, 1992; Dessart, et al., 1982; Oude Engberink, 1994; Schep & Bommeljé, 1994) have dealt with the question to what extent households with problematic debts differ from households without these problems. The authors usually try to make a profile of the overindebted households by analyzing several factors such as the age of the family head, number and age of children, budget control, income and outlay level, and number of debts. For instance, Vermeulen, et al., (1992) performed a longitudinal study on the financial situation of Dutch households and concluded that families with many children and an unemployed family head under sixty-five years of age are a high risk group for ending up in a PPD-situation. Contrary to this conclusion, Dessart, et al., (1982) found that institutional rather than personality factors determine the risk of ending up in a PPD-situation. Particular important institutional factors are: the credit acceptance system (i.e. granting persons, who already have one or more credit(s), with another credit), the credit rating system (i.e. the non-use of an objective credit rating system, so that certain issues are overlooked), and the distribution channel of credit (i.e. arrangements of credits by intermediaries such as insurance agents).

Whereas Vermeulen and Dessart sketch a picture of overindebted households in all income groups, most Dutch authors have dealt with the position of low income groups, particularly the beneficiaries (Oude Engberink, 1984/1987/1994; Engbersen & Van der Veen, 1987; Brand, 1989; Hoekstra, 1990; Schep & Bommeljé, 1994). The conclusions of these authors are alarming: over 40 percent of all beneficiaries cope with financial problems. Brand (1989) and Hoekstra (1990) empirically found that beneficiaries with financial problems differ from other beneficiaries in that they have a greater number of children, lower standard of education, more expensive houses and higher aspirations. Moreover, in the group of beneficiaries with financial problems, there is an over-representation of migrant families, households in the age group of 30 to 45 years, and one-parent families.

The risk factors for PPD-situations in the Dutch case seem to bear a strong resemblance to those in other countries. According to Reifner & Ford (1992) who studied the rise of default in Europe, the major reasons for this rise are relatively consistent among all countries in their study. These influences are: unemployment; rising levels of divorce and relationship breakdown; growth of low wage; less secure work; illness; rising costs; and over-commitment in terms of borrowing.

American studies on PPD's deal with persons in default (Caplovitz, 1974), persons who are declared bankrupt (Sullivan, 1989), and persons who can not use credit effectively (Tokunaga, 1993; Zhu & Meeks, 1994). The seminal study of Caplovitz, 'Consumers in trouble', was one of the first studies on PPD's. In examining the causes underlying payment defaults in America, Caplovitz starts with the basic principle of consumer credit, i.e., a client should have the capacity and the willingness to meet his liabilities. From that starting point Caplovitz distinguishes between two main causes for defaults. First, he names deficiencies in the client's capacity to fulfill his obligations. These deficiencies can be caused by a sudden income reduction, an unexpected increase in outlays, family problems or obligations 'to a third party'. Second, there are deficiencies in the client's willingness to repay his debts. Deficiencies in this willingness can be caused by bad faith, or temporary absence or deficient debt collection practices by the creditor, causing low debtor morale.

Several authors have taken Caplovitz as a starting point for their study on PPD's[1]. For instance, Zhu & Meeks, (1994) employed the concepts of ability and willingness to use credit in their investigation on the use of consumer credit by low income families in America. The authors found that the amount of credit outstanding in 1986 was predominantly determined by the credit balance in 1983 and the household head's employment status and age. Furthermore, two interaction variables played a significant role, namely (a) the specific attitude towards credit, together with the head's educational level, and (b) this attitude, together with the debt balance in 1983.

Other authors who have dealt with (problematic) debts of households are: Sullivan, *et al.*, (1989); and Tokunaga, (1993). The findings of these authors will be discussed briefly because attention is paid to certain factors influencing PPD situations which are not mentioned in the previously discussed studies.

Sullivan, *et al.*, (1989) studied bankruptcies in America. They found that married women who have chosen a traditional social role (staying at home, as housewife and mother) are a group with a high risk of bankruptcy. Furthermore, they demonstrated that a substantial proportion of individual bankruptcies (ten percent of the cases, twenty-five percent of the debts) are failed entrepreneurs. Debtors who purportedly abuse the credit card system (the so called 'credit card junkies') or debtors who continually use bankruptcy to escape financial obligations (the so called 'repeaters') together form less than seven percent of the total sample.

Tokunaga, (1993), in a multidisciplinary approach, explored differences between American consumers who can, and consumers who cannot use credit effectively. Particular attention was paid to the additional predictability of psychological variables beyond variables such as demographic characteristics and recent experiences of adverse life events. It was found that psychological variables significantly increase the ability to correctly identify people with credit-related problems: unsuccessful credit users displayed

---

[1] See also the study of Boorsma, et al., (1988) 'Door de bank geregeld'.

an external locus of control (i.e., believed that their lives were controlled by forces outside of their own), lower self efficacy, viewed money as a source of power and prestige, took fewer steps to retain their money, displayed lower risk-taking and sensation-seeking tendencies, and expressed greater anxiety about financial matters than successful users.

FORMS OF DEBT ASSISTANCE AS INSTITUTIONS

In most European countries, some sort of assistance for persons with PPD's is provided. This assistance can take various forms and each of these can be regarded as an institution in the policy field of problematic debts. In this section, two categories of such institutions will be distinguished: debt assistance out of court, and legal debt settlement regulations. The discussion will concentrate on the institutions in the Dutch case, especially the institutions regarding the debt assistance out of court. Furthermore, attention will be paid to the effectiveness of these institutions.

Debt assistance out of court

Generally speaking, four different kinds of debt assistance out of court, viz. four institutions, can be distinguished in the Netherlands. First, debtors can ask debt assisting agencies for *budgetary advice*. This advice aims at changing the debtor's spending pattern. Usually the debtor is taught how to write up a cash book and how to make an estimate of receipts and expenditures. Second, debtors may request an agency to carry out *budgetary control*. This means that the agency withholds a certain amount of benefits or wages from the debtor and uses it to pay the debtor's fixed costs of living. For both institutions discussed, the agency is (mainly) involved with the debtor, not with the creditors.

The other two institutions refer to arrangements in which the agency negotiates with the creditors on the debtor's behalf. These arrangements are commonly denoted as 'debt settlements'. Two forms are possible: debt mediation and debt consolidation. Both of these forms may include a partial remission of the debts. *Debt mediation* refers to an arrangement whereby a debt assisting agency acts as an intermediary between both parties in order to achieve a debt settlement. This arrangement deals with the amount which has to be repaid and the period of redemption. In the case of *debt consolidation*, the agency not only acts as an intermediary between debtor and creditors but also grants the debtor a special loan with which the creditors are paid immediately. In the Netherlands, only one debt assisting agency can grant these loans, namely the municipal loan bank (MLB). These loans will therefore be denoted as 'MLB-loans'. When debt consolidation has been done, the debtor only has to deal with one creditor: the municipal loan bank.

In realizing a debt settlement, the agencies commonly use the Debt Regulation Code of Conduct, developed by the umbrella organization of the municipal loan banks (NVVK). Important elements of this Code are:

a. agencies do not assist in debt settlements if only part of the debt package is involved;
b. the debtor has to put all his repayment capability at the disposal of solving of his debts;
c. the maximum term of a debt settlement is 36 months.

The various institutions in the policy field of problematic personal debts, as has been described above, are characterized by a low level of effectiveness: 75% of the debtors do not get in touch with the debt assistance agencies or can not be helped by it. Households who do not get in touch with the debt assistance agencies can be subdivided into two groups. The first group refers to households which find a solution for their problematic debt situation without the aid of a debt assisting agency, but with the help of family or friends for example. The second group, however, is permanently pursued by creditors, and is often confronted with visits of bailiffs, or attachment on wages or benefits.

Besides the aforementioned households that do not get in touch with the debt assistance agencies, there is a group of households that cannot be helped by it. In 1993, for example, about 23,000 requests for debt settlement were submitted to the municipal loan banks. Approximately 50% of these requests were refused (NVVK 1994). This percentage was also found in a large scale research of Boorsma, *et al.*, (1988), which will be discussed in more detail.

Boorsma, *et al.*, reviewed the (mainly Dutch) literature on debt settlements by MLB's (hereinafter called 'MLB arrangements') and distinguish between factors which influence the realization of such arrangements, both theoretical as well as empirical. The following *a priori* classification of factors are used: personality characteristics, behavioral characteristics, budget characteristics, debt characteristics, municipal bank characteristics and other factors.

According to an IVA study (Baayens & Verstegen, 1985) personality characteristics which are important in realizing an MLB arrangement are: gender, nationality, residence, age, civil status, family and profession. The impact of these factors have not been empirically tested in this study. Caplovitz (1974) found empirical evidence for the impact of ethnic background, age, profession and schooling. One or more of these factors were also found by: Van Nieuwburg, (1982): De Vos, *et al.*, (1983): and De Greef, *et al.*, (1985). In the Netherlands in 1982, race could, of course, not be expected to play such an important role as it does in the USA (apart from central cities like Amsterdam and Rotterdam), but it could play an increasing role in the nineties and beyond. Furthermore, empirical research indicates that family phase, civil status, religion, length of employment, and unemployment affect the realization of an MLB arrangement (Dessart, *et al.*, 1982; De Vos, *et al.*, 1983; De Greef, *et al.*, 1985).

Theoretically, the following behavioral characteristics are indicated as having an impact on the realization of an MLB arrangement: former credit experience, personal budget control, morality, blameworthy conduct, and concealment of information. The impact of the first two characteristics has been empirically demonstrated (Van Nieuwburg, 1982; and Dessart, *et al.*, 1982, respectively). With regard to the budget characteristics, the factors indicated by theory are: income, outlay level, financial reserves, changes in income and/or outlay level, wealth, and house ownership. The empirical relevance of the first three factors has been demonstrated by several authors (Caplovitz, 1974; Van Nieuwburg, 1982; Dessart, *et al.*, 1982; De Vos, 1982; De Greef, *et al.*, 1985). Debt characteristics which, according to theory, might have some impact are: attitudes of creditors; and number, size and nature of outstanding debts. Other than the creditors' attitude, all of these factors have an empirical impact on the realization of an MLB arrangement (Dessart, *et al.*, 1982; De Greef, *et al.*, 1985).

As can be seen in this review, only scant attention has been paid to the characteristics of the providers of debt assistance. In the IVA study, the characteristics of the MLB play a theoretical role. These characteristics are: the policy field they primarily focus on, their degree of autonomy, their profitability, and some other factors such as the complexity of the surroundings. Bank characteristics as an influential factor are also mentioned in the study by Dessart, *et al.*, (1982). These characteristics are specified as credit acceptance policy and credit rating system. They turn out to be empirically relevant. Apart from these bank characteristics, "other" factors are mentioned in two studies. Only one of the reviewed studies mentions other debt assisting agencies via a factor which they name 'contact with welfare work' (De Greef, *et al.*, 1985).

Boorsma, *et al.*, (1988) start with the following model for an MLB arrangement (see figure 1).

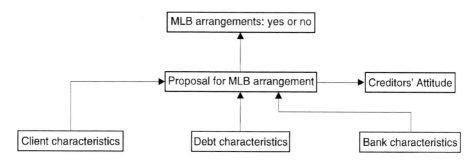

Figure 1: Model for a debt solving arrangement (Boorsma *et al.* 1988)

In this model the 'client characteristics' category covers the first three characteristics mentioned above (personality, behaviourial and budget). The bank characteristics are divided into two groups. Group 1 consists of the factors related to the willingness of the MLB to cooperate with the client: bank targets and bank vision (although these two are logically closely connected). Group 2 consists of the factors related to the bank's capacity to cooperate with the client: various financial factors, the ties with the municipality, the selection of instruments used, and some environmental characteristics.

Boorsma, *et al.*, (1988) have performed two types of empirical research. First, a large survey of the empirical relation between the realization of an MLB arrangement on the one hand, and clients' characteristics and debt characteristics on the other has been done. Secondly, the bank's characteristics have been researched. Some of the conclusions are:

a. Of the personality characteristics, only the clients' residence may have some influence;
b. Behavioral characteristics, taken together to construct a scale variable 'morality', are significant;
c. Of the budget characteristics, only the repayment capacity has an impact;
d. Of the debt characteristics, the size and character of the outstanding debts is significant;
e. Due to the lack of necessary data, the influence of bank characteristics can not be determined.

In addition to this large scale research by Boorsma, *et al.*, some other authors have also studied the effectiveness of debt assistance in the Netherlands. De Greef (1992) has done Ph.D. research on the factors influencing the realization of an MLB arrangement. He distinguishes three factors that may have a theoretical impact on this realization: the working methods of the public actors providing debt assistance, the intensity of cooperation between these actors, and the characteristics of the households in debt. In determining the influence of the working methods, De Greef makes a distinction between four welfare orientations: the allowance model, the self sufficiency model, the guardianship model and the support model. Each model refers to the attitude of a debt assistance agency towards the debtor after the realization of an MLB arrangement.

In the allowance model, the debt assistance agency withholds a certain amount of benefits or wages from the debtor on preventive grounds. This means that the agency pays the fixed costs and the debtor only receives some housekeeping money to live on. In the self sufficiency model, the agency assumes that no further aid is necessary after the MLB arrangement is realized. The household is expected to keep itself out of financial trouble. The guardianship model refers to long-lasting and intensive assistance by the agency. The responsibility for the debt problem is taken away from the debtor. Finally, the support model aims at changing the debtor's behaviour. The agency provides budgetary advice and psychosocial aid.

In the empirical part of his study, De Greef demonstrated that public stakeholders/actors consider the self sufficiency model to be the most effective assistance model, whereas households consider the allowance model to be the most effective one. With regard to the intensity of cooperation between the public stakeholders/actors, the empirical results in this study indicate that a project approach to debt assistance does not lead to more debt problems being solved than a non-project approach. Finally, the inventory of household characteristics led to the conclusion that both the households and the public actors believe that the debt problems of those who are lowest on the social ladder (unemployed single parents) are solved least often, while the debt problems of couples (unemployed with children) are solved most often.

Hulshof (1993) investigated the effects of different models of cooperation on the effectiveness of the debt assistance process. She concluded that the effectiveness of a certain model largely depends on the specific municipal situation. It is thus not possible to point out one best model of debt assistance. It should be noted that this study lacks a rigorous scientific approach: by studying just a few cases, it was impossible from the outset to draw any general conclusions.

In the preceding, four institutions regarding debt assistance out of court in the Netherlands, have been discussed. One or more of these institutions are also present in other West European countries. For instance, in Germany and Britain debt assistance is mainly offered by means of budgetary advice and debt settlement. Furthermore, Britain introduced the National Debtline, viz. a telephone helpline for people with debt problems throughout the country, and a consultancy service to other advisers. The National Debtline provides clients with self help kits, information and support over the telephone to enable them to negotiate with creditors and courts themselves (National Report on Britain, 1994).

Although in Ireland the field of debt assistance is very underdeveloped and mainly confined to budgetary advice, some pilot projects dealing with moneylending and debt counselling are in the pipeline. Furthermore, the Irish Minister for Social Welfare has established a guarantee fund with the support of financial institutions. The purpose of this fund was to guarantee loans from Credit Unions to borrowers who were in debt to moneylenders, in order to allow them to normalise their credit situation (National Report on Ireland, 1994). In Denmark, Spain, Italy, and Greece, institutions regarding debt assistance are almost absent.

Legal debt settlement regulations

In most West European countries, there are (draft) regulations concerning the settlement of consumers' debts. The present form of these regulations has been shaped by the development of the economic bankruptcy law, which was intended for commercial debtors. Some countries (like Denmark, Germany, and the Netherlands) have amended this traditional bankruptcy legislation by developing their own philosophies on how to cope with overindebted consumers. They nevertheless used the tools of the traditional bankruptcy procedures. The French model seems to be an exception: the model developed from consumer credit and mortgage loan legislation. From the outset, the French law aimed at preventing people from falling into overindebtedness, rather than at the distribution of property to creditors (see Reifner in Huls, *et al.*, 1994).

Although the technical design of (draft) consumer overindebtedness regulations differs between the West European countries, the models adopted broadly embody the same philosophy. The common elements of the various models will be presented below. First, a short summary of the Dutch model as proposed in the new Bankruptcy Act will be given.

In December, 1992, the Dutch government introduced a proposal concerning the amendment of the Law on Bankruptcy as regards the settlement of debts of natural persons[2] (Second Chamber, Document 22969, nr. 1-9, 1992-1993 / 1993-1994). This proposal is commonly denoted as the legal debt settlement regulation[3]. Its aim is to prevent natural persons with problematic debts from being pursued by creditors for the rest of their life. The outline of the regulation is as follows.

A natural person who has run into a problematic debt situation can request the Court to apply the legal debt settlement regulation. When the prospects that the debtor will positively cooperate in the implementation of a repayment plan are satisfactory, the Court will declare the regulation applicable. From that moment, a moratorium with regard to the rights of the creditors applies. This means that creditors can not demand the recovering of their claims and can not take other measures such as attachments on property, wages, or benefits. The debtor is obliged to submit to the Court a draft repayment plan and is allowed to submit a draft settlement.

After at most three months of declaring the regulation applicable, a verification meeting is held. At this meeting, the necessary verification of the creditors' claims takes place. Furthermore, the creditors give their opinion on the draft repayment plan and vote on the draft settlement (if submitted by the debtor). There are no strong demands as to the number of creditors which have to vote in favour of the draft settlement. Under the circumstances, the official receiver may pass a rejection and pronounce the draft settlement to be accepted. An accepted settlement has to be sanctioned by the Court.

If no draft settlement is submitted, *or* if the submitted draft settlement is rejected (and also not pronounced to be accepted by the official receiver), *or* if the homologation is refused, the Court first decides if the legal debt settlement regulation will be continued. In the affirmative case, the Court decides on a repayment plan. The plan always indicates the terms during which the regulation is effective. These terms may vary between a very short period and at most five years, counting from the moment that the regulation has been declared applicable. Furthermore, the plan may indicate a fixed nominal sum to increase the amount of money that will not be part of the estate.

Through the assessment of the repayment plan, the estate becomes bankrupt and payment of the creditors can take place. This payment occurs according to a certain distributive code by which (juridical) preferential creditors receive a percentage on their claims that is three times as high as the percentage ordinary creditors receive. When the debtor has fulfilled the obligations resulting from the legal debt settlement regulation and the repayment plan, the remaining debts will be turned into natural obligations which can not be enforced by creditors.

As was noted before, the models of (draft) consumer overindebtedness regulations in West-European countries broadly embody the same philosophy. Reifner (in Huls *et al.*, 1994) summarizes the following common elements:

---

[2] In Dutch: 'Wetsvoorstel tot wijziging van de Faillissementswet in verband met de sanering van schulden van natuurlijke personen'.
[3] In Dutch: 'Wettelijke schuldsaneringsregeling'.

- *Need*: all countries agree on the need to admit that their traditional bankruptcy legislation can not effectively confront the problems of private individuals.
- *Eligibility*: nearly all procedures restrict access for private individuals in non commercial activity, even though it is acknowledged that private debtors may have old commercial debts.
- *Debtor's initiative*: all procedures can only be instigated by the debtor.
- *Wage earner's plan*: with the exception of East Germany and Great Britain, all countries include the future earnings of a consumer within debt rescheduling (repayment plan).
- *Discharge*: all countries allow for discharge from those debts that are included within the plan and which will not be paid off in the given time limit.
- *Abuse*: all schemes have provisions to exclude those persons who abuse the scheme, both at the time of application as well as when considering the practical benefits available under the procedures.

In this section, it was shown that the assistance offered to the Dutch debtor takes various forms: budgetary advice, budgetary control, debt mediation, and debt consolidation. In the near future, this assistance will be extended when the legal debt settlement regulation becomes operative. Furthermore, it was shown that various authors have studied the effectiveness of the debt assistance process. The conclusions of these authors concerning the factors which influence this effectiveness, more or less point in the same direction. Nevertheless, some might question if the complex of ideas used is a theory at all: yet it definitely looks as if there is a phenomenon in search of a public policy theory. It is clear that various authors with different backgrounds have dealt with an empirical issue -problematic debts- and with some institutions related to the solving of these debts.

DEBT ASSISTING AGENCIES AS INSTITUTES[4]

The previous section has shown that in the Dutch literature on the effectiveness of the debt assistance process, attention has focused on the creditors, the debtors and the debt characteristics. Furthermore, the previous section demonstrated that some, albeit scant, attention has been paid to the characteristics of the MLB involved, and even less attention to other debt assisting agencies. If one is interested in the debt assistance process and its effectiveness, one should obviously study the process itself, with its organization, its different stakeholders/actors and their interplay. To that end this section of the chapter describes the role of the different actors with particular attention to the various debt assisting agencies - the institutes in this public policy arena in the Netherlands. The following institutes play a role in this case: the municipal loan bank (MLB), the munici-

---

[4] This section is mainly based on the findings of the Boorsma Committee, which was set up by the Department for Social Affairs and Employment in the Netherlands in order to offer advice on future policy on PPD-situations. The authors were the chairman and the assistant to the chairman, respectively.

pal social service (MSS), welfare work and private agencies contracted by the municipality.

It should be noted that cities are likely to differ in the types of institutes playing a role, and the specific roles played by a specific type of institute. For example, not all Dutch cities have their own MLB. Instead, some cities might participate in intermunicipal loan banks. Citizens from cities with no MLB, might demand service from an MLB in another city. In some cases there is a prior formal agreement that such an MLB will operate as an intermunicipal bank. However, citizens of one city may apply to the MLB in another city even in the absence of such an agreement. In the last case, the city which provides the service will have to deal with the issue of charging the local authority where the service recipient resides for the services provided.

In a problematic debt situation the actors involved are: the debtor, the creditor and the debt assisting agencies. The attitude of these actors, provisions in Dutch legislation and the organization of the process of debt assistance, influence the interplay among these actors and thereby the effectiveness of the debt assistance process. In the following we discuss the findings of the Boorsma Committee with regard to these subjects. This committee was installed by the Ministry of Social Affairs and Employment in the Netherlands and was charged with analyzing the area of problematic household debts. It should be emphasized that the approach of the committee was a qualitative one, based on expert opinion.

The Boorsma Committee concluded that there are several bottlenecks in the process of preventing and solving PPD's. This is due to the attitude of *debtors and creditors*. With regard to the preventive aspect: debtors do not use the existing provisions for income support and (especially public) creditors fail to set up adequate debt collection practices[5]. With regard to the solution aspect: debtors are not willing to meet the demands of a debt settlement (e.g., selling the car or cutting down expenditure) and creditors are not willing to accept less than the total amount of the outstanding debts (i.e., no partial remission of the debts). It should be noted that this tough attitude of creditors is sometimes caused by provisions in law and regulation. For instance, the General Social Security Act obliges municipal social services to reclaim the amount of excess welfare paid from the beneficiary. As a result of this, the MSS does not have much opportunity to give partial remission of this claim c.q. debt. Another example concerns the instructions to housing associations from the Ministry of Housing, Regional Development and Environment. According to these instructions, housing associations have to spend all their resources on public housing. This means that, except under special circumstances, they are obliged to reclaim the total amount of rent in arrears.

The Boorsma Committee paid special attention to the attitudes and working methods of the *debt assisting agencies*. The Committee distinguished four main actors. In the first place there are the municipal loan banks. One of the key activities of these banks is the provision of social loans, usually small loans, at a low rate. More important for the

---

[5] The importance of an adequate debt collection system is shown for instance in the article 'Managing Consumer Credit Delinquency in the US Economy: A Multi-Billion Dollar Management Science application' by Makuch, et al. (1992).

subject of this chapter, however, these banks provide assistance in a PPD-situation. As stated before, the MLB is the only debt assisting agency that grants loans to debtors by which the creditors are paid immediately (MLB-loans). Next to debt consolidation by means of these loans, they offer debt assistance in the form of debt mediation, budgetary advice and budgetary control. The MLB's consider themselves to be an intermediary between debtor and creditor. They apply a bank's vision in accepting clients and approach the client in a less personal way. Most MLB's share the opinion that immaterial assistance, given by other public actors, should be complementary to the material assistance of the bank.

Next, there are the municipal social services. One of the main tasks of these services is the implementation of social security laws. As a result, the debt assistance is primarily focused on low income groups. The MSS give debt assistance by means of debt mediation, budgetary advice, and budgetary control. They also provide supplementary benefits for debts, e.g., by standing surety for the debtor's repayment of an MLB-loan, or by granting an incidental loan to a beneficiary in debt in order to prevent eviction or the disconnection of gas, water and electricity. If necessary, the MSS refers the client to other debt assisting agencies. Unlike the MLB's, social services approach their clients in a more personal way. The so called 'safety-net' function of the MSS plays a role in this, i.e., people can appeal for welfare when there is no alternative.

Thirdly, local welfare work agencies provide debt assistance by means of debt mediation, budgetary advice and, if necessary, by referring clients to other agencies. Furthermore, they offer a form of assistance which is characteristic of welfare work, namely psychosocial aid. According to the welfare workers, financial problems are caused by and are connected with other problems such as alcoholism, divorce and psychological problems. Therefore, budgetary advice and psychosocial aid are taken up simultaneously. The achievement of a healthy financial situation is not the first, or only, objective.

Finally, there are some private agencies contracted by the municipality. Unlike the welfare work agencies, their main objective is to achieve a healthy and stable financial situation for the households. As a result, a lot of attention is given to budgetary advice. Other tasks of these private agencies are debt mediation and advising on the debt problem.

The foregoing shows that the activities of the main institutes in the field of problematic debts are complementary as well as overlapping. According to the Boorsma Committee, this situation calls for close cooperation between these institutes. Nowadays however, this cooperation is usually missing. As a consequence, various bottle-necks in the process of debt assistance occur. Just to mention some (see also Hulshof, 1993):

- There is a lack of clarity about the division of tasks;
- There is no adequate reference to other organizations;
- The available expertise, experience and resources are not optimally allocated;
- The total offer of debt assistance is not known to the clients;
- The material and immaterial debt assistance are badly matched to each other.

The Boorsma Committee concluded that these bottlenecks involve a loss of effectiveness in the process of debt assistance. The committee thus pleads for an 'integrated approach'. This means that the various stakeholders/actors have to work together on the basis of an univocal philosophy and policy. The committee presented several steps in order to come to a successful implementation of such an approach. Summarized:

- Municipalities should develop and realize a debt policy which is based on an integrated approach (as described above), combined with a plain central direction.
- The detailed design of this policy should be a matter of local businesses. The same goes for the decision as to which agency or agencies should carry out this policy.
- The integrated debt policy should be based on a Code of Conduct, which is approved by both the debt assisting agencies as well as the creditors.
- The organization and objectives of the integrated debt assistance should be committed to paper.
- The Minister for Social Affairs and Employment should supervise the development and realization of an integrated debt policy by municipalities.
- The costs of an integrated debt policy will vary between municipalities. Those municipalities that have already realized a comprehensive policy will not be confronted with extra costs. The remaining municipalities will. They have to reallocate the resources of the municipal budget.

Up to now, four Dutch institutes in the policy field of problematic personal debts have been discussed. These institutes referred to specific debt assisting agencies offering some kind of help to the overindebted person. In most of the West European Countries these specific agencies are lacking. Exceptions are Great Britain and Germany. In Great Britain, specialized debt assistance is offered by the Citizens Advice Bureaux and by agencies within local authorities such as Welfare Rights Units and Social Services. Furthermore, there are independent Advice Centres such as the Birmingham Settlement Money Advice Centre. The Birmingham Settlement pioneered the debt assistance specialism and has continued to develop new methodologies and directions for debt assistance services. One of these developments was the National Debtline as discussed in the previous section (National Report on Britain, 1994). In Germany, specialized debt assistance is offered by various institutes such as welfare associations, ecclesial institutes, agencies within towns and regions, agencies set up by private initiatives, and consumer unions. Furthermore, debt assistance is offered by the consumer centres of the states and by many organizations as part of their usual welfare work (National Report on Germany, 1994).

In Ireland and France there exist no specialized debt assisting agencies. In Ireland, a debtor with rent arrears can seek council at the housing advice service (Threshold). An overindebted employee can ask advice from the social worker within his organization. Furthermore, some legal advice on the debt problem should be provided by legal organizations such as the Legal Aid Board and Coolock Community Law Centre. (National Report on Ireland 1994). In France, debt assistance is provided by the locally based Communal Center of Social Aid which houses all social workers as well as by the consumer centres and the trade unions (Aucliar in Reifner & Ford, 1992). In Denmark, Spain, Italy, Greece, and Belgium almost no institutes in the policy field of debt assistance exist. This assistance is provided mainly, or only, by credit institutions themselves (Haane in Huls, *et al.*, 1994).

EFFECTIVENESS AND NEO INSTITUTIONAL ECONOMICS

The previous section discussed the findings of the Boorsma Committee. This committee concluded that the relations between the debt assisting agencies affects the effectiveness of the process. On the basis of expert opinion, a plea was made in favour of an integrated approach, relative to other advice which may be given.

In this section it will be demonstrated that the impact of the various relations between actors and stakeholders on the one hand, and effectiveness on the other, also has a theoretical foundation. This foundation can be found in the theory of neo institutional economics, in particular, Principal Agent Theory. After a brief summary of this body of literature, its importance to the process of debt assistance will be illuminated. The concept of effectiveness will also be discussed.

The central issue in neo institutional economics concerns the question of the extent to which the performance of economic activities is determined by the specific institutional context in which those activities take place. The approach aims at a generalization of micro economic theory (e.g., weakening the assumption of complete information and free exchange), while retaining the core of the micro economic approach (stable preferences, rational choice model, equilibrium structures of interaction). Just like the neo classical theory, the basic assumption concerns the notion of a rational actor. This actor chooses elements of his opportunity set that will maximize his utility function. An opportunity set consists of the collection of alternatives which are feasible for the individual, given certain constraints. In neo institutional economics, these constraints not only refer to issues such as income, physical and technological limits, but also to the institutional context. Moreover, the institutions themselves may become the dependent variable and become 'endogenized'.

The neo institutional approach emphasizes these institutional constraints in different ways (see, e.g., Furubotn & Pejovich, 1974; De Alessi, 1983; Eggertsen, 1990). As a result of this, three movements ('theories') within this approach can be distinguished. First, Property Rights Theory, which stresses the different kinds of property rights associated with scarce commodities and their allocation between actors in different institutional arrangements. Second, Transaction Cost Theory, which emphasizes the different costs of exchange relations in markets and hierarchies. Third, Principal Agent Theory, which stresses the role of information asymmetry in economic relations where the agent possesses certain discretionary powers.

The impact of the relations between actors on the one hand and the effectiveness of a process on the other, can be theoretically demonstrated by taking a closer look at Principal Agent Theory. In this theory, attention focuses on the relation between a principal (i.e., the actor who is the owner of a company) and an agent (i.e., the actor who carries out some function on behalf of his principal). There is a case of information asymmetry in this relation when the agent's performances are difficult to observe (moral hazard), and when the agent is better informed about the production process than the principal (adverse selection). In this situation, discretionary powers for the agent come into being. The agent can use these powers to pursue his own objectives, which are possibly not the same as the objectives of the principal. As a result of this, there will be a divergence between the effectiveness wanted by the principal, and the effectiveness achieved. This divergence involves agency costs. According to Jensen & Meckling (1976), agency costs are the sum of monitoring costs, bonding costs and agency loss. The monitoring costs are all expenditures by the principal to limit those activities of the agent that diverge from the principal's interest. The bonding costs are all expenditures by the agent "to guarantee that he will not take certain actions which could harm the principal or to ensure that the principal will be compensated if he does take such actions" (Jensen & Meckling, 1976). Finally, the agency loss refers to the extent that agents, despite monitoring and bonding activities, succeed in pursuing their own (non-productive) objectives. In other words, there is a trade off in an agency relation between monitoring and bonding costs on the one hand and agency loss on the other. The central issue in agency theory concerns the question of how to structure the relationship between principal and agent in order to minimize the total agency costs.

Several authors have carried out empirical research on the existing agency relations in organizations. Only a few of these studies relate to financial institutions and are for that matter important for this chapter. For instance, Nicols (1967) and O'Hara (1981) investigated savings and loan associations (SLA's) in the United States. They both concluded that differences in ownership control strongly affect the performance of these associations: SLA's which were organized as stock companies had a better score on most performance indicators than SLA's which were organized as mutuals.

Principal Agent Theory offers an interesting perspective for analyzing the process of debt assistance. Since an alderman of a municipality formulates policy and provides funds for agencies, he can be considered a principal. The agency itself, in our case a debt assisting agency, can be considered the agent who carries out a function on behalf of the alderman. Because of information asymmetry, the principal does not know the organization as well as the agent does. Therefore, the principal has to devise the means to minimize agency costs, e.g., by monitoring the agent's behaviour.

Just to give an illustration of what can happen when monitoring is absent, let us take a look at the Dutch city of Zwolle (Boorsma Committee II, 1994)[6]. In Zwolle the head of the MLB had great discretionary powers. He attempted to use these powers to fulfill the objectives of politics and management (namely: putting more products on the market). On his own initiative, the head started the 'business credit facility' product. He was, how-

---

[6] In the Dutch city of Groningen almost the same situation occurred.

ever, careless in performing his task and did not apply the 'four-eyes principle'. Furthermore, he did not adequately make up files of transactions and exceeded his credit limit competence. Neither the alderman nor the director of the sector did anything to restrict the discretionary powers of the MLB head. Like everyone else, they relied on the good reputation of the head too much and did not engage in any monitoring. The head of the MLB went his own way, resulting in an unprepared, incompetent, inefficient and (considering the risks) irresponsible granting of business credits.

In this illustration, an MLB was identified as agent. There are, of course, more organizations in the process of debt assistance which are agents as well: municipal social services, welfare work agencies, and private agencies. Moreover, practice shows that more than one alderman may have the final responsibility for this process (e.g., the alderman for Social Affairs, as well as the alderman for Finance). Thus, in applying Principal Agent Theory to the process of debt assistance, we find more principals and more agents. This is quite a unique situation: the great majority of applications in theory and empirical research relate to situations with only one principal and one agent. When there are more agents, e.g., many housing corporations (Neelen, 1993) or universities (de Vries, 1992), the studies do not deal with the interrelations between these agents and the effects of these interrelations upon the principal.

The aggregate of principals and agents, and the relations between them, within a municipality can be termed a *debt assistance constellation*. As stated before, there will be differences between cities in the type of public actors who play a role, and between the specific roles played by a certain type of actor. Therefore, various kinds of constellations will occur. The constellations may differ with regard to: (a) the number of principals in charge of the debt assisting agency/agencies, (b) the number of agents providing debt assistance, and (c) the jurisdiction in which the agents operate. When the agents work in different jurisdictions, e.g. different cities, there is no form of cooperation or competition between them.

Schematically, the various debt assistance constellations may be presented as follows:

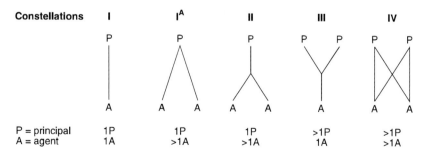

Figure 2: Different kinds of debt assistance constellations I

Constellation I^A refers to a situation where the agents operate in different jurisdictions. As was stated before, most literature refers to constellations such as I or I^A. Constellations such as II through IV are characterized by more agents and/or principals, who operate in the same jurisdiction. According to the Principal Agent Theory, the central question is: to what extent do the agents possess discretionary powers which can cause a divergence from the principals' objectives? Usually these objectives are defined in terms of effectiveness or efficiency. The term effectiveness refers to the relation between output and outcomes. The term efficiency can refer to: (a) the relation between inputs and outputs: this is economic efficiency, and; (b) the relation between inputs and outcomes: this is allocative efficiency.

Schematically:

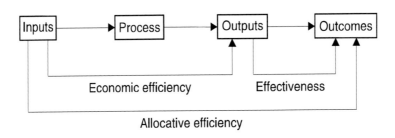

Figure 3: Efficiency and effectiveness

Because the process of debt assistance provides products c.q. outputs, which are difficult to identify and to define, effectiveness and efficiency will also be difficult to determine. This means that the principal lacks an essential monitoring device, namely an adequate performance indicator (PI). (Of course, the same is true for many other public services, such as police or education).

At this point, it should be noted that the PI used has to refer to the debt assistance constellation as a whole. The different organizations in this constellation are connected because of the intermediary character of the products provided. This means that the output of one organization (e.g., psychosocial aid by welfare workers) is the input for another organization (e.g., an MLB, trying to realize a debt settlement). Because of the connection between these organizations, their PI's should also be connected. In his paper on the criminal justice system, Boorsma (1995) mentions two problems with the common use of PI's. First, many organizations devise their own PI's without paying attention to the usefulness of the selected indicators for other, related organizations. Second, many PI's are given for subsequent parts of a system, without placing a priority on certain indicators.

With regard to the debt assistance system, these problems can be avoided by taking an 'overall performance indicator' of the process. An example of such an indicator in this policy field is the reciproke of the number of recidivists, i.e., the percentage of people who get into financial trouble more than once, despite the debt assistance provided.

HYPOTHESES

As was shown before, the reviewed literature on problematic personal debts mentions many variables which influence such a situation, and many variables which influence the realization of a debt settlement by a municipal loan bank. Only a small amount of literature deals with the role of other debt assisting agencies in the field, or with the relations between them in a specific constellation. Furthermore, it has been shown that authors who chose Principal Agent Theory as an explanatory body of theory, narrowed down the state of the art to situations of 1 principal ($x=1$) and 1 agent ($y=1$), or situations where there are more, but isolated agents, neither competing nor cooperating. These gaps in the literature may be filled by analyzing the effectiveness of the whole municipal debt solving system for different constellations (x,y) where $x \geq 1$ and $y \geq 1$. This research manuscript ends with some hypotheses on this matter.

In the former constellation IV (regarding a situation with more principals and more agents), it was assumed that every agent had more than one principal. In figure 4, situations with more principals and more agents are divided into situations in which not all agents have more than one principal (superscript s: 'single' bonds) and situations in which each agent has more principals (superscript d: 'double' bonds). Thus, (some) agents have single bonds in the new constellations IV and IV^A; they all have double bonds in the new constellations V and V^A.

Furthermore, in the former constellations II and IV (with regard to situations with more agents operating in the same jurisdiction) it was assumed that each agent will operate independently, according to his own institutional goals (and his own personal goals). Now we may introduce the probability of cooperation, hereby meaning that agents choose the same goals and positions. In figure 4, situations with more agents are divided into situations with cooperation (C) and without cooperation (NC: no cooperation). The rectangles show whether the actors are cooperating or not. Thus, agents cooperate in constellations II^A, IV^A and V^A; they do not in constellations II, IV and V.

Because constellations I and III refer to situations with only one agent, there can not be a case of (absence of) cooperation. The same is true for constellation 1^A where isolated agents are working in different jurisdictions. In figure 4, these constellations are termed $C*$ (which means: cooperation between agents not applicable).

Figure 4 presents the new 'catalogue' of possible constellations. The subscripts (x,y) denote the number of principals and agents respectively.

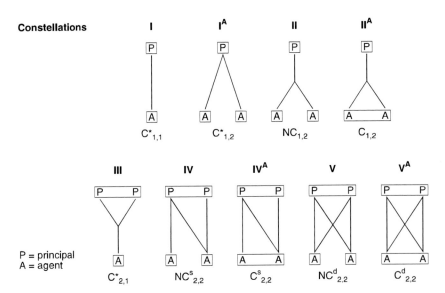

Figure 4: Different kinds of debt assistance constellations II

For symmetrical reasons the question arises whether constellation III can be distinguished from another constellation III, say III^{NC}. In figure 4, constellation III refers to a situation in which principals cooperate (see the rectangle round the principals); constellation III^{NC} can refer to a situation in which this cooperation is absent. In figure 4, this distinction between constellations is not made because it is assumed that in this case the alderman will always operate in the same institutional setting of one 'college' of a mayor and aldermen. In the Dutch situation such a 'college' is responsible as a group for all kinds of municipal policy. Therefore, by introducing constellation III next to constellation I, the element of cooperation has already been introduced. In other settings, where principals have the choice between working independently or cooperatively, the distinction between a constellation III (cooperation between principals) and a constellation III^{NC} (no cooperation between them) may be useful. The same applies to constellations IV through V^A which all could be distinguished from a constellation with no cooperation between principals. In that case, the following constellations would be super-added to figure 4: IV^{NC}, $IV^{A, NC}$, V^{NC}, $V^{A, NC}$.

The various constellations presented in figure 4 imply different levels of efficiency/effectiveness[7]. This is due to differences in monitoring costs, bonding costs and agency loss. Monitoring and bonding costs can well be interpreted in the perspective of Transaction Cost Theory. This theory was developed *inter alia* to explain why some transactions are executed on markets and others in organizations (Coase, 1937; Williamson, 1975). The concepts of this theory, however, enable us to analyze other

---

[7] We do not make a choice between the concepts of effectiveness or efficiency; as was stated before, we take a performance indicator such as the reciproke of the number of recidivists.

subjects as well, such as the choice of specific procedures[8] or, more importantly to this subject, the differences in efficiency/effectiveness of various constellations. Transaction costs can be globally defined as the costs involved in the coordination of activities. Williamson (1985) distinguishes *ex ante* and *ex post* transaction costs. According to his definition, *ex ante* costs are 'the costs of drafting, negotiating and safeguarding an agreement' and *ex post* costs are, for example, 'the set up and running costs associated with the governance structures' or 'the bonding costs of effecting secure commitments' (Williamson, 20, 21).

The magnitude of the agency cost is, next to the monitoring and bonding costs, also determined by the agency loss. The agency loss refers to the money equivalent of the reduction in the welfare experienced by the principal, in spite of the monitoring and bonding activities. These activities do not fully counterbalance the divergence between the decisions that would maximize the principal's welfare and the decisions that are taken by the agent. In other words, the agent is still realizing his non-productive goals, viz., engages in shirking behaviour[9]. The foregoing implies that the most effective debt assistance constellation does not refer to the one which realizes the lowest monitoring and bonding costs, but the one which realizes the lowest total agency costs.

As the number of principals and/or the number of agents increase, we expect a rise in agency costs due to disputes over areas of responsibility, problems of coordination and (because of this) waste of time. Furthermore, these disputes and problems of coordination will result in a less effective control of the agent by the principal, leading to more discretionary powers (more possibilities to shirk) for the agent. In other words: efficiency/effectiveness will decrease as the number of principals and/or agents increase. The efficiency/effectiveness hypotheses now evolve into:

Hypothesis 1:
Constellations with one principal and one agent (constellation I) are the most efficient/effective.

Hypothesis 2:
Constellations with cooperation between agents (C-constellations) are, *ceteris paribus*, more efficient/effective than constellations without cooperation (NC-constellations).

From hypotheses 1 and 2, it follows[10]:
$$E_I \rangle E_I^A \ E_I \rangle E_{II}^A \rangle E_{II}$$

---

[8] In this respect, Transaction Cost Theory overlaps with Constitutional Theory (e.g., Buchanan & Tullock 1965).

[9] The residual loss occurring in a constellation might be determined through multivariate regression by which differences in effectiveness/efficiency between constellations are (partly) attributed to monitoring and bonding activities. The remaining difference in effectiveness/efficiency then refers to the residual loss, viz., is due to the shirking of the agent, plus some small random effects.

[10] The presented rankings in efficiency/effectiveness are only valid when variations in x and/or y are equal for all constellations to be compared.

$E_I \rangle E_{III}$ $E_I \rangle E_{IV}^A \rangle E_{IV}$ $E_I \rangle E_V^A \rangle E_V$
Where E_i = efficiency/effectiveness of a constellation and $i = I, I^A, II,...V^A$.

Hypothesis 3:
Constellations in which all agents operate under the command of one principal are, *ceteris paribus*, more effective/efficient than constellations with different principals, some of them being in charge of more than one agent.
Thus: $E_{II} \rangle E_{IV}$ and $E_{II} \rangle E_V$

Hypothesis 4:
Constellations in which not all agents have more than one principal (C^s-constellations) are, *ceteris paribus*, more efficient/effective than situations in which each agent has more principals (C^d-constellations).
Thus: $E_{IV} \rangle E_V$ and $E_{IV}^A \rangle E_V^A$

Summarized:
$E_I \rangle E_{IIa} \rangle E_{IV}^A \rangle E_V^A$
$E_I \rangle E_{II} \rangle E_{IV} \rangle E_V$

In the end, it suffices to say that distinguishing so many different constellations is a heavy burden on the availability of sufficient data for empirical testing. In practice, just a few constellations might be subjected to these hypothetical effectiveness rankings.

REFERENCES

Auclair, E. (1992). 'Unemployment and Consumer Debts in France', in: Reifner & Ford (eds.), *Banking for People*, Berlin/New York, pp.471 ff.

Baaijens, J., R. Verstegen. (1985) *Schuldregelingen en de rol van gemeentelijke kredietbanken, Een verslag van een vooronderzoek*, Tilburg.

Boorsma, P.B., F. Kaiser, C. Petersen, H. de Ruig. (1988). *Door de bank geregeld, Factoren van invloed op het oplossen van problematische schuldsituaties door gemeentelijke kredietbanken*, Universiteit Twente, Faculteit der Bestuurskunde, Enschede.

Boorsma, P.B. (1995, March). *(Un)connected performance indicators in the criminal justice system*, discussion paper for the Conference on Social Reengineering and Performance Indicators in the Criminal Justice System, organized by the Western Australian Ministry for Justice and the Working Group on Public Productivity of the IIAS.

Brand, A. (1989). *Minima en schulden in de Maasstad, Een vergelijkend onderzoek naar de huishoudvoering van 150 Rotterdamse minima mèt en 60 zonder problematische schuld*, Gemeentelijke Sociale Dienst, Rotterdam.

Buchanan, J., G. Tullock. (1965). *The Calculus of Consent*, Michigan.

Caplovitz, D. (1974). *Consumers in trouble, A study of debtors in default*, New York.

Coase, R.A. (1937). 'The nature of the firm', *Economica*, New Series, Vol. 4, pp.331-351.

De Alessi, L. (1980). 'The economics of property rights: A review of the evidence', *Research in Law and Economics*, vol. 2, pp. 1-47.

Dessart, W.C.A., A.A.A. Kuylen, T. de Vries. (1982). *Ja, nee, geen lening, Oorzaken, omvang en achtergronden van problematische schuldsituaties*, Den Haag.

Eggertson, T. (1990). *Economic behavior and institutions*, Cambridge.

Engbersen, G., R. van der Veen, K. Schuyt. (1987). *Moderne Armoede, Overleven op het sociaal minimum*, Een onderzoek onder 120 Rotterdamse huishoudens, Leiden/Antwerpen.

Furubotn, E.G. and S. Pejovich. (1974). 'Introduction: The New Property Rights Literature', in: E.G. Furubotn & S. Pejovich (Eds.), *The economics of property rights*, Cambridge (Mas.), pp. 1-9.

Greef, M.H.G. de, L.J. Middel, W. van Rossum. (1985). *Kenmerken van problematische schuldsituaties, Vooronderzoek*, Rijksuniversiteit Groningen, Groningen.

Greef, M.H.G. de. (1992). *Het oplossen van problematische schulden, Een analyse van de invloed van hulpverlening, interorganisationele samenwerking en huishoudkenmerken op de effectiviteit van schuldregelingen*, dissertatie, Rijksuniversiteit, Groningen.

Haane, B. (1994). 'Quantitative data on credit, debt and overindebtness', in: N. Huls (Ed.), *Overindebtness of Consumers in the EC Member States: Facts and Search for Solutions, Part I*, Diegem, pp. 9-62.

Haane, B. (1994). 'Debt counselling institutions in Europe', in: N. Huls (Ed.), *Overindebtness of Consumers in the EC Member States: Facts and Search for Solutions, Part I*, Diegem, pp. 87-98.

Hall, P.A., R.C.R. Taylor. (1994, September). *Political Science and the Four New Institutionalisms*, Paper prepared for presentation at the Annual Meeting of the American Political Science Association, New York.

Hoekstra, L. (1990). *Minima en schulden: de etnische factor*, Gemeentelijke Sociale Dienst, Rotterdam.

Huls, N. (ed.). (1994). *Overindebtness of Consumers in the EC Member States: Facts and Search for Solutions*, Collection Droit et Consommation 29, Diegem.

Hulshof, M.E. (1993). *De integrale aanpak van problematische schulden*, Ministerie van Sociale Zaken en Werkgelegenheid, Den Haag.

Jensen, M.C., W.H. Meckling. (1976). 'Theory of the firm: Managerial behaviour, agency costs and ownership structure', *Journal of Financial Economics*, vol. 3, p. 305-360.

Jepperson, R.L. (1991). 'Institutions, Institutional Effects, and Institutionalism', in: W.W. Powell & P.J. DiMaggio (Eds.), *The New Institutionalism in Organizational Analysis*, The University of Chicago Press, Chicago, pp.143-163.

Künneke, R.W. (1991). *Op armlengte van de overheid, Een theoretisch en empirisch onderzoek naar de effecten van verzelfstandiging op de efficiëntie van openbare nutsbedrijven*, disseratie, Universiteit Twente, Enschede.

Makuch, W.M., J.L. Dodge, J.G. Ecker, D.C. Granfors, G.J. Hahn. (1992, January-February) 'Managing Consumer Credit Delinquency in the US Economy: A Multi-Billion Dollar Management Science Application', in: *Interfaces*, vol. 22, pp. 90-109.

National Report on Belgium, in: N. Huls (ed.). (1994). *Overindebtness of Consumers in the EC Member States: Facts and Search for Solutions, Part II, Annexes*, Diegem.

National Report on Britain, in: N. Huls (ed.). (1994). *Overindebtness of Consumers in the EC Member States: Facts and Search for Solutions, Part II, Annexes*, Diegem.

National Report on Denmark, in: N. Huls (ed.). (1994). *Overindebtness of Consumers in the EC Member States: Facts and Search for Solutions, Part II, Annexes*, Diegem.

National Report on Germany, in: N. Huls (ed.). (1994). *Overindebtness of Consumers in the EC Member States: Facts and Search for Solutions, Part II, Annexes*, Diegem.

National Report on Ireland, in: N. Huls (ed.). (1994). *Overindebtness of Consumers in the EC Member States: Facts and Search for Solutions, Part II, Annexes*, Diegem.

Nederlandse Vereniging voor Volkskrediet. (1987). *Gedragscode Schuldregeling*, Amsterdam.

Neelen, G.H.J.M. (1993). *Principal-agent relations in non-profit organizations, A comparative analysis of housing associations and municipal housing companies in the Netherlands*, dissertatie, Universiteit Twente, Enschede.

Nicols, A. (1967). 'Stock versus mutual savings and loan associations: some evidence of differences in behaviour', *American Economic Review*, vol. 57, pp. 337-346.

Nieuwburg, M.J.T. van. (1982). *De persoonlijke lening, Statistische methoden als hulpmiddel bij de beoordeling van kredietaanvragen*, Leiden.

North, D.C. (1986). 'The New Institutional Economics', *Journal of Institutional and Theoretical Economics*, vol. 142, pp. 230-237.

O'Hara, M. (1981). 'Property Rights and the Financial Firm', *Journal of Law and Economics*, vol. 24, pp. 317-332.

Oude Engberink, G. (1984/1987). *Minima zonder marge*, Gemeentelijke Sociale Dienst, Rotterdam.

Oude Engberink, G., B. Post. (1994). *Grenzen van de armoede, Risico's en risicogroepen op het sociaal minimum*, Dienst Sociale Zaken en Werkgelegenheid, Rotterdam.

Powell, W.W., P.J. DiMaggio, 'Introduction', in: W.W. Powell & P.J. DiMaggio (eds.). (1991). *The New Institutionalism in Organizational Analysis*, The University of Chicago Press, Chicago, pp. 1-38.

Powell, W.W., P.J. DiMaggio (Eds.). (1991). *The New Institutionalism in Organizational Analysis*, The University of Chicago Press, Chicago.

Rapport van de Commissie Schuldenproblematiek. (1994). *Schulden:naar, Nieuwe impulsen in de schuldenproblematiek*, Ministerie van Sociale Zaken en Werkgelegenheid.

Rapport van de Externe commisssie Stadsbank Zwolle. (1994, December). *Stadsbank Zwolle, Zakelijke kredietverlening en toekomstperspectief*, Zwolle.

Reifner, U., J. Ford (eds.). (1992). *Banking for People*, Berlin/New York.

Reifner, U., 'Debt arrangements', in: N. Huls (ed.). (1994). *Overindebtness of Consumers in the EC Member States: Facts and Search for Solutions, Part I*, Diegem, pp. 99-121.

Schep, G.J., Y.B. Bommeljé. (1994). *Een kwestie van geld, Over de financiële positie van cliënten van de sociale dienst*, Ministerie van Sociale Zaken en Werkgelegenheid, Den Haag.

Shepsle, K.A. (1986). 'Institutional Equilibrium and Equilibrium Institutions, in: H. Weisburg (ed.), *Political Science: The Science of Politics*, New York, pp. 51-82.

Sullivan, T.A., E. Warren, J.L. Westbrook. (1989). *As We Forgive Our Debtors, Bankrupty and Consumer Credit in America*, New York.

Tokunaga, H. (1993). 'The use and abuse of consumer credit: Application of psychological theory and research', in: *Journal of Economic Psychology*, vol. 14, pp. 285-316.

Tweede Kamer. (1992-1993/1993-1994). 22969, nr. 1-9, *Wijziging van de Faillissementswet in verband met de sanering van schulden van natuurlijke personen*, Den Haag.

Vermeulen H., H.J. Dirven, A. Kersten and R. Euwals. (1992). *Financiële problemen, schulden en problematische schuldsituaties in Nederland, Omvang, verdeling, determinanten en dynamiek*, Ministerie van Sociale Zaken en Werkgelegenheid, Den Haag.

Vos, K. de, A.J.M. Hagenaars. (1986). *Inkomens, bestedingen en schulden in Nederland in 1983, Verslag van een aantal resultaten van de GPD-enquete*, Ministerie van Sociale Zaken en Werkgelegenheid, Den Haag.

Vries, P. De. (1992). *De lastige verhouding tussen departement en agent, De departementale bekostiging in het licht van de principaal agent benadering*, dissertatie, Universiteit Twente, Enschede.

Williamson, O.E. (1975). *Market and hierarchies: Analysis and antitrust implications*, New York.

Williamson, O.E. (1985). *The economic institutions of capitalism*, New York.

Zhu, L.Y., C.B. Meeks. (1994). 'Effects of Low Income Families' Ability and Willingness to Use Consumer Credit on Subsequent Outstanding Credit Balances', in: *The Journal of Economic Affairs*, vol. 28, No. 2, pp. 403-422.

PART III

ENTREPRENEURIAL QUALITY, ETHICS AND GOVERNANCE

In Chapter 12 of Part III, *The Greening of Industry through Government-Supervised Self Regulation*, Daniel Press and Dan Mazmanian discuss the greening of industry, a topic that has emerged in recent years as an important topic among business, environmental, and governmental leaders. Moving forward, a major transformation in business and industry practices will be necessary. The authors emphasize that industry greening is a serious public problem in need of a public policy solution. To illustrate the different opinions on industrial greening, the authors present four broad approaches based on governmental imposed restrictions, self-regulation, market-based incentives, and volunteerism.

Press and Mazmanian discuss the likely resistance and avoidance from businesses in a "green transformation," as there are real costs associated with this transformation, and it is in the best interest of businesses to minimize and avoid costs. The authors use the example of the 1970's compulsory environmental laws and the progress that ensued, but point out that unnecessary costs incurred by both business and government could be avoided under a different approach.

As the chapter moves forward, Press and Mazmanian continue to analyze how to bring about significant changes that are in the best interest of all stakeholders. Green industry is presented as a collective action dilemma to approximate the close relationship between the public and private sectors. The authors apply this analysis to regulatory experiments in industrial greening, and find that attention has begun to shift from pollution reduction to pollution prevention by incentive-based, self-regulatory, and voluntary policy approaches. Press and Mazmanian find that bolder experiments in self-regulation have pushed industry closer to a zone of cooperation. The chapter ends with an assessment of how to accomplish the much-needed green transformation of America's business and industry by embracing the strategy of "government-supervised self-regulation."

Chapter 13 of Part III, by Albert C. Hyde and Dorothy Olshfski, is *Service Quality in the Public Sector in the Internet Economy.* Hyde and Olshfski start by noting that increasing demand for quality by customers and researchers began in earnest about 1990. They explain that the path towards service quality improvement has not always been easy for consumers, even though America is considered the "greatest bastion" of consumer capitalism. Service quality improvement has been difficult for the public sector, and the efforts to increase quality were taken up by the private sector. The public sector was slower to respond until Gore's National Performance Review in 1993.

Hyde and Olshfski go on to develop the emergence of the quality movement in the public sector, noting obstacles like the Grace Commission and anti TQM interests. They link TQM to reinventing adjustments and subsequent problems which unfolded along the way. The question of citizens as clients is addressed. And the evolving role of the customer is explored. "Process quality" and "buyer beware" become matters to be dealt with as the entrepreneurial environment increasingly manifests itself. As the internet era emerged, a technical side to service quality became necessary for both public agencies and service quality. Increasingly, the better the technical quality, the more important process quality becomes as a differentiator of better service.

The authors analyze the Internal Revenue Service for its quality of administration which leads to a discussion of reinventing customer service and the reorganization of the IRS. In searching for new strategies, Hyde and Olshfski address the remarkable advances made in recent customer service quality research. They note increasing requirements for dealing with customers by their governments, and how important choice, convenience, access, and speed are becoming...towards virtual service equality. The authors end with a significant section dealing with converting strategy to action, emphasizing that change is necessary for survival in the future.

Linda de Leon is the author of Chapter 14, *Ethics and Entrepreneurship.* This chapter addresses a fear of many in both the public and private sectors: entrepreneurship as a potential danger to the public interest. She addresses the problems raised when entrepreneurs emerge in the public sector. Traditional entrepreneurial behavior is not usually perceived to be synchronous with democratic governance. The author reviews entrepreneurship in both the public and private sectors and discusses how a string of corporate scandals has tarnished the image of the private sector entrepreneur. She notes that egotism, domination, opportunism, waywardnesss, and selfishness are actually functional as the emerging entrepreneurial reality increasingly unfolds. This is because there is a link between entrepreneurial behavior and a type of policy problem where goals are found to be conflicting or ambiguous, and where the means for achievement are uncertain or even unknown.

Author deLeon develops an exceptional model for analyzing ethical behavior and relating it to community, bureaucracy, and certain networks. She explores the ethical implications of competition. She concludes that there is a place for entrepreneurs, especially where innovation is necessary; further, she finds that entrepreneurship can be seriously ethical. It is important for reinventors to manage them, however, and to monitor appropriate behavior carefully. The chapter concludes with a discussion of how to encourage ethical entrepreneurship in bureaucracies, communities, and in anarchic networks.

In Chapter 15, *The Perception of Evil in Market Driven Academic Governance Systems,* Professor William L. Waugh, Jr. analyzes the crisis in governance that is unfolding on academic campuses affected by Hurricanes Katrina and Rita. It is a manifestation of entrepreneurialism and managerialism which have overflowed their boundaries. For the majority of the educational institutions affected by the Hurricanes, the recovery process has been painful with limited campus resources, loss of facilities and equipment, changes to funding streams, and changes in demand from enrollment and service reductions.

To further simultaneously aggravate manners, the very essence of professionalism in academia is also under assault. Means and ends become not only confused, but manipulated in an attempt to drive efficiency to the forefront of academic endeavors. The market is increasingly used as an excuse to diminish the integrity of academic governance systems. Traditional academic leadership, reward structures, human resources strategy, and governance in academia have defaulted towards minimal support by market driven academic administrators.

As faculty lose control of academic programs, as tenure is proactively attacked by administrators, and as salaries become inverted, Waugh explores the perceived "evil" manifested by the conflict laden changes being increasingly witnessed across market driven academia in America today.

Waugh also notes that Hurricanes Katrina and Rita have created an opportunity to change the character of educational institutions. This opportunity calls for entrepreneurial leadership, effective management, and consensus-building.

In the final chapter of Part III, Chapter 16, Van Johnston takes on *Professional Performance Priorities after the Privatization and Entrepreneurial Management Transformation.* He addresses the assault on sovereignty and governance protections, and analyzes the transition of citizens to customers. The author then inspects the entrepreneurial management transformation, paying particular attention to the change in managerial mission and the goal displacement that is often caused.

Johnston develops an analytical entrepreneurial conflict management model and stresses the increasing importance of professional ethics which become more important as we find the guidelines of the past less useful. We need to learn from cynicism and its residue which result from the chaos and turbulence of transitioning from citizens to customers. This will require efforts towards greater stewardship, wisdom, leadership, trust, and credibility. Increased competition, manifested as privatization, reinventing, franchising, and outsourcing requires new innovative and responsible professional priorities to deliver services by private or public sector organizations to customers and/or citizens in the transformed world of entrepreneurial management that is unfolding before us.

Chapter 12

THE GREENING OF INDUSTRY THROUGH 'GOVERNMENT-SUPERVISED SELF-REGULATION'

Daniel Press
Dan Mazmanian

The greening of industry has emerged as an important topic among business, environmental, and governmental leaders only since the mid-1980s. At this early stage in what will require a profound transformation by the time it is complete, debate exists over which business and industry practices are most in need of change and how to bring these about: To what extent is it at the stage of waste management, air and water pollution control, or energy usage that policy intervention is best applied? Is it in production methods, product design, or the end products themselves that the most change can be realized? It is at the stage of consumption and usage of products that the strongest drive for change will come?

Equally unclear is the best position for society to adopt in order to promote the most comprehensive while cost-effective transformation. Four broad approaches to this question illustrate the differences of opinion about how best to achieve industrial greening. They start with government imposing on all business and industry prescribed environmental protection technologies and methods of emissions reduction. A second, more flexible approach, would allow businesses to select their own most cost-effective strategies for reducing emissions, under the watchful eye of government. A third way is to use market-based incentives approaches that provide bottom-line rewards for environmentally-friendly business behavior, leaving change to the natural workings of the marketplace. The fourth is to rely largely on volunteerism, wherein businesses commit to environmental goals that match and/or exceed those required in exchange for relief from the prescribed technology and command-and-control regulations that would otherwise be imposed.

Since the mid-1990s the amount of research on these approaches has expanded rapidly and heated debate has ensured about which approaches or mix of approaches to use. At one side of the debate, attention is mainly focused on the shortcomings of the nation's long-standing environmental policies—variously referred to as "command-and-control," "top-down," "deterrence-based" policies for air, water, land-use, noise, and endangered species protection—and the need to roll back these policies. Others focus mainly on the growing importance of the corporate responsibility and quality management movements within and across industries—domestically and internationally—and how this is moving many businesses towards a greener path. All reformers want to know how best to accelerate this trend through various flexible governmental and voluntary policies, particularly in light of the unrelenting challenges to the environment posed by modern technological society and a growing worldwide population.

In assessing the contending positions and approaches, it is reasonable to assume that all else being equal, business and industry owners, managers, and workers would prefer to live and work in a cleaner, more environmentally-sustainable world. Yet seldom is "all else equal." The market economy in which businesses operate has a long history of freely using natural resources and nature's goods, such as clean air, water, and soil, food and fodder, and shielding both producers and consumers from the environmental pollution and resource degradation associated with the extraction of these goods, their use in production, and their consumption. This is the very same market economy, after all, that nurtures consumer tastes and expectations, ultimately their "demands," for ever-more goods and services, resulting in the extraordinary material consumption of today's modern lifestyle (Princen, Maniates, and Conca, 2002).

Consequently, the greening of industry is neither a private business matter nor a minor marketplace imperfection so much as a serious "public" problem, in need of a public policy solution. Since there are real costs associated with transforming into a green business we do not expect businesses to automatically or enthusiastically assume these costs. Indeed, it is typically in a firm's best interest to minimize if not avoid the additional costs of transformation to the extent that doing so does not demonstrably improve its near-term market position. This is precisely why the first generation of environmental laws, starting in the 1970s in the United States, were compulsory for all business, creating the "command-and-control" regulatory regime of the first environmental epoch. As this chapter shows, a good deal of progress resulted, but at great expense; arguably many unnecessary costs were incurred by both business and government, costs that arguably can be avoided under a different approach.

THE DILEMMA OF COLLECTIVE ACTION FOR ENVIRONMENTAL PROTECTION

How to bring about significant changes that are in the best interest of all sectors can be understood as one of a category of problems known as "collective action problems" or "collective action dilemmas" (Pellikaan and van der Veen, 2002; Dolšak and Ostrom, 2003). These occur when individuals would be better off if they cooperate in pursuit of a common goal, but for one reason or another each chooses a less optimal course of action; one that typically satisfies some other highly important goal. The challenge to policymakers when facing collective action problems is to devise an approach that anticipates and counteracts the normal (in the language of game theory, the "rational") tendency of actors to forego the better *joint* gain for a nearer-term assured and secure, but lesser *individual* gain.

The collective action "dilemma" in the case of the greening of industry has been portrayed by Matthew Potoski and Aseem Prakash (2005) as a two dimensional game theoretic problem, which we have adopted in Figure 1. The four-fold table and choices they represent show the options available to each player and the four cells represents the combinations of each. Each cell represents the payoff (or benefits) and risk (or costs) to each of the actors should they decide to cooperate in order to maximize the gains to each (cell B), or to not cooperate and avoid the possibility of being taken advantage of by the other and/or incurring some other cost (cell C); such as the loss of public confidence and trust on the part of government and market share and profitability on the part of business.

Figure 1: Green Industry as a Collective Action Dilemma

GOVERNMENT'S CHOICE *Flexible Regulation*	CELL A Government as potential "sucker"	CELL B Win-win: superior outcomes for government and industry
	CELL C Sub-optimal for both government and business, but a typical outcome	CELL D Green industry initiatives of the 1980s – today, with industry as potential "sucker"
Deterrence (through command-and-control)		
	Evasion FIRM'S CHOICE	*Self-policing*

Source: Potoski and Prakash, 2004.

Although simplified, the game situation closely approximates the real world of the relations between business and government. Consequently, if left to its own devices business would chose to have little or no governmental requirement placed upon it to protect the environment. This would be only reasonable ("rational") for a business trying to maximize its profits in a market economy. This is represented by the "evasion" position of the horizontal dimension, on the "Firm's choice" axis. However, if compelled by law to provide environmental protection and safeguards, and possibly go even further to transform itself into a green company, business would prefer an approach that allowed for self-policing and regulatory flexibility. It would find this superior to being heavily regulated by a command-and-control government bureaucracy.

Government, in turn, has the choice of opting for a policy of "deterrence," which experience has shown to be workable based on the command-and-control regulatory approach to environmental protection of the past thirty-five years. The downside, as experience has also shown, is that it has required the growth and support of a large government bureaucracy to carry out the oversight and regulation of businesses, the suppression of the creative energy on the part of firms that could be used to develop their own green business strategies, and ultimately the less than promised and far less than imaginable transformation of industry than could have occurred. Conversely, government could chose to be more flexible and lenient on industry, relying instead on a modest amount of monitoring combined with market forces, consumer demands, and new technology to ensure greater protection of the environment. There is risk in this approach for the government. Although it embraces the promise of an eventually large payoff, as market forces and modest oversight combine to bring about the desired green transformation of business in the short term, absent stringent regulation some, if not most, businesses will not change their behavior or will do so insufficiently or slowly.

And this is the dilemma: As the logic of game theory suggests and a fair amount of experience affirms, under flexible regulatory systems that rely on market forces to bring about changed behavior, the market forces are insufficient and many businesses do not change or do so only minimally. When firms know that they are unlikely to be detected or penalized even when caught, they too often opt for evasion over committing the capital required to transform themselves. The result is that government (and thus the public) ends up being betrayed, realizing even less movement toward the green transformation than under a command-and-control approach: Government finds itself in the position of the "sucker," which is the worst possible outcome in a collective action game.

Armed with the insights of game theory, it is logical that, left to its own resources and absent compulsion, business will choose evasion over greening. Government, in turn, will choose command-and-control over flexibility, not because it is optimal but in order to avoid the risk of ending up a sucker. Thus, game theory tells us that most of the activity surrounding environmental protection can be expected to take place in the lower left cell of Box 1, cell C, the zone in which government regulates with a heavy hand in order to prevent business from evading environmental protection laws and regulations. This is precisely where the action took place throughout the first environmental epoch, which began in the 1970s (Mazmanian and Kraft, 1999).

A second epoch began in the 1980s and continues today, characterized by recognition of the collective action dilemma and efforts to extricate government and business from its grasp. The challenge is how to combine flexible regulatory strategies with market forces to move the central theater of action out of the lower-left cell C to the upper right cell B.

A number of pilot and experimental programs by government and business have been initiated. The experience underscores how difficult it has been to dislodge the players from their long-standing positions. This should not come as a surprise in light of the dilemma they face, and the now thirty-five years living and working under the command-and-control approach. The crux of the matter remains that, by-and-large, government is loath to relinquish its reliance on deterrence, and by-and-large business can be expected to evade when circumstances allow.

Yet the need for society to find a win-win solution – a more optimal mix of flexibility and self-policing – continues and has motivated the continuing search for the needed policy breakthrough. A growing body of research evidence on strategies that appear to work is guiding these efforts, at least on an experimental basis among self-motivated businesses. Thus, devising a new hybrid public policy approach seems feasible; feasible in principle, that is, within a game theoretic framework. Of course, the direction of public policy is set by the politics of policymaking, not simply the logic of policy analysis, so this too will be considered in our final assessment.

What follows is a brief sketch of the more than three decades of effort to address the problems of environmental pollution and the degradation of our natural resources base by greening the practices of business and industry. This moves through the strict command-and control environmental policy epoch, located schematically in cell C. It then turns to the market-oriented and flexible regulatory strategies that reflected a significant change in the understanding of the problem. In actuality, the debate and center of activity has moved only part way, with the innovative action today taking place "under the shadow of regulation," in cell D. The chapter ends with an assessment of how we can best accomplish the much-needed green transformation of America's business and industry by embracing the strategy of 'government-supervised self-regulation" promulgated by Marc Eisner (2004), a long-standing student of the greening process.

REGULATORY EXPERIMENTS IN INDUSTRIAL GREENING

Command-and-control approaches have clearly resulted in better environmental practices in business and industry practices in the United States and a significant curbing of traditional patterns of environmental pollution, but they ultimately fall short of the fundamental transformation in business and industry needed. The best end-of-pipe pollution management has not sufficiently reduced the overall pollution load generated by an ever-expanding economy to satisfy the needs of a global population projected to grow by fifty percent over the next 50 years (Miketa and Mulder, 2005; Worrell, Price, Martin, Farla, and Schaeffer, 1997).[1]

Therefore, attention has begun to shift from pollution reduction to pollution prevention, and to do so by devising incentive-based, self-regulatory and voluntary policy

---

[1] Despite the important improvements in energy efficiency and pollution prevention achieved by American manufacturing since 1970, U.S. industrial sectors generally lag well behind Japanese and European industries on a wide variety of energy and environmental performance indicators. This suggests that U.S. industrial greening could improve significantly even with real-world technologies and processes already in use elsewhere. By way of illustration, consider the startling differences in environmental performance between U.S. and other sectors: In the pulp and paper sector, energy intensities differ by 60% between the most efficient country (Germany) and the least efficient (Portugal); the U.S. lies in between, far from the leading performers. Other sectors, such as automobiles, exhibit similar differences, with two of the largest producers (Germany and the U.S.) differing by 45%. Other scholars have noted these variations across countries (e.g., Worrell et al., 1997, who demonstrated that the German and Japanese iron and steel industries consume 45% and 26% less energy per ton than in the U.S.) and across sectors (e.g., Miketa and Mulder, 2005, who showed persistent cross-country differences in energy productivity of 10 manufacturing sectors).

approaches. Building on the successes and limitations of command-and-control regulation, American industry and government moved on a limited basis towards an industrial greening approach (cell D in Box 1). Characterized by industry self-policing and government deterrence, this approach has achieved some successes, but is clearly sub-optimal – from economic and environmental perspectives – to the relationship that could exist if moved to cell B (across-the-board cooperation by both business and industry).

A first phase in the movement toward greening has employed market incentives, self-reporting, and environmental management systems to improve corporate environmental performance. More recently, bolder experiments in self-regulation have advanced industry closer to the cooperative zone.

Phase I: Market Incentives, Self-Reporting and Environmental Management Systems

Incentive-based approaches to environmental policy – such as emissions taxes, tradable permit systems and deposit-refund programs – can be both effective at preventing pollution and more economically efficient. The U.S. EPA and many states experimented with a wide range of market incentives, mostly since the 1980s, many of which have demonstrated promising results (Rosenbaum, 2005). Experimentation with these "efficiency-based regulatory reforms" characterize the second epoch of the environmental movement (Mazmanian and Kraft, 1999).

The most well-known experiments with market incentives include the Acid Rain program of the 1990 Clean Air Act and the RECLAIM tradable permits program in the Los Angeles basin. By most accounts, the Acid Rain program made good on economists' predictions: emissions decreased and industry spent less money overall. RECLAIM has worked less well, at least in keeping down pollution control costs (Dale, 2000).

In the case of the Acid Rain program, the Clean Air Act allowed sulfur dioxide emissions trading throughout the Midwest (where power plants burn a great deal of acid-rain-producing coal). Prior to the Acid Rain program, new plants were required to "scrub" – remove at the smokestack – 90 percent of their sulfur dioxide emissions. They thus were only motivated to reduce costs to meet the standard, not to increase the effectiveness of their scrubbers or find less costly methods. After the program began, however, and as was predicted, de-sulfurization rates increased substantially, because now power plants could reap the economic benefits of scrubber technology innovations (Popp, 2003). Overall, EPA estimates that the Acid Rain program is responsible for reducing sulfur dioxide emissions by 35 percent over 1990 levels at a cost of only one-quarter what was expected under the old command-and-control regulation (Environmental Protection Agency, 2002).

Another significant second-epoch regulatory experiment consisted of self-reporting, auditing and disclosure requirements, beginning in 1986 with the Superfund Amendments and Reauthorization Act. This legislation created the Toxics Release

Inventory (TRI), the first major federal environmental program that moved away from the traditional command-and-control approach (characterized by heavy fines, specified emissions levels, and mandatory pollution abatement technologies) toward a "softer, gentler" self-reporting and cooperative framework. The TRI requires companies that have ten or more employees, and use significant amounts of any one of the hundreds of listed chemicals, to report their annual releases and transfers of these chemicals to the EPA, which then makes these data available to the public through an annual report – the TRI *Public Data Release.*

The overall record of the TRI program has been mixed. First, total production-related waste (TPRW) – the amount of toxics produced before any treatment, recycling or release occurs – is down by about 10 percent from the early 1990s to 2002. Industry is producing less total toxics, but releasing more to air, land and water. Ten percent over a decade constitutes relatively little fundamental reduction. Second, not all sectors are responding equally well to the challenge of toxics reduction. Although the original industries required to report to the TRI have decreased their chemical releases, they have not changed the amount of chemicals they generate as waste, which must then be recycled, used as a source of energy, treated, or released.

The TRI is the most widely-known and used database of self-reported information, but it is not unique. Thousands of companies around the world implement corporate environmental reports (CER) every year, and submit annual documents similar to their financial reports. These include "…management policies and systems; input/output inventor[ies] of environmental impacts; financial implications of environmental actions; relationships with stakeholders; and the [company's] sustainable development agenda" (Annandale, Morrison-Saunders, and Bouma, 2004).

Despite the appealing logic of self-reporting and auditing, it is exceedingly difficult to tell what such information achieves. Firms may be reluctant to accurately disclose potential problems with their facilities, fearing that regulators or third-party organizations (such as environmental litigants) may seize on the data to impose fines, facility changes in equipment and operation, or both (Pfaff and Sanchirico, 2004). The relatively small amount of research done on self-reporting suggests that, at best, CER systems improve company data collection and internal management, while possibly rendering environmental issues more transparent to government and the public (Annandale, Morrison-Saunders, and Bouma, 2004).

The third innovation of industrial greening actually modifies company management philosophies and practices. To implement green strategies, firms have adopted Environmental Management Systems (EMS) that include corporate environmental pledges, internal training programs, environmental education programs, and use of cradle-to-grave systems of management control such as full-cost accounting, total quality management (TQM), and other environmental management systems (Willig, 1994; Coglianese and Nash, 2001; Eisner, 2004).

Given their interest in avoiding environmental protection costs, why do firms adopt EMS? After all, it is costly – in terms both of money and staff time – and opens private firms to external scrutiny that may not be welcome. Potoski and Prakash (2005) report that annual third-party audits for ISO 14001 certification (an international EMS discussed later in this chapter) can cost a small firm from $25,000 - $100,000 and much, much more for larger firms.

In their survey of over 200 U.S. manufacturing plants, Florida and Davison found that the three most important reasons included management "commitment to environmental improvement ...corporate goals and objectives..., and business performance." Compliance with state and federal regulations, as well as improved community relations, were also frequently cited as reasons for adopting EMS (Florida and Davison, 2001).

Firms that go green can also be rewarded by the financial markets. Some investment brokers have begun to respond to the greening movement with socially responsible environmental investment portfolios, although they are only a small part of the investments market. In 2003 the Social Investment Forum reported that socially responsible investment portfolios, those which select companies through a wide range of social screens, include shareholder advocacy or invest in communities, had reached $2.16 trillion in assets, or a little over 11 percent of the total investment assets under U.S. management (Social Investment Forum, 2003).

Do EMS make a difference? Because of the difficulty linking management changes to verifiable, objective environmental outcomes, the jury is still out on that question. Some researchers conclude that EMS are effective when they enjoy strong support from top management, who in turn, rely on EMS to greatly improve company environmental awareness and to better track the flow of raw materials, energy, labor, quality, and costs throughout the firm's operations (Annandale, Morrison-Saunders, and Bouma, 2004; Smart, 1992). And "EMS adopters" report that they recycle more, release fewer air, water and waste emissions and use less electricity than non-EMS firms, but such findings are not based on third-party audits (Florida and Davison, 2001).

Phase II: Self-Regulation

More recently, greening includes voluntary self-regulation efforts by firms around the world, some of which are "invited" by regulators, while others are initiated and implemented by corporate leaders themselves. The primary attraction of voluntary, self-regulation is cost. Regulators simply cannot keep up with the cost of regulating many thousands of large firms; industries should adopt environmental programs if, by doing so, they can lower their operating costs.

Since the mid 1980s, the U.S. EPA has launched about two dozen voluntary programs; these are managed by the agency's Office of Policy, Economics and Innovation (formerly the Office of Reinvention) and its Partnership Programs Coordinating Committee. One of the most successful includes the 33/50 toxics reduction program.

The 33/50 Program. The 33/50 program was the first of several new voluntary programs launched in the early 1990s. The EPA launched in 1991 the 33/50 program, named for its goal of reducing releases of seventeen high-priority chemicals by 33 percent by 1992 and 50 percent by 1995. The seventeen chemicals included were selected from the TRI list based on "their relative toxicity, volumes of use, and the potential for pollution prevention opportunities" (Environmental Protection Agency, 1997). Significant decreases in the release levels for these chemicals were not the program's only objective. The EPA also wanted to promote flexibility by challenging corporations to reduce toxic emissions by whatever means they felt most appropriate. Participants were encouraged to adopt source reduction rather than end-of-pipe control methods. More than 8,000 companies were identified as potential program participants and invited to enroll in the program. According to the *1995 TRI Public Data Release*, roughly 1,300 companies signed up more than 6,000 facilities for the 33/50 program.

The EPA reported that the cumulative reduction achieved by participants during the program's first five years (1988—1993) totaled 46 percent (Environmental Protection Agency, 1995). The 1996 TRI report indicated a 60-percent overall reduction in the releases and transfers of the seventeen chemicals between 1988 and 1996 (Environmental Protection Agency, 1998).

In many ways, the 33/50 program is a success story. Not only were the reduction goals achieved, but also an EPA-sponsored study revealed that source reduction accounted for 58 percent of the decrease in releases and transfers for the 33/50 chemicals (Environmental Protection Agency, 1997). In 1997 the program was recognized by the Innovations in American Government Award program as one of the twenty-five best government innovations in the country. At the same time, caution is warranted. Many of the reductions in 33/50 program chemicals cannot be directly attributed to the program because 26 percent of the 1988—1991 reductions were reported by non-participants, and 40 percent of the reductions occurred before the program was established (U.S. General Accounting Office, 1994).

The EPA is not alone in its efforts to promote green management. The International Standards Organization (ISO), founded in 1947 and based in Geneva, Switzerland, is a nongovernmental organization made up of the national standards bodies of 149 countries. Since 1996, the ISO has promulgated standards for environmental management systems (EMS); these underwent a major revision in 2004. A company registering for ISO 14001 certification must (1) develop an environmental management system, (2) demonstrate compliance with all local environmental laws, and (3) demonstrate a commitment to continuous improvement (see Box 1). As of December 2004, 90,569 companies had received 14001-certification in the world; Japan had the most with 19,584, more than four times that of the United States (4,759) (International Standards Organization, 2005). The U.S. continues to lag behind most other developed countries in the proportion of its companies that sought and obtained this voluntary certification (International Standards Organization, 2002). Increasingly, large manufacturers require that their suppliers become ISO 14001 certified as well. Ford Motor Company led the way in the mid-1990s, but was soon followed by all the major automakers (Eisner, 2004).

The ISO develops *management* standards, not environmental *performance* standards; as such, ISO 14001 is only effective if EMSs truly guide regulatory compliance and facility process decisions. The ISO doesn't actually conduct the certification process itself. Rather, it first relies on national accreditation bodies to evaluate private, third-party certifiers. In the U.S., the American National Standards Institute (ANSI), based in Washington and New York, and the ANSI-ASQ National Accreditation Board (ANAB), based in Milwaukee, provide the formal recognition that a third-party auditor is competent to provide ISO 14001-certification. Some 60 certifiers operate in the U.S., catering to the wide range of industries that have sought ISO 14001 certification in the last decade.

Potoski and Prakash (2005) analyzed ISO 3000 "major sources" of air emissions in the U.S., including many that were 14001-certified. They asked whether toxic air emissions were significantly lower in certified versus non-certified firms – and indeed they were. Their explanation is that, on the spectrum of voluntary measures, ISO 14001 represents a "weak sword," because it requires only third-party audits. A "strong sword" system, like the EPA's Performance Track program, requires third-party monitoring, public disclosure of audit information, and sanctions by program sponsors (Potoski and Prakash, 2005). In another study, Philippe Barla at the Université Laval, found no difference between ISO 14001-certified paper mills and non-certified mills in Quebec; however, he did not look at "strong" versus "weak" implementation (Barla, 2005). These conflicting conclusions mirror the literature's uncertainty; it thus still remains to be seen just how much more environmental performance strong sword environmental management systems can spur over weak sword programs.

Industry trade associations also lead voluntary self-regulation efforts by their member companies; the chemical industry provides one notable example. In response to extensive and highly negative media coverage, the Synthetic Organic Chemical Manufacturers Association (SOCMA) adopted its Responsible Care program in 1988. This sectorwide code of conduct is now required of all CMA members and has been adopted in some form by chemical manufacturers in forty-six countries (Synthetic Organic Chemical Association, 2004). It consists of ten guiding principles and six management practice codes. The guiding principles emphasize responding to community concerns; ensuring safety in all phases of production, transportation, use, and disposal; developing safe chemicals and supporting research on health, safety, and environmental effects of products, processes, and wastes; and helping to create responsible laws and regulations. The management codes are designed to improve each facility's emergency response capabilities; pollution prevention efforts; and safety in production, sales, distribution, and final disposal. The CMA has been adopting quantitative benchmarks to measure its members' progress on each of these codes (Ember, 1995).

The Responsible Care program has also spawned an extensive mutual assistance network within the chemical industry, a network that includes very senior management. Companies that are far along in their implementation of the codes are asked to help those companies having difficulty complying. Through its Partnership Program, CMA actively pushes the envelope of Responsible Care beyond the chemical industry. Partners are industries and associations that are not CMA members, but that make, use, formulate, distribute, transport, and/or treat or dispose of chemicals (Ember, 1995).

Early assessments about the Responsible Care program revealed disappointing progress. In one study of sixteen medium- to large-sized firms, about half took the

Box 1: Environmental Management Systems and ISO 14001 Certification

What is an EMS?

As one recently certified high-tech firm described it, the following components make up of the core of EMS:

Environmental Policy: This is a statement from top management that identifies the organizations commitment to continual improvement, prevention of pollution, and a commitment to comply with all relevant environmental legislation and regulations.

Planning: Companies are required to identify ways in which they impact and interact with the environment and identify goals for improvement. In addition, companies need to identify all environmentally related legal requirements.

Implementation and Operation: Documented procedures must be in place to control and monitor all of the ways in which the company impacts and interacts with the environment, including emergency preparedness and response. This includes an assurance that employees are trained and competent in their jobs that may interact with the environment.

Checking and Corrective Action: Documented procedures that monitor and measure key characteristics of operations and activities that may impact the environment must be specified.

Management Review: Requires top management to actively participate in reviewing the EMS. (http://www.zilog.com/quality/iso14001.asp)

How does the ISO 14001-certification process work?

Every certifier operates in their own way, but they generally follow similar steps. A certification will begin with a review of company documents policies and procedures, identifying where these 1) fail to guarantee compliance with environmental regulations and, to some degree, 2) miss opportunities for encouraging best environmental practices. The second step generally involves an on-site audit consisting of many interviews and document reviews. Finally, certifiers work with companies to train employees and develop new policies or procedures until adequate EMSs are in place, after which they grant the ISO 14001 certificate.

Resources: A complete description of ISO 14001 environmental management standards and list of certifiers operating in every country is available from the International Standards Organization (www.iso.org); for an example of a private certifier, see Smithers Quality Assessments (www.smithersregistrar.com).

Responsible Care codes seriously--mostly by adopting environmental management systems and integrating environmental principles throughout the firm (Howard, Nash, and Ehrenfeld, 2000). A study comparing the environmental performance of firms adopting Responsible Care with those that had not revealed essentially no difference, a discouraging result suggesting that management changes may not be resulting in measurable environmental improvements (King and Lenox, 2000). Other critics point to a large gap between improvements to which CMA members have committed themselves and what companies have actually achieved. Part of the problem is that some of the management codes lack clear performance indicators and company statistics are not yet independently validated by third-party observers (Ember, 1995).

All critiques aside, the U.S. chemical industry certainly pollutes less for each gallon of product than it did in prior decades. Toxic releases, energy consumption and air emissions data all show that the industry's total production has grown faster than its pollution levels.

BUILDING ON PILOT PROGRAMS AND POLICY EXPERIMENTS

Overall, the national effort to reduce the air pollution emitted by business and industry, particularly in major urban areas across the nation, under the CAA, has been reasonably successful. Significantly helping this effort there has been a dramatic reduction of emissions per automobile on the road today versus thirty-five years ago. Many of our most polluted waterways have been cleaned up over this time period as well.

Balanced against this record, there is little evidence that the emissions reduction and cleanup was accomplished in the most cost-effective manner. Possibly more important in looking forward, three decades of experience did not result in any visible commitment by the majority of businesses in the United States to a comprehensive, green transition.

We therefore cannot be sure to avoid continuing, large-scale pollution, nor that American industry's emissions, in aggregate, will not return us to previous levels. That is, there is little commitment by businesses to moving beyond the long-standing command-and-control regulatory approach to a life-cycle environmental analysis of their products. We are even less likely to see widespread closed-system toxics management in manufacturing or product use, sustained attention to more global and growing problems such as greenhouse gases emissions, destruction of natural habitats, or depletion of ocean resources. Equally important, there exists no U.S. national policy goals or mandated regulations to move industry in this direction.

An instructive lesson from the voluntary programs of the past fifteen years is that when businesses form an alliance within their sector, either voluntarily or under the pressure of government policy, significant reductions can be realized, as illustrated by the experience of chemical industry. Yet this very example suggests that chemicals may be the proverbial exception to the rule since the change in that industry was due to the extraordinary public pressure brought to bear in the early 1990s as a result of the few colossal environmental disasters that were experienced in the United States and abroad and the fact that the industry is fairly well concentrated. Thus cooperation was brought about among a relatively few number of actors. In effect, the conditions for moving into a "win-win" game position for both government and the chemical industry existed, where flexible regulation and volunteerism could be achieved, and the action moved into cell B, of Box 1. Today, few other such examples among major business and industrial sectors can be found.

How might this situation be changed? After a thorough review of the pilots and experiments in flexible regulation, self-regulation, and voluntary approaches of the past decade, Marc Eisner (2004) has woven together the best components from each into a promising synthesis. His approach is designed to overcome the natural ("rational") reticence of business and industry, and move the greening agenda beyond cell D, into cell B. He focuses on bridging the gap between business and government, on "harnessing the market and industrial associations to achieve superior results by creating a system of government-supervised self-regulation" (Eisner, 2004).

The central propositions of his policy synthesis are:

- Market rewards should be the primary motivator (placing emphasis on the carrot) while retaining in reserve the traditional regulatory stick;
- Reliance should be placed on trade and business associations; these sectoral and quasi-governmental organizations can serve as the central implementers of greening policy (they are "quasi" in that they are non-profit organizations though they would be imbued with governing authority);
- Emphasis should be placed on disclosure and "sunshine" provisions over government prescribed techniques of emissions reduction and on-site government inspection;
- Sectoral associations would serve as intermediary entities, both to implement policy and "assure" the government that policy would be carried out as intended;
- The proposal does not require significant new public laws or the creation of new government bureaucracy since they can be woven together from existing programs and authority.

The critical virtue of the approach is that, if adopted as the overall framework for greening, it would mitigate the fear of becoming a "sucker" on the part of government and the fear of an overbearing regulatory regime on the one hand and of other businesses "evading" their responsibilities to go green, on the other. In short, we have in Eisner's proposal a game theoretic- and pragmatically-attractive approach to moving government and business into cell B. As we mentioned at the outset, policy is set by the politics of policymaking not simply the logic of policy analysis, as attractive as it may be, to which we now turn.

MIXED SIGNALS FROM INDUSTRY AND WASHINGTON

Despite the good image nurtured by corporate public relations officers, many industry lobbyists still work assiduously at blocking or rolling back environmental mandates (Reisch, 2004b). Industry political action committees are keeping up a steady stream of campaign contributions to anti-environmentalist legislators, just as they have done for years (Makinson and Goldstein, 1994). Indeed, the chemical industry's strong political lobbying to weaken existing environmental protection legislation and to prevent new legislation undermines the credibility of its own Responsible Care program. The American Chemistry Council became concerned enough with its industry's poor reputation to adopt third-party auditing as part of a newly-reinvigorated Responsible Care initiative (Reisch, 2004a).

For its part, the current administration of George W. Bush has done little to move industry and the government toward win-win outcomes depicted in cell B; rather, the administration's general retreat from regulatory enforcement moved the country further into cell A (in which the federal government can end up being a "sucker").

From the start of the Bush administration, pro-enforcement advocates took a back seat while the EPA was instructed to drop air pollution lawsuits that were close to successful settlement, relax standards for mercury in air emissions and arsenic in drinking water, and advance energy production goals over conservation and habitat protection (Drew and Oppel, 2004; Rosenbaum, 2005; Cohen, 2004). The most significant retreat from command-and-control regulation came when the administration yielded to industry pressure on the subject of "new source review." New source review, rules in place for decades, required new, better pollution controls when industries upgraded or expanded their facilities. Led by electric power utilities burning coal in old plants, lobbyists argued that new source review would impose hundreds of millions of dollars in new, unnecessary costs – and could prevent much-needed expansion of the country's electric power generating capacity (Barcott, 2004). In the end, the revised regulations "...said utilities would not have to add new pollution-control devices if upgrades and construction projects did not cost more than 20 percent of the plant's value – a loophole all sides said was huge" (Drew and Oppel, 2004). The inevitable conclusion is that not even conventional deterrence, much less win-win strategies, will be pursued without a change of administrations or a much more aggressively-environmental Congress.

REACHING BEYOND "WIN-WIN"

We assume that devising ways to improve protection of the environment will need to build on the several generations of existing law and public policy, and any thought of disregarding these and starting anew is unrealistic. It is for this reason that the synthetic approach conceived by Eisner, designed to harness the core self-interested impulses of business and government on behalf of protection of the natural environment, is appealing. To be successful, these policies require business to improve the production of material goods and services while reducing to a minimum the adverse impacts on the natural environment. Indeed, this is not only the win-win of game theory but the "double bottom-line" aspiration of industrial ecology today. As a blueprint for a politically-realistic, near term policy goal, we believe Eisner provides an ambitious though realizable approach to environmental protection and the greening of industry.

Not even the best policy ideas succeed in the real world, of course, short of dedicated political and corporate leaders to guide the way. Given the gravity of the environmental and pollution challenges, in the United States and even more so around the globe in rapidly developing economies of Asia and Latin America, we can only hope that the emerging generations of new corporate and political leaders will better understand the respective positions they are in within the game-theoretic framework, and extricate themselves through the strategy of government-supervised self-regulation.

REFERENCES

Annandale, D., Morrison-Saunders, A., and Bouma, G. (2004). The Impact of Voluntary Environmental Protection Instruments on Company Environmental Performance. *Business Strategy and the Environment, 13*, 1-12.

Barcott, B. (April 4, 2004). Changing All the Rules. *The New York Times*.

Barla, P. (2005). *ISO 14001 Certification and Environmental Performance in Québec's Pulp and Paper Industry*. Retrieved February, 2006, from http://econpapers.repec.org/paper/lvllagrcr/0503.htm

Coglianese, C., and Nash, J. (Eds.). (2001). *Regulating from the Inside: Can Environmental Management Systems Achieve Policy Goals?*. Washington, D.C.: Resources for the Future.

Cohen, M.J. (2004). George W. Bush and the Environmental Protection Agency: A Midterm Appraisal. *Society and Natural Resources, 17*.

Dale, T.B. (Summer, 2000). Political Obstacles to the Implementation of Emissions Markets: the Lessons of RECLAIM. *Natural Resources Journal*.

Dolšak, N., and Ostrom, E. (2003). *The Commons in the New Millennium Challenges and Adaptation*. Cambridge, MA: MIT Press.

Drew, C., and Oppel, Jr., R.A. (March 6, 2004). How Industry Won the Battle of Pollution Control at E.P.A. *The New York Times*.

Eisner, M.A. (April, 2004). Corporate Environmentalism, Regulatory Reform, and Industry Self-Regulation: Toward Genuine Regulatory Reinvention in the United States. *Governance: An International Journal of Policy, Administration, and Institutions, 17*(2), 145-167.

Ember, L.R. (May 29, 1995). Responsible Care: Chemical Makers Still Counting on It to Improve Image. *Chemical and Engineering News*, 12.

Environmental Protection Agency. (1995). *1993 Toxics Release Inventory Public Data Release*. (EPA Publication No. 745-R-95-010). Washington, D.C.: U.S. Environmental Protection Agency.

Environmental Protection Agency. (1997). *1995 Toxics Release Inventory Public Data Release.* (EPA Publication No. 745-R-97-005). Washington, D.C.: U.S. Environmental Protection Agency.

Environmental Protection Agency. (1998). *1996 Toxics Release Inventory Public Data Release.* (EPA Publication No. 745-R-98-005). Washington, D.C.: U.S. Environmental Protection Agency.

Environmental Protection Agency. (2002). *Acid Rain Program, 2002 Progress Report (EPA-430-R-03-011).* Retrieved November 29, 2006, from Environmental Protection Agency Web Site: http://www.epa.gov/airmarkets/cmprpt/arp02/index.html

Florida, R., and Davison, D. (2001). Why Do Firms Adopt Advanced Environmental Practices (And Do They Make A Difference)? In C. Coglianese, and J. Nash (Eds.), *Regulating from the Inside: Can Environmental Management Systems Achieve Policy Goals?.* Washington, D.C.: Resources for the Future.

Howard, J., Nash, J., and Ehrenfeld, J. (2000). Standard or Smokescreen? Implementation of a Voluntary Environmental Code. *California Management Review, 42*(2), 63-82.

International Standards Organization (ISO). (2002). *Twelfth Cycle: The ISO Survey of ISO 9000 and ISO 14001 Certificates.* Retrieved November 29, 2006, from ISO Web Site: http://www.iso.ch/iso/en/iso9000-14000/pdf/survey12thcycle.pdf

International Standards Organization (ISO). (2005*). The ISO Survey of Certifications.* Retrieved November 29, 2006, from ISO Web Site: http://www.iso.org/iso/en/iso9000-4000/certification/isosurvey.html

King, A., and Lenox, M. (2000). Prospects for Industry Self-Regulation without Sanctions: A Study of Responsible Care in the Chemical Industry. *The Academy of Management Journal, 43*(4), 698-716.

Makinson, L., and Goldstein, J. (1994). *The Cash Constituents of Congress.* Washington, D.C.: Center for Responsive Politics.

Mazmanian, D.A., and Kraft, M.E. (1999). The Three Epochs of the Environmental Movement. In D.A. Mazmanian, and M.E. Kraft (Eds.), *Toward Sustainable Communities Transition and Transformations in Environmental Policy.* Cambridge, MA: MIT Press.

Miketa, A., and Mulder, P. (2005). Energy Productivity Across Developed and Developing Countries in 10 Manufacturing Sectors: Patterns of Growth and Convergence. *Energy Economics, 27,* 429-453.

Pellikaan, H., and van der Veen, R. (2002). *Environmental Dilemmas and Policy Design.* New York: Cambridge University Press.

Pfaff, A., and Sanchirico, C.W. (Summer, 2004). Big Field, Small Potatoes: An Empirical Assessment of EPA's Self-Audit Policy. *Journal of Policy Analysis and Management, 23*(3).

Popp, D. (2003). Pollution Control Innovations and the Clean Air Act of 1990. *Journal of Policy Analysis and Management, 22*(4), 641-660.

Potoski, M., and Prakash, A. (March/April, 2004). The Regulation Dilemma: Cooperation and Conflict in Environmental Governance. *Public Administration Review, 64,* 137-148.

Potoski, M., and Prakash, A. (2005). Covenants with Weak Swords: ISO 14001 and Facilities' Environmental Performance. *Journal of Policy Analysis and Management, 24*(4), 745-769.

Princen, T., Maniates, M., and Conca, K. (Eds.). (2002). *Confronting Consumption.* Cambridge, MA: MIT Press.

Reisch, M.S. (2004a). Track Us, Trust Us: American Chemistry Council Says Will Supply the Facts to Earn the Public's Trust. *Chemical and Engineering News, 82*(23).

Reisch, M.S. (2004b). Twenty Years After Bhopal: Smokescreen or True Reform? Has the Chemical Industry Changed Enough to Make Another Massive Accident Unlikely? *Chemical and Engineering News, 82*(23).

Rosenbaum, W.A. (2005). *Environmental Politics and Policy* (6th ed.). Washington, D.C.: CQ Press.

Smart, B. (Ed.). (1992). *Beyond Compliance: A New Industry View of the Environment.* Washington, D.C.: World Resources Institute.

Social Investment Forum. (2003). *2003 Report on Socially Responsible Investing Trends in the United States.* Retrieved November 29, 2006, from Social Investment Forum Web Site: http://www.socialinvest.org/areas/research/

Synthetic Organic Chemical Association (SOCMA). (2004). *Responsible Care Program.* Retrieved February 27, 2006, from SOCMA Web Site: http://www.socma.com/ResponsibleCare/index.htm

U.S. General Accounting Office (GAO). (1994). *Toxic Substances: Status of EPA's Efforts to Reduce Toxic Releases.* Washington, D.C.: GAO.

Willig, J.T. (Ed.). (1994). *Environmental TQM* (2nd ed.). New York: McGraw-Hill Executive Enterprises Publications.

Worrell, E., Price, L., Martin, N., Farla, J., and Schaeffer, R. (1997). Energy Intensity in the Iron and Steel Industry: A Comparison of Physical and Economic Indicators. *Energy Policy, 25*(7-9), 727-744.

Chapter 13

SERVICE QUALITY IN THE PUBLIC SECTOR IN THE INTERNET ECONOMY

Albert C. Hyde and Dorothy Olshfski

"IRS to Close Walk-in centers As Agency Faces Tighter Budget".... "After widely publicized hearings seven years ago, Congress passed a law ordering the Internal Revenue Service to enhance services that were financed by cutting enforcement of the tax laws to make sure telephones were answered and that forms were readily available. That era is ending..."

-New York Times, David Cay Johnston April 10, 2005

"No Thanks; we prefer shopping..."..."Britain is unusual in having set explicit targets for making all government services available electronically. What is far more worrying is that where such services have already been put on-line, hardly anyone seems to be using them. "Citizens have so far barely used the government's own online services offerings, noted one official glumly. Worse...usage of e-government services has not grown in the past two years and has even fallen in some cases".

-The Economist, January 4, 2005

"Farmers Rage Against the Dying of the County Office.... Farmers are famously resistant to change, and that goes for a recently announced U.S. Department of agriculture plan to close as many as 713 of the 2,351 county offices of the Farm Service Agency. .. It's a terrible idea in the view of one Illinois farmer...'consolidation, that's government bull. They're closing offices and ...there will be a lot of upset people..."

-The Washington Post, Dan Morgan October 18, 2005

"YOU CAN'T ALWAYS GET WHAT YOU WANT!"

The path towards service quality improvement has not been easy for consumers; even in an America generally consider the greatest bastion of consumer capitalism in the world. It has been especially difficult for governments and consumers of public services. It is now 15 years since three marketing professors issued their infamous management challenge to American industry in an article in the *Sloan Management Review*. They charged: "It is time for U. S. companies to raise their service aspirations significantly and for U S. executives to declare war on mediocre service and set their sights on consistently excellent service." (Berry, Zeithaml, and Parasuraman, 1990, p. 29).

They based their indictment of industry service quality on a significant body of marketing and customer service measurement research that demonstrated that customers do differentiate between satisfactory and unsatisfactory service quality. It is customers who define service quality and their assessment is based on a comparison of the actual service they receive against their expectations. The SERVQUAL model, as this research was called, produced a wave of further studies, discussion, and initiatives as American firms struggled with their global counterparts in Japan and Europe for competitive advantage using service quality. In the private sector, the debate moved rapidly to how to measure, improve, and use excellent service quality to retain customers and increase market share.

By the mid 1990's, most businesses fully understood the importance of overall customer satisfaction and its linkages to product quality, service quality, and ultimately corporate image. American corporations from Sears to FedEx built service quality models that demonstrated how important front-line employees were to ensuring business success. As more corporations understood and researched quality further, many businesses shifted the frame of reference from customer quality to brand quality. It was the perception or image of the brand that was seen as key to retaining customers and sustaining an image of quality. Ironically, one of those three upstart marketing professors (now an Associate Dean at a prominent American Business school) – charges in a recent issue of Harvard Business Review that brand management so dominates business thinking about customer relationships that it imperils progress. She and her colleagues advocate a return to basics by developing a concept of customer equity that requires business "focus on growing the lifetime value of their customer relationships" (Rust, Zeithaml, and Lemon, 2004).

All this debate about the why and the how of service quality in the private sector is in marked contrast to its reception in the American public sector. Service quality in government also had its moment of discovery in the early 1990's. Then Vice- President Gore's National Performance Review team in its first report in September of 1993 made improving customer service one of its top priorities. All federal agencies that provided services directly to the public were required to create service standards, survey and report on customer satisfaction, and publish their customer service plans. An Executive Order confirming these good intentions was even issued.

Government never really got to the service quality research part – much less the "corporate or brand image issue." Instead, critics challenged the wisdom of a commitment to service quality objective. Critics openly questioned first whether it merited being one of the top principles of the reinventing government movement. Secondly, there was a very strong reaction to even using the word "customer" in assessing public sector performance. That debate raged through out most of the 1990's. (Pegnato, 1997; Gilbert and Nichols, 1999). But to understand where the public sector is on its journey to realizing service quality improvement, it is best to provide some background. One must examine how the public sector has reacted to the overall quality movement or Total Quality Management or TQM as it is known in the management lexicon. Seen in this light, the rather hostile reaction against service quality, especially at the federal level, is perhaps more understandable, though still rather lamentable.

PUBLIC SECTOR QUALITY MANAGEMENT: A BRIEF HISTORY

The quality management movement in the United States normally traces its roots to those first attempts in the 1970's to make quality circles work in American industry. Quality circles were efforts to import a Japanese management concept adapting employee participation by creating voluntary groups of workers to address problems of product quality and cost control.   More importantly they created a new awareness of the importance of quality and the involvement of those in the workforce who were closest to the production and supply processes.

By the time quality circles were introduced in the public sector in the early 1980's, however, they were already being abandoned in the private sector in favor of a much broader effort, namely TQM.   Organizations that adapted TQM invested heavily in measurement systems, training, problem solving team efforts, program coordination and consulting assistance. When organizations adapted TQM successfully, they installed new core processes that integrated quality measurement with participative management efforts, customer feedback techniques with supplier contractor partnerships; all linked to continuous improvement goals. Unsuccessful efforts, on the other hand were typically those that saw quality as a quick start up program and created a paper process to advertise the importance of quality initiatives without really making any investment in measurement systems or workforce training on participative management.

When TQM first emerged upon the American public management scene in the mid 1980's, it found a federal government deeply divided over political issues involving deficit reduction, privatization, and cut back management. The Reagan administration set the tone in its Grace Commission Report subtitled "War on Waste" followed by centrally directed management initiatives on increasing contracting or outsourcing and mandating productivity improvement.   With the active and effective backing of a Congress controlled by the opposition party, many federal agencies stonewalled or ignored what most perceived as at best poorly conceived management directives, or worst politically motivated reforms, masquerading as efficiency improvement.

Quality attempted to take a different route in the public sector. Given the failure of previous management reforms, or management through budget systems reform efforts, the adoption of quality management was left up to agency choice as opposed to administrative fiat. Government quality management efforts were first led by defense agencies and other public organizations that did extensive contracting with the private sector. Logically, they picked up quality from their suppliers and contractors who had adopted quality to promote competitive advantage. In keeping with this new ideal of grass-roots reform, the Federal Quality Institute under the auspices of the Office of

Personnel Management was established to serve as clearinghouse, coordinator, and consultant for federal quality efforts.

By the early 1990's, there was sufficient attraction to the quality management movement that it was found throughout government. The General Accounting Office, which itself had undertaken a major effort to adopt quality, [1] surveyed federal agencies in 1992 and found that almost 80% of all federal agencies had established some type of TQM program or effort. Similar surveys of state and local government found that quality efforts were found in the majority of larger governments and progressive. smaller governments. But the flip side of this, the large presence at the federal level, was its veneer like applicability. GAO noted that TQM had only reached about 17% of the federal workforce in terms of direct involvement in the quality process or participation on a quality team (GAO, 1992). Only a quarter of those surveyed by GAO recognized the existence of the Federal Quality Institute. Likewise, many state governments had established quality teams in most departments but actual involvement by the workforce was slight (Hyde, 1995a).

Still, expectations were high in the public sector. Quality advocates in government had great hopes with the election of President Bill Clinton. Clinton as governor of Arkansas was generally credited as being the first state governor to establish a formal TQM program and put quality teams into nearly every state agency. When the National Performance Review (NPR) was announced in March of 1993, many felt that quality management would be the cornerstone for the reinvention effort. The resulting document from the NPR was a philosophical victory but a titular defeat. TQM was not adopted as the official management philosophy of the reinvention movement. Quality advocates could rightly claim that the customer service orientation (to be discussed in the next section) was all TQM; but clearly NPR avoided any and all management labels.

In retrospect, avoiding management labels proved to be an excellent strategy. By the mid 1990's, a backlash to TQM in the private sector was already forming, led by the Business Process Reengineering movement. At the same time, as previously mentioned, the response to the central importance of customer service as a cornerstone of the reinvention was highly critical. TQM was simultaneously being labeled a management fad in some quarters and revered in others as the quality management movement. A quote explaining TQM from a standard casebook on public management at the time aptly summed up this confusing situation. According to Golembiewski, Stevenson, and White, "TQM is a controversial management technique now popular in business and industry. TQM's success has forced managers to examine possible applications in public agencies. Concurrently, TQM has failed in some organizations and has many detractors" (Golembiewski et al., 1997, p. 119).

What the Clinton Administration did put in place was the already referred to executive order mandating customer service quality improvement. Again, this should be

---

[1] GAO's experience with quality management is a classic case study in itself on the "quality divide" over government quality adoption. After implementing a number of features of TQM within GAO, the National Academy of Public Administration was asked to do a 'review" of the effects of TQM on GAO's performance. Their very negative assessment of both the appropriateness and the results of TQM at GAO led to its abandonment as a formal program.

seen in context. Another executive order issued along with the publication of the National Performance Review reports mandated labor management partnership. Federal unions throughout the 1980s were not enthusiastic supporters of TQM, primarily because of tension over the participative management. In some cases, unions even filed suit, unsuccessfully, to stop quality teams from being formed. While a detailed discussion of this issue is beyond the scope of this chapter's charge, a fair conclusion might be that the federal experience with service quality mirrored the more successful experience of many state governments of the early 1990's with quality. States like Ohio, Pennsylvania, Florida and others with solid records of successful labor-management cooperation were some of the benchmark examples of adopting quality management in government. Labor-management partnership under Clinton made quality management much more acceptable and hence viable as the Defense Department's championing of quality management throughout the 1990's clearly demonstrated.

In 2000, when the Bush administration came to office, quality was still a major consideration in their management plan, but with differences. The stated goal of the Bush administration's agency reform was to provide government that was more customer-focused, results-oriented, and market-driven. Citizens would become aware of the change in service quality and citizen satisfaction would result (U.S. Office of Management and Budget, 2002). Yet at the same time, Bush's strategy of limiting government by devolving program costs and responsibility to the states and curtailing federal efforts, especially in the social service sector, would work counter to many agencies' quality improvement efforts. Simply put, the goal of providing the best service quality possible has limited impact when it must compete with the goal of reducing the overall level or quantity of service.

One would expect that the budget restrictions that have accompanied the "limited government approach" to have a negative impact on the capacity of government to perform even some of its core functions. Yet government capacity has been affected by two seemingly contradictory trends. Swiss (2005) has argued that capacity has been enhanced by improvements in communication and information technology, while Ingraham (2005) is concerned that capacity has been negatively impacted by the scant attention paid to workforce recruitment, planning and training. However, this is a reoccurring theme in both sectors: focusing on technology while neglecting the people who employ that technology stymies quality improvement efforts. Advances in e-government have led to governmental efficiencies while at the same time neglectful personnel policies threaten to undermine these gains. Ingraham argues that capacity is a precondition for performance, so too it must be a precondition for quality. Nonetheless, quality, especially how it manifests itself in concern for citizen satisfaction with government services, survives because quality has become ingrained as a part of the thinking about government performance.

This "technology-provided" versus "personal-provided" service issue is especially significant for governments and their public consumers. Behind that Washington Post headline on farmers' anger about closing county farm offices is an actual program – entitled "FSA tomorrow" with stated goals of making services more efficient, re-skilling the agency employees to do business on-line ;.. and most controversial of all- "bringing the country's farmer into the Internet Age." No one doubts that internet service is more efficient, faster, more accessible, and possibly more convenient. But what about customer equity, especially for public consumers? And what happens if what government wants is not what the public customer wants?

This is the focus of the second debate and it is a long ways from the original debate about service quality. It seems hard to believe that in the 1980's, conventional thinking was that the quality movement would be hard-pressed to shift from its initial application in manufacturing/production to the service arena. Many pointed out that Japan, the acknowledged world leader in quality, was not even applying quality management to its services and public sectors. James Swiss noted in his now seminal *Public Administration Review* article that finding solutions to the problems of applying TQM to services (i.e., that services are very labor intensive, are produced and consumed often simultaneously, and vary greatly in uniformity) would be elusive (Swiss, 1992).

Many public managers agreed and adopted the position that while quality management was fine for making widgets, it couldn't and wouldn't work for hospitals, legal clinics, schools, social services, etc. In reality, that transition wasn't the problem. Much of the evidence in the private and now public sector even suggests that services may have a natural advantage in applying quality management. This is not to suggest that there aren't major problems to be dealt with in service quality improvement and innovation. But most organizations saw the "quality is just for widgets" argument as a red herring. Since the "SERVQUAL" challenge was issued, customer service improvement has become a well developed territory with well defined roads and discernible destination points. And those public managers who say that service quality is not applicable to their operation are likely to find a growing line of private sector, non-profit, and even other public sector agency service providers who would welcome the opportunity to take that operation over, either as prime contractor or direct manager.

Nevertheless, the contention is strongly made that customer service is much more complicated in the public sector. (One would hope that it would be). The core question to be faced is: How does the public sector reconcile the often-competing needs of its customers or program/service consumers with its ultimate customer "the citizen," or perhaps more discerning, the public taxpayer? This issue has deeply divided the public administration community between those who see the customer service concept as going too far and those who see it as only the first step of a much more ambitious agenda to change the way governments do business.

THE PUBLIC ADMINISTRATION CRITIQUE OF CUSTOMER SERVICE

To be fair, the customer service concept introduced by the National Performance Review was not the only tenet of that executive reform effort that drew heavy fire from the public administration academic community. Reinventing Government was subject to numerous criticisms, from it being labeled nothing more than a downsizing effort to more serious concerns about failing to understand the problems it was attempting to fix, to scathing rebukes of the various solutions being offered up as executive reform. In the middle of this rather fierce debate was the citizen-customer problem. If public sector bureaucrats were unsure of who their customers were, and what they were supposed to do about improving customer service, many academics were quite sure that the entire notion of the citizen as customer corrupted the basic ideals of government and their relationships with the public.

This critique often begins with exactly that charge: that the concept of customer marginalized the idea of citizenship and distorted the basic meaning of the Constitution. In a 1996 symposium review of the NPR in the *Public Administration Review,* the academic contributors lambasted the idea of customer service orientation as unacceptable. One suggested that to recast citizens as customers is to accede to the notion that the government is no longer accepted as "we, but they" (Fox, 1996, p. 260). Another saw customer service as merely another wedge in the privatization effort in which "the empowered customer makes individual (or family) choices in a competitive market, thus breaking the bureaucratic service monopoly" (Fredrickson, 1996 p. 265). Still another viewed customer service based on any idea of a market model completely ignorant of the realities of what government is all about and what it is responsible for. This critique concluded that clients are treated differently by private firms, "the bigger the client, the better the service;" and nonclients are obviously less, if at all, important. Citizens, however, demand equal and fair treatment for all from their governments. Lest we forget "one person's red tape is often another's due process." (Peters and Savoie, 1996, p. 280).

These are serious criticisms in the sense that governments cannot ignore their responsibilities to citizens and clients. But what are we really talking about here? Does improving customer service really mean that the U. S. Constitution is being changed to "We, the customers?" Proponents argue that service quality is a much more modest proposition. It merely starts an assessment in which public servants (as service providers) examine the processes they use to provide products and services (be they tax collection payments, social security checks, library books, drivers licenses, payloads on the space shuttle; or permits, licenses, patents, whatever) and include the concept of process quality in that assessment. When service quality uses the word customer it means "consumers" any party that receives goods and services along some chain of distribution or process.

Essentially, there is a technical side to service quality that all public agencies (and private firms) must provide (is it correct and is it in conformance with the stated requirements and rules) that is basically the same. However, in the service sector, there is a process side (considerations like convenience, access, cost, professional courtesy, and even a procedure to hear and fix complaints) which is also important. And, the better the technical quality, the more important process quality becomes as a differentiator of better service.

There should always be a balance. Having an effective complaint procedure does not mean that when revenue officials make a mistake on your taxes, they are going to allow you a free year without paying taxes to make up for your inconvenience. There are real limits on the IRS that the staff at the Ritz Carlton hotel chain doesn't face. Ritz Carlton, as one of its service quality tenets, gives its employees levels of cash credits to fix customer problems they find on the spot.

This idea of process quality was what reinventing government was striving for when it declared putting customers first was one of its core tenets. It meant simply that government had to understand the expectations of a consumer oriented society that expects service hours tailored more to their convenience, more accessible locations to access the service, more mediums (telephone, fax, and internet) to conduct service transactions; and perhaps most of all being treated with courtesy and even a degree of empathy, especially when government is doing business. Perhaps that's the key distinction.

Henry Mintzberg's classic examination of these distinctions suggested that there are four such categories of relationships between the public and the government: customers, clients, citizens, and subjects (Mintzberg, 1996). He argued that as customers and citizens, we enjoy a reciprocal, give-and-take relationship with government "Government's customers receive direct services at arms length; its citizens benefit more indirectly from the public infrastructure it provides. As subjects and clients, we have relationships with government that are more one-sided" (Mintzberg, 1996, p. 77).

But, does this overlap mean that public sector agencies must take a hands off approach to service quality? That's not really possible since even a non-policy of bare minimum, no frills, first come-first served service favors some over others. If National Parks, as an example, based admission and obtaining campsites based on whoever they found lined up outside their gates each day, the results might be "fair," but very inequitable. Visitors to national parks – as customers - want a quality tourist experience, which means preserving the park environment, limiting the number of visitors at any one time, and now even regulating the transportation modes they may use to access the parks. The Parks Service also wants a mix of visitors that is both local and national- hence the need for a reservation system and potentially one that equalizes opportunity but respects the desires of local citizens who live nearby the Park. Lastly, as citizens and subjects, we want the parks to be accessible and well managed, as well as preserving our natural and historical heritage.

How does the National Parks Service reconcile all of those demands and relationships? Just as they make investments by different programs: one for reservation systems, one for visitors and concessions, one for park maintenance, one for cultural and historical preservation, and one even for the acquisition of new parks; they also can segment their customers and clients in terms of their consumer preferences, i.e., who desires to use what service at what cost, and with what restrictions. Similarly, the National Parks have an interest in being good, or at least respectful, neighbors with those who live or make their livings next to the park lands. All of these relationships can be segmented by risk; meaning that public agencies can attempt to serve customers, clients, citizens, and even subjects by articulating their service goals in conjunction with their policy, program, and budget objectives. And that service policy can be adjusted as various customers change behaviors, expectations, and loyalties.

Mintzberg is right in pointing out that the type of *caveat emptor,* "let the buyer beware," often associated with business transactions is an inappropriate philosophy for the public sector. The fact is, increasingly, such a strategy is unacceptable; certainly for the long run, even for the private sector. One should not underestimate the difficulty in creating customer service standards or service guarantees for public sector transactions. However, if governments are going to be in the business of providing direct services to consumers of those services, they need to understand what customer service really means and what are the most appropriate methods for measuring satisfaction and value. They too must segment customers and their transactions by risk, volume, cost, and most importantly, by value and all the other dimensions that make service quality such a critical aspect of organizational performance.

But segmentation in public sector customer service is entering a new phase in development in the internet era. Governments are rapidly working out the difficulties of providing equal and secure access (namely overcoming the digital divide and addressing the security issues that make administering entitlement programs, collecting taxes, enforcing regulations, and sharing information with all the public a more difficult task than what the private sector encounters). As they do, more and more customer service quality will be refocused and reshaped within three core domains – B2B, B2C, and B2E: - which more properly should be labeled G2B, G2C, and G2E. or government to business, customers, and employees (Figure 1).

Figure 1 – Innovation in Public Service Quality

Service Domain	G2E – Government to Employee	G2B – Government to Business	G2C^2 – Government to Customer/Citizen
Core Concept	E-Management through "Portfolio" for self-management	E-Management through "Enterprise Accounts"	E-Management through Client "E-Record"
Service Quality Goal	Consolidate all administration actions into Employee Accounts for transparency, efficiency, and knowledge management	Create two-way business relationships with current and potential contractors, suppliers, agents, and networks of bidders—E-Procure lean services and products	Provide better service with complete record of transactions, requests ofr service, effects (accountability and compliance) – data mining of trends and impacts
The Next Big Thing: Service Innovation for 2010	E-Folio (master records of all administrative actions and decisions for each employee, section, and organization)	E-Sourcing (two-way bidding auctions and sourcing for service provision)	E-Records (Electronic medical records)
Customer Equity Issues	Security & Fraud issues versus grid administrative service concept (better systems accountability, leaner operations)	Open Competition versus waste reduction, environmental improvement, lower overhead costs	Privacy issues versus Improving Nations Health & Controlling Health Care Costs

- Where the internet has been most effective is in taking advantage of efficiencies created by establishing business to business (B2B) communications networks. G2B- "government to business" simply allows select businesses that "opt in" to set up accounts, share business and transaction data, and order, supply, bill, reconcile – in short conduct business over the internet between a government agency and a corporate or non-profit entity. This is already a reality in many federal and state agencies with their "contractors" or vendors.

- Government to customers (G2C) is now entering the space where B2C is. Buying (and selling) goods and services over the internet has already grown rapidly in business from the successes of Amazon to E-Bay. In government, a first plateau – establishing useable websites and single points of access to individuals has been reached. The next plateau- conducting transactions (from registering motor vehicles to making tax payments) – is still a work in progress. Agencies are just now addressing how to incentivize public transactions over the net. What they don't yet know is whether they can follow the example of the airlines (well maybe just the ones in bankruptcy) who after a brief period of providing incentives for customers to purchase tickets online, now charge customers who call to talk to a real person and purchase a ticket. Agencies aren't quite ready for the outcry if social security was to charge for office visits and phone calls or the postal service was to charge more for stamps purchased over the counter than those offered online. Of course, one might ask if "consolidating the number of offices" a la the headline examples cited of IRS and the AFS isn't tactically the same approach.

- One would think the third domain – government to employee (G2E) would be the easiest. High tech firms like Microsoft require their employees to do online most personal management functions. i.e., travel, training, IT upgrades and repairs, purchasing, performance reviews) as part of daily self-management. Intricate software systems then "mine" the corporate business to leverage purchasing power or diffuse innovative practices. The reality is that there is still reluctance (call it lack of trust) to put the potential of B2E action in play within government. Part of the issue is multiple data bases and separate systems within the management functions but another is surely the mindset of managers, many of whom are unwilling to do their own administrative work.

The G2B, G2C, G2E domains raise a larger question about which should come first. For the Government re-inventors in the early 1990's, improving public service quality was largely a tactical question of how to improve the image of government. The current question is much more strategic. Should we on the one hand first figure out how governance is going to work in cyberspace in terms of impacting citizens, interest groups, and society and then construct a new model for virtual management and customer service. Or- should we accept that IT has so fundamentally altered management processes, organizational structures, workforce capabilities, and knowledge management that public sector management and by extension service quality should track and adapt innovations developed as strategic necessity. It is all the more ironic that the debate in business has shifted to whether or not IT provides strategic advantage and whether it is or is not like a common utility (Carr, 2004).

Clearly- E-government, using the internet to post information, provide services, collect data and encourage democratic participation, is already one of the most important innovations in the way government conducts business. Creating new solutions to improving service quality using technology was one of the stated purposes of the E-government Act of 2001 which required departments and agencies at the federal level to use internet technology to achieve savings, improve results and increase customer service levels (U.S. OMB, 2004). This was akin to bursting through an open door since the World Wide Web had already permeated all levels of government. By 2000, every state had installed a state government web portal and all had designated a chief information officer (Bretschneider, 2003). At the local level Ho (2002) reports that large municipalities have been moving away from a traditional department oriented web design toward a "one-stop shopping" and more customer-oriented Web design. E-government is new design for customer service and quality enhancement.

Thomas and Streib (2003) have reported that most citizen contact with government on the Web has been to obtain information and the citizens were generally pleased with the service they obtained there. The potential for moving up the chain of participation to delivering services and eventually facilitating participating in government decision-making and planning are within the realm of the possible. But this is not without cost. Generally, the digital divide persists. Those who use the Web to communicate with government are not representative of the country. Although examining only Georgia, Thomas and Streib (2003) found that visitors to government web sites were generally "wealthier, better educated, younger, more urban and whiter" than the rest of the population (p. 98). The mode of service delivery then would be determined by socio economic status.   Furthermore, the capacity problem again influences future developments in e-government as insufficient staff and lack of funding hamper efforts to extend the tasks and reach of Web based citizen services.

THE INTERNAL REVENUE SERVICE AND QUALITY SERVICE: A CASE STUDY IN RELATIVITY

Earlier the example of Park Service was used to explain how the public generally accepts the limitations applied by the Park Service in visiting and using parks. It helps also that the public generally likes the Park Service. In terms of quality, one might say they have a surfeit of brand and corporate image quality. How does customer service work when the agency provides a service people don't like and worse ... when the public doesn't like the agency either?

The case example here is easy to find. In a nation where the public basically distrusts government and dislikes taxes, one would expect the public to dislike the tax collection agency. And Americans have always seemed to dislike the IRS very much. Back in 1998, based on a Pew Research Center Study on Americans' View of Government, the

IRS was the only major federal agency with a higher unfavorable rating than positive. 60% rated the IRS negatively compared to 38% who view it positively (Pew Research Center: 1998). The same year, an ABC News.com Poll found that 61% of respondents saw the IRS as "too harsh" on average people compared to 29% responding "about right." Those ratings came at a point where most federal agencies were showing some increases in public ratings over the last decade. IRS's favorable ratings had dropped 11% in the same period.

To be fair to the IRS and its employees, they are not the sole creators of the tax code which even President Clinton, in a rare moment of candor and who was not campaigning for tax reform, admitted was too complicated to understand. The IRS is also unlike other agencies in that elected officials don't make a habit of indicting the Post Office or the National Park Service as part of our economic and political woes. IRS also suffers from "communication aversion" in that the majority of taxpayers want the IRS to be basically invisible and to have minimal contact with them. Lastly, it should be pointed out that the IRS has not been sitting by idly over the past twenty years in terms of management effort. It has long been a leader among public agencies in the quality management arena. Along with its union, IRS was one of the first public agencies to embrace the quality management movement and to introduce quality concepts in government.

That having been said, IRS began in the late 1990's to take very aggressive steps to deal with its customer service problem. In a report entitled *Reinventing Service At The IRS* (Report of the IRS Customer Service Task Force, 1998) it provided a very frank assessment of what the IRS thought it knew and didn't know about customer service. First, it acknowledges publicly that the majority of taxpayer mistakes are caused by the complexity of the tax system and the lack of clarity of the forms, instructions, and communications issued by the IRS. The full realization of this comes when IRS admits, as it does with this report, that the fact that nearly half of taxpayers hire a tax preparer to do their taxes is itself a serious customer service issue. Likewise, another candid admission noted: "In another example of the agency's internal focus, the task force found that the IRS often tested its notices for clarity on employees already familiar with the subject of the notice, rather than on customers" (IRS, 1998, p. 64).

In the rather paternalistic world of the public sector, this is often the product of an internally focused mindset. The IRS Task Force report showed what rethinking the "how" and "why" of service quality can lead to. The report discussed in depth customer segment profiles (individual, small businesses, corporations, etc.), and future customer market projections (seniors, older-working age, self-employed, foreign language speaking, etc.). Then it addressed the special needs and expectations of each segment. Once you start thinking about providing better service, promoting easier and faster access, and helping customers, you've got to be able to differentiate levels of risk with current and future groups of customers and their needs before you start dictating service solutions. That's the start of an external focus.

Perhaps the most interesting new dimension to reinventing customer service was the new reorganization strategy to restructure the IRS into three core business units: one for individual taxpayers, one for small businesses, and one for corporations. In service quality, that would be called aligning the organization around a more holistic set of customer service needs and priorities. It's also the way several major corporations in communications and finance have organized their business units to service needs. If direct and close product-service-customer line of sight is the goal, that's the total concept.

How should the fruits of service quality reinvention be assessed at the IRS? There is a bottom-line gauge and IRS is one of the few federal agencies that is on it. Customer satisfaction levels for many corporations are measured each quarter by the ACSI (American Customer Satisfaction Index) through the University of Michigan. The IRS, the U.S. Postal Service, and an aggregate sample of urban and suburban police and public works departments, at that time were the few public sector agencies measured on an indexed 100 point scale, combining customer ratings of: expectations, quality, value, satisfaction, complaint handling, and loyalty. (Since then, a number of federal agencies are included in the ACSI scoring, as will be discussed).

IRS's rating was at 54 in 1997, was still quite low, but up 8% from 1996. The Postal Service rated a 69 in 1997, down 7% from 1996. To establish the corporate range for comparison purposes, in 1997, the highest rated company was Mercedes at 87, while MacDonald's was lowest at 60 (University of Michigan, 1998). Fast track forward to 2004 and considerable improvement is evident as the scorecard below shows.

ACSI Public Sector Scores	Public Administration (overall)	Local Government (Solid waste, Police)	Internal Revenue Service
1994	64.3	65.9	55.0
1995	61.9	66.2	54.0
1996	59.2	65.0	50.0
1997	62.4	67.7	54.0
1998	64.6	69.6	53.0
1999	68.7	68.7	*51.0
2000	67.0	65.7	*56.0
2001	69.3	67.9	*60.0
2002	67.9	66.3	*62.0
2003	68.3	66.5	*63.0
2004	65.8	62.7	*64.0

* Score Revised as Average for measured customer segments

What IRS did after 1999 through ACSI was break out service quality scores for six categories of customer segments. Taking the 2004 highpoint rating of 64 - this breaks out as:

Individual Electronic tax Filers	Individual Paper tax Filers	Small Business Corporate Tax Filers	Tax-Exempt Organizations	Large & Midsize Business Corporate tax Filers	Employee Plans
78.0	52.0	60.0	59.0	51.0	51.0

(http.//www.theacsi.org/government/govt-all-04.html)

IRS may never reach the level of Mercedes, but simply having a bottom-line customer service metric provided by an outside entity means that IRS now knows whether it is getting better or getting worse compared to a field of other service providers where the pace is continually changing. Does improved customer service translate into more of the public liking the IRS? There has been, in fact, a gain in IRS's corporate image quality. A Gallup poll in 2005 showed 48% of respondents rating the IRS as good in enforcing the tax laws so that everyone pays what they should. Not bad perhaps when one considers that 54% of same poll respondents rated the federal income tax system as basically unfair. Of course, overall tax burden has decline in the past 5 years. Since 1999, when 45% regarded their income tax payments as unfair; the seeing their income tax payment as fair is now 61% (Gallup Poll, 2005). That's the problem with using polling data to track quality and why the IRS example is such a good illustration of how public agencies can segment their customer bases and begin to overhaul their service approach. One can even defend closing walk-in centers when the IRS can demonstrate that electronic filing is not only more efficient but a better source of customer satisfaction and quality.

SEARCHING FOR NEW STRATEGIES IN THE INTERNET ECONOMY

So the real task confronting public sector managers in this pivotal decade of transformation is to understand just how significant the private sector's new pursuit of service quality will be, and thus how it will affect public sector "competitiveness." Service quality transformation promises to speed up dramatically. Robert Woodruff in a future projecting article in a forum on Marketing for the 21st Century asserted that past improvement attempts by organizations that were internally focused on themes like TQM, reengineering, downsizing, and restructuring would be viewed as insufficient. The thrust for "competitive advantage" would be largely externally focused on what he called delivering customer value. Successful organizations would have to focus on their markets, target customers and transform their customer knowledge into specific performance improvements by brand and by customer segment (Woodruff, 1997).

Woodruff was right in predicting that few would see the relevance of the late 1980's when a few service quality gurus, like Karl Albrecht (1990), and numerous tradebooks written by corporate directors of service or consultants expounded on the virtues of Total Quality Service as an offshoot of TQM. The customer value and subsequently the brand value literature has simply exploded as market and business researchers have covered all facets of defining, analyzing, and predicting customer attitudes and behaviors: segmentation, satisfaction, expectations, retention, loyalty, benchmarking, internal and external organizational aspects, metrics, and complaint processes. Likewise, there are articles examining service quality impacts and issues in various industries from welfare offices, hospitals and clinics, police stations, and janitorial services, to tax collection and post offices. Unfortunately, the research base in public sector service quality is simply not keeping pace. (Probably, this should be expected given that most schools of public administration do not have a marketing research area which is a driving force in this area among business schools.)

When the Bush administration announced its Presidential Management agenda for fiscal year 2002, it made "competitive sourcing" the second of five government-wide initiatives. It was, along with e-government, the two real strategic differences from Clinton's NPR agenda as the graphic below overviews:

	Reinventing Government (1993-2000)	Improving Government Performance (2001-present)
Vision Statement	"Creating a government that works better and costs less"	"Improve the Management and Performance of the Federal Government"
Core Strategies and Key Principles	Create Entrepreneurial Organizations focused on: ❑ Cutting Red Tape ❑ Putting Customers First ❑ Empowering Employees to get Results ❑ Cutting Back to Basics	Reform Government Operations focused on: ❑ Citizen-centered, not bureaucracy-centered, ❑ Results-oriented, ❑ Market-based, actively promoting rather than stifling innovation through competition
Source	Report of the National Performance Review 1993	The President's Management Agenda 2001

In the new arena of managed competition, public sector managers (not just federal) must incorporate service strategy into their managerial competencies. This means seeing customer service as a core value; not as a competing priority or a program initiative. This goes beyond simply rethinking the formula for providing services to the public by expanding business hours or locating offices in more convenient locations. The Post Office is the next great test case for understanding how to rethink service strategy as it struggles to compete with UPS and FedEx and the disappearance of first class mail from its core business. Postal services all across the globe are facing the prospect that 80% of their letter mail currently from businesses to individuals (billing and monthly statements) will disappear once businesses provide the right incentives for virtual billing and statements. Private mail is already under 10% of letter volume and half of that comes during the Christmas holiday season. As junk mail grows (now at almost a third of letter volume) customer satisfaction with the mail system will surely decline as fast as customers are. But the future of public postal services is actually quite bright. E-commerce will be increasingly dependant on parcels, express deliveries, and convenient pick-up locations. There's no reason that the post office, if it identifies its competition and where it can develop customer value, can't develop a strategy to compete in the internet economy.

What will be required are new strategies to take public managers beyond the conventional customer service requirements identified with the issuance of Executive Order 12862 in 1993. The National Performance Review should be seen as setting the baseline for taking what were clearly the right first steps in having agencies create basic standards of service, and survey customers on levels of compliance and satisfaction. But the core steps of Executive Order 12862 should be updated, much as we urged in the first edition of this article. What follows is a table that attempts to depict how the 1993 requirements might be transformed for "21C"- or the 21st Century Internet economy.

Executive Order 12862 Customer Service Requirements (1993)	Customer Service Requirements Transformed for the Internet Economy –
A. Identify the customers served by the agency.	*A.* Identify current & future customers served by their industry – create profiles for services and assess demands & needs – for service, mode of access, service delivery.
B. Survey customers to determine demand & satisfaction	*B.* Survey customers about what they value now and project for the future – develop customer segments around customer value concept
C. Post service standards & measure compliance	*C.* Continuously improve service standards and performance for both customer and customer segment
D. Benchmark customer service performance against business	*D.* Benchmark customer service performance with partners (suppliers, other providers, service representatives)

Executive Order 12862 Customer Service Requirements (1993)	Customer Service Requirements Transformed for the Internet Economy –
E. Survey front line employees on barriers/suggestions	*E*. Realign and train front-line employees into service teams – to manage accounts – develop service policy improvements
F. Provide customers with choices (sources and delivery)	*F*. Provide customers "choices" based on value – that respect economy & need, privacy, but capture segment trends
G. Make information, services, complaint systems accessible.	*G*. Reengineer information/services/complaint tracking systems so citizen can follow status of request for service or change
H. Provide means to address customer complaints	*H*. Leverage customer complaints - refocus on customer and customer segment needs and issues

Even if Executive Order 12862 had been rigorously implemented in all agencies, which of course it wasn't, it would still require major steps forward to reach the next plateau of competition. With the exception of the benchmarking requirement, most of the customer service steps are based on the standard quality model which is much too internally focused. It doesn't look outward enough at different kinds of customers and market factors, their expectations, or their priorities. A few comments are in order to explain how the first era of customer service requirements might be transformed to the next and why.

Public sector managers must begin by ensuring that their surveys of customers examine demographics, future market factors, potential new customers, and even departed customers. Even more important, public sector agencies must look beyond their organizational or functional boundaries and see customers from the "industry" or "community" perspective. Following the IRS example, they must carefully assess the prospects for developing customer segments and realigning service teams to become more expert in delivering services to the segment. They may even want to rethink their customer service value proposition. Conventional thinking requires a sufficient number of consumers who need the service before a jurisdiction would produce and provide it. The economics of the internet have generated a new business market scenario – what is referred to as the "long tail." If potential consumers of a product or service can be identified and accessed via the internet, a niche marketing or customer service segment can be created and made affordable. What would be unthinkable because no one organization has enough consumers in their area alone who want the product or service; a "niche item" is feasible if one government agency could provide the service to consumers in different jurisdictions.

Further, customer needs are not static. Public sector managers must plan to serve needs in transition. This is more than factoring in the accelerating impacts of technology change. It isn't just that more people will be willing and able to use the internet to access services- it is that the public will have more information and be more knowledgeable about what they want (or worse, what someone else received that they think they want) and want access to more information about what services they've received in the past.

Regarding customer service standards, the historical tendency was to establish a minimum level of service that the agency knows it can guarantee and cover 99% of the time. Even when an agency knows it can do significantly better, there weren't incentives to continually improving service standards when a service can be delivered in half the time "promised." That simply no longer works. Customer's expectations are shaped by all their service experiences, not by what one organization proclaims as their service standards. Even as business pushes more and more of service to call-in centers in who knows where to match their on-line offerings, response cycle time is going to be shorter and shorter.

Like it or not, public sector managers are going to be compared to other providers who offer better choice, convenience, access, and above all speed. Consumers of public services will take a day off to come in person to public offices, sit in waiting rooms, or wait in long lines for hours, and accept delays and excuses; but don't expect them to like it when the norm is automated tellers, guaranteed next day delivery, set appointments, one-call service response, and faster and faster turn-around on service actions. The real need is for public managers to continually raise the bar and announce and demonstrate to customers how much service is improving and will improve across multiple fronts.

So little real benchmarking of public sector agencies service performance is going on now that it seems ridiculous to call for next steps. But there is much to be gained by agencies working as partners with other agencies and even private sector firms in this arena. Benchmarking also needs to be viewed as a potential joint endeavor designed to augment the size of the market or improve core capabilities. With the rapidly approaching revolution of e-commerce and other new forms of Internet based services, this will be essential. The real purpose behind benchmarking is diffusion of best practice. Public agencies will come to see that service innovation in the private sector will have to be copied in 3-6-9 months as opposed to the couple of years excuse so often used in the public sector regarding any change.

In addressing the input of front-line employees, corporations are already emphasizing – "time with the customer" as a key organizational value. Indeed, many corporations have learned that it is the front-line employees (and indirectly their morale) that have the most direct impact on customer satisfaction. Raising the bar means paying attention to the incentives that encourage the public employee to really strive for improved quality and service. The impediments to trying harder are both personal (resistance to change, lack of understanding, or preference of personal goals over organizational ones) and organizational (politician preference for symbolic outcomes, no profit incentive, or short time frames). Swiss (2005) argues that for incentives to work the reward or punishment must be tied to results and the system must be viewed by the employees as fair. These two criteria are not usually present under the current civil service arrangements.

Employees will also need direct access to customer data to examine the gaps between what they think the customer values and what customers say they think. More importantly, front-line employees will need better training and direct involvement in designing and improving service systems, including the creation of new types of new technology supported service teams. Tied to this active role of employees is interaction with customers about a range of choices on the technical and process quality of service, at what cost. Choice means dialogue and ongoing market research about what customers value. But none of this will happen until agencies set up systems to share employee knowledge about customer service process and outcomes.

The impacts of technology are already apparent. At some point, there will be a collision between service systems controlled by software generated menu-based phone answering protocols and service response efforts that tie up more and more personnel hours before providing a real human voice. Clearly there will be more choices provided to consumers, and those choices will probably include costs. What public sector managers must seek out are ways to reassess the relationship between accounts and transactions.

There are a number of options, but they begin with the agency thinking about tracking the services provided to categories of consumers as opposed to simply counting the services by category. Banks are already showing some of the possibilities as they shift from a phone call based transactions menu to reach a person to more on-line banking, prompted by a recording informing you of how much longer you have to wait to talk with someone and what the internet address is for you to handle your transaction on-line. Many banks have even realigned their physical space to make them less attractive and more crowded places to be in to encourage consumers to do their routine business on-line or by ATM.

In summary, for all the controversy Executive Order 12862 has generated, it is no longer adequate for customer service strategic thinking. Service quality strategy requires a much more advanced premise. It begins with the organization listening and doing ongoing research about different kinds of customers in a dynamic flow. Of course, that's easy to say, but very hard to do. It's especially hard to do in the public sector in many cases because agency missions are often fragmented, and services are shared with other providers. For example, providing services for the homeless may seem straightforward until you see the proliferation of agencies which are in this arena at different levels of government trying to cope with a "consumer population" that is 30% veterans, 30%-40% alcohol or drug dependent, and other percentages encompassing single parents with young children, young adults coming out of foster care, or sick persons coming out of hospitals or mental health facilities. Even if every agency from the police, welfare, housing, veterans, and health care agencies had a specific service plan for performing their role in helping the homeless, they would still fall short on providing the continuum of care that can only come from an integrated service strategy that plans for different segments of the growing number of citizens at risk in this country who live on our streets.

If a customer base can be established, public sector agencies must then develop knowledge about current and future customer expectations and understand consumer experiences and perceptions of cost, quality, responsiveness, and even the organization's corporate image. Current thinking about service quality differentiates among first time, short term, long term, and even lost customers; and sees each with different values regarding transactions, and even their relationship with the service provider. (Parasuraman, 1997). All of this affects the ultimate idea of customer value, which extends beyond products and services provided to a consumer, to include the relationship and "emotional bond" between the customer and the producer (Butz and Goldstein, 1996).

Finally, the strategy must translate service quality knowledge into superior performance. This means more than creating a marketing group or a new service department, or increasing awareness about the importance of service at all levels of the organization. It also means more than tracking customer satisfaction levels. Superior performance means the deployment of new ideas, new products, and new service choices and features, while maintaining superior cost. In short, the competitive organization must be highly adept at knowing what customers need now and in the future, and how to get better at delivering those products and services.

CONVERTING STRATEGY TO ACTION

Having addressed what the next level of creating a new service quality strategy means for public managers, there remains a final obstacle: making change happen. One should not underestimate the problems inherent in interpreting customer feedback. It is just as easy to use customer service quality information to perpetuate the pursuit of last year's objectives or lock the organization into a static set of service standards, reducing the capability to change and respond to external forces, and desensitizing the organization to the needs of the future marketplace. In a tight budget environment, any agency can use customer focus to become market blind.

To avoid this problem, public sector agencies are first going to have to rethink their planning horizons. In fact, the argument can be made that in today's' accelerating technology-driven environment, planning in the conventional sense may have to be abandoned altogether. For all the progress made, since the passage of the Government Performance Results Act, by federal agencies putting together their five-year strategic planning processes, there may have to be a recognition that product and service innovations operate within 12 to 18 month time frames and require a very different mindset. Shona Brown and Kathleen Eisenhardt in their book *Competing on the Edge* describe one corporation's problems: ".... [the organization's] managers simply did not understand that in high velocity markets, a strategic plan is an emotional rallying point and a resource roadmap. It is not anything more and it certainly does not provide any insight about the future" (Brown & Eisenhardt, 1998, p. 159). The point of this chapter is hopefully equally clear in asserting for public sector managers that a dynamic and effective customer service strategy must always be about the future.

A second demand will be for public sector agencies to rethink their managerial mindsets. Improving public service customer quality is not the same as service quality innovation. One of the most compelling reasons to make service quality a cornerstone of any organization's management philosophy is the opportunity to move to the cutting edge of change. Increasingly organizations are realizing that their attempts to do research and development and technology transfer are failing badly. Even when the R&D group comes up with a worthwhile development, it often is flatly rejected or resistance to adoption greatly diminishes its value. Management theorists now argue that entire new model for innovation is needed that portrays innovation as a customer-client relationship.

To be successful, organizations have to customize innovation, develop relationships with lead-users and user-innovation communities, and develop relationships with users to be a partner, not dictator in change (Von Hippel, 2005). That same prescription can be used for service quality. To generate real customer service quality and effective performance, public agencies need to move into an entirely different arena where the services they provide are less important than the relationships they create and the opportunity to create the next generation of products and services are more important than simply regulating who gets what from the public domain.

Third, improving quality begins at the transaction level. First line employees are the gatekeepers of the clients' evaluation of the quality of the interaction and their impact on the process has been greatly underestimated. Just as most people quit their boss before they quit their organization, individuals will resent the way they are treated by a public servant before they begin to hate the department of motor vehicles, the IRS office or the department of human services. Purchasing technology results in a tangible product, the result of investing in training is less apparent. But it makes no sense to invest in technology yet neglect the training of those who are to use it. It is also to the detriment of service quality to over-manage, under-resource and under-value the front line workers because they are the face of the government office to the clients and citizens. It is trendy to talk about employees as a resource and not a cost, but enhanced service quality cannot become reality until government actually understands and believes in their front line employees.

Finally, as public administration debates how we wish to shape our conceptualization of that strategy and what service quality is and should be, it is time to jettison our normal defensive posture. This is not about fads; this is about survival in the future. Paraphrasing a saying from one of the great classics of modern Italian literature, if public managers want things to stay the same, things will really have to change.

REFERENCES

Albrecht, K. (1990). *Service Within*. Homewood, Ill: Dow Jones Irwin.

Ambrose, M. (1997). A new way of thinking about customer service. *Business Communications Review*, *27*(7), 51-55.

Arora, R. and Stoner, C. (1996). The effect of perceived service quality and name familiarity on the service selection decision. *The Journal of Services Marketing*, *10*(1), 22-34.

Asubonteng, P., McCleary, K.J., and Swan, J.E. (1996). SERVQUAL revisited: a critical review of service quality. *The Journal of Services Marketing*, *10*(6), 62-81.

Babin, B.J., and Griffin, M. (1998). The nature of satisfaction: an updated examination. *Journal of Business Research*, 41, 127-136.

Berry, L.L., Zeithaml, V.A., and Parasuraman (1990). Five imperatives for improving service quality. *Sloan Management Review*, Summer, 29-38.

Bretschneider, S. (2003). Information Technology, E-Government, and Institutional Change. *Public Administration Review,* (63) 6. 738-741.

Brown, S.L and Eisenhardt, K.M. (1998). *Competing on the Edge*. Boston: Harvard Business School Press.

Bryant, B.E. (1996). Customers are different: satisfying all types is a challenge. (Working paper #9690-04). University of Michigan Business School, Ann Arbor, MI, 1-13.

Butz, H.E. and Goodstein, L. (1996). Measuring customer value: gaining the strategic advantage. *Organizational Dynamics*, *24*, (Winter), 63-77.

Canadian Centre for Management Development (1997). Citizen/Client Surveys: Dispelling Myths and Redrawing Maps, Ottawa.

Carr, N.G. (2004) Does IT Matter? (2004) Boston: Harvard Business School Press.

Chen, W.H. (1998). Benchmarking quality goals in service systems. *The Journal of Services Marketing*, *12*(2), 113-128.

Clow, K.E., Kurtz, D.L. & Ozment, J. (1998). A longitudinal study of the stability of consumer expectations of services. *Journal of Business Research*, *42*, (63-73).

Day, G.S. (1998). What does it mean to be market driven? *Business Strategy Review*, *9*(1), 1-14.

Fox, C.J. (1996). Reinventing government as postmodern symbolic politics. *Public Administration Review*, *56*(3) 256-261

Frederickson, H.G. (1996). Comparing the reinventing government movement with the new public administration. *Public Administration Review*, *56*(3), 263-269.

Gilbert G.R, and Nicholls, J.A.F. (1999). Measuring public sector customer service satisfaction. *The Public Manager*, *27*(4), 21-26.

Golembieski, R.T., Stevenson, J., and White, M. (1997). Cases in Public Management. Itasca: F. E. Peacock, p 119.

Hallowell, R. Schlesinger, L.A., and Zornitsky, J. (1996). Internal service quality, customer and job satisfaction: linkages and implications for management. *Human Resource Planning, 19*(2), 20-32.

Ho, A.T. (2002). Reinventing Local Governments and the E-Government Initiative. *Public Administration Review*, (62)4, 434-444.

Hyde, A.C. (1992). Feedback from Customers, Clients, and Captives. *The Bureaucrat, 22*(4), 35-40.

Hyde, A.C. (1995). Quality, Reengineering, and Performance: Managing Change in the

Public Sector. Halachmi, A. and Bouckaert, G. (Ed.), *The Enduring Challenges in Public Management.* San Francisco: Jossey-Bass, 150-176.

Hyde, A.C. (1995). Improving Customer Service Quality: Changing Concepts, Goals, and Methods. *The Public Manager,* Fall, 1995, *24*(3), 25-28.

Ingraham, P. (2005). Performance: Promises to Keep and Miles to Go. *Public Administration Review, 65*(4), 390-395.

Johns, N. & Tyas, P. (1997). Customer Perceptions of service Operations: Gestalt, Incident or Mythology. *The Services Industry Journal, 17*(3), 474-488.

Lewis, B. R. & Gabrielson, G.O.S. (1998). Intra-organizational aspects of service quality management: the employees perspective. *The Services Industry Journal, 18*(2), 64-89.

Macdonald, S. (1995). Too close for comfort? The strategic implications of getting close to the customer. *California Management Review, 37*(4), 8-28.

Mangold, W. G. & Babakus, E. (1991). Service quality: The front stage vs back stage perspective. *The Journal of Services Marketing, 5*(4), 59-70.

Mintzberg, H. (1996). Managing government, governing management. *Harvard Business Review,* (May-June), 75-83.

Parasuraman, A., Zeithaml, V.A. & Berry, L.L. (1985). A conceptual model of service quality and its implications for future research. *Journal of Marketing, 49*(3), 41-50.

Parasuraman, A. (1997). Reflections on gaining advantage through customer value. *Journal of the Academy of Marketing Science,* (25)2, 154-161.

Pegnato, J. A. (1997). Is a customer a citizen? *Public Productivity and Management Review,* (20)4, 397-404.

Peters, G.B. & Savoie, D. 1996. Managing Incoherence: The coordination and empowerment conundrum. *Public Administration Review, 56*(3), 281-289.

Powpaka, S. (1996). The role of outcome quality as a determinant of overall service quality in different categories of services industries: an empirical investigation. *The Journal of Services Marketing, 10*(2), 5-24.

Reeves, C.A., Bednar, D.A. & Lawrence, R.C. (1995). Back to the beginning: what do customers care about in service firms. *Quality Management Journal, 3*(1), 56-72.

Sturdy, A. (1998). Customer care in a consumer society: smiling and sometimes meaning it? *Organization, 5*(1) 27-53.

Swiss, J.E. (1992). Adapting Total Quality Management (TQM) to Government. *Public Administration Review, 52*(4), 356-362

Swiss, J.E. (2005). A Framework for assessing Incentives in Results-Based Management. *Public Administration Review 65*(5), 592-602.

Thomas, J.C. & Streib, G. (2003). The New Face of Government: Citizen-Initiated Contacts in the Era of E-Government. *Journal of Public Administration Research and Theory,* (13), 1, 83-102.

U. S. Government, *National Performance Review* (1994). Putting Customers First: Standards for Serving the American People, U.S. GPO: Washington.

U. S. Government, *National Performance Review* (1998). Reinventing Service at the IRS U.S. GPO: Washington.

U.S. OMB. (2004). Expanding E-Government: Partnering for a Results-Oriented Government. Retrieved from, http://www.whitehouse.gov/omb/budintegration/ expanding_egov12-2004.pdf

U.S. Office of Management and Budget. (2002) The President's Management Agenda. Retrieved from http://www.whitehouse.gov/omb/budintegration/ pma_index.html

Wayland, R.E. & Cole, *P. (1997). Customer Connections: New Strategies for Growth.* Boston: Harvard Business School.

Webb, D. (1998). Segmenting police customers on the basis of their service quality expectations. *The Service Industries Journal, 18*(1), 72-100.

Woodruff, R. B. (1997). Customer value: the next source for competitive advantage. *Journal of the Academy of Marketing Science, 25*(2), 139-153.

Zimmerman, D., Zimmerman, P., and Lund, C. (1997). Customer Service: the new battlefield for market share. *Healthcare Financial Management, 51*(3), 51-55.

Chapter 14

ETHICS AND ENTREPRENEURSHIP

Linda de Leon

An important criticism of public entrepreneurship has been that its precepts and practices are not consonant with democratic values. This chapter examines the meaning of entrepreneurship as defined in both the public and the private sectors, suggesting that some attributes of entrepreneurs that are commonly deemed undesirable -- egotism, selfishness, waywardness, domination, and opportunism -- are actually functional for entrepreneurial activity. This is because entrepreneurship plays an essential role in addressing a particular type of policy problems (here called "anarchic"), those where goals are ambiguous or conflicting and where the means to achieve them are unknown or uncertain. The ethical implications of excessive competition are explored. Finally, methods of encouraging ethical entrepreneurship, whether it is undertaken in an anarchic setting or within an organizational matrix that is communitarian or bureaucratic, are suggested.

Since the 1980s, the pressure on government to "do more with less" has become increasingly fierce; the road to administrative reform is littered with bashed bureaucrats, dashed hopes, and political casualties. Critics of the public sector have contrasted its "bungling" and inefficiency with the flexibility, creativity, and innovation of private business. The have lauded business for its entrepreneurial spirit, an intrepid willingness to accept risk in pursuit of greater gain. They have touted the private sector as either a model for public organizations to copy, or as an alternative means of service delivery -- the privatization of public functions. Stung by such rhetoric, and proving once again that necessity stimulates invention, public managers began to develop increasingly innovative approaches to their tasks. Thus was born "public entrepreneurship," in which (as so often happens) a concept from business was adapted to the public sector (Johnston, 1993; Osborne and Gaebler, 1992; Perlmutter and Cnaan, 1995; Tewes, 1983).

The first wave of recent reforms grew out of the "total quality" movement, which American business copied from Japanese management and which gradually made its way into the public sector. Although many critics bridled at applying the term "customer" to those who consume government services, the concepts of quality, continuous improvement, and user satisfaction found a receptive audience among beleaguered bureaucrats. The second wave of reform brought "reinvented" government, which caused far more ambivalent reactions than had quality. On the one hand, reinvention provided the public service with an opportunity to be seen as innovative, creative, efficient, and customer-oriented. Also, it was leverage for obtaining increased room for maneuver, for managerial discretion and employee empowerment. On the other hand, the price was high: the clear expectation of citizens and elected officials was that "savings" will be produced, usually from workforce reductions. And as critics of reinvention have pointed out, the RIFs are required, but investment -- in technology and training -- has not been forthcoming (DiIulio, Garvey and Kettl, 1993; Kettl, 1994).

Another important criticism of the reinvention initiative has been that its precepts and practices are not consonant with democratic values (Caiden, 1994; deLeon, 1998; Moe, 1994). For example, Bellone and Goerl (1992) charge that public entrepreneurship is based upon values -- such as autonomy, personal vision, secrecy and risk-taking -- that are opposed to democratic accountability, participation, openness and stewardship. In reply, Terry (1993) goes even further to suggest that any attempt to reconcile democratic values with entrepreneurship is misguided, since the latter implies a mindless disrespect for tradition and a reliance upon domination and coercion as a management style. Bellone and Goerl address these ethical concerns by proposing "civic-regarding" entrepreneurship, involving transparent operations by government and support for extensive citizen involvement at all stages of the policy process.

In recent years, moreover, a long string of scandals has tarnished the image of the private sector entrepreneur. Overpaid CEOs, get-rich-quick schemes, the dot-com bubble and other issues called into question the ability of the competitive marketplace to curb its own excesses. Some of the largest, most profitable and most admired firms were implicated: Adelphia, Arthur Anderson, Crédit Suisse, Dynergy, Enron, Global Crossing, Imclone, Qwest, Martha Stewart, Merrill Lynch, Rite Aid, Tyco and Worldcom are now in a rogues' gallery of transgressors. Their CEOs have done the "perp walk," their pension funds are bankrupt (leaving many former employees destitute), their stock prices have fallen, and in some cases, their doors have closed.

This chapter addresses the fears of many in both the public and the private sectors that entrepreneurship is dangerous to the public interest. It argues that entrepreneurship plays an essential role in both sectors as an engine of innovation and that, further entrepreneurship can be entirely ethical. But eternal vigilance is, for both markets and polities, required to prevent the dark side of entrepreneurship from obscuring its benefits. Beginning with an analysis of what entrepreneurship means, this discussion explores the role that ethical considerations play in entrepreneurial activity and the values that are congruent with it. It concludes by suggesting a variety of ways that public entrepreneurship can be held to high ethical standards and deployed to serve the public interest.

THE VIRTUES AND VICES OF ENTREPRENEURS

In French, the word *entreprendre* means to undertake. French economist J.B. Say, in 1800, used the term entrepreneur to signify a person who "shifts economic resources out of an area of lower and into an area of higher productivity and greater yield" (Drucker, 1985, p. 21).[1] Contemporary theorists, however, have amended this definition, primarily to focus on the entrepreneur's role as an innovator. Drucker, for example, considers entrepreneurship to be spotting opportunities and marshaling resources to produce innovation. In one of the first applications of the term to the public sector, Lewis identifies an entrepreneur as "a person who creates or profoundly elaborates a public organization so as to alter greatly the existing pattern of allocation of scarce public resources" (1980, p. 9). Fisher (1983) sees the entrepreneur as one who takes shrewd risks in order to break through the encrustations of bureaucracy. Stever considers entrepreneurship "an adaptive, opportunistic, and individualistic response to the chaos and fragmentation of post-Progressive public administration" (1988).

In all these definitions of entrepreneurship, innovation is a common theme, but this is not to say that all entrepreneurs are geniuses struck by the fire of the gods.[2] An innovation need not be something entirely new; rather, it could be the creative recombination of familiar elements, that is, known intervention used in a new way or a new setting (Khademian, 1995; Levin and Sanger, 1994). An engaging case study of a private-sector entrepreneur is the autobiography of Joseph J. Jacobs, founder of Jacobs Engineering, who illustrates the point:

> I am an entrepreneur by definition, but not in any heroic sense. I had no brilliant flashes of inspiration, no spectacular recognition of market need, no marvelous coincidence of being in the right place at the right time. I slugged it out in my chosen profession, making lots of errors and, fortunately, lots of good decisions. But my story is more representative of the entrepreneurial process than that of the more celebrated examples one reads about....(Jacobs, 1991 p. 3)

An entrepreneur, however, is someone who is able to spot market signals regarding opportunity for potential profit or beneficial change (Boyett, 1996). Entrepreneurs have keen ears to hear opportunity knocking; they see, more clearly than the rest of us, something interesting in an unexpected event, in changes in industry or market structure (particularly those that reveal as-yet-unmet new needs), in demographics, in public perceptions, in technological developments (Drucker, 1985). They are champions of innovation.

---

[1] According to Inger Boyett (1996), Richard Cantillion first employed the term in 1734, in his *"Essai sur la Nature du Commerce en General."*

[2] Innovation is a requisite of organization survival, particularly in chaotic, turbulent environments, so the entrepreneurial function must be performed. Although the romantic notion of the heroic entrepreneur is common, it should be noted that – like leadership – entrepreneurship is not necessarily the work of a single individual but may be the product of collaborative activity.

A good idea, however, is not enough. As suggested by Edison's famous quip that "genius is 1% inspiration and 99% perspiration," entrepreneurs also must pull together a variety of resources in order to realize the good idea in practice. This may involve locating and mobilizing financial and human resources, persuading others to use their influence and credibility in support of the innovation, and sustaining collaborative efforts to market the new enterprise. It may also involve findings ways to circumvent impediments – particularly important in the case of public entrepreneurs (Kobrak, 1996). Casson (1991) called the entrepreneur an "optimizing agent," in that s/he identifies opportunities for innovation in the organizational environment and then exerts influence on the organization itself to implement the entrepreneurial vision. Boyett (1996) comments that Casson's conceptualization of entrepreneurship has the advantage of being as clearly applicable to the public as to the private sector.

Entrepreneurs share much in common with other managers. They are risk-takers, but they are not the only businesspersons who take risks – in fact, all economic activity involves uncertainty (Drucker, 1985; Khademian, 1995; Osborne and Gaebler, 1992). They innovate, but in Drucker's view, all managers have the potential to produce innovations. What distinguishes entrepreneurs -- whether in the public sector or the private -- is that innovation is much more central to their role, and they exhibit a greater-than-average willingness to take risks in pursuit of their project (Fisher, 1983; Jacobs, 1991). In Drucker's formulation, they "search for change, respond to it, and exploit it as an opportunity" (1985, p. 28). Or to use Lewis' definition of the public entrepreneur, they alter existing resource allocations by expansion or by the creation of entirely new organizational entities (1980).

Despite the conventional view that the public sector is the refuge of the risk-averse, daring initiatives occur there, which sometimes succeed – as was true for the heroes profiled by Lewis (1980) or Doig and Hargrove (1987) – but sometimes fail. For example, in 1982, the State of Michigan's Treasury Department decided to invest part of its pension fund in venture capital intiatives (Osborne and Gaebler, 1992). These investments lost money, however, and pressure from pensioners forced the policy to be phased out (Kobrak, 1996). In another case, Ted Gaebler's successor as city manager of Visalia, California, entered into an agreement to build a Radisson Hotel with a land developer who turned out to be unreliable. By the time the project was completed, the city had paid out an unexpected $20 million to keep the project afloat (Gurwitt, 1994).

As important as what entrepreneurial innovation does entail, however, is a understanding of what it does not (Drucker, 1985). For example, it is not simply a new business. Some new businesses merely undertake in a new location an enterprise that already exists in hundreds of other places, as when partners open a fast-food franchise. Such small businesspersons are owner-managers, but they have not done much that is new. Nor is entrepreneurship merely the process of bringing a new invention to market, as when Thomas Edison tried to make money from a variety of his own bright ideas (he did not succeed with most of them; it was left to others to draw profit from his brilliance). Drucker calls this "high-tech" entrepreneurship and argues that it often fails because inventors may be quite innocent of managerial skills.

In America, entrepreneurs often seem larger than life. The brilliant loner, the outsider who "pulls a fast one" on the entrenched powers, the sly maverick who lives by his wits on the edges of civil society, have enduring appeal. Public entrepreneurs evoke the same images of derring-do, Robin Hoods of the bureaucracy, winning our secret approval even as we castigate their techniques. And castigate them we do. Critics of public entrepreneurship look askance at the private-sector variety, concerned that if civil servants become entrepreneurial, then "individualism, profit, selfishness and shrewd calculation become the norms for public agencies as well as private business" (Stever, 1988, p. 99). Among the aspects of the entrepreneurial character that elicit concern are egotism, selfishness, waywardness, domination, and opportunism. The following sections discuss these characteristics and suggest for each why it is in fact *functional* for the entrepreneurial role.

Egotism

Individualism is often cited as a core trait of entrepreneurs (Fisher, 1983; Lewis, 1980; Stever, 1988). The three public-sector innovators profiled by Lewis -- Hyman Rickover, J. Edgar Hoover, and Robert Moses -- demonstrated single-mindedness in the pursuit of their own ends, rather than "corporate 'good behavior'" (p. 235). Each was iconoclastic and egoistic, mavericks who strove for power, sometimes veiling the true nature of their goals in order to win approbation and rewards from others. Fisher (1983), however, points out that "the effective entrepreneur works the fringes and not the mainstream of societal ventures," for it is on the margins that opportunities for innovation lie. From a vantage point on the margin, the entrepreneur can "constantly scan the boundaries of the system and figure ways to poke holes in it" (p. 14).[3] That is, it is the egotism of the entrepreneurs that gives them the confidence to assert their unique and innovative vision.

Selfishness

There is probably a good-sized element of truth to the charge of self-interest: even Joseph Jacobs avers that the entrepreneur's motives are entirely self-centered, though he is quick to point out that social good is a by-product of his efforts and that this is often overlooked by the many critics of businessmen (Jacobs, 1991, p. 4). But although Jacobs acknowledges his self-interest, he also describes how it is moderated by concern for others: when required to lay off employees in the bust that followed the oil boom of the 1970s, he justified these painful decisions by noting that the survival of the business -- and the livelihood of the majority of his employees -- required it (p. 96). Lewis too sees self-interest at work in the careers of his public-sector entrepreneurs. "The public

---

[3] Interestingly, those on the margins of an enterprise appear to those in the mainstream to be almost, if not completely, "deviant." Again, entrepreneurship has both desirable and undesirable connotations.

entrepreneur," he writes, "sees the organization as a tool for the achievement of *his* [sic] goals" (1980, p. 237 [italics in the original]), which are substantive, involving more than merely a quest for status and power. Extreme selfishness was certainly characteristic of many of the CEOs in the business firms that have caused recent scandals: between 1960 and 2000, the ratio between the pay of CEOs and the average worker grew from 1:12 to 1:531 (Anderson, *et al.*, 2001).

Self-interest, however, is not the same as selfishness. Solomon (1992) offers the example of eating dinner. One's self-interest dictates that one should do it, but to do so is not selfish. It *would* be selfish, however, to try to eat someone else's dinner, too. In a sense, however, the charge that entrepreneurs may act in self-interest is specious. *Everyone* acts in his/her self-interest, as is widely recognized in the literature on organization behavior. For example, "goal displacement" means that bureaucrats have placed their own (or their agency or department's) interest above the public interest (the mission of the organization). Politicians, too, have been characterized by Lasswell (1977) as displacing repressed impulses onto political life and rationalizing their private drama as the pursuit of the public interest.

In fact, what probably occurs most often is what Freud called the "overdetermination" of actions. Most people prefer to act when their behavior is determined *both* by self-interest and by higher ideals. Stever (1988) seems to scorn this process ("Indeed, the entrepreneurial ideal encourages a merger of the general good with individual or agency interest," p. 94), as he goes on to describe how agencies and individuals use the rhetoric of crisis to manipulate legislative or public opinion.

Waywardness

Because entrepreneurs are often stereotyped as loners or mavericks, they are sometimes regarded with the suspicion commonly accorded "outsiders" or "aliens." Of course, not all entrepreneurs operate outside organizations: the famous "skunk works" at 3M Corporation is an example of corporate "intrapreneurs," and other innovators have simply been creative managers working within traditional bureaucratic or corporate structures. Wayward entrepreneurs are not only self-interested (or worse, pursuing goals of their own *rather than* or *at the expense of* public goals), but they are willing to use any means necessary to achieve them. Certainly the executives at Enron and WorldCom started out believing that their creative accounting, which helped push up the price of their stock, would thereby promote the interests of their employees who owned stock or relied on their pension plan. Under financial and then investigative pressure, however, they resorted to increasingly devious and illegal schemes (Eichenwald, 2005).

Public entrepreneurs, too, may be wayward; Lewis' depiction of Rickover, Hoover and Moses shows them to have this quality.

> This is not to suggest that [they] were criminals in any conventional sense. Rather, they were "rule benders." They were crafty, and they pushed the limits of

what was legal and permissible time after time without getting caught or, when caught, without serious punishment (p. 243).

Entrepreneurs are wayward, however, because they require some freedom to innovate or experiment, outside the boundaries of the usual rules and procedures. Lewis (1980) cites examples of the "buffering and autonomy-seeking strategies" employed by Rickover, Hoover and Moses. Hoover, for example, successfully argued that the FBI personnel system should be separate from the rest of the civil service, which provided him with greater control over personnel selection and discipline, and thus facilitated his bending the organization to conform to his vision of it. But Bellone and Goerl (1992), for example, worry that entrepreneurial autonomy threatens to obstruct democratic participation. While it is certainly true that the entrepreneur, as the first to sense the opportunity to innovate, needs a degree of autonomy in order to pursue the possibilities, this activity does not inherently require autonomy above and beyond that normally allowed by an organization. Every manager, in fact every employee, has some degree of autonomy and discretion, with many public organizations permitting a fairly broad scope for it, particularly to professional-level workers. Innovations, particularly important ones, need space in which to flourish.

Domination

Like the auteur filmmaker, whose personal style and tight control over all aspects of production impress his/her unique stamp on each film s/he makes, the entrepreneur seeks to realize a personal vision in the business or governmental sphere. Critics of public entrepreneurship fear that this tendency will lead to tyrannical domination within what should be democratically-run agencies of government (Terry, 1993). The three public-sector entrepreneurs profiled by Lewis (1980) all managed to follow, according to him, strategies leading to undisputed domination over their respective organizations. Three data points are not sufficient to prove the case, however. The auteur analogy does suggest that entrepreneurs, in following their personal vision (and from their position of power as the originator or builder of their organization), would have a great degree of influence over organization culture and climate. Nevertheless, the same is likely to be true of *any* CEO, witness the universal admonition of consultants and organization development specialists that change will not occur unless it has "support from the top."

Opportunism

Stever considers opportunism one of the defining characteristics of an entrepreneur (in addition to adaptiveness and individualism), and he clearly places it in opposition to traits and values appropriate to a public servant. The opportunistic entrepreneur, he suggests, is the antithesis of the cautious bureaucrat (1988, p. 92), suggesting that the opportunist is fickle, a careless risk-taker, heedless of the welfare of his/her clients and associates.

An opportunist, of course, is someone who takes advantage of opportunity, and, cast in that light, it is obviously a virtue. The contrast between the two points of view suggests that there are two types of entrepreneurs whose very different characteristics may help account for the different moral judgments of those who value and those who fear entrepreneurship. The two types might be called the "opportunistic" and the "tenacious" entrepreneur. The opportunist seizes upon trends and straws in the wind, hoping to profit from them. These adventurers believe the proverb that achieving success depends upon knowing when to admit failure, quickly moving on to other avenues if success does not come early and easily or if they simply tire of the particular effort.

Drucker makes a somewhat similar contrast in his discussion of "high-tech" and "low-tech" entrepreneurs. He faults high-tech entrepreneurs for their typical deficiencies in organization and discipline. High-tech industries, he says, "follow the traditional pattern of great excitement, rapid expansion, and then sudden shakeout and collapse." He accuses these Silicon Valley supernovae of being "still inventors rather than innovators, still speculators rather than entrepreneurs" (1985, p. 12). By contrast, the low-tech entrepreneur relies upon systematic, purposeful (we might add, tenacious) management.

Tenacious entrepreneurs hold fast to a vision despite others' lack of interest; they pursue their goals despite many obstacles. Jacobs, who possessed no "brilliant flashes of insight," but rather "slugged it out in his chosen profession," is a superb example of the tenacious entrepreneur. Opportunistic entrepreneurs are probably the type that critics have in mind, for they have less incentive to behave ethically than tenacious ones. While working for an insurance brokerage firm, I once discussed with our CEO the apparent amorality of some members of our sales force. His observation was that those who stand to make money by brokering insurance services to many small businesses, with whom they have brief and slight relationships, will tend to take good business ethics more casually than those who hope to serve the very few large businesses in their region. In the latter case, it is critical to maintain the client's respect and trust, for there are few alternative buyers of one's services. For tenacious entrepreneurs, who intend to stay in a line of endeavor for the long term and who will therefore prefer to develop lasting alliances with suppliers and customers, a reputation for ethical conduct is important. Opportunistic entrepreneurs, who shift restlessly from one venue to another, may be less concerned with niceties of conduct.

Whatever the virtues and vices of particular entrepreneurs, private sector theorists find much to admire in entrepreneurship because of the importance of its role in the broader context of business. At root, the reason the entrepreneur is valued is that his/her activity creates value. "Successful entrepreneurs," writes Drucker, "whatever their *individual* motivation -- be it money, power, curiosity, or the desire for fame and recognition -- try to create value and to make a contribution" (1985, p. 34, italics added). Solomon (1992), a business ethicist, argues that the true purpose of business is productivity and general prosperity (Solomon, 1992). He notes that many contemporary images of business redirect attention away from this view. Some confuse wealth with success, others portray business as war ("It's kill or be killed!"), or as a game (with "winners" and "losers"), or as a grueling necessity without point or purpose. Where Adam Smith saw quality, efficiency, and the general welfare as by-products of competition (and it does not matter that competitors do not act out of benevolence or love of their fellow man), Solomon sees these as the real object of business. Business competition occurs within a framework of mutual interest and a considerable level of trust, recent destructive tendencies (hostile takeovers, downsizing with no end other than profitability) being the exception that proves the rule.

WHEN IS ENTREPRENEURSHIP NECESSARY?

According to the myths of business, entrepreneurs are the heroes of the economist's fairy-tale world, the perfectly competitive market. Utilizing their resources -- contacts, knowledge, a bright idea, perceptive analysis of changes in the environment -- they parlay their own money, and investment dollars cadged from other people, into a profitable enterprise. Like all myths, this one contains many half-truths: not all entrepreneurs are mavericks, and they don't produce all the innovation that occurs. But there is an important element of truth in their identification with the market: their true value does lie in the role they play in solving problems that can be called "anarchic."

Elsewhere (deLeon, 1993) I have argued that the kinds of problems public organizations are attempting to solve affect the choice of organizational forms used to solve them. While bureaucracy is well-designed to solve *routine* problems (where goals are unambiguous and the means to achieve them involve familiar technologies (Thompson, 1967; Thompson and Tuden, 1959), relatively few public problems are now thought to be so simple. Instead, most problems are more complicated. For example, there may be disagreement about goals (should a dam be built in order to supply downstream municipal power needs, or should it be stopped because it would destroy a species of fish?), even though means (how to build a dam) are well understood. Naturally, problems of this type need to be dealt with in the political system, which is designed to resolve conflicts over goals through the articulation and aggregation of competing interests. Other problems are difficult because, while goal consensus is relatively strong (everyone wants the next generation to be well-educated), the means to achieve those objectives are uncertain (should schools use "back-to-basics" instruction in the three "R's" or "outcomes-based education"?). Most often, these problems are consigned to the discretion of professionals, whose advanced training and depth of experience give confidence that they are better able than laypersons to resolve them. Frequently, administrative activity is thought to lie in this problem-space and thus to be the province of professionals. Romzek and Dubnick (Dubnick and Romzek, 1991; Romzek and Dubnick, 1987) prefer professional accountability over bureaucratic, legal or political forms precisely because they believe most administrative tasks are of the professional variety.

Finally, the most intractable problems lie in a field where neither goals nor means are known. Thompson argues that decisions regarding problems of this type are made by "inspiration" (Thompson and Tuden, 1959).   A more recent description, however, has been offered by Cohen and March in their portrayal of "organized anarchies" (Cohen and March, 1986; 1972), which they also call "the garbage can model." In their words,

> An organization [can be viewed as] a collection of choices looking for problems, issues and feelings looking for decision situations in which they might be aired, solutions looking for issues to which they might be the answer, and decision makers looking for work (p. 1).

Organized anarchies produce decisions when a problem (something that needs to be done) meets a choice (a program that could potentially solve the problem). In a chaotic problem-space, where preferences are conflicting and technologies uncertain, more than one problem might attach itself to a particular solution, or more than one solution to a particular problem --which is merely another way to say that there would be extensive experimentation in search of effective responses to policy issues.

The term anarchy is in fact a judicious choice (..., 1994). Political theorist Michael Taylor (1982) defines an anarchy as a "stateless" polity, in which there is no specialization of political roles (a particular individual can take on the role of "leader," for example, but cannot make a habit of it) and no enforcement of collective decisions. In other words, sovereignty inheres in each individual. The organization structure appropriate to this situation is a *network* (think of a fishnet, or the Internet), with no center and nodes of equal size (power).

It is not difficult to see a role for entrepreneurship in this kind of situation. In the absence of group consensus on goals, personal vision finds room for expression; in the absence of knowledge about means, the entrepreneur must experiment; in the absence of sufficient budget allocations, s/he must scrounge for resources. To go one step further, in an anarchic problem situation, the entrepreneur's personal vision is a *necessary* precondition for action. Problems and technologies roil around in the "garbage can," and the entrepreneur is the catalyst that connects them. S/he makes the "entrepreneurial leap" (Lewis, 1980) that sees the possibility of connection, then pours energy and resourcefulness into making it happen.

The parallels to the conventional image of the entrepreneur, and to business theorists' portrayal of that role, are abundant. "Inspiration" suggests the bright idea, the invention, of Drucker's high-tech entrepreneur. The anarchic context resonates with Schumpeter's view of entrepreneurship as a sort of creative destruction (1911). In his view, the entrepreneur not only exploits change, s/he creates it, generating dynamic disequilibrium by the pursuit of innovation. Public-sector entrepreneurs are described by Stever (1988) as having traits such as courage, shrewdness and individualism -- and he emphasizes that these qualities are an adaptive response to the "chaos and fragmentation" (anarchy) of post-Progressive public administration.

Table 1
Varieties of Problems, Decisions, Structures
and Associated Ethics

	(1) **Hierarchy**	(2) **Competitive Pluralism**	(3) **Community**	(4) **Anarchy**
Goals:	Clear	Unclear	Clear	Unclear
Means:	Certain	Certain	Uncertain	Uncertain
Decisions by:	Computation	Bargaining, majority rule	Consensus	Inspiration
Structure:	Pyramid	Playing field	Web	Network
Example:	Bureaucracy	Partisan politics	Professions	Markets
Ethic:	"Discipline, obedience, service"	"Play by the rules"	"One for all, and all for one."	"Live and let live"

Source: de Leon, L. (2008).

ETHICAL ARENAS

Drucker (1985), for one, is very clear that entrepreneurship is fundamentally a moral enterprise, for which the goals (or values) that characterize it are more important than means:

> [It] is neither a science nor an art. It is a practice. It has a knowledge base, of course. But...[it] is a means to an end. Indeed, what constitutes knowledge in a practice is largely defined by the ends (p. viii).

Each of the types of problems discussed here engender a characteristic ethic (..., 1993). For a bureaucracy (including corporations), the ethical "prime directive"

(Trekkies will understand) could be expressed as "Discipline, obedience, service." The bureaucrat lives by the rules, willingly sacrificing autonomy and submitting to hierarchical control of his/her conduct in order to permit the organization to achieve its goals, as well as in return for organizational rewards. In a competitive pluralistic arena, the directive is to "Play by the rules." The gamesman (Maccoby, 1976), on the playing field of pluralistic competition, submits to the discipline of his/her team and the control of the coach, in return for the chance to enjoy membership in a winning organization. When politics is the arena, winning implies gaining the right to shape government policy and to enjoy the advantages of the majority party. For communities (or collegial organizations), the directive is "One for all and all for one." Members of communities share goals and values, putting the benefit of the community before their personal advantage. In collegial decision making (such as the traditional professions), the individual's training and expertise are honored by permitting him/her to exercise discretion over how to serve clients, while accountability is served by requiring him/her to act in accord with professional norms and be answerable to his/her peers.

For anarchies (which include the perfectly competitive market), the prime directive is to "Live and let live." In anarchic systems, creative self-actualization (the injunction to "Live!") is highly valued. Individuals have freedom to choose, to act, to maximize their personal growth, development and expression. The injunction to "Let live!" suggests the fact that there is no enforcement of collective decisions. This means the individual has no accountability to outside authority, nor can s/he call others to account for their actions. Freedom of this sort is justifiable in a situation where goals are unclear or conflicting, for where there is no agreement on what results should be obtained, there can be no accountability for results. And where cause-effect knowledge is minimal, an individual or group cannot justifiably be penalized for selecting the wrong means to achieve an objective, since no one else could have known what choice was better.

If "live and let live" were the sum total of the entrepreneurial ethic, there might be cause for concern. In the abstract, this admonition is nothing more than the Golden Rule. An organization or a society based upon the Golden Rule would probably work quite well, if everyone in it could reason out the consequences of their actions, and if everyone in it possessed impeccable impulse control. But this "best of all possible worlds" does not exist, and theories of public policy and administration must deal with the real one that does. Therefore, it is important to consider that the anarchic zone in which entrepreneurship thrives is normally embedded within some more "orderly" system, often a bureaucratic one.

Lewis (1980), in fact, argues that this encystation is an essential corollary of the "entrepreneurial leap": the entrepreneur must create a buffering boundary that seals off his part of the organization from potential threats in its task environment. (Of course, this separation poses problems of accountability, for the buffers that shelter the entrepreneur's experiment also block normal mechanisms of political or bureaucratic control [deLeon, forthcoming].)

A buffered zone in which entrepreneurial maneuvering is possible is an enduring feature of American government and administration. Stever (1988) calls the conditions to which entrepreneurship is a response "chaos" and "fragmentation." Fragmentation refers to multiplicity of governments; chaos is the result of the lack of clear directives from the legislature. Marshall Dimock (1980) -- who wrote while the bureaucratic paradigm still held sway, pointed out a relatively narrow zone of discretion, in the space left by the inability of legislation to specify every detail of implementation. His premise, like that of most early writers in public policy and administration, was that disagreements over the goals of public policy were fought out in the legislature; the winning view was incorporated into legislation, together with some specification of the means for achieving them. (Policies can be viewed as hypotheses about the connection between ends and means: "If we adopt Policy X, then we will be able to achieve Goal Y.") Administrators did not have the right to determine overall goals -- that was the province of politics. This is the sense in which politics and administration are separate. (But, during implementation, they did have opportunity to decide many subordinate goals. This is the sense in which administration and politics interpenetrate.)

Other analysts (Lewis, 1980; Lynn, 1987) emphasize the way the organization (for any manager) imposes constraints but also offers resources. In Lynn's analysis, the "indeterminacy of the political process creates a potentially significant sphere of executive autonomy and allows public executives and other civil administrators to be a creative force in government" (p. 76). Similarly, the fluidity of organization structures -- even bureaucracies -- provides room for maneuver. Autonomy is something the public executive can work to increase: "possibilities" are inherent in the complex relationships among environment, structure, technology, tasks, financial and human resources, and organization culture. Similarly, Doig and Hargrove (1987) suggest that the fragmentation, decentralization, and pluralism of the American political system opens up space for experimentation, where entrepreneurs can attempt to create innovative new programs. In Elmore's (1986) phrase, the realm for executive leadership in public management is at the "seams of government," in the relationships -- messy, ill-defined and often problematic -- where action can occur and republican government be made to work. In her analysis of institutional entrepreneurs in local governance in the United Kingdom, Lowndes (2005) shows that they exploit ambiguities in the "rules of the game" in order to respond to changes in the environment (as well as to protect or further their own interests).

Harlan Cleveland (1972) -- who wrote as the vision of public organizations as existing with a highly turbulent environment was seizing the imagination of many theorists -- saw a larger area for discretion, resulting from the chaos and complexity of modern life. Complexity arises both because technology (knowledge of means) has become so advanced as to be esoteric, and because increasing diversity of opinion (agreement on goals) means there are no simple principles for action nor collective norms of behavior. Into this vacuum steps the "future executive," who must use his own personal judgment as to what is in the public interest. "Hence, in entrepreneur-like fashion, the civil servant ventures out into uncharted waters armed with little more than his own individual energy, wit and judgment" (p. 93). Similarly, Levin and Sanger (1994) argue that where legislation is vague and confusing, the public manager *must* turn to his/her personal understanding of the public interest in order to create a mission for the agency, and thus channel the energies of its members. Without entrepreneurial energy, government agencies could never be more than stultifying bureaucracies churning through their standard operating procedures.

Encouraging Ethical Entrepreneurship

The importance of the fact that anarchic zones are encysted within a bureaucratic or organizational matrix is that the surrounding organization can be deployed to ensure that entrepreneurial activity is directed toward public purposes. In a bureaucracy, the "enterprise zone" can be walled off from the surrounding organization, keeping the entrepreneur within bounds. When the entrepreneur is a member of a professional community, the norms and values shared by all members of that community serve as an important check on his/her choice of ends and means. And even in an anarchic setting, there are restraints on entrepreneurial action.

In a Bureaucracy

A variety of methods can be used to wall off entrepreneurial activity within a bureaucracy. DiIulio, Garvey and Kettl (1993) contend that giving public officials room to fail is the only way to encourage the sort of risk-taking necessary to solve problems instead of merely falling back into the safety zone of standard operating procedures. Without prudent risk-taking and experimentation, without pushing the envelope of current practices, government will be unable to realize the dramatic increases in productivity necessary if it is to recover public trust and confidence.

Another way to encourage entrepreneurship while at the same time limiting its effects is to use pilot programs to test the workability of innovations. The Navy Demonstration Project to experiment with "broad banding" in compensation is one example (Ban, 1991). In Colorado, recent legislation (HB 95-1178) permitted experimentation in the state personnel system, even providing a mechanism for allowing deviations from state law for the purpose of trying out potentially beneficial reforms.

Levin and Sanger (1994) propose a differentiation of roles between a program executive and a chief executive as a way to permit entrepreneurship while containing it within acceptable bounds. The program executive is the entrepreneur, pushing the envelope and bending the rules. The chief executive is charged with reining in the hard charger and holding him/her accountable for results and within proper bounds of process. This strategy should be undertaken with full cognizance of its drawbacks, however. First, controlling an energetic, free-wheeling program executive is time-consuming and psychologically taxing for the chief executive. Constant vigilance is required if the entrepreneur has a tendency to break, not just bend, the rules; fretting over where the boundaries must be drawn (to give the entrepreneur, in effect, the freedom *not* to worry about this) and holding the entrepreneur inside them takes stamina.

Second, envelope-pushing inevitably leads to failure, with all its possible consequences for the agency, its clients, and its political supporters. In his wittily-titled book *To Engineer is Human*, Henry Petroski (1982) explains that innovative engineers face this problem. An engineer who is not content simply to continue using conventional designs and familiar technologies can take on one of two challenges: either build the conventional designs much more cheaply, or essay an unconventional design. But whichever direction one pushes the envelope, the only way to know when one has reached the edge is by experiencing a failure. Each engineer, in trying to reach for greater efficiency or greater design daring, pushes farther than his/her predecessor. The one who reaches the edge (and steps over it) takes the fall. Innovative management works the same way. Innovative managers will feel the challenge to improve upon familiar methods and conventional programs. As they push the design envelope, they too find the edge only when a failure occurs.

Finally, it is impossible to monitor every action of an energetic entrepreneur. In giving a generous grant of discretion, the organization (and the public) trust that entrepreneurs will act honestly and prudently. In his tale of the shenanigans at Enron, Eichenwald (2005) writes, "Ultimately, it was Enron's tragedy to be filled with people smart enough to know how to maneuver around the rules, but not wise enough to understand why the rules had been written in the first place" (p. 11). Respect for organizational rules and procedures, a classic characteristic of bureaucratic organizations, is needed if entrepreneurship is to stay within reasonable bounds.

In a Community

Whether they operate inside a bureaucracy or not, entrepreneurs who are members of a community will try to adapt their behavior to the norms and values to which they have been socialized. In reflecting upon his life and work, Joseph Jacobs (1991) recounts a number of incidents that taught him valuable ethical lessons, indicating what he believed were the most pervasive influences on his moral development. It is striking how often he locates the wellsprings of his actions in the values of his family and community, as well as in the practical necessities of business:

> As I considered [my forebears'] values, ethical standards, moral fiber, courage, and the need to reach for seemingly unattainable goals in an attempt to define my inner drive, I kept coming back to family and community. ...The strong emphasis upon character, morality, and the sanctity of one's "reputation" that I learned from my parents and the Lebanese ethnic enclave in which I grew up was a source of strength that nurtured the entrepreneurial accomplishment (p. 2).

Or, again, he refers to "pride, and reputation, and integrity" as the qualities ingrained in him by his family and community. "I often wonder," he says, "where the myth arose that a necessary ingredient for successful trading is dishonesty or deviousness. Nothing could be further from the truth" (p. 21). Rather, the good businessman seeks to engage in win-win situations, obtaining good value because he is willing to give good value.

In attempting to show that anarchy can work (remain stable and produce social order), Taylor argues this is possible only if the anarchic society is also a community. Relationships in a community are based on reciprocity, which is expressed in mutual aid, cooperation, and sharing. The glue that holds together an anarchic society (in which there is no mechanism for the *enforcement* of collective decisions) is social pressure. The presence of community generates the social pressures that can restrain the self-interest of individuals without resorting to formal institutions of government. As an illustration, consider Joseph Jacobs' moral tale of how community norms constrained a businessman's self-interest. During wartime, his father had opportunity to make exorbitant profits on goods he traded. The war had cut off supplies to his competitors, but Jacobs, Sr. chose to ration the goods to his regular customers rather than allow demand from others to bid up the price. "The lesson," says Jacobs, Jr., "was clear. To take inordinate advantage of a temporary situation was as reprehensible as not making a profit" (1991, p. 25). The audience for this good behavior was the Lebanese community; it was their approbation that this self-restraint was intended to win. For Jacobs, maintaining his reputation in his ethnic, professional and business community sometimes meant going to extraordinary lengths to correct deficiencies in a project, even when there was no legal obligation to do so. "Honor and principle are not as incompatible with success in business as many people think" (p. 27).

Honor and principle were in short supply at Enron, however. A key factor in the deception practiced upon regulators, stockholders, and the Board of Directors was that both internal accountants and external ones (the firm of Arthur Andersen) violated the ethical norms of their profession (Carson, 2003). The lesson for public management is that providing appropriate bounds on public entrepreneurship necessitates encouraging ethical consensus within that professional community and attending carefully to the professional education that aspirants receive.

In an Anarchic Network

Another factor that helps trammel the entrepreneur's self-interest and willingness to break or bend rules is consideration of the consequences. In their analysis of the anarchy that is world politics, Axelrod and Keohane (1985) maintain that, absent mechanisms for the enforcement of collective decisions, the major factor inhibiting nations from reneging on their agreements is the fear that like will answer like. In an evocative phrase, they call this effect "the shadow of the future" (p. 232). When future payoffs have a high value relative to current ones, there is little incentive to defect today, since the other side might retaliate tomorrow. In short, the states are accountable as a group, each to the others. (Of course, when future payoffs have a relatively low value compared to current ones, or where actors can leave a group without cost, anarchic accountability may not work.)

Similarly, if a businessperson does not act cooperatively, s/he incurs the risk that others will respond in kind. If one does not act trustworthily, one will not be trusted (for example, with a loan). Game theorists have x-rayed these cases to see their bones: the classic game of this sort is the Prisoners' Dilemma. In the payoff matrix of that game, cooperative behavior brings a modest reward, while betrayal yields greater benefit...but only if one's partner acts the patsy. If *both* attempt betrayal, the worst payoff occurs. Iterative play (modeled by computers) proves that there is, in fact, one best strategy, called "tit for tat." If one always acts cooperatively, one is vulnerable to an unethical partner. If one always seeks to maximize self-interest at the expense of the other, a recurring cycle of betrayals will occur. So perhaps the ethics of entrepreneurship adds a codicil to the Golden Rule: "Do unto others as you would have them do unto you...the first time -- and after that, tit for tat!"

Where the shadow of the future is not effective, where community is weak, or where mistrust is high, the only remaining constraint on public entrepreneurs may be that proposed by Bellone and Goerl (1992; 1993): civic-regarding, participative entrepreneurship. Perlmutter and Cnaan (1995) suggest that it may be necessary that entrepreneurial efforts in the public sector be accompanied by citizen boards that are more than advisory in nature, as a vehicle for control and a way to ensure equity and due process. In fact, participation would be virtually unlimited: since technologies are unclear in anarchic decision situations, every citizen's expertise would be potentially valuable. Any individual or group with sufficient energy and interest could involve themselves in the work of public organizations, cooperating with like-minded others. They would not be able to hold the organization to account *ex post* but would have shaped its decisions as they were made. To achieve this goal, public entrepreneurs must operate openly and transparently, allowing citizen input into and review of innovative new ventures (Kobrak, 1996).

SUMMARY AND CONCLUSIONS

Public entrepreneurs are neither knights on white horses nor wolves in sheep's clothing (Bellone and Goerl, 1993; Terry, 1993). They are, however, necessary agents of innovation in a business or governmental arena that would otherwise remain static. They are catalysts who bring together problems and solutions that would otherwise bubble chaotically in the convection currents of modern policy streams. Many of the attributes that provoke criticism -- their egotism, selfishness, waywardness, opportunism and domineering style -- are the extremes of qualities that are functional for their role as innovators.

Entrepreneurship is not the appropriate response to all social problems, just as bureaucracy is inadequate for dealing with many of today's issues (Lewis, 1980, p. 253). But for the particularly difficult situations where goals are in conflict and means are in doubt, entrepreneurship is perhaps the only way to bring about helpful change. For entrepreneurship to flourish, a protected zone of autonomy -- a touch of anarchy -- is needed. Thus we must recognize, with Koch (1995), that introducing entrepreneurialism into a public arena probably cannot be achieved without also changing organizational structures. At the very least, the creation of a buffer between the entrepreneurial unit and its bureaucratically-organized host may be required, to permit and protect the innovative initiative while it is being set up and tested. In addition, incentive structures within the organization may need revision, in order to provide rewards for entrepreneurial activity and some measure of protection for well-conceived experiments that nevertheless fail.

Acknowledging both the hopes of government's reinventers and the fears of their critics, the public sector should encourage entrepreneurship but focus it on those situations to which it is appropriate and necessary. Simultaneously, however, we should ensure that it remains ethical. Three methods were discussed here: first, the setting of limits, so that entrepreneurs do not transgress nor wreak undue harm; by nourishing professionalism in the public service, so that entrepreneurs have enough autonomy to realize their vision but their actions are held in check by their own sense of public interest and public welfare; and by facilitating widespread public participation in all aspects of the policy process so that entrepreneurial activity is transparent and accountable. Doing more with less may be necessary in today's climate of public opinion, but (as one wag put it) taken to extremes, government would eventually have to do "everything" with "nothing." Ethical entrepreneurship remains a useful and important means of finding better ways to achieve public purposes.

Notes: The author is indebted to her colleague Chris Koziol for this idea and these labels.

REFERENCES

Axelrod, R., and Keohane, R.O. (1985). "Achieving cooperation under anarchy." *World Politics, 38*(3), 226-253.

Ban, C. (1991). "The navy demonstration project: An 'experiment in experimentation.'" In C. Ban and N. M. Riccucci (Eds.), *Public Personnel Management -- Current Concerns, Future Challenges* (pp. 31-41). White Plains, NY: Longman Publishing Group.

Bellone, C.J., and Goerl, G.F. (1992). "Reconciling public entrepreneurship and democracy." *Public Administration Review, 52*(2), 130-134.

Bellone, C.J., and Goerl, G.F. (1993). "In defense of civic-regarding entrepreneurship or helping wolves to promote good citizenship." *Public Administration Review, 53*(4), 396-398.

Caiden, G.E. (1994). "Administrative reform -- american style." *Public Administration Review, 54*(2), 123-128.

Carson, T.L. (2004). "Self Interest and Business Ethics: Some Lessons of the Recent Corporate Scandals." *Journal of Business Ethics*, *43*(3), 389-394.

Cleveland, H. (1972). *The future executive.* NY: Harper and Row.

Cohen, M.D., and March, J.G. (1986). *Leadership and ambiguity.* (2nd ed.). Boston, MA: Harvard Business School Press.

Cohen, M.D., March, J.G., and Olsen, J.P. (1972). "A garbage can model of organizational choice." *Administrative Science Quarterly, 17*, 1-25.

de Leon, L. (forthcoming). Accountability in a 'reinvented' government." *Public*

Administration (an International Journal).

de Leon, L. (1993). As easy as 1, 2, 3 ... and 4: Ethics and organization structure. *Administration and Society, 25*(3), 293-316.

DiIulio, J.J., Jr., Garvey, G., and Kettl, D.F. (1993). *Improving government performance: An owner's manual.* Washington, DC: The Brookings Institution.

Dimock, M. (1980). *Law and dynamic administration.* NY: Praeger Publishers.

Doig, J. W., and Hargrove, E.C. (1987). *Leadership and innovation: a biographical perspective on entrepreneurs in government.* Baltimore, MD: The Johns Hopkins University Press.

Drucker, P. (1985). *Innovation and entrepreneurship.* NY: Harper and Row, Publishers.

Dubnick, M.J., and Romzek, B.S. (1991). *American public administration: Politics and the management of expectations.* NY: Macmillan.

Eichenwald, K. (2004) *Conspiracy of Fools.* New York: Broadway Books (Random House).

Elmore, R.F. (1986). "Graduate education in public management: working the seams of government." *Journal of Policy Analysis and Management, 6*(1), 69-83.

Fisher, F. (1983). "The new entrepreneurs." In B. H. Moore (Ed.), *The entrepreneur in local government* (pp. 9-14). Washington, DC: International City Management Association.

Jacobs, J.J. (1991). *The anatomy of an entrepreneur.* San Francisco: ICS Press.

Johnston, V.R. (1993,). "Improving quality and productivity by implementing TQM and creative entrepreneurial organizational innovations in public sector organizations." Paper presented at the International Institute of Administrative Sciences, Toluca, Mexico.

Kettl, D.F. (1994). *Reinventing government? Appraising the national performance review* (CPM Report 94-2): Center for Public Management, The Brookings Institution.

Khademian, A.M. (1995). "Reinventing a government corporation: professional priorities and a clear bottom line." *Public Administration Review, 55*(1), 17-28.

Koch, R. (1995). "Public managers and entrepreneurialism." Paper presented at the Annual meeting of the European Group in Public Administration (EGPA), Rotterdam, The Netherlands.

Lasswell, H.D. (1977). *Psychopathology and politics.* Chicago: The University of Chicago Press.

Levin, M.A., and Sanger, M.B. (1994). *Making government work.* San Francisco, CA: Jossey-Bass Publishers.

Lewis, E. (1980). *Public entrepreneurship.* Bloomington: Indiana University Press.

Lynn, L.E., Jr. (1987). *Managing public policy.* Boston: Little, Brown and Company.

Maccoby, M. (1976). *The gamesman.* NY: Simon and Schuster.

McLean, B., and Elkind, P. (2003). *The Smartest Guys in the Room: The Amazing Rise and Scandalous Fall of Enron.* New York: Portfolio-Penguin Group.

Moe, R.C. (1994). "The 'reinventing government' exercise: misinterpreting the problem, misjudging the consequences." *Public Administration Review, 54*(2), 111-122.

Osborne, D., and Gaebler, T. (1992). *Reinventing government*. Reading, MA: Addison-Wesley Publishing Company.

Perlmutter, F.D., and Cnaan, R.A. (1995). "Entrepreneurship in the public sector: the horns of a dilemma." *Public Administration Review, 55*(1), 29-36.

Petroski, H. (1982). *To engineer is human: The role of failure in successful design*. NY: St. Martin's Press.

Romzek, B.S., and Dubnick, M.J. (1987). "Accountability in the public sector: Lessons from the Challenger tragedy." *Public Administration Review, 47*(3), 227-238.

Schumpeter, J. (1911). *The theory of economic dynamics*.

Solomon, R.C. (1992). *Ethics and excellence*. NY: Oxford University Press.

Stever, J.A. (1988). *The end of public administration*. Dobbs Ferry, NY: Transnational Publishers, Inc.

Taylor, M. (1982). *Community, anarchy and liberty*. Cambridge, England: Cambridge University Press.

Terry, L.D. (1993). "Why we should abandon the misconceived quest to reconcile public entrepreneurship with democracy." *Public Administration Review, 53*(4), 393-395.

Tewes, J.E. (1983). "The new entrepreneurship." In B. H. Moore (Ed.), *The entrepreneur in local government* (pp. 15-20). Washington, DC: International City Management Association.

Thompson, J.D. (1967). *Organizations in action*. New York: McGraw-Hill.

Thompson, J.D., and Tuden, A. (1959). Strategies, structures and processes of organizational decision. In J. D. Thompson (Ed.), *Comparative studies in administration*. Pittsburgh: University of Pittsburgh Press.

Chapter 15

THE PERCEPTION OF EVIL IN MARKET DRIVEN ACADEMIC GOVERNANCE SYSTEMS

William L. Waugh, Jr.

There is a crisis in governance that is unfolding on academic campuses affected by Hurricanes Katrina and Rita. It is a manifestation of entrepreneurialism and managerialism which have overflowed their boundaries. For the majority of the educational institutions affected by the Hurricanes, the recovery process has been painful; with limited campus resources, loss of facilities and equipment, changes to funding streams, and changes in demand from enrollment and service reductions.

To further simultaneously aggravate matters, the very essence of professionalism in academia is also under assault. Means and ends become not only confused but manipulated in an attempt to drive efficiency to the forefront of academic endeavors. Traditional academic leadership, reward, and governance systems have been increasingly coopted by market based bottom line administrative decisions and values. As faculty lose control of academic programs, as tenure is proactively attacked, and as salaries become inverted, Professor Waugh explores the perceived "evil" manifested by the conflict laden changes being increasingly witnessed across market driven academia in America today.

Dr. Waugh notes that Hurricanes Katrina and Rita have created an opportunity to change the character of educational institutions. This opportunity calls for viable entrepreneurial academic leadership, effective management, and consensus-building.

THE PERCEPTION OF EVIL IN THE RECOVERY OF COLLEGES AND UNIVERSITIES AFFECTED BY HURRICANES KATRINA AND RITA

Catastrophic disaster exerts extreme pressure on colleges and universities, their administrators, faculties, staffs, and students and extreme pressure on their governance processes. Disaster brings demands upon limited campus resources, loss of facilities and equipment, threats to funding streams such as tuition and state budgets, and changes in demand caused by reductions in enrollment and other services. Disaster may discourage decision processes that include faculty, alumni, and other interest groups. The stakes may be huge. Institutional missions may be affected, programs may be eliminated, and faculty and staff may be laid off. Some of the changes may be dictated by circumstances and some may be the result of choices that could have gone the other way. Disaster affords rare opportunity to make fundamental changes in an institution for the better and for the worse. The faculty governance questions that arise are whether the faculty has a central role in decisions that affect academic programs and faculty affairs and whether the faculty has a role in deciding what the new institution will look like. Recovery seldom means simply rebuilding the old institutions.

When Hurricanes Katrina and Rita cut a swath of destruction across Louisiana, Mississippi, Alabama, and Texas in August and September of 2005, many colleges and universities were damaged, some severely, and thousands of students, faculty, and staff were evacuated. The storms and the breaches in the levees around the City of New Orleans, in particular, damaged that city's numerous college and university campuses, including the medical centers associated with Tulane University and Louisiana State University.

For the most part, institutions in Texas and Alabama sustained minimal damage and reopened within weeks. Some institutions in Mississippi suffered the loss of campuses along the coast, but managed to shift students to other campuses or to online programs, so that they could also open quickly. However, the prognosis for institutions in New Orleans has not been as positive. Figure 1 provides information on some of the institutions in Louisiana that were affected by the storms and levee breaks. In most cases, officials announced that classes would resume or facilities would reopen in time for the spring term of 2006, meaning that the institutions were closed only for their fall terms. In some few cases, officials were uncertain about reopening at any time in the future. Smaller institutions with smaller endowments, smaller enrollments, and few other resources, like small businesses, might be bankrupted by the disasters and unable to rebuild. Larger institutions, particularly those with multiple campuses, simply shifted students to other facilities. The University of New Orleans escaped most of the flooding and was able to reopen for a short fall term, although not all buildings were able to open that quickly.

Figure 1
Louisiana Colleges and Universities Damaged by Katrina and Rita
and When Their Classes Are Expected to Resume

Affected Institutions in Louisiana	Estimated Resume Classes
Delgado Community College	Spring 2006
Dillard University	Spring 2006
Herzing College – New Orleans	October 31, 2005
Louisiana State Univ – Health Sciences Center	Uncertain reopening date
Loyola University – New Orleans	January 9, 2006
NcNeese State University	October 27, 2005 – depending , building availability
Our Lady of Holy Cross College	January 2006
Our Lady of the Lake College	New Orleans campus closed indefinitely
Remington College – New Orleans	Closed until further notice
Southern University – New Orleans	January 17, 2006
Tulane University	Spring 2006
Tulane University School of Medicine	February 2006 (est.)

Source: CampusRelief.org

For most of the institutions, the recovery process has been painful. Faculty and staff, as well as students, have been among the storm and flood victims. Xavier University, an historically black institution in New Orleans, was severely damaged and announced that over one half of its faculty and staff were being laid off. Xavier officials also announced that the university's nationally known pharmacy program would be open in the spring of 2006, but its radio and television program would be closed because its equipment was lost in the flooding. Some choices will be driven by institutional priorities, but some will be driven by outside pressures. For state colleges and universities in Louisiana, for example, there is discussion of the consolidation of institutions and programs that may have profound effect upon their faculties and staffs. The state institutions in Louisiana have lost an estimated $54 million in tuition and fees and, because of the state budget shortfall, each can expect a 6% budget reduction if the governor's recommendations are accepted. Because faculty and staff represent 70 to 75% of university operating budgets, layoffs are expected (Fischer, 2005). Hurricanes Katrina and Rita will victimize even more people, in other words.

All of this is to say that Hurricanes Katrina and Rita have created challenges for college and university administrators, faculty, staff, students, alumni, and other stakeholders. The rules of university governance change as institutions declare financial exigency and extraordinary circumstances permit extraordinary choices. The disasters create an opportunity to change the very character of institutions. On the positive side, there may be funding for new facilities and the elimination of weak programs. On the negative side, the loss of student enrollment may cause serious financial strain and even the elimination of high quality and popular programs.

In the case of New Orleans, it is uncertain that the students who evacuated will return. Many enrolled under special programs at other institutions and may choose to remain at those institutions. For large, well-endowed institutions, like Tulane University, it is likely that the institutions will recover quickly and their students will return. For smaller institutions, the expected loss of population in New Orleans may mean a loss of their current and future student bodies, i.e., their market. There is some expectation that the changing demographics in New Orleans after Katrina may mean that some programs, perhaps some institutions, may not be needed and some programs and institutions may be consolidated to save money (Fischer, 2005).

How will faculty, as well as the college and university stakeholder groups, participate in the critical recovery and rebuilding decisions? It is a situation that calls for entrepreneurial leadership, effective management, and consensus-building. The processes may be viewed as equitable, reasonable, and necessary even if the outcomes are negative for faculty and staff. Unfortunately, while collegial processes can promote consensus, they may be eschewed in favor of more expedient and less sensitive processes. The temptation for some administrators will be to eliminate weak programs and those programs not central to the college or university mission and to lay off their faculties and staff with little or no input. The question is whether, in the end, the processes will be viewed as evil because they violated expectations concerning shared governance.

American Association of University Professors, *Hurricane Katrina and New Orleans Universities: A Report of an AAUP Special Committee* **(Washington, DC: AAUP, May-June 2007).**

The potential for university officials to use a catastrophic disaster as pretext for eliminating faculty and programs without appropriate consultation and due process was a concern of the American Association of University Professors following the Katrina disaster in 2005. A special committee reviewed the processes used to "downsize" universities in New Orleans and determined that there are reasons for concern. While there were significant differences in how the universities handled the crisis, the AAUP committee's report (2007) noted:

- Failures to follow stated policies to protect academic freedom and to preserve due process (AAUP Report, 2007, page 120).

- Lack of congruence between institutional justifications and the extent of the measures taken (AAUP Report, 2007, page 121).

- Issuance of notifications of adverse personnel actions to more personnel than necessary to meet minimum institutional needs (AAUP Report, 2007, page 121).

- Failures to meet minimal AAUP standards for faculty consultation as well as the levels that could have been met (AAUP Report, 2007, page 122).

- Failures to meet minimal AAUP standards for the notification and timing of personnel actions which increased uncertainty and stress among those affected (AAUP Report, 2007, page 122).

- Failures to meet AAUP standards for alternative placement of affected faculty or even the levels that the institutions had the capacity to meet (AAUP Report, 2007, page 122).

- Failures to meet accepted standards for the internal review of adverse actions as well as the institutions' own review procedures (AAUP Report, 2007, page 122)

The report also cited "far less deference" to faculty tenure than the AAUP or the institutions' own practice prior to Katrina should have warranted (AAUP Report, 2007, page 123). In short, the institutions made more draconian cuts in personnel and programs than their own statements seemed to justify, failed to provide adequate due process to faculty and staff, failed to consult faculty as much as they could have, gave short notice of personnel actions with little opportunity for appeal, and failed to provide as much placement and other assistance to those affected as they could have. There were significant differences in how the institutions dealt with the need to downsize, but none followed policies consistent with the protection of academic freedom and due process. Pre-disaster policies and procedures were not followed. Faculty consultation varied among institutions with some providing little or no opportunity for faculty either to participate in decision making or to question administration policies. There was a perception among faculty that officials used the Katrina disaster to make programmatic and personnel changes that they could not make or would have had to spend a lot of time making prior to the disaster (AAUP Report, 2007, page 120). "A question that has troubled the Special Committee … is whether Katrina created an opportunity to make major changes —specifically, to terminate the appointments of certain tenured faculty members—that could not have been made in the absence of such devastation" (AAUP Report, 2007, page 121). There were allegations that the disaster was used, in at least a few cases, "as a subterfuge to rid the institution of faculty troublemakers or critics of the administration…." (AAUP Report, 2007, page 121). The committee observed that it seemed that officials did not trust faculty to understand the dire situation or to provide advice on how the institution might recover from the disaster. Clearly, adherence to AAUP's policy of having at least twelve months notice of termination might have been impractical, but the institutions failed to provide as much notice as they could have and even removed faculty who had been assigned and were preparing for classes. At one institution, faculty access to offices, computing facilities, library, and even parking was terminated without explanation (AAUP Report, 2007, page 123). The perception was that university officials simply took advantage of the situation to get rid of faculty and programs. As the special committee noted, "[g]iven the manner in which these decisions were made—the malleability of standards, the absence of meaningful faculty involvement, the disregard for tenure, and, often, the inadequacy of review—it is almost inevitable that such would be a common perception" (AAUP Report, 2007, page 123).

ENTREPRENEURIALISM AND MANAGERIALISM PERCEIVED AS EVIL IN UNIVERSITY GOVERNANCE

Articles in the *Chronicle of Higher Education* have decried the "de-tenuring" of university faculty, the centralization of university decision making, and the "outsourcing" of university functions (see, e.g., Nicklin, 1997, and Healy, 1997). The larger issue, however, is the declining role of faculty in university governance. While the threats to tenure systems may seem to strike at the heart of the academic enterprise, the real threat is the administrative changes that are causing faculty to lose control over academic programs. As one article described it, there is a "war against the faculty." The author warns that viewing the faculty as simply a human resource to be "managed" and "deployed with originality and attention to institutional mission," when many faculty believe "that they are the institution," is creating serious conflict (Nelson, 1999, B4).

Responses to the "war" article in the subsequent issue of *The Chronicle* criticized the author's call for active resistance to such change as being insensitive to the financial realities that universities face today. Judging from the letters to *The Chronicle's* editors, "war" may be being waged on some campuses, but clearly it is not being waged on all. Nonetheless, given the number of articles on the subject in recent years, growing numbers of faculty members on many campuses are concerned about the changing status of faculty and their role of faculty in university governance. The concerns are being fed by proposals from some state and university officials to end the "scam" of tenure and to make universities more sensitive to market forces. For example, one article recommended that universities apply "lessons from ... companies that have 're-invented' themselves during the past decade" by focusing on their core missions and eliminating or deemphasizing peripheral activities, cutting their bureaucracies, sharing functions with other organizations to achieve economies of scale, and simplifying operating procedures to save money (Mahoney, 1997). But, while "re-invention" is touted as a panacea for university budget limitations despite growing disillusionment with its promise, the real culprit may be natural administrative processes.

CULTURAL CHANGE AND CONFLICT IN UNIVERSITY GOVERNANCE

A first question might concern the nature of the threat to university governance. A recent article in *Policy Studies Review* (Waugh, 1998) argued that traditional university governance processes are being affected by a number of changes in university administration, including: (1) the centralization of authority and decisionmaking; (2) the use of strategic planning and management techniques; (3) the use of quality management techniques; (4) the professionalization of university administration; (5) the bureaucratization of university administration; (6) the entrepreneurialism of university leaders and administrators; (7) the general distrust of the academy by the public and public officials who fund higher education; and (8) fundamental changes in the organizational cultures of universities.

In brief, the *PSR* article argued that university decisionmaking is being centralized because university presidents are being held more accountable to governing boards and state legislatures and are afraid to entrust their careers to traditional university governance processes that are dominated by faculty. The defense of disciplinary prerogative and departmental budgets can result in quite parochial views on the role of the university. Although the booming economy has provided some respite, shrinking budgets or, at best, tight budgets have made it difficult to maintain programs, let alone expand and improve them. As a consequence, academic leaders have been forced to redistribute resources among programs and to eliminate programs when they become too expensive to maintain, too small to be viable, or too peripheral to the university mission. In short, economics have intruded upon the university and economic criteria are supplanting academic criteria in university policymaking.

Economics does not explain all of the problem, however. Within university administrations, professional financial and human resource administrators are replacing faculty administrators. The same professionalization process is occurring in hospitals as accountants and business managers replace doctors, and in other institutions where financial managers and lawyers are replacing administrators drawn from the core technology of the institution. The result is greater attention to efficiency and management technique and less attention to the core mission of the institution. As one might expect, professional managers often do not fully understand the value system of the institution if their education and experience was acquired in a different setting. As the *PSR* article (Waugh, 1998) points out, allocating resources on the basis of corporate values and having a reward system based on corporate values creates a corporate cultural conflict. For senior administrators, accountability to faculty and the university as a whole is replaced by accountability to the chief executive or chief administrative officer. Even providing information to the faculty may complicate the decision process and make it more difficult for the president to pursue his or her agenda.

Also, demands for greater efficiency are encouraging the adoption of business management techniques that are ill-suited to traditional bottom-up academic planning and policymaking processes. For example, strategic planning is essentially a top-down management technique in which senior executives guide the development of the mission statement, the identification of strategic issues, and the development of objectives and action plans to achieve the objectives. Participation may be broad, communication may be relatively open, and there may be a genuine interest in reading the internal and external environments and developing reasonable and even ambitious goals. But, the management technique lends itself to controlled participation, a preference for values set at the top, and the reallocation of resources based on economic measures to implement action plans. While faculty may be involved in strategic planning processes, they are just another stakeholder group, rather than the central technology of the university responsible for its core mission. In effect, they are marginalized in the process, because they become just another set of stakeholders, along with alumni, external constituencies, and staff. The marginalization is all the more problematic because some faculties and departments may fall victim to a redefined mission.

The customer focus engendered by quality management techniques is also having negative and positive effects. Relatively few faculty object to an emphasis on quality teaching, although many object to an over-reliance on student evaluations and are concerned about the quality of the other measures of classroom effectiveness. To the extent that customers, i.e., students, are driving program development and administrators are relying more on measures of customer satisfaction and less on standards set by the faculty, traditional faculty control over academic programs is eroding. Credit hour-driven budgets encourage the weakening of standards to keep enrollments up and may well spell doom for degree programs and departments that are less popular. To be sure, the pursuit of grants and contracts and the overhead that they bring may be affecting the allocation of university resources, as well. But, many departments and faculties may fail the market test if that is a principal criteria for allocating resources.

Similarly, a natural bureaucratization of administrative processes is creating new organizational structures and values. The natural tendency is for the number of staff to grow as they take the place of faculty in support services. Student advising, internship supervision, and other critical functions are being turned over to staff who have more time to spend on such roles. Bureaucratization produces its own pathologies. Classical Weberian bureaucratic structures are by their very nature slow moving and slow changing. While routine tasks may be very efficiently carried out (the principal value of classical bureaucracy), nonroutine matters find little solution. The more aggravating characteristic is that as administrative processes ossify the proverbial "tail wags the dog." The manifestations are familiar to most faculty (indeed to most people who work in large organizations of any sort). The paperwork becomes more important than the task. Meetings are scheduled during breaks when administrators have to be on campus, but faculty do not. Meetings are scheduled early in the morning when faculty teach at night. And, there may be an explicit expectation that all will be at their desks from 9 to 5 when faculty may well work at different times or need to be at other locations, such as the library. Business attire, business hours, and business values may become the central themes of faculty meetings, when credit hour generation is not the focus of discussion. In some cases, the effect may be more amusing than otherwise, although sinister purposes may be inferred when important meetings are scheduled when faculty are away. Explaining to a 9-to-5 administrator that one's distribution of effort among teaching, research, service and other activities is based on a 60 or even 70 hour work week or that the work week includes Saturday and, for the untenured and especially productive, Sunday and holidays can be a challenge.

Ironically, businesses long ago learned that their more creative units may have to be located away from their more traditional "factory" units because of differences in organizational culture and operational imperatives. Research and development units are often located in different buildings or in wooded industrial parks, away from the headquarters, so that creativity will be nurtured rather than managed. The cultures of some of the most technologically creative firms in our society have become the stuff of legend. As a result, creative organizations may now be more closely associated with nonhierarchical structures, informal relationships, casual attire, and little attention to the clock. In short, business "campuses" have come to look very much like traditional university campuses. Given that university faculty are generally considered the creative technology of the university, the logical answer might be to relocate the more "factory-like" operations to the fringe of campus or to another site altogether to prevent contamination.

THE EVILS OF ENTREPRENEURIALISM AND MANAGERIALISM

In March of 1999, the faculty at Morris Brown College in Atlanta received notices of their status following a review by a committee of administrators, faculty, trustees, and students appointed by the college's new president. The nine-member committee recommended that 16 of the college's 98 faculty be fired, and another 3 be retired by the end of the academic year, and that 20 others be put on probation until June, 2000; and another 6 be retired by that time. In all, the committee recommended removing or putting on probation over a third of the Morris Brown faculty (Magner, 1999). For a college with a history of financial and academic troubles, the president's radical actions might appear justified. Morris Brown is a private college, dependent upon enrollments for revenue, but financial exigency was not the reason given for the firings and retirements. The reason given by college officials was that the targeted faculty did not fit into the administration's plans for the college, rather than that they were academically unqualified. Presumably, the faculty will be replaced by others more in tune with the college's new mission. Without information on the review process and the criteria used to identify those to be removed, it is difficult to judge whether the actions are justified or not. Nonetheless, it is clear that the actions reflect a managerial approach that is significantly different from the traditional shared governance approach to human resources and personnel decisions. The actions may also reflect the entrepreneurial bent of the new president. The important point is not that the change itself is good or bad; rather the point is that the change was made without the normal participation of faculty. Only time will tell whether the institution and the faculty will be served by the terminations.

Fortunately, few college and university faculty have faced the same threat to their livelihoods. The Morris Brown case illustrates the growing trend towards more entrepreneurial presidents and governing boards, mission-driven university decisionmaking, and the supplanting of traditional university governance processes by hand-picked task forces and business management techniques. The case also illustrates the external and internal factors that are affecting decisionmaking in many universities and encouraging entrepreneurialism by many university presidents and chief academic officers and managerialism in university administration. Whether the changes are good for universities in the long run or represent an evil that will ultimately damage academe, is uncertain. What is certain is that entrepreneurialism and managerialism are affecting the structures and processes of university governance in ways that are reducing the roles and influence of faculty in academic and administrative decisionmaking. They are changing the very values that have historically guided academic decisions.

Unfortunately, the values guiding the entrepreneurialism of university presidents and governing boards, and inherent in the managerialism of staff, may not be as apparent to faculty and staff, or even university officials, as they should be. While most would acknowledge that entrepreneurial leadership can have good and bad impacts on institutions and individuals, the impact on university governance may be more bad than good. Even scholar-kings and scholar-queens with the best of intentions do not always know what is best for students, faculty, and their institutions. Pragmatic approaches may benefit the students, faculty, and their institutions; but they also damage the trust and the commitment of the faculty.

Managerialism, on the other hand, is often presumed to be almost value-free, beyond the explicit objectives of efficiency and cost effectiveness. However, the pursuit of rationality and efficiency, without regard for the impact on human beings and social institutions, may well be a form of what Adams and Balfour (1998) call "administrative evil." In effect, the application of management techniques in universities may be saving money or more rationally allocating resources, but it may also be having a detrimental effect on students, faculty, staff, and other constituents. As long as efficiency is the sole criteria against which the techniques are measured, their effects on university governance will not be accurately assessed.

To be sure, the centralization of university decisionmaking also may be problematic. In large measure, university administrators may not fully understand what they are doing. While they read a management literature that extols rational techniques for resource allocation, human resource development, and any number of other organizational changes, they do not consider either the nature of the processes or the fundamental assumptions on which they are based. In many cases, the techniques have to be adapted to the academic setting, and in others they are inappropriate altogether. If the techniques are used without considering their impact, the result may well be "administrative evil" (Adams and Balfour, 1998). "Administrative evil" is the product of bureaucratic rationality when managerial values are carried to their extreme, without regard for their effects. Adams and Balfour trace the pursuit of efficiency and focus on mission by the German civil service through the Holocaust and by American authorities through the space program that was lead by former Nazi scientists. They find "evil" in a number of current policy areas, most notably on the welfare reformers who focus on efficiency (i.e., reduced welfare rolls) and not on the effects experienced by families and children when welfare checks are not replaced with adequate jobs and adequate health benefits.

While there is no Holocaust in American higher education, the changes in university governance may well be "administrative evil" in the sense that the academy and higher education are damaged. Certainly careers can be damaged by the lack of attention to the impact of managerial values and the values inherent in management techniques. The impact of change on university governance may not be readily apparent because there is so much going on on campus. The clearest indication of change is in the language of university administration. Universities are being "re-invented." University presidents are becoming more "entrepreneurial." University decisionmakers are paying more attention to "cost centers." Decisions are "mission-driven." University services are becoming more "customer friendly." In large measure, the same changes that have occurred in private industry over the past decade are being visited upon universities. With the changes in the language of university administration has come a change in fundamental values and, thereby, change in the culture of the institution. While some of the terminology actually means very little, the impact of all the change means a great deal, in other words.

Some of the changes are clearly for the better in terms of more considered allocations of resources and greater efficiency in their use. Universities, administrators and faculty, are realizing that they cannot be all things to all people, and painful choices may have to be made to assure that the quality of at least some programs is protected, if not enhanced. The designation of "centers of excellence" in many universities is a manifestation of that change, as is the choice by some institutions to focus on traditional liberal arts programs rather than professional programs (or vice versa). But, some of the changes are decidedly not for the better. While some are easier to live with than others, such as the bureaucratization of university administration, some are very much contrary to the role of universities in modern society.

The change is occurring in the administration of universities elsewhere in the world, as well as in the U.S. Proposals to eliminate tenure in favor of term appointments, require post-tenure reviews for some or all faculty, "outsource" staff operations, eliminate programs and faculty not central to university missions, "refocus" faculty and staff on university and departmental missions, and shift the burden of keeping up with technological change to students by requiring that they buy their own computers (thereby freeing up university funds for other purposes) are but a few of the many suggestions that have been made. Some of the changes are cosmetic and some are affecting the core values of the academy. Some of the changes are very visible, such as the increasing reliance on part-time and nontenure-track faculty and on graduate teaching assistants to teach large sections of undergraduate service courses, and some are not.

While some of the administrative changes are very apparent, the profound change in how universities are governed is less so. The distinction between administration and governance is important; and it is a distinction that is increasingly overlooked as university presidents and governing board members extol the virtues of business management techniques in higher education, and leaders seek to affect fundamental change in mission and method. Administration is: those processes that are related to the allocation of resources, including planning, human resource management, and particularly financial management. Governance is: those processes related to the technology of the university, including the academic programs, faculty, and scholarship. Preserving the distinction, so that the dog wags the tail, is essential for maintaining healthy academic institutions.

CONCLUSIONS

What is the answer? As the articles and letters to the editor of *The Chronicle* indicate, not all faculty are experiencing a loss of power or influence, nor do all those who are being marginalized regret the loss of responsibility for academic programs. Faculty have different expectations. In fact, it may be that one of the major changes affecting university governance is the declining interest among faculty members in university policymaking. Pressures to publish, consult, and write grants may be distracting faculty from their traditional roles. Such pressures are clearly making it difficult to spend time with students outside of class, and to devote more than a little time to university governance. Reward systems that encourage individual effort and punish university service weaken faculty commitment to institutions. That has been the experience of large corporations with similar reward systems, and there is no reason to think it will be different in universities.

In some measure, the threat to traditional university governance is localized, as well. A president eliminates faculty because they do not fit his or her vision for the university. A department chair presumes to change curricula to disempower some faculty and/or to empower others (or him - or herself). Or, a dean chooses to reallocate faculty lines and, thereby, reduces course offerings and the coverage of a discipline. The problem is not that the entrepreneurial president, dean, or chair made a strategic decision. The problem is that that decision was made with little or no faculty input and may well have been motivated by baser values than efficiency or academic quality or financial exigency. The faculty responsibility for such matters has been wrested away.

Responsibility for guiding change is becoming an administrative task, rather than a faculty responsibility. To the extent that faculty prerogatives and even careers are at stake, change can be a scary thing. It can be very scary for the untenured and for those in programs with declining enrollments, peripheral missions, and/or poor academic reputations. It is less scary for those who have market value and can find more accommodating circumstances. As corporations have found out during reductions-in-force, the best leave first and often when the corporation wanted them to stay. For that reason, the literature on organizational development often recommends reassuring those whose positions or roles may be affected by proposed changes and providing them with more job security in exchange for their participation in the adoption of new organizational structures and purposes. While "grandfathering" (or "grandmothering") people in so that they will not lose their positions may be difficult, particularly in small departments, alternatives can usually be found.

Cary Nelson, a professor of English at the University of Illinois at Urbana-Champaign, calls for a "resistance" movement to fight back (1999: B4). Indeed, the ethical choice may be to resist threats to academic freedom and to protect faculty prerogatives in curricular matters, i.e., the traditional method of university governance. The ethical choice also may be to draw attention to the "evil" results of administrative action. To do less would amount to complicity. Although budget cuts, resource reallocations, and mission redefinition may be necessary to the health of the institution, the choices should be made with full understanding of their implications.

Distrust of the academy makes it difficult to find sympathy or understanding when concerns about governance processes are voiced. Faculty may scoff at the perception of some that they only work a few hours a week, but that perception may be all too common. The perceptions among administrators that faculty are "loose cannons" or lack understanding of the "real world" operations of the university also makes it difficult to find common purpose. One of the more problematic aspects of the change in university governance is the presumption that executive or centralized control is a good idea. "It's good to be king," as Mel Brooks said in the *History of the World Part II*. Being king affords perquisites. It gives license to do good, while it affords opportunity to do evil. However, centralization is seldom a good idea. It facilitates decisionmaking, but it results in much poorer decisions. It is often the choice of those who confuse leadership and decisionmaking. It is sometimes the choice of those who overestimate their own knowledge and experience. It is too often the choice of those motivated by power. University officials should be encouraged to exercise leadership and to take advantage of the expertise within their institutions.

While the title of this chapter may suggest that entrepreneurialism and managerialism are evil, the thesis here is that both represent good and evil in university governance. The problem is that too little attention is being paid the evil aspects of entrepreneurial leadership and professional management. The pathologies that are reducing the faculty role in university governance are not exotic conditions. It is common for large organizations to need periodic reaffirmations of their core missions to reduce the tendency for the "tail to wag the dog." It is common for bureaucracies to grow and to clog decision processes with standard operating procedures, regulations, and other impediments to innovation and flexibility. It is common for reward systems to encourage perverse behaviors. It is common for rational decisionmaking techniques to be utilized without a full understanding of the assumptions that underlie their method. In those regards, universities are suffering the same problems that other large organizations have suffered after long periods of growth. It is also common, however, for large organizations to disintegrate when they lose touch with their core values.

The conflict between the new culture of university administration and the traditional culture of university governance is understandable and should have been anticipated. The arrogance of expertise and technical specialization has permeated Western culture for centuries (see, e.g., Saul, 1992). An unwavering belief in rational (bureaucratic) approaches is rooted in our national history and, unfortunately, limits our capacities to deal with problems in new and innovative ways (see, e.g., Silberman, 1993). And, the assumption that professional expertise provides a better foundation for policymaking than democratic or consensus-building processes has been commonly held since the Progressive Era, if not earlier, and has proven a serious problem in American governance more than once (see, e.g., Schiesl, 1977: 191-196). In large measure, traditional university governance processes, as aggravating as they may be for all involved, may be far more appropriate to the university role in society than centralized, bureaucratic processes; and, in the long term, will be more effective in maintaining the health of academe.

REFERENCES

Adams, Guy B., and Balfour, D. L. (1998). *Unmasking Administrative Evil.* Thousand Oaks, CA: SAGE Publications.

American Association of University Professors (May-June, 2007). *Hurricane Katrina and New Orleans Universities: A Report of an AAUP Special Committee.* Washington, DC: AAUP.

CampusRelief.org. (2005). Affected Campuses. Retrieved November 21, 2005 from http://www.campusrelief.com/x6.xml

Fischer, Karen. (November 18, 2005). Louisiana Governor's Order to Cut State Spending Could Cost Colleges $71 Million and Force Layoffs. *The Chronicle of Higher Education*, p. A24.

Healy, P. (1997, November, 14). Mass. Leader to Seek Abolition of Tenure, *The Chronicle of Higher Education* p. A36.

Magner, D.K. (1999, March, 26,). Morris Brown Tells a Third of Faculty Members That Their Jobs Are at Risk, *The Chronicle of Higher Education,* p. A18.

Mahoney, R. J. (1997, October, 17,). 'Reinventing' the University: Object Lessons from Big Business, *The Chronicle of Higher Education*, p. B4-B-5.

Nelson, C. (1999, April, 16,) The War Against the Faculty, *The Chronicle of Higher Education*, pp. B4-B5.

Nicklin, J. L. (1997, November, 21,) Universities Seek to Cut Costs by 'Outsourcing' More Operations, *The Chronicle of Higher Education*, pp. A35-A36.

Saul, J. R. (1992). *Voltaire's Bastards: The Dictatorship of Reason in the Wes.,* New York: Vintage Books.

Schiesl, M. J. (1977). *The Politics of Efficiency: Municipal Administration and Reform in America: 1880-1920.* Berkeley: University of California Press.

Scott, J. V. (1996). The Strange Death of Faculty Governance, *PS: Political Science and Politics,* (December), 724-726.

Silberman, B. S. (1993). *Cages of Reason: The Rise of the Rational State in France, Japan, the United States, and Great Britain.* Chicago: University of Chicago Press.

Waugh, W. L., Jr. (1998) Conflicting Values and Cultures: The Managerial Threat to University Governance, *Policy Studies Review,* 15 (Winter), 61-73.

Chapter 16

PROFESSIONAL PERFORMANCE PRIORITIES AFTER THE PRIVATIZATION AND ENTREPRENEURIAL MANAGEMENT TRANSFORMATION

Van R. Johnston

Traditional sovereignty and governance protections have been under assault for some time now. Privatization, reinventing, franchising, and re-engineering have brought private sector demands for managerial efficiency and accountability to the public sector. Customers emerge from their citizen roles. Efficiency replaces effectiveness. The nature of the managerial mission changes.

Entrepreneurial conflict management replaces more traditional and more benign public policy and administration behaviors. Professional ethics becomes increasingly important as public managers, citizens and politicians find themselves without the guidelines of the past, and yet to discover the unfolding professional ethical standards of the future. Turbulence and changing reward systems create very significant professional and ethical concerns and dilemmas. Sovereignty and governance as we have known them are disappearing. We need new mechanisms to govern and enhance the behavior of the emerging customers while providing stewardship, wisdom, and leadership for our citizens.

Government employees, of course, are caught in the middle. With privatization, reinventing, franchising, and downsizing, there are not only fewer employee positions; the ones that exist are less secure, more efficiency and competition oriented, and clearly more complex overall. This chapter explores and analyzes this transformation of the public sector and focuses as well on the threats to sovereignty, governance and ethics for citizens, customers, public sector employees, and consultants. It also addresses the new skills and caveats needed to be able to optimally deliver government services, whether by government agency or private contractor, to both citizens and customers in a transformed, reinvented, and privatized world.

Privatization, Reinventing, and Public Policy

In implementing public policy in the privatization/contracting arena, government's role has been transformed. Private partners are relied upon by government to get the work of the public done. The balance between the government vs. the market is increasingly part of this exercise in dynamic change.

Underlying this evolution are the latent interests of the public sector for effective implementation of the public will, and the interests of the private sector for increased efficiency and competition. There is little doubt, however, that we will continue to witness the merging of the sectors. Contract management expertise is increasing in importance. We will also be unable to avoid the serious concerns that managing the public interest forces upon us. (Kettl, 1993).

It should not be forgotten that there are those who argue that privatization allows government to focus on what it dose particularly well, while adjusting what it doesn't do so well towards contractors in the private sector. The partnerships created therein can emphasize quality alliances and network capitalism. Such benefits are usually far more positive than the laissez faire that is often attributed to government in privatization cases.

The reality, nonetheless, is that there are privatization situations that are praised by a wide range of supporters. Liberals value a government presence in services which can continue to exist, even if privatized, when government budgets are increasingly scarce. Conservatives see more market influence and less government intrusions. Progressives can argue that the government is becoming more effective. (Clark, Heilman, Johnson, 1995 / 1996).

Citizens, Customers and the Constitution

Citizens and Constitutional Democracy

Under the Constitution, we view citizens as having rights and interests. Government has sovereignty, which manifests itself in terms of both duties and protections. Duties could be seen as a requirement to provide for basic health, welfare, defense and education, etc. One example of a sovereign's protection would be the right not to be sued by citizens unless such right is granted by government. The Constitution, in accordance with the principles of sovereignty, also grants the government powers such as eminent domain, which it is to use on behalf of the citizens (Johnston, 1990).

Over the years, our notion of government, based on constitutional democracy, has functioned with a number of underlying values and principles at its core. Besides sovereign duties and obligations, we've valued: legitimacy, accountability, governance priorities, the public interest, stewardship and access to the governance system. Clearly, different eras have emphasized strengths and weaknesses in these orientations, but overall, citizens had a pretty reasonable notion of the differences and/or predictions involved when they received their services from government as opposed to receiving them from business, industry, or other private sector firms and organizations. Citizens had legal rights and access to the governmental system which allowed them to have an impact.

1. The Public Interest	7. Constitutional Rights
2. Sovereignty	8. Authority/Responsibility Linkages
3. Due Process	9. Legal Rights
4. Legitimacy	10. Participation
5. Accountability	11. Equity
6. Governance Priorities	12. Stewardship

Figure 1: Citizens and Constitutional Democracy

Nagel noted that those managing the public's interests have noticeable priorities. These priorities, based on constitutional democracy, empower citizens to be able to perform their roles in the unfolding manifestation of democracy as time moves on. Those citizen priorities, according to Nagel (1989) include: public participation, predictable rules, due process, political feasibility, effectiveness, efficiency, and equity.

1. Public Participation
2. Predictable Rules
3. Due Process
4. Political Feasibility
5. Effectiveness
6. Efficiency
7. Equity

Figure 2: Citizens Priorities - Nagel

Before the dramatic shifts towards deregulation and more stringent efficiency oriented entrepreneurial management in government that started with California's Proposition 13, and President Carter's deregulation of the airline industry in 1978, government typically delivered services to our citizens by way of government organizations. Citizens elected political representatives, by way of our political party system, to their various offices. These legitimately elected politicians then appointed professional senior administrators to manage the financial and administrative systems. The arrows on the Citizens Model (Figure 3) indicate how that system worked. Before the entrepreneurial changes launched by Proposition 13, Carter's deregulation of the airlines, and shortly thereafter by Reagan's Reaganomics in the early 1980's, citizens were much closer to the political and financial accountability provided by the constitution.

Citizens Model

Politician
Administrator

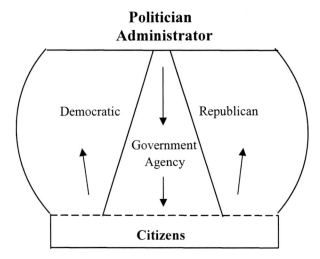

Figure 3: Citizens and the Citizen Model

THE ENVIRONMENT SHIFTS

Contemporary scholars refer to the onset and surge of market based competitive managerial values and priorities (Halachmi, 1994) as a change in the political economy (Halachmi and Boydston, 1994). The ominous harbinger was proposition 13. Then came the budget limitations. Increasing demand for government services, at the same time, pressured public policy makers and administrators to search for innovative alternatives to provide for citizens' needs and desires...with increasingly shrinking budgets.

Contracting out and privatization (Savas, 1982) were used to escape the fiscal pressures (Donahuc, 1989). Reengineering (Hammer and Champty, 1993) and reinventing (Osborne and Gaebler, 1991) were embraced by private sector managers and public sector administrators.

Efficiency, economy and competition became increasingly valued. De-regulation enhanced their viability as the environment was increasingly transformed towards an entrepreneurial arena. Many of the values of total quality management (Johnston, 1995 a) such as customer satisfaction (Gore, 1993) were increasingly adopted.

Along the way, both the game and the players (formerly actors, now stakeholders) began to change dimensionally. Citizens were becoming customers and government was acting more like business (Johnston, 1995b; Johnston and Seidenstat, 2007). As the transformation unfolded, the rules of the game became more occluded. The rights, protections, and contributions of both sectors became less clear (Bozeman, 1987). Efficiency begins to dominate effectiveness. And contracts, which public sector professionals could improve their skills on, and entrepreneurial public managers became more valued. Conflict and competition are injected into the business of government.

CUSTOMER MODEL

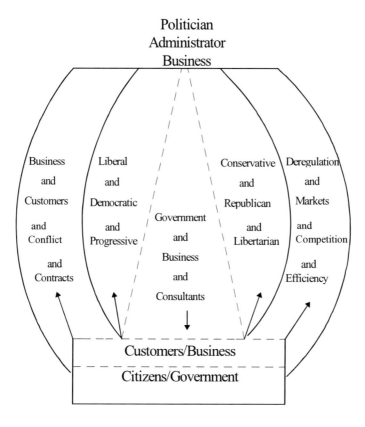

Figure 4.

LOSS OF TRUST

As the entrepreneurial revolution took hold (Johnston, 1996 a, b, c), and as citizens became customers (Johnston, 1995b), many of the protections of constitutional democracy for its citizens faded significantly. Competition, conflict, efficiency and economy reoriented the behavior of citizens, politicians and administrators. Zero sum engagements emerge where collegial or even bargained interactions used to reign. Partisan participants increasingly appear to be plundering the public realm for predatorily captured spoils. One of the more cogent representations of this unfolding reality is captured in the following. "Government is broke and politics is broken." (Newland, 1997).

The increasingly uncontrollable competition is focused on our collective public mission, goals, and problems less and less. Frontal confrontation, especially as manifested in the special prosecutor wars, diverts our energies from providing public sector based services to citizens or customers. This certainly doesn't reduce the credibility of those who claim that government is the problem. Yet numerous potential problems for customers and competition oriented management emerge.

1. Sovereignty issues	9. Quality control problems
2. Accountability problems	10. Service interruptions: profit declines
3. Due process	11. Lack of competition
4. Contract naiveté	12. Fraud
5. Secrecy	13. Loss of capital investment
6. Political considerations	14. Corruption
7. Sector blurring	15. Labor strikes
8. Skimming	16. Lost job benefits

Figure 5. Potential Problems of More Competition, Conflict and Customer Oriented Management

As the business of government took on a unique entrepreneurial flavor based on competition, conflict, efficiency and economy; and as winning, money, and power were reified, people lost their trust in government. Citizens lost. Customers lost. Yet savvy customers will probably cope with the changes more adequately than citizens without viable customer skills.

The transformation of government towards its new privatized, reinvented and entrepreneurial image doesn't seem to have lessened the sense of alienation. It has actually stimulated many to seek greater control over the increasingly market oriented approach that government is pursuing. Those with customer skills want more. Those without customer skills are seeking ways to become more viable in the new game.

Government reacts to the increased pressures by attempting to focus on the truth when debatable controversy erupts. It also prepares to deal with more hostility and even outright violence. Yet, it is also realizing that, with the increasing variety of service delivery mechanisms, many will perceive government as increasingly less viable (Kingsley, 1997).

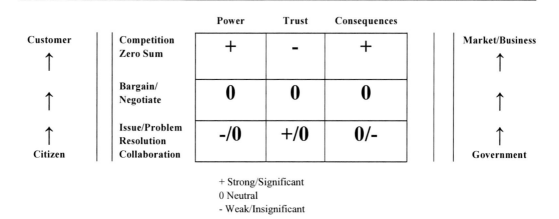

Figure 6. The Emerging Entrepreneurial Management and Public Policy Model

CITIZEN CYNICISM

It has been popular to refer to the press and the media as being cynical for some time now (Starobin, 1995). It is also understandable since the media reports on the events unfolding on the public policy and administration stage. As the entrepreneurial emergence manifests itself more fully, interesting new twists are examined which reveal not only innovative market based mechanisms for dealing with matters, but the loss of variably cherished public priorities as well.

Focusing on citizen cynicism, however, seems more profound and more problematic. Citizens, after all, are the heroes of our democratic system of government. We have one of history's great constitutions to guarantee their viability in our successful but increasingly troubled democracy. It is downright problematic to think of citizens as alienated and disenchanted. As entrepreneurial mechanisms for delivering public services and protections replace citizen oriented provision, production and governance systems, however, increasing numbers find themselves left out. They are not credibly represented any more. It is less than surprising that many feel betrayed. Some simply do not have the skills necessary to become viable players in the emerging entrepreneurial public arena.

Berman (1997) notes that current research indicates public cynicism regards public officials and government policies as being inept, corrupt, and taking advantage of citizens. When analyzed in the context of the theories of social capital and trust, it becomes apparent that cynicism dampens the spirit and participation of the citizenry. Manifestations of citizen cynicism include: disappointment, alienation, disengagement, lower trust, diminished public spirit, and an overall experience of disenfranchisement.

Government as:

Corrupt
Inept
Taking advantage of citizens

Causing:

Disengagement
Alienation
Disappointment
Low Trust
Diminished Public Spirit
Experience of disenfranchisement

(adapted from Berman)

Figure 7. Citizen Cynicism

PRIORITY PRESSURES AND GOVERNANCE GUIDELINES

There are enormous pressures to change traditional democratic governance guidelines and to bring them more into line with the increasingly competition and conflict oriented public (and increasingly private) sector arena. Franchising (Halachmi, 1996) has been added to privatization (Seidenstat, 1996) and reengineering. De-regulation still has strong promoters and contracting out is here to stay. We live in the residue of the private sector's merger, acquisition, and hostile takeover influences. Reinvention (Osborne and Gaebler, 1991) has transformed America (Gore, 1994) and downsizing is a threat still looming on the horizon for so many in America, even after the millennium. We continue to be confronted with entrepreneurial ethics. The names of individuals (Ken Lay, Jeff Skilling, Joe Nacchio, Bernie Ebbers, The Rigas', et al); and companies (Enron, Andersen, Qwest, Global Crossing, Tyco, Adelphia, and others) have become household names…warning us of the need for constant vigilance (McLean and Elkin, 2003).

1. Reinventing	7. Hostile Takeovers
2. Privatization	8. Contracting out
3. Franchising	9. De-Regulation
4. Reengineering	10. Downsizing
5. Mergers	11. Competition
6. Acquisitions	12. Conflict

Figure 8. Priority Pressures

CITIZENS

Americans, as citizens, are taking a beating. They no longer have the heroic standing they did when constitutional democracy was embraced so much more strongly. Many feel betrayed. Others fall through the cracks. Some simply lack the skills to navigate through the increasingly market based maze in order to secure what they believe to be their citizens' rights and interests.

Guidelines could be developed to identify problem areas and orient citizens regarding how to exercise their rights and interests. How can they now meaningfully participate? Who is accountable? How does a citizen get due process any more? Health, safety, defense and education are still accessible, aren't they? The environment and economy are still very important; but how do we deal with them with our new innovative public partnerships and government — business collaboration? Citizens, as citizens, do have governance concerns and priorities.

CITIZENS	
1. Accountability	8. Defense
2. Participation	9. Education
3. Due Process	10. The Environment
4. Citizen Rights	11. The Economy
5. Citizen Interests	12. Government, Business Collaboration
6. Health	13. Innovative Public Partnerships
7. Safety	14. Public Interest

Figure 9. Citizen Governance Priorities

CUSTOMERS

As citizens transition into customers, quality and choice become far more important. Who is accountable for making sure they exist? Honest advertising and sensitive marketing move to the forefront so our transformed citizen/customers will know what is available. Where does the budget for this come from? Services must be administered fairly and customer dignity needs to be respected. Is there a selection of alternatives available? There is increasing leverage to get the word straight, and out, e.g., through public information offices. Since customer satisfaction (Gore 93, 94) continues to be increasingly important especially after the turn of the century, customer complaint resolution mechanisms need to be put in place. Customer governance priorities add the following to citizen governance priorities.

CUSTOMERS	
1. Choice	6. Sensitive Marketing
2. Quality	7. Responsible Marketing
3. Selection of Alternatives	8. Administer Services Fairly
4. Honest and Credible Advertising	9. Customer Complaint Resolution
5. Respect Customer Dignity	10. Public Information Offices

Figure 10. Customer Governance Priorities

CYNICAL CITIZENS

Many citizens are not satisfied with their increasingly forced transformation to customer status, however. They are frustrated with government abandoning many of their governance values and lurching toward the simpler and more zero sum oriented market model. There are a number of strategies and practices that can be employed to engage them and to deal with their frustrations and concerns. Among those available are the strategies noted below, as extrapolated from Berman (1997).

General Strategies
Communicate awards of distinction
Encourage positive statements by managers
Respond to negative media
Inform citizens of high ethical standards
Media campaigns

Participation Strategies
Open meeting policies
Citizen surveys
Citizen panels
Citizen referenda
Citizen task forces
Meet with neighborhood activists
Citizen advisory boards

Respond To
Citizen complaints
Citizen queries
Preferences on surveys
Dialogue with community leaders

Reputationial Strategies
Pride programs
Performance awards
Service excellence rewards
Media coverage

per Berman

Figure 11. Strategies and Practices for Dealing with Citizens

We can also cope with citizen cynicism by organizing sets of strategic responses. Berman notes three sets in particular. It can be shown that government uses its power primarily to help citizens, even though, in the experience of many this is questionable. Comparisons can be made and explanations given to contrast positive government contributions with negative or even indifferent or uncaring government activities. Getting information on this to citizens is important.

Government also needs to integrate citizen contributions regarding public decision making. Participation is important and the array of opportunities available should be positively exploited. Government also needs to enhance performance, document it, and get the information to the citizens (Berman, 1997). These sorts of adjustments can have a positive impact on citizen cynicism.

Based on 3 Sets of Strategies

I. Show government uses power to help citizens
    (vs. to harm; or even as indifferent)
    -- Government information campaigns
        - how government helps citizens
        - e.g. mailings

II. Incorporate citizen input into public decision-making
    -- Public hearings
    -- Panels
    -- Focus groups
    -- Citizen surveys
    (Let citizens know these are available)

III. Enhance government's efficiency and competence reputation
    -- Improve and document performance
    -- Communicate improvements to citizens

                                                IAW Berman

Figure 12. Coping with Citizen Cynicism

Citizens will be less cynical when they believe their rights and interests are valued and managed well. The short term, bottom line approach of the market place can improve efficiency and economy. But government has a tougher task. Out of sovereignty and the public interest come a duty to act for and on behalf of the citizen. Carrol and Lynn (1995) also focus on : ... domestic tranquility, the general welfare, justice, liberty, the common defense, and ... a more perfect union. The more citizens perceive these as somehow again adequately valued, and implemented, the less visible citizen cynicism will be. As we approach the 2008 presidential election, it is becoming increasingly apparent in the polls that neither the current federal administration nor the congress has done a good job of dealing well with citizen cynicism.

GOVERNANCE PRIORITIES FOR CONTRACTORS, COMPETITORS AND SUPPLIERS

Competition must be monitored so we can be fair in dealing with contractors, competitors and suppliers. We need to be truthful, open, non coercive (Caux, 1995) and have clear contracts. Ethics and integrity must be integrated into the system. Conflict resolution mechanisms are important and should guarantee that all parties are fairly represented in legitimate disputes. Human dignity and high professional standards should be inherent in honest competition linked to state of the art licensing, pricing, and performance standards.

Contractors, Suppliers and Competitors	
1. Clear and Open Competition	9. Employment Practice Standards
2. Clear Contracts	10. Pricing Standards
3. Non-coercive Competition	11. Licensing Standards
4. Truthful Competition	12. Human Dignity
5. Participatory Planning Process	13. Clear Communication
6. Ethics	14. Open Communication
7. Integrity	15. Honest Competitiveness
8. Conflict Resolution Mechanism	16. Transformed Financial Control

Figure 13. Governance Priorities

IMPOSED CONTROL PRIORITIES FOR CUSTOMER ORIENTED PUBLIC MANAGEMENT PERFORMANCE

Privatization, contracting out, reinventing, reengineering, TQM, downsizing, rightsizing, efficiency, and franchising are now all factors in the public management equation (Johnston, 1996a). Since proposition 13 in June of 1978, voters across the nation have been increasingly relentless in sending the clear message that they want more results and services from government with demonstrably more efficiency and economy. The impact on public management and their managerial control systems is dramatic. Budgets have increasingly come to provide control mechanisms for results produced...if they are produced. They also impose control priorities on public managers.

As we move from the traditional citizens model towards the customer model, we should again be aware that budgets now provide more thorough screening and prioritizing mechanisms for policy makers and managers alike. Back when the work of government really was primarily the work of government, Pressmann and Wildavsky (1974) addressed the complexity of joint action. There was incompatibility with other commitments between and among governmental units, preferences for other programs, commitments to several projects simultaneously, dependence on those with no sense of priority, value differences regarding organizational roles and leadership differences, procedural priorities and considerations, and varying degrees and perceptions of lack of power.

Today we have also added: severe budget constraints, increased demand for services, typically fewer employees, more private sector contractors, more participating citizen customers, more review, more noticeable privatized organizations and operations, public-private partnerships and joint ventures, more public mandates (including the unfunded variety), more contracts, more consultants, more market interaction, more deregulation, more business, and the seemingly ubiquitous customer (Johnston, 1996b). To say the management control responsibilities of public managers are more complex really doesn't even begin to address the reality that the entire game has changed; not just the players, but the rules, the results, and the very nature of the game itself.

An existing set of lessons and examples for state and local public managers can be seen in the evolution of customer oriented managerial control adjustments at the federal level. In the last few years there has been a major effort to increase accountability for providing results to customers. Starting in 1990 the Chief Financial Officers Act provided for CEO positions in two dozen federal agencies. It also required, similar to the case in private companies, that annual reports be prepared and submitted revealing financial conditions and reviewing management control systems. The Government Performance and Results Act of 1993 applied requirements to use performance measurement to improve results. These were to be grounded in a strategic planning effort as well.

The Government Management Reform Act of 1994 broadened the 1990 Act requirements delineated above to require audited financial statements to each of the two dozen CFO agencies. The 94 Act also required a review of progress towards goals and objectives based on performance measurement within each organization. For fiscal year 1997, the Comptroller General audited a consolidated government wide financial statement prepared by the Secretary of the Treasury and the Director of the OMB.

The Information Technology Management Reform Act of 1996 required the use of information technology in improving the efficiency and effectiveness of organizational operations. These agencies accounted for their goal setting and performance measurement and reported on their progress via information technology.

The acts highlighted above were at the core of the federal government's National Performance Review spearheaded by former Vice President Al Gore. The focus and energy were on improving performance, former accountability and results for the customers of government services. The examples above are federal; yet we know that similar customer oriented management transformations are unfolding in cities, counties, and states as well (Gore & Brandt, *et al.*, 1996).

Clearly the federal government, in implementing its version of Osborne and Gaebler's reinventing, employed the TQM model with its emphasis on customers. As the sequence of acts delineated above indicates, it also increasingly employed strategic management and planning, typically used in sizable private sector organizations. While these developments are certainly in the tradition of entrepreneurial private corporations, they are not always so. Mintzberg writes about how smaller sized entrepreneurs tend to want to optimize their freedom in the decision making process and notes that planning, plans, and planners themselves are not valued by many of those with such market oriented behavioral preferences (Mintzberg, 1994). Nonetheless, larger public sector organizations implementing privatization, contracting out, and reinventing; and customers making the kinds of adjustments reviewed above, are likely to need significantly more planning to cope with the turbulence that they not only have been drawn closer to, but indeed have become intimately embroiled in.

As public policy is transformed with the surge of privatization, contracting out, and reinventing, performance measurement limitations have been accentuated. As the stakes rise and the stakeholders become more proactive, performance priorities are also highlighted. In order to clarify both our thinking and our actions in this transformed arena, work is now being done to develop public service production measurements. Based upon a view of public policy, as policy formation and implementation, to include production of services for stakeholders in specific domains, analytical mechanisms can be developed to determine performance profiles in various policy domains. The networks developed along the way can also then be scrutinized. In the end, we will get better, more precise analytical tools for analyzing both production and consumption, for reviewing multi stakeholders costs and benefits, and for balancing our concerns for efficiency and effectiveness (Kirchoff, 1997).

The entrepreneurial organizations now manifesting themselves have public policy makers and administrators alike, including those in managerial control systems, identified more clearly as primary players. They are much closer to the center of the unfolding action. Their roles are increasingly critical. They must be better prepared and disciplined. They must be more optimal team members. Organizations must be better synchronized and coordinated in order to be more clearly efficient and effective. This usually means more planning and more strategic management. Success, while a function of standards, is often more attainable with the more autonomous, well led, strongly supported, and fiscally viable organization. Strategic management and/or TQM have been adapted to the public sector from private sector organizations. They will likely increase as public sector policy makers, managers, and budgeters are forced to increase performance and produce greater results for their customers and other stakeholders with shrinking revenues (Vinzant & Vinzant, 1996).

We have come quite a way since Peter Senge's book (1990) on the learning organization. It is increasingly clear, however, with the acceleration of entrepreneurial activity and the increasing emergence of public organizations in the market place, that strategic management, TQM, and the emerging learning theory will play an increasing role in the public policy, management, and control systems of public sector organizations. The case examples for applied organizational learning lean toward the private sector yet again. Nonetheless, by its very nature, learning theory places an emphasis on people and organizations structuring environments in which they can proactively grow and learn, as opposed to having to be taught, or trained, or constantly guided.

By including as many significant stakeholders as possible, and by providing a genuinely supportive environment with appropriate resources and leadership, organizations can optimize their learning potential. Learning team practices include involving "customers" in organizational decision making, and having customers and suppliers interact with an organization's managers in problem solving experiences. There are numerous training techniques, of course, but a major concern is that the organizations and individuals involved value the learning, trust the environment, utilize collaborative practices, and be supported by adequate resources and leadership (Dilworth, 1996) as they develop and employ 21st century skills (Johnston, Haynes and Schulz, 2006).

There is little doubt that, as we find ourselves immersed in the privatization, competition, deregulation, reinventing, and quality based transformation with strong new entrepreneurial messages, constraints and opportunities for the participating players and stakeholders, both now and in the future; that we will witness (or help develop) an adjusted paradigm for public sector policy making, management, control and governance systems (Rosenbloom & Dubnick, 1996). It is likely that the theoretical underpinnings or roots of such a transformed organization theory set will reflect learning theory, strategic management and dynamic planning, performance measurement and decision making, and the customer and quality emphases which have emerged from quality management theories and concepts.

The challenge is to sort out and provide, as wisely as possible, the best of what both the private and public sectors have to offer. Customers usually do better when dollars and market skills are preeminent. Government has a larger charge. Providing legitimacy, due process and stewardship in a sovereign environment for all citizens is a difficult sort of pursuit. The struggle will be to optimally merge the best that each sector has to offer in the interest of both customers and citizens. Strong examples of success would include: Denver's Transportation Expansion Project (T-REX) completed in 2006 (Johnston, Haynes, and Schulz, 2006); and the new Department of Homeland Security, along with the Transportation Security Administration to manage the terrorism threat after 9/11 (Johnston, 2003; and Haynes and Wright, Chapter 17). Strong examples of failure would include FEMA's collapse in its response to Hurricane Katrina (see Chapters 8, Johnston and Schulz; and Haynes and Wright, Chapter 17; and Johnston, Chapter 18); and NASA's mismanagement of the Columbia disaster (see Chapter 18, Johnston).

REFERENCES

Berman, E. M. (March-April, 1997). Dealing with Cynical Citizens, *Public Administration Review, 57,* 105-112.

Bozeman, B. (1987). *All Organizations are Public; Bridging Public and Private Organizational Theories*. San Francisco: Jossey Bass.

Carroll, J. D., and Lynn, D. B. (May-June, 1995). The Rhetoric of Reform and Political Reality in the National Performance Review, *Public Administration Review, 55,* 299-304.

Caux Roundtable. (1995). Principles of Business, *SBE Newsletter, 6.*

Clark, C., Heilman, J.G., and Johnson, GW. (Fall 95/Winter 96) Privatization: Moving Beyond Laissez Faire, *Policy Studies Review*, 14, 395-406.

de Leon, L. (Autumn, 1996). Ethics and Entrepreneurship, *Policy Studies Journal*, *24*, 495-510.

Dilworth, R. L. (June, 1996). Institutionalizing Learning in the Public Sector, *Public Productivity and Management Review, 19*, 407-421.

Donahue, J. D. (1989). *The Privatization Decision: Public Ends, Private Means.* New York: Basic Books, Inc.

Gore, A. E. Jr. (1993). *From Red Tape to Results: Creating a Government That Works Better and Costs Less.* Report of the National Performance Review. Washington D.C.: U.S. Government Printing Office.

Gore, A. E. Jr. (September, 1994). *Creating a Government That Works Better and Costs Less: Status Report, September, 1994.* Washington D.C.: U.S. Government Printing Office.

Gore, A. E. Jr., and Brandt, T. (October, 1996). *Reaching Public Goals: Managing Government for Results.* National Performance Review. Washington D.C.: U.S. Government Printing Office, 1-6.

Halachmi, A. (1994). The Challenge of a Competitive Sector. *In the Enduring Challenges in Public Management: Surviving and Excelling in a Changing World.* San Francisco: Jossey-Bass, 220-223.

Halachmi, A., and Boydston, R. (1994). The Political Economy of Outsourcing. In Khan, A. and Hildreth, B. *Public Budgeting and Financial Management.* Dubuque, IA: Kendall Hunt Publishing Company.

Halachmi, A. (Autumn, 1996). Franchising in Government: Can a Principal - Agent Perspective Be a First Step in the Development of a Theory? *Public Studies Journal, 24,* 478-494.

Hammer, M. and Champty, J. (1993). *Reengineering the Corporation.* New York: Harper Business Books.

Johnston, V. R., (Winter, 1990). Privatization of Prisons: Management, Productivity, and Governance Concerns, *Public Productivity and Management Review, 14*, 189-201.

Johnston, V. R., (1995a). Increasing Quality and Productivity: Strategic Planning, TQM, and Beyond, In Halachmi, A., and Bouckaert, G. (Eds.), *Public Productivity Through Quality and Strategic Management,* Brussels: IOS Press, 83-97.

Johnston, V.R., (Fall, 1995b). Caveat Emptor: Customers vs. Citizens, *The Public Manager - The New Bureaucrat, 24*, 11-14.

Johnston, V. R. (Ed.), (Autumn, 1996a). Privatization and Entrepreneurial Management, A Symposium in *Policy Studies Journal, 24*, 437-510.

Johnston, V.R. (Autumn, 1996b). Optimizing Productivity Through Privatization and Entrepreneurial Management, *Policy Studies Journal, 24*, 439-443.

Johnston, V.R. (Autumn, 1996c). The Entrepreneurial Transformation: From Privatization, Reinventing, and Re-engineering, To Franchising, Efficiency, and Entrepreneurial Ethics, *Policy Studies Journal, 24*, 444-463.

Johnston, V.R. (Spring, 2002). Competition, Conflict, and Entrepreneurial Public Managers: The Legacy of Reinventing Government, *Public Administration Quarterly*, 26, 9-34.

Johnston, V.R. (2003). Terrorism and Transportation Policy and Administration: Balancing the Model and Equations for Optimal Security, *Review of Policy Research*, *21*(3), 275-291.

Johnston, V.R., Haynes, W., and Schulz, C.L. (2006).   The T-REX Megaproject: Denver's Showcase for Innovation and Creativity, *The Public Manager*, 35(2), 3-8.

Johnston, V.R., and Seidenstat, P. (2007). Contracting out Government Services: Privatization at the Millennium, *International Journal of Public Administration*, *30*(3), 231-247.

Kettl, D.F. (1993). *Sharing Power: Public Governance and Private Markets.* Washington, DC: The Brookings Institution.

Kingsley, G. (March-April, 1997). Reflecting on Reform and the Scope of Public Administration, *Public Administration Review, 57,* iii-iv.

Kirchoff, J.J. (September 1997). Public Services Production in Context: Toward a Multilevel, Multistakeholder Model, *Public Production and Management Review*, 21, 70-85.

McLean, B., and Elkind, P. (2003). *The Smartest Guys in the Room: The Amazing Rise and Scandalous Fall of Enron.* New York: Portfolio-Penguin Group.

Mintzberg, H. (1994). *The Rise and Fall of Strategic Planning: Reconceiving Roles for Planning, Plans, Planners.* New York: The Free Press, a division of Macmillan, Inc., 410-411.

Nagel, S. S. (1989). *Higher Goals for America.* Lonham, MD: University Press of America, Inc.

Newland, C. A. (March-April, 1997). Realism and Public Administration, *Public Administration Review, 57,* ii-iii.

Osborne, D. and Gaebler, T. (1991). *Reinventing Government: How the Entrepreneurial Spirit is Transforming Government.* New York: Addison Wesley.

Pressman, J. L., and Wildavsky, A. B. (1974). *Implementation.* Berkeley: University of California Press, 87-124.

Rosenbloom, D. H. and Dubnick, M. J. (November-December, 1996). Farewell from the Catbird Seat, *Public Administration Review, 56,* 503-505.

Savas, E.S. (1982). *Privatizing the Public Sector.* NJ: Chatham House.

Seidenstat, P. (Autumn, 1996). Privatization: Trends, Interplay of Forces and Lessons Learned, *Policy Studies Journal, 24,* 464-477.

Senge, P. (1990). *Fifth Discipline: Mastering the Five Practices of the Learning Organization.* New York: Doubleday Currency.

Starobin, P. (March-April, 1995). A Generation of Vipers: Journalists and the New Cynicism, *Columbia Journalism Review,* pp. 25-32.

Vinzant, J. C., and Vinzant, D. H. (Summer, 1996). Strategic Management and Total Quality Management: Challenges and Choices, *Public Administration Quarterly, 20,* 201-219.

PART IV

THE ENTREPRENEURIAL MANAGEMENT AND PUBLIC POLICY MODEL

In Chapter 17, *The Department of Homeland Security and the Entrepreneurial Management and Public Policy Model: A Work in Progress*, Wendy Haynes and Robert J. Wright use the Johnston Entrepreneurial Management and Public Policy Model to analyze the complex collaborative systems forming the core of the interdisciplinary problem-solving and safety/security challenges facing the Department of Homeland Security, and the nation. In the future, comprehending and managing these increasingly complex collaborative systems will continue to challenge students, scholars, and managers of public policy and administration.

The authors provide a cross-disciplinary approach to the examination of the Department of Homeland Security to enhance both the understanding and response to recent, current, and future events. Haynes and Wright begin with a professional literature review comprised of multidimensional perspectives. This comprehensive review focuses on intergovernmental relations, budgeting for homeland security, organization theory, human resources management, and macro to micro-implementation. After setting up this framework, Haynes and Wright provide a history of the Department of Homeland Security.

The authors then apply the Johnston Entrepreneurial Management and Public Policy Model to several of the initiatives of the Department of Homeland Security. The analysis of the authors focuses on the creation of the Department of Homeland Security, with two FEMA-initiatives as examples (see also Chapter 8 on FEMA and Katrina), the Department of Homeland Security response to border protection, and attempts to reform the public personnel system in the Department of Homeland Security.

The authors conclude with observations about the applicability of the Johnston Model. Haynes and Wright emphasize the importance of managing the several different interdependent dynamics in changing environments. The authors find that significant changes will be necessary to bring about greater safety and security, and note that stakeholders react with resistance and sometimes "cooperative enthusiasm."

In Chapter 18, *Re-Setting the Entrepreneurial Management and Public Policy Model for Optimal Effectiveness and Efficiency*, the concepts and ideas discussed throughout this book ultimately culminate in Professor Johnston's analysis of implementing public policy and using business decision making and management practices. Johnston analyzes four different catalytic events in both the public and private sectors with his Entrepreneurial Management and Public Policy Model.

Johnston begins with a discussion of resetting the model for transportation security following the September 11, 2001 terrorism attacks. He traces the flow of events, trends, processes, services, and decisions that resulted in a shift from effectiveness to efficiency. He discusses the implications and viability of both a partial reset and a full reset from efficiency towards effectiveness.

The author then shifts to an analysis of resetting the model for financial policy and administration, with a comprehensive overview of how over emphasis of efficiency led some of the players and stakeholders in the corporate world far beyond prudent and responsible behavior in the late 20th and early 21st centuries. Johnston reminds us that this was not the first occurrence of serious financial and unethical misbehavior, noting the savings and loan crisis of the 1990's; and he applies his model to explore how these financial disasters could occur so closely together.

Through his discussion of the NASA Challenger and Columbia disasters, Professor Johnston provides another example of how the world of management and public policy continues to shift towards a more entrepreneurial orientation with catalytic consequences. Johnston specifically emphasizes the conflict between effectiveness and efficiency, and how a full reset is necessary to restore effectiveness to NASA.

The final situation analyzed differs from Johnston's other analyses of business and public policy case situations. In the case of FEMA, a full reset from the efficiency environment to an effectiveness environment occurred after Hurricane Andrew and before the Northridge Earthquake. Then, a paradigm shift in government management and leadership essentially reversed this reset, leaving FEMA without the benefit of the more collaborative effectiveness management that was in place for the Northridge Earthquake response.

Throughout this last chapter, Johnston reminds us that too much emphasis on efficiency diminishes effectiveness and increases the likelihood of catalytic events. Johnston concludes with the caveat that a balance of collaboration oriented effectiveness and competition oriented efficiency is necessary for the implementation of professional entrepreneurial management and public policy.

Chapter 17

THE DEPARTMENT OF HOMELAND SECURITY AND THE ENTREPRENEURIAL MANAGEMENT AND PUBLIC POLICY MODEL:
A WORK IN PROGRESS

Wendy Haynes
Robert J. Wright

INTRODUCTION

The emergence of the Department of Homeland Security (DHS) provides profound insights into the core components of public policy and administration: budgeting/finance, human resource management/public personnel, organization theory, research methods, program evaluation/public policy analysis and implementation, among others.[1] Indeed, one could conceivably treat the creation of DHS as a case study that crosses course boundaries throughout a student's journey through a Master of Public Policy and Administration (MPPA) program, or some variation on that graduate degree theme.

A review of the literature reveals a tantalizing array of lenses through which one might view the creation of the Department of Homeland Security. This chapter explores the possibility of using a single mega-case – the emergence of the Department of Homeland Security – across the boundaries of the typical MPPA common curriculum components (Haynes and Wright, 2005). Indeed, the DHS has been the subject of formal learning within a diverse set of educational settings (Smith, 2005). These settings range from those with a policy sciences, entrepreneurial management, emergency management, or public administration focus to those with an orientation toward national security, the military, and terrorism (Smith, 2005). A central notion emerges: The complexity of the

---

[1] We draw the topical areas of study – the shared curriculum components – from the standards for accreditation issued by the National Association of Schools of Public Affairs and Administration. http://www.naspaa.org. Most recently accessed September 2005.

DHS provides a rich interdisciplinary petri dish and merits "mega" status among case studies for MPPA and professional management programs. As will be seen throughout this chapter, the DHS phenomenon gives new meaning to Pressman and Wildavsky's concept of the "complexity of multi-action" (1984).

The recently botched management efforts surrounding Hurricane Katrina underscores the challenges facing DHS administrators. How does one comprehend and manage the immensely complex collaborative systems that now form the core of the interdisciplinary problem-solving and safety/security challenges facing our nation? The question will challenge students, scholars, and practitioners of public policy and administration for years to come.

This chapter begins with an interdisciplinary literature review, organized along several key components of the world of public policy and administration, followed by a brief history of the DHS. The discussion then moves to the chapter centerpiece: application of the Johnston Model discussed elsewhere in this book to several DHS-specific initiatives. Finally, the chapter concludes with preliminary observations about the applicability of the Johnston Model and suggestions for further research.

PROFESSIONAL LITERATURE

Multidimensional Perspectives

For purposes of this chapter, the following areas appear to offer the most diverse, yet discrete, vantage points for applying Johnston's analytical model: (1) the phenomenon of the creation of the DHS, generally, and using two FEMA-related initiatives as specific examples; (2) DHS response to difficulties in border protection; and (3) attempts at public personnel system reform in DHS. Core areas of study in public policy and administration provide an interdisciplinary underpinning for the discussion of the tortuous road to implementing the congressionally-mandated department. By embracing a cross-disciplinary approach to the examination of the DHS, we hope to enhance our understanding of recent events and eventually learn how the response to future events might be improved.

Intergovernmental Relations

The scope of the DHS enabling legislation, as well as existing local and state laws pertaining to emergency management and response, recognizes a sharing of power between governmental organizations. In this context, two intergovernmental relations concepts offer particularly relevant insight. First, the "cooperative federalism" theory underscores the value of cooperation among levels of government, arguing that joint efforts may produce better results than any one level acting alone (Kincaid, 1990). A diffusion of power should occur among the different levels of government so that power does not become isolated in and monopolized by one level of government. The theory further asserts the importance of all responding organizations viewing the others' interest and role in the mitigation effort as legitimate. In cooperative federalism, there is a line that responding organizations should not cross. To do so may well cause an organizational breakdown, at least from an intergovernmental perspective.

The notion of "compound implementation" provides a second theoretical framework. This theory goes to the administrative and operational components of the DHS and its programs. Compound implementation occurs when national legislation establishes specific standards or conditions and then delegates administrative responsibility to states or localities. Compound implementation presumes that DHS grants a measure of flexibility to states and localities commensurate with their level of involvement in implementing relevant DHS programs. It also assumes a degree of oversight and monitoring among the various levels of government. If not properly regulated (and balanced) then relations between the various levels of government may become toxic.[2]

Budgeting for Homeland Security

Wrangling over the DHS budget certainly provides insights into the volatility of the federal budget process, especially when the nation's policymakers clash with the nation's airlines and airports. For example, the proposal to increase fees paid by airline passengers was blasted by the Air Transport Association, the largest trade organization representing domestic airlines. Similarly, the 2003 FAA Reauthorization Act ordered the Transportation Security Administration (TSA) to cover 90 percent of certain security improvements at airports, but TSA only intends to pay 75 percent under the 2006 budget proposal (Strohm, 2005). Although the case study focus may begin with the DHS, it must inevitably extend beyond the organizational borders to include the impact throughout the nation.

Some observers find that today's federal programs – including DHS – transfer resources to the states, but devolve program responsibilities to local governments. In difficult economies, such delegation can prove disastrous (Anders, 2003). And others observe that the inherent challenges in complex undertakings such as emergency management require great care in making decisions about reform spending or federal fiscal assistance. Policymakers must remain cognizant of the varying functional capabilities and interests of the various responders to a critical, mass-casualty incident (Donahue, 2004; Donahue and Joyce, 2001).

---

[2] Deil Wright (1990) and others (e.g., O'Toole, 1999; Rosenbloom and Kravchuk, 2005; Shafritz and Russell, 2005) give fairly extensive treatment to the topic, which receives only summary attention in the text of this chapter.

Organization Theory and Human Resource Management

Many of our younger students have a difficult time relating to the classical works of public policy and administration and find the complexities of the civil service system nearly impossible to penetrate, much less appreciate as a significant reform in the history of their country. The creation of the DHS, however, qualifies as a current event that is unfolding in attention-getting ways even as students read the works of such antiques as Weber, Taylor, Maslow, Herzburg, Mintzberg, Simon, Gulick, Follett, and their esteemed colleagues throughout the relatively young life of the field.

In their remarkably approachable text (*Reframing Organizations: Artistry, Choice, and Leadership, 2003*), Bolman and Deal focus in on four lenses for examining the vicissitudes of organizational behavior: structural; human resources; political; and symbolic. The ongoing saga of DHS's emergence provides ample opportunity to view the process and its implications from these four frames, with the aim of fostering in students the ability to move nimbly from one perspective to another.

Van Johnston's Model provides a similar opportunity to gain analytical proficiency with a thoughtful eye on the changing world around us. One hopes that the experience will enhance our students' future performance as managers, particularly in local governments where the policies made at the federal level profoundly affect the capacity of communities to respond effectively to disastrous events.

Macro to Micro-Implementation

Large and complex topics – including the creation of DHS and its mission to secure the homeland – raise equally complex issues about how best to evaluate the implementation process and results. Many have explored the topic of evaluative criteria (Palumbo and Calista, 1990, to name but one team) and perspectives differ, as one would expect. Scholars in the field, however, appear to agree that implementation factors surface from the design of policy and the institutional settings within which policy is applied (Bardach, 1977; Goggin *et al.*, 1990; Lipsky, 1980; Mazmanian and Sabatier, 1989; Pressman and Wildavsky, 1984; Scheirer, 1990).[3] Scheirer elsewhere explains the use of the macro-implementation approach in studies of large-scale government programs, "in which the focus is on the connecting links between the government agency or other umbrella organization and multiple layers of lower-level organizations. . . . (1994, p. 62)."

A variety of variables impact upon the micro-implementation process – that is, in a particular agency at the local or "street" level. These variables include the type of department or agency, leadership characteristics of a manager, level and scope of training, technical capacity, in-service or continuing training, various administrative

---

[3] Jodi Sandfort does a nice job of succinctly distinguishing between micro and macro-implementation in her contribution to a policy series at the Center for Policy Research at the Maxwell School of Citizenship and Public Affairs (Paper No. 20, April 1999) and we rely upon her work, among others cited in the text.

arrangements for receiving technical assistance, and amount of peer assistance, among others.   Successful adoption of a program at the local level has also been found to be positively related to a variety of in-person and other related contacts (Scheirer, 1990). This notion implies that the micro-implementation process can help to realize the aims of the macro-implementation process if the implementers (the decision makers, managers, etc.) understand and anticipate the needs, capacities, and challenges encountered by their clientele at the other end of the implementation continuum.

Inevitably, the DHS must implement its programs and policies. The implementation process is complex, and at times, chaotic. One of the unique challenges for the DHS is that despite its significant scope and power, the department must, especially in times of crisis or attack, deliver effective safety and security services at a micro, granular level. The impact of DHS services must be felt at the individual level.

Within the scope of the DHS, the macro-to-micro-implementation path can also engender further complexity as the following networking elements emerge during more involved stages of the implementation process: federal/state-government political support; federal/state-government supported research and program validation; materials and information developed by various federal/state staff; state and local officials and interagency and intergovernmental committees/boards; agency support and commitment; and the end-user community involvement and support (Scheirer, 1990). At the micro-implementation level evaluation techniques and considerations assume a more critical role in the large-scale adoption process. If the DHS program components, for instance, have not been clearly articulated and tested for efficacy, at least on a small scale, then perhaps it will be premature for large-scale implementation. No doubt Scheirer would concur with the authors' conclusion that the various components of the policy or program should be tested *prior* to widespread implementation within the operating and service delivery level of the DHS.

HISTORY OF THE DEPARTMENT OF HOMELAND SECURITY

Before advancing further into this chapter, the reader may find a brief narrative summary of the history of the DHS helpful. A detailed timeline follows the brief history and is included to intrigue those who may feel moved to continue the exploration undertaken by the authors.

Complex Landscape[4]

Since the tragic events of September 11, 2001, we have witnessed the remarkable flurry of activity launching the national effort to protect the American homeland against terrorist attacks. Indeed, the creation of the new Department of Homeland Security (DHS) has been heralded as "the most significant transformation of the U.S. government since 1947, when Harry S. Truman merged the various branches of the U.S. Armed Forces into the Department of Defense to better coordinate the nation's defense against military threats."[5] Signed into being by President George W. Bush on November 25, 2002, the new DHS combines at least 22 agencies -- and an estimated 170,000 employees -- including such disparate organizations as: the new Transportation Security Administration (Transportation), the Secret Service (Treasury), the Federal Emergency Management Agency (FEMA), the Federal Law Enforcement Training Center (FBI), and the Critical Infrastructures Assurance Office (Commerce).

Each of the 22 agencies brought its own unique array of existing management challenges and program risks to the new mega-agency. The U.S. Comptroller General noted, at the time, that many of the major components merging into the new department, including the TSA, already faced major problems such as strategic human capital risks, information technology management challenges, and financial management vulnerabilities (US GAO, 2003). Informed observers have feared during each appropriation cycle since its creation that budgets proposed come any where near providing the funds and the foresight to successfully implement the President's July 2002 *National Strategy for Homeland Security* (Bush, 2002) and or deal with the challenges posed by recent natural disasters as Hurricanes Katrina and Rita.

Although the massive political mobilization effort required to gain support for and now to implement the DHS may have drawn more public attention, there were other significant restructuring efforts afoot, including realigning the FBI and CIA Counter Terrorism operations and reforming certain elements of the Intelligence Community, to say nothing of incomplete efforts to transform the U.S. Department of Defense and restructure the congressional oversight framework. Many feared that the turf wars among these agencies would draw attention and funds away from the critical job of turning information collection and analysis into knowledge for protecting the nation (Markle, 2002; US GAO, 2003; Brookings, 2002).

Add to the mix the role complexities of the Homeland Security Council and the President's Office of Homeland Security, a bewildering mix of congressional oversight and appropriations committees (Gilmore, 2002), the challenge of meeting a grueling implementation schedule…and the absence of a culture of cooperation within the

---

[4] The entire "HISTORY" section draws heavily on an earlier article by one of the authors, entitled "Seeing around Corners: Crafting the New Department of Homeland Security," which appeared in the *Review of Policy Research*, volume 21, Number 3 (2004), in a symposium edited by Van R. Johnston. The Figure that follows the narrative history in this chapter builds upon the sequence of events discussed in that earlier article.

[5] This quote was drawn from the DHS web site (http://www.dhs.gov/dhspublic/theme_home1.jsp in 2003 and may no longer appear at the web site.

Intelligence Community, and a daunting homeland security agenda begins to look more like an impossible and potentially catastrophic dream. We are witness to a mind-boggling demonstration of the "complexity of joint action" (Pressman and Wildavsky, 1984).

Figure 1 on the following page provides a time line of selected events that have occurred following the terrorist attacks of 9/11. This chapter does not attempt to track through each of the developments of the last four years, but rather to highlight several that are especially relevant to this discussion. By providing a more detailed timeline than the discussion requires, we hope to provide a context for the examples we offer and entice others to explore further the inquiry this chapter pursues.

DHS as Mega-agency

The DHS is an entity that is "mega" in scope and, surprising few observers, stands already in the midst of significant re-organization initiatives. By virtue of the breadth of its missions, DHS leaders must reconcile a diverse array of stakeholder interests. The DHS has, in part, responded to these various pressures by managerial change strategies. One critical strategy emerged during the summer of 2005. This planning effort, termed the Second Stage Review, utilized 18 action teams – involving more than 250 members of the DHS staff – and evaluated specific operational and policy issues.

The Review examined nearly every element of the DHS for improved risk and security management, consequence management, and overall preventive and protective purposes. The *Homeland Security Act of 2002 (HSA)* empowered the Secretary to undertake the Review and provides Secretary Chertoff with a measure of flexibility to establish, consolidate, alter or discontinue organizational units within the DHS. The planning effort associated with the Second Stage Review was driven by a six-point agenda, focusing on organizational adjustments that would accomplish the following objectives:

1. Increase overall preparedness, particularly for catastrophic events;

2. create better transportation security systems to move people and cargo more securely and efficiently;

3. strengthen border security and interior enforcement and reform immigration processes;

4. enhance information sharing with our partners;

5. improve DHS financial management, human resource development, procurement and information technology; and

6. realign the DHS organization to maximize mission performance.

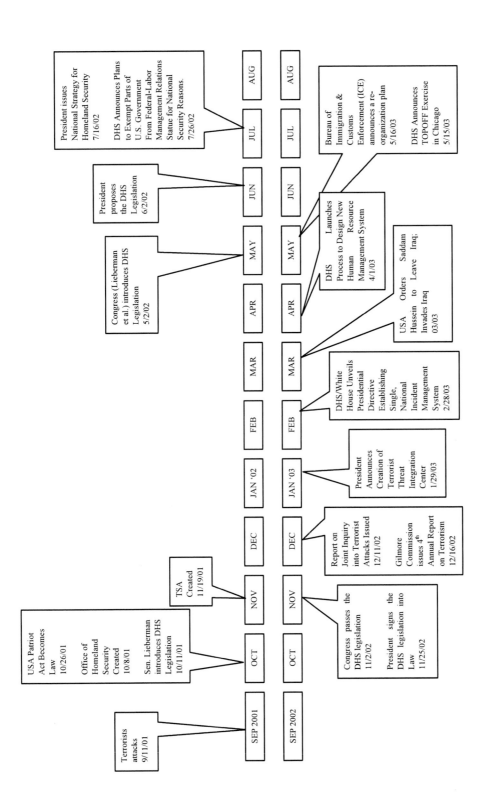

Figure 1: Department of Homeland Security Implementation Time-Line: January 2001-September 2005[6]

6 The timeline was compiled from multiple sources by the authors, and especially Robert Wright, who so ably ferreted information from government documents, the media, and the works of colleagues in the field

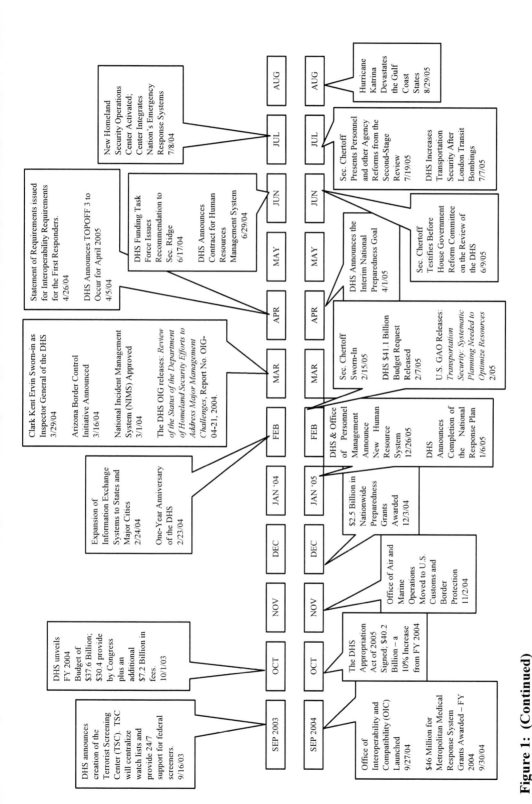

Figure 1: (Continued)
Department of Homeland Security Implementation Time-Line: January 2001-September 2005

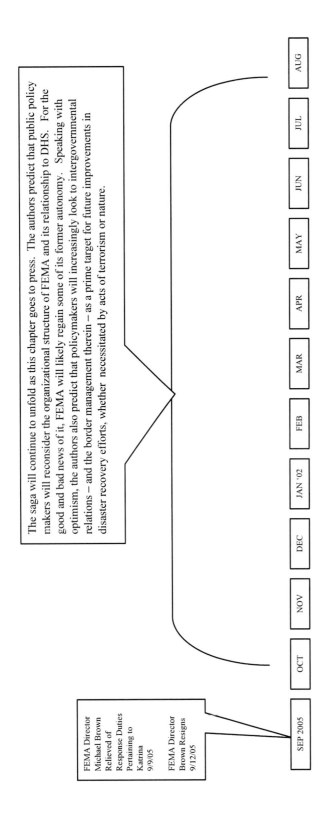

The saga will continue to unfold as this chapter goes to press. The authors predict that public policy makers will reconsider the organizational structure of FEMA and its relationship to DHS. For the good and bad news of it, FEMA will likely regain some of its former autonomy. Speaking with optimism, the authors also predict that policymakers will increasingly look to intergovernmental relations – and the border management therein – as a prime target for future improvements in disaster recovery efforts, whether necessitated by acts of terrorism or nature.

FEMA Director
Michael Brown
Relieved of
Response Duties
Pertaining to
Katrina
9/9/05

FEMA Director
Brown Resigns
9/12/05

| SEP 2005 | OCT | NOV | DEC | JAN '02 | FEB | MAR | APR | MAY | JUN | JUL | AUG |

Figure 1: (Continued)
Department of Homeland Security Implementation Time-Line: January 2001-September 2005

Implementing the overall intent of this six-point agenda required realigning certain components of the DHS (see **Figure 2**). The overall aim of this realignment has been to improve the preparedness and response capacity of the DHS to terrorist attacks and other emergencies and to better equip the DHS employees for achieving their mission.

The results of the Secretary's initiatives bear watching, but the review itself lacks the insights that students of public policy and administration could glean from a perspective that steps back from the agenda of a particular administration. The post-catalytic setting in which DHS is evolving is captured most effectively through the frame of reference offered by Van Johnston's *Entrepreneurial Management and Public Policy Model* (the Johnston Model).

The frame of reference provided by the Johnston Model (see Figure 3) offers us important, wide-ranging insights relating to the powerful variables that have been, and continue to be, encountered by the DHS leadership as it attempts to provide security and safety for the United States on the domestic front. The remainder of this chapter turns attention to three key areas of DHS programming: FEMA, focusing on field exercises and Hurricane Katrina efforts; border protection; and personnel systems reform. Topics of particular interest to the field of public policy and administration – budgeting, organization theory, public personnel, intergovernmental relations, and related areas – permeate the examples. Before describing the topical areas, however, the discussion turns to a brief overview of the Johnston Model as recently developed from previous publications (Johnston, 2004).

From the bottom of the Model we see a flow with emphasis on safety and security to the top of the Model with priorities for freedom, and risk, and innovation and creativity (Johnston, 2004). The movement highlights a transformation from an effectiveness based managerial culture to an efficiency-oriented one, based on privatization and contracting out. The Model portrays the changes ascribed to a move from a regulated environment evolved to a more deregulated one. Such an adjustment involves the increase in efficiency and business orientation associated with a market model, which engenders more of the traits associated with an entrepreneurial government model in terms of the challenges related to the implementation of an effective governance system (Johnston, 2004). From the perspective of the DHS, this would mean an orientation that places high value upon the effective delivery of security and safety systems.

Examining the Model from the bottom and flowing toward the top, we find problem/issue resolution strategies, including: (1) issue/problem resolution and collaboration; (2) bargain/negotiate; and (3) competition/zero-sum. On the top, we see that the variables of power, trust, and consequences related to the risk inherent in a free-market approach to the regulatory (or lack thereof) process. Often we experience a catalytic event if we deregulate too much. Events around 9/11 and Katrina offer examples of this phenomenon. Usually, we then reset the model by following the arrows on the right down toward more effectiveness. As we proceed to the bottom of the Model, we see elements and traits inherent in a heavily regulated environment of a major (mega) bureaucratic entity. The flow toward the highly regulated, more effective, security and safety environment also engenders greater trust within the general public as risk factors are diminished (Johnston, 2004).

The flow of events and Model adjustments following a "catalytic event" (such as 9/11 or Hurricane Katrina) create pressure to return to the bottom part of the Model and "back to a more regulated security and safety zone where citizens demand their governments step in and step up to more optimally manage the disaster at hand" (Johnston, 2004, p. 269). Upon return to the bottom section of the Model, a need to examine the root cause of the catalytic event emerges as an ongoing imperative at both the organizational and individual levels.

In the case of Hurricane Katrina, the catalytic event was the hurricane – an act of nature, and thus of known origin. The challenges and purported failures of the recovery efforts that followed were significant. The catalytic event thus focuses attention and public resources upon strategies to prevent its recurrence. The interest of the public and the citizen drive this focus and this condition will remain as long as threat conditions, similar to those encountered before the catalytic event, prevail. In sum, governmental effectiveness is a preferred condition over market efficiencies when managing catalytic events.

MODEL STRUCTURE ELEMENTS & IMPLICATIONS

The Model represents a re-balancing and/or re-setting following the catalytic event and suggests that there is a remedy available to mitigate the possibility of a similar event. The Model also depicts a circular process, emerging from one state to another. The Model further suggests that after a re-setting, a period of maintenance prevails during which smaller-scale resetting actions occur. These actions could include the introduction of innovations, more sub-agency reorganization initiatives, or issuance of contracts without following sole-sourcing procedures. Many of the analytical tools offered by the field of public policy and administration can be used to plumb the depths of the Model's implications, including such common curriculum components as: entrepreneurial management, budgeting, organization theory, program evaluation, innovation, intergovernmental relations, legitimacy, bureaucratic accountability, agential public management, and other related areas of scholarship.

Some observers of highly complex public undertakings (e.g., megaproject public works such as the BigDig in Boston) have noted that public policymakers must grapple with the huge challenge of reconciling the conflicting values and objectives that underlie the managerial, technical and political players' agendas (Haynes, 2004). In keeping with that notion, the Model could provide several tracts upon which analysis can proceed. Each of the cases that follow could be viewed from the standpoint of conflicting objectives in these three realms. It could also reasonably be argued that at any point in time, one bundle of values and objectives prevails over the others and is, thus, reflected in the policy instrument that emerges.

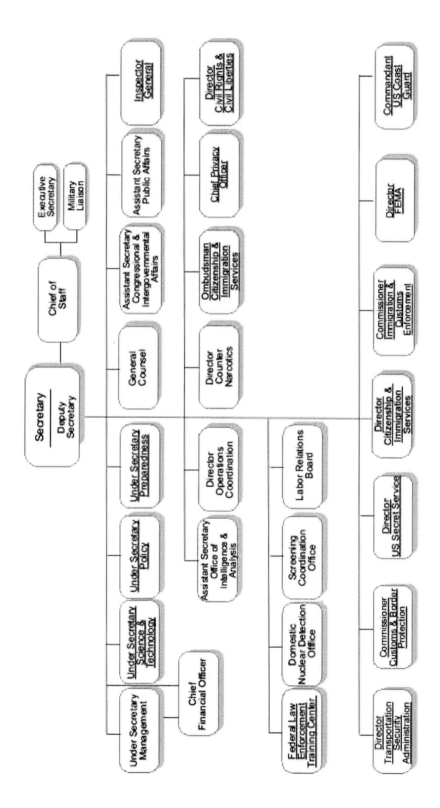

Figure 2: The Department of Homeland Security Organizational Chart (proposed end state, released 7/13/05)

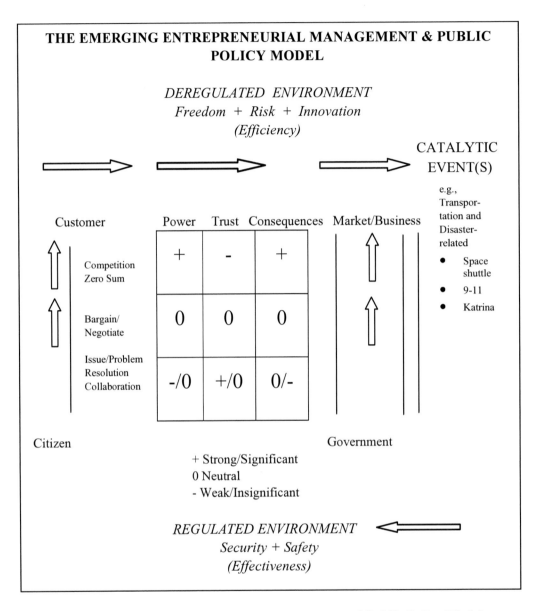

Figure 3: The Entrepreneurial Management and Public Policy Model

AREAS OF MODEL APPLICATION: FEMA, BORDER PROTECTION, AND DHS PERSONNEL SYSTEM

Application One

FEMA faces critical challenges, including effective delivery of incident management and stabilization services as well as integration with the state and local jurisdictions and their response systems. Trust plays an important role and revolves around the extent to which FEMA can deliver services and positively impact upon the safety and security challenges encountered by the DHS. For example, FEMA must be cognizant concerning the positive and negative impacts of the large scale field exercise upon those participating state and local jurisdictions. Considerations must be evaluated in terms of the relevancy of the training to the participants and the manner in which performance measures are calculated and assessed. Performance measures are not an end unto themselves; however, managers within FEMA must carefully review the key elements they wish to change or impact in terms of the performance (behavior) of their organization. A clear understanding and perspective concerning the manner in which performance measures can help foster organizational improvement must be understood before undertaking those initiatives the FEMA managers believe will catalyze such improvements.

Waugh (2003) posits that the creation of the DHS was undertaken while ignoring the nation's existing capacity to mitigate large-scale disasters. Waugh asserts that the DHS has not been able to effectively integrate the critical aspects of the nation's emergency management systems, on both human and material dimensions, as it contemplates and fashions a response system to a terrorist-sponsored, critical incident. Waugh's article importantly notes that the DHS command-and-control posture may hamper overall planning and implementation of key DHS components and sub-components. For instance, he provides that areas relating to the technical and non-technical (cultural) elements of interoperability, within the context of critical incident response and mitigation, may surface as one of the glaring operational gaps impacting upon both short and long-term efforts to diffuse the innovations associated with the DHS.

Moreover, the limited scope of this preparedness can also impact upon the networks crafted and the manner in which these networks represent regional approaches to preparedness. Those involved in the critical incident/emergency management function – the managers, fire/police chiefs and other actors and stakeholders – have been found to have a profound effect as to the manner by which resources are expended and the nature of the response system (Donahue, 2004).

The many ancillary nuances associated with critical incident response – culture, techniques, and macro inter-organizational cooperation – deepen the complexity of the DHS developmental canvas. Emergency management functions can be characterized as a set of complex undertakings that transpire at many levels of government through which various incentives emerge and impact upon human behavior at the individual or group levels (Donahue, 2004). These actions are also linked to preparedness activities. Murphy (2004) highlights four administrative and coordinating measures that can serve as barriers to successful preparedness efforts: lack of community involvement; insufficient response staff training; deficient information technology-based tools; and little deliberation regarding the need for additional staff and equipment.

FEMA initiatives corroborate Murphy's thesis. For instance, in spite of FEMA work on the various TOPOFF (top official) exercises from 2003-2005, the 2005 approval of the National Incident Management System (NIMS), the Nation's first standardized management plan that creates a unified structure for federal, state, and local lines of government for incident response, or the latest implementation of a new state-of-the-art Homeland Security Operations Center (HSOC), there remained criticisms and concerns related to the scope of work undertaken by FEMA and related DHS entities (see **Figure 1**). During 2005 congressional hearings, several Congressmen expressed reservations relating to the outcomes of FEMA-sponsored field exercises.

We can see how the Johnston Model offers a path to insights, as outlined below, about how the field exercises can be adjusted to enhance the effectiveness of FEMA's emergency management services. The right side of the Johnston Model below the catalytic event focuses primarily on model reset management.

Example: Major FEMA-Sponsored Field Exercise

According to a fact sheet issued by the U.S. Department of State in 2002,[7] TOPOFF is a national-level, multi-agency, multi-jurisdictional, real-time, limited-notice weapons of mass destruction response exercise, designed to better prepare senior government officials to effectively respond to an actual terrorist attack. The TOPOFF exercises were mandated by Congress and involved local, state, national, and international public, private, and non-profit entities. In the late nineties, the TOPOFF exercise initiative was inspired by the 1995 Tokyo subway sarin gas attack. The first exercise was conducted pre-9/11 in May 2000 in Denver, Colorado and Portsmouth, New Hampshire. Denver participants faced a simulated chemical attack, while Portsmouth participants were confronted with a biological attack.

The second exercise occurred in 2003, in the post-9/11 era, and provided further basis for performance management and overall program evaluation. A central challenge for FEMA entailed the need to make these exercises meaningful to participants who functioned at different safety and security levels. This challenge proved difficult for FEMA, particularly as it faced a substantial organizational change as federal officials crafted the new DHS.

The U.S. Government Accountability Office, in a variety of reports (2005, 2004, 2003), as well as the DHS Office of Inspector General (2004), have identified some of the central management challenges facing the DHS. The challenges involve developing and implementing effective communications and information exchange systems and include both administrative and technical concerns. These challenges revolve around DHS's internal operational components as well as the need to connect effectively the local and state entities that are crucial to an integrated response and incident management system. The TOPOFF exercise graphic (Figure 4) and summary that follow uses the Johnston "re-setting" concept to illustrate the struggle that ensued between a command and control, highly regulated exercise and the need to employ techniques of net-working, collaboration, and cooperation at the local level.

---

[7] The fact sheet may be accessed at www.state.gov/s/ct/rls/fs/2002/12129.htm. The DHS website (http://www.dhs.gov/dhspublic) provides additional information

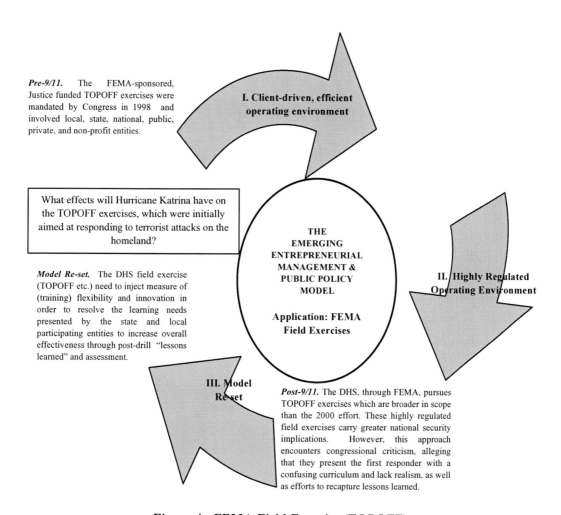

Figure 4: FEMA Field Exercise (TOPOFF)

- **Post- 9/11 IMPERATIVE:** DHS requires training (TOPOFF etc.) to assess the effectiveness of incident (first) response and the degree to which effective safety/security conditions can be attained, in part, by simulating a critical, all-hazard response and incident mitigation/stabilization effort.

- **GOAL:** This field exercise would test the manner in which local response adheres to the National Incident Management System (NIMS). All technologies and other such tools used at the local level should support the response per the NIMS protocols (**re-setting of the Model**). The TOPOFF exercises highlighted training, drills, field exercises that were expansive and involved many public, private, and non-profit entities in order to test effectiveness of incident response, mitigation, and stabilization services.

- **Problems:** DHS-sponsored field exercises reveal some measure of **problem resolution** and some **level of negotiations**. But command and control posture is difficult (can be overly regulated) and lacked flexibility for innovation in the local response.

- **The directional "up" arrows (see Figure 3 discussion)** suggest that FEMA, the U.S. Department of Justice, and the TOPOFF exercises will evolve to a **less regulated environment** as notions **of innovation** are introduced in the DHS field exercise environment. Ongoing **techno-administrative** challenges may call for innovative technologies to deal with the "marble cake" communications among federal, state, and local officials engaged in emergency preparedness and recovery.

Example: FEMA & Hurricane Katrina

Hurricane Katrina represents one of the first major challenges encountered by the DHS where the aftermath of destruction approached that of 9/11. The challenges overwhelmed FEMA's capacity to respond effectively. The scope of the storm called for the highest level of preparedness that could be marshaled from all actors inside and outside of FEMA's organizational boundaries. But the agency and its counterparts have been widely criticized as inept and unprepared, despite the kind of advanced meteorological warnings that terrorist attacks do not enjoy. FEMA Director Michael Brown resigned in the wake of Katrina. State and local officials lambasted FEMA's performance. Those who desperately needed FEMA action during the early stages of the incident mitigation and stabilization effort – and those of us who looked on -- lost confidence and trust in national and subnational government's capacity to respond effectively.

FEMA's inability to deliver its core coordinating services to the state and local jurisdictions contributed to a public perception – or, perhaps, public realization – that inadequate safety and security systems put the public at grave risk. This example – the early stage incident response (or lack thereof) effort undertaken by FEMA – demonstrates that those efficiency measures so well documented in many public papers and most notably codified in the National Response Plan issued in January of 2005, may be moot or meaningless absent an urgent and prolonged commitment to achieving the goals therein.

Post-assessment of the Katrina recovery effort – no doubt complicated by the Hurricane Rita efforts that followed close on Katrina's heals – is still unfolding. The following graphic (Figure 5) and summary uses the organizing principles of the Johnston Model to begin to understand and predict how these events may play out and eventually alter FEMA's role and approach in the context of the DHS agenda.

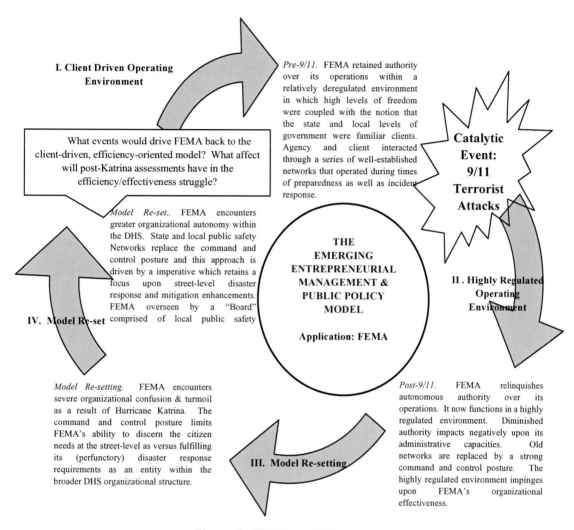

Figure 5: FEMA and Katrina

- **Post-911 IMPERATIVE:** DHS requires FEMA to provide a central coordinating role within the scope of the incident response and mitigation effort(s) relating to a critical, all-hazard incident.

- **GOAL:** FEMA is to effectively implement key planning components (coordinating functions) from federal policy statements, such as the National Response Plan, during a critical, all hazard incident to maintain the overall security and safety of the homeland (**re-setting of the Model**).

- **Problems:** DHS – and FEMA, specifically – did not appear to achieve a high level of **problem resolution capacity** and **negotiation ability** with the various state and local levels of government operations. It could be claimed that the command and control posture assumed by the DHS leadership emerged as an area of operational difficulty, since such a posture does not invite innovation and/or flexibility in the local response effort. The FEMA response effort to Katrina highlighted severe deficiency in terms of interagency and intergovernmental coordination at the local and state levels. This situation undermined trust and faith in FEMA's ability to ultimately contribute effectively to the safety and security of those citizens negatively impacted by Katrina and future threats, whether natural or not.

- **The directional "up" arrows**, suggest that FEMA and its role in disaster recovery and homeland security may experience another re-setting phase. Post-Katrina commentators have called for a return to greater autonomy or a different level of integration for FEMA in securing the homeland. It will be interesting to see whether as a catalytic event, Katrina causes a clockwise or counter-clockwise movement in the model. Surely, public officials will see a need to re-examine the role of the state and local networks, which may emerge as a qualitative enhancements to restore public trust in the capacity of public agencies to respond to public disasters. These network relationships – with innovative technology support structures – may also provide fodder for richer analysis and metric development for improving FEMA's performance under the National Response Plan.

Application Two

In 2005, congressional testimony reflected concern about the performance of the U.S. Citizenship and Immigration Services, USCIS, a component of the relatively new Bureau of Immigration and Customs Enforcement (ICE) (Chertoff, 2005). Mounting criticism has assailed the DHS and leaderships' attempts to accomplish the new agency's mission, much of it focusing on information technology systems. This criticism provided the impetus for the House Government Reform Committee to launch an aggressive review of the U.S.-VISIT program and its implementation by DHS.

We can, again, see how the Johnston Entrepreneurial Management Model offers insights relating to how the administrative and technical apparatus can be better positioned to enhance the effectiveness of the safety and security environment created by the DHS through its many organizational elements.

EXAMPLE: RE-STRUCTURING & RE-TOOLING OF BORDER PROTECTION

When the DHS announced the creation of the ICE in 2003, a variety of challenges emerged relating to the service structure of the new entity, as well as technical hurdles that loomed in the organizational arena (see Figure 1 for sequence of events). In 2004, the DHS encountered technical challenges relating to the enhanced border technology it positioned for implementation via the US-VISIT program. The US-VISIT was designed to enhance the nation's security while facilitating legitimate travel and trade across our borders. New entry procedures affected most foreign visitors with non-immigrant visas at 115 airports and cruise ship terminals at 14 seaports. As designed, the system was to utilize biometrics technologies for personal identification and verification purposes.

From an internal organizational perspective, 2005 congressional testimony revealed that DHS was faced with exploring a more holistic approach to dealing with the mounting challenges of border protection. Figure 6, below, provides a visual depiction of the re-setting process from pre to post-911. The narrative following the figure supplements the verbal snapshots already included in the graphic display.

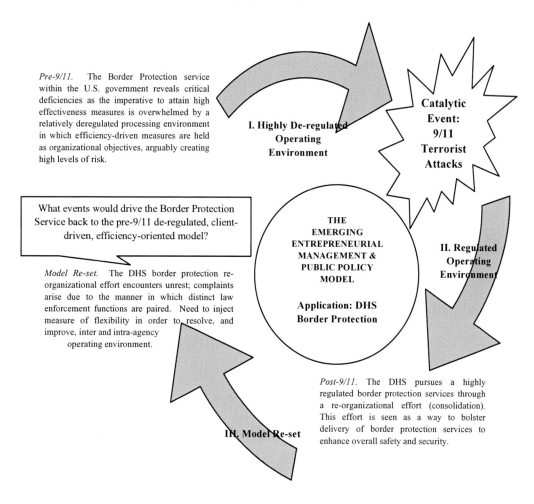

Pre-9/11. The Border Protection service within the U.S. government reveals critical deficiencies as the imperative to attain high effectiveness measures is overwhelmed by a relatively deregulated processing environment in which efficiency-driven measures are held as organizational objectives, arguably creating high levels of risk.

I. Highly De-regulated Operating Environment

Catalytic Event: 9/11 Terrorist Attacks

What events would drive the Border Protection Service back to the pre-9/11 de-regulated, client-driven, efficiency-oriented model?

THE EMERGING ENTREPRENEURIAL MANAGEMENT & PUBLIC POLICY MODEL

Application: DHS Border Protection

II. Regulated Operating Environment

Model Re-set. The DHS border protection re-organizational effort encounters unrest; complaints arise due to the manner in which distinct law enforcement functions are paired. Need to inject measure of flexibility in order to resolve, and improve, inter and intra-agency operating environment.

III. Model Re-set

Post-9/11. The DHS pursues a highly regulated border protection services through a re-organizational effort (consolidation). This effort is seen as a way to bolster delivery of border protection services to enhance overall safety and security.

Figure 6: Border Protection

- **Post 9/11 IMPERATIVE:** Re-organize Border Patrol in the aftermath of 9/11. DHS leadership creates ICE (the Bureau of Immigration and Customs Enforcement) to facilitate improved border patrol services. Organization appears entrenched and in need of change via a top-down approach. This approach did not incorporate much, if any, **negotiation and/or problem-solving,**

collaborative approach with those entrenched historical members of the organization.

- **GOAL:** Effective delivery of border patrol services (re-setting of the Model).

- **PROBLEMS:** Lack of response and input with technologies from older organizational members increased the **regulatory environment,** without concomitant operational integration of technology tools designed to enhance border security. The failed IT innovations, caused in part by lack of negotiations with key stakeholders, illustrates a classic problem highlighted by the public policy and administration literature in the context of organizational development.

- The Johnston Model (Figure 3) suggests a need to reach across the matrix to collaborate with key "pre-organizational" entities (former organizational sub-agencies) – **to rebalance** – key elements of each area and regain **trust** within the oversight (executive) components of the Border Patrol organization and sub-organization.

Application Three

From another organizational vantage point, we can see that the restructured personnel system proposed by the DHS also contributes to the organizational challenges linked to the smooth development of the DHS as a public (mega) agency. The Homeland Security Act of 2002 accorded the administration a very broad grant of authority to reform the public personnel system. The act amended Title 5 of the U.S. Code, which covers federal civilian personnel matters, by specifying that the secretary for homeland security and the director of the Office of Personnel Management (OPM) could at their discretion establish a new personnel system for the department. . .[that must be] "flexible" and "contemporary. . . .[g]reater flexibility in collective bargaining. . . [and much more]. (Kellough and Nigro, 2005; 67f). The flexibility granted DHS, especially in light of the post-catalytic tendency toward greater regulation suggested in the Johnston Model, presented a recipe for dissension and resistance.

EXAMPLE: DHS PERSONNEL SYSTEM

In 2004, the DHS awarded a blanket purchase agreement (BPA) to Northrop Grumman Information Technology to provide a full range of services needed to assist Homeland Security in implementing and maintaining a new human resources management system, known as MAXHR. By mid-2005, during congressional hearings, criticism of the proposed personnel system rose to new heights, based in part on the expressed fear that the changes would needlessly undermine the nation's long-standing commitments to employee protections, independent arbitration, and collective bargaining rights.

Earlier, in January 2005, four federal employee unions filed suit alleging that DHS had exceeded its authority under the statute establishing the DHS human capital system (*National Treasury Employees Union v. Ridge*, No. 1:05cv201). A federal judge subsequently ruled that key personnel regulations poised for implementation by DHS were illegal and could not be installed. The decision effectively halted DHS from implementing its new labor relations system in October 2005 as it had earlier planned. The U.S. District Court for the District of Columbia, in striking the regulations, concluded that "significant aspects of the HR System fail to conform to the express dictates of the Homeland Security Act."[8]

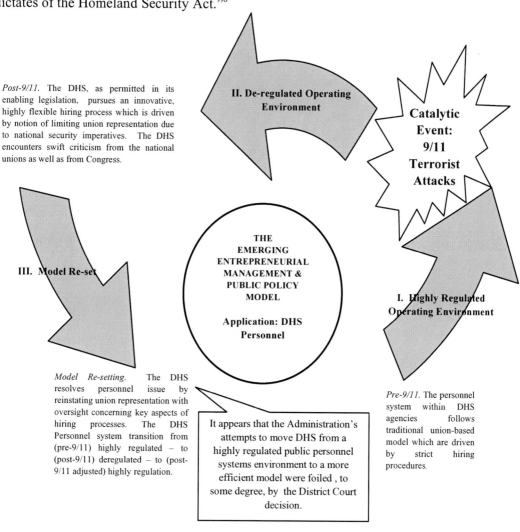

Post-9/11. The DHS, as permitted in its enabling legislation, pursues an innovative, highly flexible hiring process which is driven by notion of limiting union representation due to national security imperatives. The DHS encounters swift criticism from the national unions as well as from Congress.

II. De-regulated Operating Environment

Catalytic Event: 9/11 Terrorist Attacks

III. Model Re-set

THE EMERGING ENTREPRENEURIAL MANAGEMENT & PUBLIC POLICY MODEL

Application: DHS Personnel

I. Highly Regulated Operating Environment

Model Re-setting. The DHS resolves personnel issue by reinstating union representation with oversight concerning key aspects of hiring processes. The DHS Personnel system transition from (pre-9/11) highly regulated – to (post-9/11) deregulated – to (post-9/11 adjusted) highly regulation.

It appears that the Administration's attempts to move DHS from a highly regulated public personnel systems environment to a more efficient model were foiled , to some degree, by the District Court decision.

Pre-9/11. The personnel system within DHS agencies follows traditional union-based model which are driven by strict hiring procedures.

Figure 7: DHS Personnel System

---

[8] Case 1:05-cv-00201-RMC, Document 41. Filed 10/07/2005 by Judge Rosemary M. Collyer, U.S. District Court.

- **Post 9/11 IMPERATIVE:** Need to recruit the best and the brightest for service within the newly created DHS.

- **GOAL:** Develop and implement a re-tooled personnel system that will provide greater flexibility in recruitment and retention and minimize the impact of collective bargaining. The goal as reflected in the law (although not necessarily here) appears to have been a continuation of the new public management reforms of the nineties, initiated in part through the Clinton/Gore government reinvention reforms, which decried the limitations of the civil service system and attempted to increase hiring flexibility in the public service.

  An entrenched organization and the need to re-organize/re-tool personnel via a top-down approach ensued. This approach did not incorporate much, if any, **negotiation and/or problem-solving, collaborative approach** with those bargaining unit members.

- **PROBLEM:** Re-tooled personnel system, due perhaps to lack of effective collaboration/negotiations with key stakeholders, runs the risk of not serving the needs and interests of the public, thus jeopardizing public trust and credibility.

- **The directional arrows** in Figure 3 would predict what is initially depicted in Figure 7: The regulatory trend following a catalytic event runs contrary to the earlier reforms that tilted toward less government control, arguably less worker protection, and greater managerial flexibility. One might surmise a need to reach across the philosophical divide toward key "pre-organizational" entities (former organizational sub-agencies) – **to rebalance** – key elements of each area and regain **trust** within the street-level bureaucrats and other key union and related bargaining unit leaders.

CONCLUSIONS

Model Application to DHS: Preliminary Observations

The six key elements of the emerging model (Figure 3) – power, trust, consequences, competition/zero sum, negotiation, and problem resolution/collaboration – should be construed as dynamic and multi-dimensional rather than linear in nature. The DHS issues and problems discussed briefly in the preceding examples may require us to view the post-catalytic dynamics as incremental "re-settings" as we seek optimal effectiveness in response to the changing environment. Typically, the incremental adjustments in the tension between efficiency and effectiveness – broadly defined earlier in the discussion of the model – occur under the radar of public attention. But catalytic events, such as 9/11 and Hurricane Katrina, cause several inter-dependant dynamics: public officials make radical changes to bring about a greater feeling of safety and security; and stakeholders both internal and external to organizations directly affected by the changes react, sometimes with resistance and sometimes with great cooperative enthusiasm.

A Few Lessons to be Learned

In such a gargantuan undertaking, which strikes at the heart of our communities, as those in New York and New Orleans will attest, we must heed and tend to the concerns expressed by Representative Christopher Shays (R-CT), in response to DHS Secretary Michael Chertoff's testimony before the House Government Reforms Committee in June 2005:

> We saw the need to unify and coordinate scattered functions to confront a new, lethal, post-9/11 security paradigm. The truth be told, we created a fairly blunt instrument to wield against an agile subtle foe. In effect, we built a four-headed octopus and asked the behemoth to perform brain surgery the next day. . . .

> Exercises, federal counterterrorism training and exercise programs still offer first responders a confusing smorgasbord rather than a cohesive curriculum. . . .**[w]e'll never know if preparedness is improving if first responders can't answer the basic question, prepared for what?** [Emphasis added.]

It has been observed that the success or failure of mega-undertakings turns on the degree to which public leaders are able to resolve the conflicting values and objectives of political policy-makers, managers, and technicians/service (Haynes, 2002). The entrepreneurial model underscores the importance and difficulty of managing the struggle between and among various forces that would pull an implementation effort toward a business-based efficiency model or a safety/public trust-oriented effectiveness model. The balance settles, shifts, and re-sets as the worlds of internal and external forces come to bear. Wise leaders and students of business, public policy and administration would do well to serve as thoughtful observers and active guides in the events surrounding the evolution of the DHS and its struggle to protect the homeland.[9]

REFERENCES

Anders, K., et al. (2003). New federalism: Impact on state and local governments." *Journal of Public Budgeting, Accounting, and Financial Management, 15*(3), 466-486.

---

[9] George Fredrickson (2005) in a series of columns for the American Society for Public Administration, Sharon Caudle (2005) in her work on results management in DHS, Lester Salamon (2005) on "border management," Charles Wise (2002), among others have important insights on the interdisciplinary nature of public policy and administration

Bardach, E. (1977). *The implementation game: What happens after a bill becomes a law.* Cambridge, MA: The MIT Press.

Bolman, L.G. and Deal, T.E. (2003*). Reframing organizations: Artistry, choice, and leadership.* 3rd edition. San Francisco: Jossey-Bass.

Brookings Institution. (2002) *Project on homeland security—Chapter 7: Organizing for success* (pp. 99-124). Washington, DC: Brookings. Retrieved 2003, from http://www.brookings.org/dybdocroot/fp/projects/homeland/orgs.html

Bush, G.W. (2002). National strategy for homeland security. Retrieved 2003, from http://www.whitehouse.gov/homelandbooks/index.html

Caudle, S. (2005). Homeland security: Approaches to results management. *Public Performance & Management Review. 28*(3), 352-375.

Chertoff, M. (2005). Statement by Secretary of Homeland Security Michael Chertoff before the House Government Reform Committee (June 9). Retrieved June 12, 2005, from http://www.dhs.gov/dhspublic/display?theme=45&content=4536&print=true

Donahue, A.K. (2004). Managerial perceptions and the production of fire protection. *Administration & Society. 35*(6), 717-46.

Donahue, A.K. and Joyce, P.G. (2001). A framework for analyzing emergency management with an application to federal budgeting. *Public Administration Review. 61*(6), 728-740.

Frederickson, G.H. (2005). *Public administration with an attitude.* Washington, DC: American Society for Public Administration.

Gilmore, J.S.III, Chairman. (2002*). Fourth annual report to the president and the Congress of the advisory panel to assess domestic response capabilities for terrorism involving weapons of mass destruction* (a.k.a. the Gilmore Commission). Retrieved 2003, from http://www.rand.org/nsrd/terrpanel

Goggin, M.L., Boman, A., Lester, J.P., and O'Toole, L. (1998*). Implementation theory and practice: Toward a third generation.* New York: Harper Collins.

Haynes, W. (2004). Seeing around corners: Crafting the new department of homeland security. *Review of Policy Research, 21*(3), 369-395.

Haynes, W. (2002*). An exploration of the nexus of the public and private sectors in the project management organizations for two Boston megaprojects: The Central Artery/tunnel project and the Boston Harbor Cleanup.* Dissertation. Boston: Northeastern University. UMI.

Haynes, W and Wright, R. (2005). Thoughts on the department of homeland security: Border management, students, and our communities – a holistic approach. Paper presented at the 66th National Conference of the American Society for Public Administration in Milwaukee, WI (April 2 – 6).

Johnston, Van R. (2004). Terrorism and transportation policy and administration: Balancing the model and equations for optimal security. *Review of Policy Research, 21*(3), 263-274.

Kellough, J. E. and Nigro, L.G. (2005). Radical civil service reform: Ideology, politics, and policy. In Condrey, S. (Ed.), *Handbook of human resource management in government,* San Francisco: Jossey-Bass.

Kettl, D.F. (2003). Contingent coordination: Practical and theoretical puzzles for homeland security. Prepared by author for presentation at the American Society for Public Administration 2003 Annual Meeting, Washington, DC, in the Senior Scholar Spotlight: Bureaucratic Structure in a Post-9/11 Government.

Kincaid, J. (1990). From cooperative to coercive federalism. *Annals of the American Academy*, 509, 139-152.

La Porte, T. et al. (2002). Democracy and bureaucracy in the age of the web; empirical findings and theoretical speculations. *Administrative & Society*, *34*(4), 441-446.

Lipsky, M. (1980). *Street-level bureaucracy: Dilemmas of the individual in public service*. New York: Russell Sage Foundation.

Markel Foundation Task Force on National Security in the Information Age. (2002) *Protecting America's freedom in the information age* (174 pages). Retrieved 2003, from http://www.markletaskforce.org

Mintzberg, H. (1979). *The Structuring of organizations (the theory of management policy)*. Englewood Cliffs, NJ: Prentice Hall.

Murphy, J. (2004). After 9/11: Priority focus areas for bioterrorism preparedness in hospitals. *Journal of Healthcare Management*. *49*(4): 227-35.

O'Toole, L. J. (1999). American intergovernmental relations: An overview. *Public administration: concepts and cases*. Stillman, R.J. (Ed.) 8th edition. Boston: Houghton Mifflin Company, 2005.

Palumbo, D. J. and Calista, D.J. (1990). *Implementation and the policy process: Opening up the black box*. New York: Greenwood Press.

Pressman, J. and Wildavsky, A. (1984*). Implementation: How great expectations in Washington are dashed in Oakland; Or, why it's amazing the federal programs work at all this being a saga of the economic development administration as told by two sympathetic observers who seek to build morals on a foundation of ruined hopes (3rd ed.)*. Berkeley: University of California Press.

Rosenbloom, D H. and Kravchuk, R.S. (2005). *Public administration: Understanding management, politics, and law in the public sector*. 6th edition. Boston: McGraw-Hill.

Salamon, L. M. (2005). Training professional citizens: Getting beyond the right answer to the wrong question in public administration. *Journal of Public Affairs Education*. *11*(1), 7-19.

Sandfort, ,J. (2003). Exploring the structuration of technology within human service organizations. *Administration & Society*, *34*(6), 605-631.

Scheirer, J.M. (1994). Designing and using process evaluation. In J.S. Wholey, H.P. Hatry, and K.E. Newcomer (eds.), *Handbook of Practical Program Evaluation*. San Francisco: Jossey-Bass.

Scheirer, M. (1990). Studying micro-implementation empirically: Lessons and dilemmas, in Implementation and the Public Policy Process: Opening Up the Black Box. Westport, CT: Greenwood Press.

Shafritz, J.M. and Russell, E.W. (2005). *Introducing public administration*. 4th edition. Boston: Pearson Longman.

Smith, R.W. (2005). What is homeland security? Developing a definition grounded in the curricula. *Journal of Public Affairs Education. 1l*(3): 233-246.

Strohm, C. (February 9, 2005). Homeland security budget puts administration on collision course with lawmakers, airlines. Retrieved February 10, 2005, from http://www.govexec.com

Thomas, R. (1990). National-local relations and the city's dilemma. *Annals of the American Academy*, 509, 106-117.

U.S. DHS Office of Inspector General. (2004*). Major management challenges facing the Department of Homeland Security*. (OIG-05-06). December 2004.

U.S. Government Accountability Office. (2005). *Transportation Security. Systematic Planning Needed to Optimize Resources (Testimony before the Committee on Commerce, Science, Transportation, United States Senate)*. Washington, D.C., Cathleen Berrick (GAO-05-357T).

_____. (2004). *Homeland Security: Selected Recommendations from Congressionally Chartered Commissions and GAO*. Washington, D.C.: Author (GAO-04-591).

_____. (2003). Major management challenges and program risks: Department of Homeland Security (*Performance and Accountability Series*). Washington, DC: Author (GAO-03-102).

Waugh, W. (2003). Terrorism, homeland security, and the national emergency management network. *Public Organizational Review*, 3(4), 373-385.

Wright, D. (1990). Policy shifts in the politics and administration of intergovernmental relations, 1930s-1990s. *Annals of the American Academy*, 509, 60-72.

Chapter 18

RE-SETTING THE ENTREPRENEURIAL MANAGEMENT AND PUBLIC POLICY MODEL FOR OPTIMAL EFFECTIVENESS AND EFFICIENCY

Van R. Johnston

In the business and public policy arena, America has suffered from giving in too easily to the lure of the efficiency environment. Freedom and innovation have captured our spirit since about 1980 when we started, and have kept on, voting for fiscally conservative presidents who favor an entrepreneurial (and business efficiency) orientation to public policy. Implementing public policy and using business decision making and management practices, however, brings higher levels of risk into the equation. We have suffered a number of catalytic events as a result.

This chapter analyzes four sets of catalytic events utilizing the Johnston Entrepreneurial Management and Public Policy Model in the Re-Set Application (Appendix A). The four crisis arenas we explore here are: 1) Terrorism, 1993 and 2001; 2) Business, Public Policy, and Finance - the Savings and Loan Bailout of the 1990's, and the Financial Ethics collapse of the early 21st century; 3) NASA - The Challenger and the Columbia; and 4) FEMA - the Northridge Earthquake and Hurricane Katrina.

The chapter ends by analyzing collaboration (effectiveness) vs. competition (efficiency). One of the significant managerial challenges of the 21st century will be to optimally balance collaboration and competition for more professional and productive organizational performance (Appendix B).

RE-SETTING THE MODEL FOR TRANSPORTATION SECURITY AFTER THE 9-11 TERRORISM ATTACKS

Prior to 9-11

In the period leading up to September 11, 2001 America was over investing in efficiency based security. Private companies like Argenbright and Wackenhut were contractors hired to provide basic security at many of America's airports. In their efforts to control costs, they were allowed to hire low paid employees with marginal training and language skills. Some of those security screeners also had criminal records (Johnston, 2004).

This is but one example of efficiency displacing responsible provision and production of security and safety, but certainly a significant one. It represents the evaluation of management thinking and policy implementation that go back to 1978 when President Jimmy Carter deregulated the airline industry, and to 1980 when Reagan/Bush brought Reaganomics to America (Johnston, 2001, 2002a,b). This efficiency oriented Reaganomics (conservative financial policy and management) has been with us for most of the years since the Reagan/Bush election in 1980. There have been five Bush represented presidential terms of office since then: 1980, 1984, 1988, 2000, and 2004. From 1992 to 2000, President Bill Clinton, a fiscal conservative, was in office. During his administration, he and Vice President Al Gore downsized the federal government about 30% with their reinventing government efforts (Osborne and Gaebler, 1991; Gore, 1993, 1994, 1996).

The reinventing government initiatives were based on privatization and contracting out (Osborne and Gaebler, 1991; Savas, 1982; Donahue, 1996; and Johnston 1991, 2000). Taken to their private sector roots, we find connections to re-engineering, total quality management, private public partnerships and franchising (Halachmi, 1996; Johnston, 1996a,b,c). Infused in these management approaches not too distantly is the thinking and conceptualization behind mergers, acquisitions, hostile takeovers, and beyond.

Bringing private sector management thinking to the public sector has been called entrepreneurial management (Johnston, 1996a,b,c; Johnston, 2000). Entrepreneurial Management focuses on efficiency, or output over input. It is products and goods oriented. It is based on the logic of the market system and the private sector. It highlights and emphasizes quantitative measurement. As opposed to efficiency with its orientation towards short term bottom line, is effectiveness which focuses more on output over standards and providing optimal levels of service, e.g., safety and security.

Effectiveness has more of a citizen flavor to its outputs, while efficiency leans more towards a bottom line customer orientation. In the airport security situation leading up to 9-11, we definitely were emphasizing efficiency, e.g., screeners simply looking at x-ray scanners. For implementing effectiveness, employees would be better trained and educated to provide better security and safety. Increased language skills would be necessary, for instance. Effectiveness requires more infrastructure and systems integration networking and support. These were sorely missed leading up to 9-11.

9-11

With the terrorist attack on 9-11, America genuinely lost some of its innocence. We realized, as cynicism crept in (Berman, 1997), that we had over invested in trust in both our public and private sector leaders (Johnston, 1999; Wicks, Berman, and James, 1999; Bozeman, 1987). They had lost their credibility where airline security mattered (Kouzes and Posner, 1993). We found ourselves on the verge of a paradigm shift (Kuhn, 1970).

There had been a number of warnings: Mary Schiavo, as Inspector General of the United States Department of Transportation (USDOT) for instance, had run inspections on airline security that failed significantly and often. She is on record noting that both industry and government were reluctant to invest in transportation security; and, that America ignored the recommendations of the major transportation oriented security organizations on a regular basis (Schiavo, 2001).

Johnston also warned in March 2001, six months before the terrorist attack, that we were dangerously ill prepared to deal with terrorism and transportation security (Johnston, 2001).

When real security tests are run by knowledgeable security experts, the:

"holes in the system" are astounding. Guns, grenades and other weapons fail detection almost at will in the Department of Transportation audit checks (Johnston, 2001). The FAA needs to work much more closely with the FBI, the CIA and the State Department to build a much stronger net for air passenger security (US State Department, Jan, 2001). This will require the infusion of more government money. Airport authorities need to become more active in this cause as well...We probably need to build a new federal agency to deal with terrorism, and possibly general security as well. International agreements need to be generated, including bilateral and multilateral approaches... A much more sophisticated data base needs to be developed. This can help us identify, profile and track terrorists and other security risks (Johnston, 2001).

Without a macro level catalytic event however, America found it impossible to focus attention, money, time, and other resources towards getting airline security upgraded to viable standards. The World Trade Center had been attacked by terrorists in 1993. That attack was only marginally successful and we virtually ignored its lessons.

We will now take a look at the Johnston Entrepreneurial Management and Public Policy Model (JEMPP) to analyze how we got to the 9-11 disaster and what we've done about it since. We will be seeing the Model with its Re-Set application.

THE JOHNSTON ENTREPRENEURIAL MANAGEMENT AND PUBLIC POLICY MODEL: RE-SET APPLICATION

Starting at the bottom of the model (Appendix A), we have a regulated environment which focuses on effectiveness. Effectiveness is output over standards. In this case the standards relate to security and safety in transportation, especially air transportation.

Effectiveness typically relates to public or not for profit organizations. It deals primarily with services (like security and safety) rather than goods, for instance. It tends to have qualitative measures, like: is the security good enough? And, by what standards? The environment for the application of the standards also tends to be political. So, is the amount of money, and its application, considered to be "adequate to optimal" when evaluated by liberals/democrats or conservatives/republicans? If both consider a service to be either adequate or inadequate, then there is clarity. When there is disagreement, there is debate. In this case, the 9-11 terrorist attacks via air transportation, there was clear agreement that adequate air transportation security and safety were missing (Johnston, 2004).

At the top of the model (Appendix A), we find a significantly more deregulated environment for business and public policy. This is the world of efficiency. When we choose a policy and management world that is more market and business oriented, like we have been in our political elections since 1980, we are moving more towards freedom, risk, and innovation. This choice aligns us more clearly with business and market practices. Efficiency, being about output over input, exists more typically in the world of products and goods. It emphasizes quantitative measures and features private firms and private industry.

For analysis, we focus on the grid in the middle of the flow of events, trends, processes, services and results (Appendix A). The +, 0, and – symbols represent: strong to weak indicators.

At the bottom of the grid, we start with a presumption of some level of reasonably well balanced business and public policy in a world where citizens can rely on their government to protect their interests as citizens, by way of sovereignty (Johnston, 1996a,b,c), in health, education, security and so on. For our analysis in the air transportation arena for instance, let's say about 1977, before the air deregulation of 1978 which created so much competition that many airlines did not have monetary reserves sufficient to provide or produce security, or in some cases even safety. That led to a shake out in the airline industry. Government was still there for its citizens via the FAA for safety. The Civil Aeronautics Board dealt with rates and routes.

At the top of the three columns are: Power, Trust, and Consequences.

The significance of these analytical indicators changes as we select different policy and management strategies on the left of the grid: Issue/Problems Resolution/Collaboration (bottom), Bargain/Negotiation (middle), and Competition/Zero/Sum (top).

Beginning with President Jimmy Carter and his deregulation of Air Transportation in 1978; and more significantly across the business and public policy environment with Reagan/Bush in 1980, America began to move up the model away from effectiveness towards efficiency. Citizens began the transformation to becoming Customers (Johnston, 1995a). And government adopted many private sector business practices, becoming more efficient while, many would argue, also becoming less effective.

Looking at the grid for analytical feedback, we see that as we move from issue/problem resolution and collaboration through bargaining and negotiation, we changed the emphasis of the analytical indicators. So, regarding Power, we see a relatively light or insignificant emphasis on power, then becoming somewhat more significant with bargaining and negotiating, to being really significant when we get to competition and zero sum.

The trust feedback indicator also changes, from somewhat significant, e.g., passengers think airlines and airplanes are safe and secure, through being swayed in either direction with bargaining and negotiating, to a position of little trust, like after 9-11. Efficiency won. Little time, money or effort was spent on security and/or safety.

The Consequences feedback indicator for airlines is much like that for Trust, where the situation moves to a state of competition and zero sum. When the competition in the airline industry is severe enough that many airlines do not adequately invest in safety and security, then the risk has been taken on significantly.

This increased risk condition is enhanced and perpetuated when the government (now the FAA without the CAB) "contracts out" security screening to private companies like Argenbright and Wackenhut which employ low paid, ill trained, and language challenged workers.

When one considers all these factors, variables and trends as they evolve (look at the arrows going up, then across to the right on the model), we find the potential of having a Catalytic Event increases significantly. In this case it turned out to be the 9-11 air transportation Catalytic Event.

Below Catalytic Event, at the top of the grid on the model, we have the Re-Set application (Appendix A). Given any set of circumstances, in any given case, the way to resolve the risk of catalytic events is to Re-Set the Model towards effectiveness, and away from efficiency.

Efficiency can be great to grow an economy and provides opportunities to increase life style and certain indicators of quality of life, etc. It also comes with risks, e.g., air security and safety may decline significantly.

To increase security and safety, some form of re-regulation (usually a different form of regulation than in the past) could be utilized. Remember there are alternative approaches and remarkably varying changes and options to choose from.

There is also a Partial Re-Set which can take us part of the way back to a regulated environment. Or, a Full Re-Set which could provide substantial changes. Recall, for instance, that the World Trade center was attacked by terrorists in 1993. There was only a marginal, partial re-set where security and safety were concerned. Result? The 2001 terrorist attack demolished the entire World Trade Center.

So, after 2001, the response was a Full Re-Set, and launching the Transportation Security Administration with more training, education and pay for employees. The Department of Homeland Security was also created. It took in FEMA (Federal Emergency Management Agency) and over twenty other agencies. The Federal Bureau of Investigation and the Central Intelligence Agency even started a joint venture to deal with the terrorists. This Full Re-Set should be more viable than the Partial Re-Set of 1993.

RE-SETTING THE MODEL FOR
FINANCIAL POLICY AND ADMINISTRATION

Do the following corporations bring any particular sense of recognition relative to professional performance, governance and ethical behavior when they are identified? Try Enron, Qwest, WorldCom, Tyco, Global Crossing, Adelphia, and so on. How about corporate leaders like: Ken Lay (Enron), Joe Nacchio (Qwest), Bernie Ebbers (WorldCom), Joe Berardino (Andersen), John Rigas (Adelphia Communications Corporation), and Martha Stewart (Martha Stewart Living Omni Media)?

What about rampant corporate restatements, offshore corporations generated by primary corporations to get debt off the books, and stock options for corporate executives that are not expensed on the books? How about conflicts of interest like accounting firms consulting and auditing for the same corporation at the same time? Do you believe in accounting firms "blessing the books" versus professional auditing feedback? How about corporations paying for executive pensions but not for those of other employees? Or divesting the corporation of pension responsibilities by way of bankruptcy? Does the Pension Benefit Guaranty Corporation (PBGC) have enough funding and authority to be able to deal adequately with the increasing demand?

What happened to the watch dogs? Why have we been so weak in preventing, then dealing with so many of these outrages and the criminal activity connected with them? What about the SEC, FASB, Attorneys General, civil and criminal law suits, ethics organizations, and even whistleblowers?

It is clear by now that the early part of the 21st century has had more than its fair share of all of these. Business and public policy leadership and management, with a few notable exceptions like New York's Attorney General Elliot Spitzer, have been virtually missing in action. Not that no one paid attention, but our infatuation with short term bottom line, freedom, risk, and innovation (primarily efficiency – see the terrorism section above) seemed to have lead us beyond prudent and responsible behavior. Some scholars like Linda deLeon (Chapter 14) worked to get ethics and entrepreneurship thinking to relevant stakeholders. It can be hard to focus on ethical theory, however, when the rewards for pool and skim, and bait and switch, for instance, can be so great.

The government has seriously gone after Ken Lay, Jeff Skilling and Joe Nacchio; years after they walked away from Enron and Qwest...with criminal cases. Ken Lay died of a heart condition after conviction but before sentencing. Jeffrey Skilling, Enron's chief executive was sentenced to 24 years and four months for fraud and other crimes at Enron. He began serving his sentence December 13, 2006. Joe Nacchio was convicted of numerous counts of insider trading and sentenced to six years in prison in 2007. He appealed, and the SEC began its civil suit against Nacchio at the time of this chapter is being written. Various accounts credited both Lay and Nacchio with accumulating more than $100 million personally while their corporations and the stock of their shareholders and pensions of the employees of those corporations unraveled and became relatively worthless.

Eventually, Sarbanes-Oxley was passed by Congress establishing more significant accounting standards. McCain-Feingold was also passed by Congress, which brought more rigor to campaign finance. Arguably this would lessen the conflict of interest inherent in the cost of financing elections. Perhaps most significantly, however, in terms of getting after corporate executives who have performed beyond the legal threshold are Attorneys General; like Elliot Spitzer in New York, and Ken Salazar when he was Attorney General of Colorado.

This is not the first time we have witnessed corporate executives' financial misbehavior. In the late 1980's and the early 1990's America paid extensively for the misbehavior and collapse of the savings and loan industry. The FDIC (Continental Illinois Bank) and the FSLIC (Savings and Loans) worked overtime to help keep America's financial health alive. Some estimated that bailing out the savings and loan industry cost Americans over $500 billion.

So, how does the Johnston Entrepreneurial Management and Public Policy Model (JEMPP – Appendix A) work to analyze the financial policy and management that has negatively impacted so many Americans so significantly? We will examine the Re-Set application of the JEMPP model to get a clearer picture of how we got a second wave of financial disasters so close together.

It would be helpful to start with the paradigm shift (Kuhn, 1970) from effectiveness to efficiency that began about 1980 (see the theory development and the model in the terrorism section of this chapter above). In brief, as we left the 1970's, Americans began opting for a more business oriented approach in our public policy and business world. Safety and security, in the financial world gave way to the lure of more freedom and innovation, along with the inherent risk. Efficiency was embraced. This usually took the form of deregulation. Privatization and contracting out come with the adjustment. Total Quality Management, Re-Engineering and Re-Inventing were part of the paradigm shift (Johnston, 1995a; 1996a,b,c).

In part, in the 1980's, this led to a change in the rules for managing and insuring loans. Congress passed legislation giving much greater coverage for business loans than was previously available by the FSLIC. With the assistance of Congressman Fernand St. Germain, a democrat from Rhode Island with experience as Chair of the House Banking Committee, legislation changed insurance coverage per savings and loan account from $40,000 to $100,000.

Many businesses, with quite a number in the real estate development field, filed and organized their loans and investments to take advantage of the government insurance provided to multi-account situations. It was argued that what happened in part was that a situation developed whereby many were rewarded for making risky investments. After the federal government changed the insurance coverage, if companies failed after reorganizing financially to take advantage of the adjusted loan insurance procedures, the government would help pay off failed risky investments. Eventually, of course, there was so much activity that the system collapsed.

Before the changes in the loan laws, insurance was relatively simple and low risk. Looking at the lower part of the grid in the JEMPP (Appendix A), we were at or near a pretty regulated environment, e.g., the FSLIC for personal loans, or the FDIC for certain business loan coverage. The focus was on issue/problem resolution by collaboration and cooperation.

The changes passed by Congress permitting multiple business accounts to be covered much more substantially changed the risks of the game significantly. There was a clear shift for efficiency as we see it at the top of the model. Freedom and innovation, along with the inherent risk, replaced safety and security. At the grid level of analysis, competition and zero sum (along with the gaming involved in this decision making dimension) became part of a new and more risky financial environment.

As it unfolded, the accumulating risk eventually caused the financial bubble to burst, and the savings and loan industry collapsed. This was a "Catalytic Event." It eventually cost the taxpayers about $500 billion with interest.

Below Catalytic Event at the top right of the model, we see the Re-Set Arrows; Partial and Full. After the savings and loan collapse (Catalytic Event), Congress changed some laws and procedures to prevent precisely the same thing (Catalytic Event situation) and the Power, Trust, and Consequences changes, from happening again. Among the Re-Set legislation was the following: The maximum penalty for bank fraud and embezzlement was raised from 20 to 30 years, with possible life in prison. Ten million dollars became the maximum fine. The government's ability to freeze or to seize assets was expanded. And whistleblower rewards were increased up to $250,000 for information leading to conviction. It was a Partial Re-Set...limited to savings and loan types of situations.

Hence, in the early years of the 21st century we get to experience a similar implosion of trust and credibility with the collapse of confidence in America's financial leadership and management. The NASDAQ collapse is but one symbol. The names Enron, Andersen, Ken Lay, and Joe Nacchio have become symbols for financial mismanagement and the consequent pain shareholders and employees have experienced as stocks collapsed and pensions disappeared.

The Re-Set after the 1990's Savings and Loan Catalytic Event was only partial. The lessons learned were not enough to deter us from the lure of the efficiency formula.

It should be remembered, however, that the stock market increased about ten times from about 1980 over the next two decades to about 11,000 before plummeting at the turn of the century. This reality helps to provide some additional perspective.

Yet, we embraced the efficiency of the market system beyond responsible standards. We began to have to address the kinds of questions asked at the beginning of this Finance section of this chapter. We came to know all too well the names of corporations and human stakeholders like Enron, Andersen, and Qwest; and Ken Lay, Joe Berardino, and Joe Nacchio.

We went, since the Savings and Loan Crisis/Catalytic Event, back towards the bottom of the model, to behaving like citizens, believing our government would protect us financially as we worked hard collaboratively together to solve our collective financial problems and issues, such as investments and pensions.

Yet, in reality we had not Re-Set the system fully enough to that more regulated environment. The serious corporate stakeholder gamers were playing the efficiency game. Some won, some lost. Some walked away with tens and even hundreds of millions of dollars. Some lost jobs, others shareholder value, and many others lost their pensions. With related events like stock market disruption, the overall impact was truly a Catalytic Event.

So, what is going on now to Re-Set the analytical model so this doesn't happen again? And, will we Re-Set the model partially, or try for a full Re-Set? Remember, where the Re-Set conflicts occurs, and how far it goes, is part of an incredible struggle. The forces of effectiveness are often at war with the forces of efficiency. And there are many fronts, including: values, legislation, civil and criminal courts, campaign finance laws, stakeholder interventions, research and publication, whistleblowers, bankruptcy and pension tactics and strategies, and more.

To date we have seen the following model Re-Set accomplishments. Congress has passed the Sarbanes-Oxley legislation regarding accounting standards. McCain-Feingold is the newer, more restrictive law dealing with campaign finance. The SEC has even filed civil law suits. As with Qwest, the Justice Department pressed criminal charges for: Ken Lay, Jeffrey Skilling, Joe Nacchio, Martha Stewart, John Rigas, Bernie Ebbers, and more.

Attorney General Elliot Spitzer in New York has gone after corporations doing business in New York. Former Attorney General, now U.S. Senator, Ken Salazar did the same in Colorado, on a smaller scale; investigating Qwest, Invesco, and Janus, for instance.

Values and ethics, and entrepreneurial management and public policy are being taught in business and public policy professional education more now. Research is being published in ethics journals, academic books, and professional management and policy journals, and in other publications.

Political appointees are reviewed more significantly. Harvey Pitt, President George W. Bush's appointment to head the SEC, was removed after arguments were made that he was too efficiency oriented for the role he was expected to perform. Some argued he was the proverbial fox in the henhouse.

Whistleblowers like Sherron Watkins at Enron are listened to more. Had Ken Lay heeded Ms Watkins early warning, Enron might have had a greater chance of survival. Ethics boards are listened to more as well. Carl Bass was ousted from his lead role on Andersen's ethical standards board by Joe Berardino who argued that "blessing the books" was important to clients. Had he listened to Carl Bass and his board, Andersen might still be viable today.

The lawsuits have returned some money to employees. Shareholder settlements and pension funds are the usual targets. The criminal cases have convicted some executives. John Rigas, Bernie Ebbers, and Martha Stewart were among the first. Ken Lay was also convicted but died of heart failure before sentencing. Jeffrey Skilling is serving a sentence of over 24 years. Joe Nacchio was convicted of 19 of 42 counts of insider trading in 2007.

The private sector can contribute as well. A stronger FASB would be able to provide more significant professional accountancy standards. There has also been talk of another market, a premium one with higher professional and ethical standards guaranteed, beyond the New York and American exchanges.

Public interest organizations like the Center for Public Integrity now have increased visibility. There are also new governance centers and institutes being founded, like that at the University of Southern California's School of Policy, Planning, and Development. The University of Denver's Daniels College of Business has courses which include business, public policy, ethics, and law. It now also has a Department of Business Ethics and Legal Studies.

Will all this, and more, lead to a significant Re-Set of the JEMPP Model, partially, or fully? Time will certainly tell. Because of the enormous forces aligned with both the efficiency and the effectiveness interest groups however, it is clear that analysts will need to keep a watchful eye on the struggle.

When the Rewards of efficiency can be So Great, skilled stakeholders will attempt to Win the Competition. Other stakeholders, especially those who value effectiveness and collegiality more, must therefore, remain constantly vigilant.

RE-SETTING THE MODEL FOR NASA

The Challenger

On January 28, 1986 NASA launched the Space Shuttle Challenger. 73 seconds later, after being launched from the Kennedy Space Center, the Challenger blew up. All seven crew members died in the explosion.

This event became a Catalytic Event for the National Aeronautics and Space Administration. How could the world renowned NASA have such a devastating crisis happen? NASA had scientists and engineers who were acknowledged to be among the very best in the world. It also had numerous highly successful space missions.

We have seen in this chapter (above) that beginning about 1980, the world of management and public policy shifted towards a significantly more entrepreneurial orientation. Effectiveness guidelines, based on standards for safety and security for instance, gave way to the new emphasis being placed on efficiency, or output over input. In the efficiency environment, spending for "excessive safety," for instance, would be frowned on.

William Rogers, a former U.S. Secretary of State, chaired what became known as the Rogers Commission. This investigative body analyzed what happened in the Challenger situation.

It did not take long to discover the following. The O rings, which sealed hot gases in, preventing the burning gases from destroying the Shuttle, had been suspect for a long time. Up to 43 different solutions to the O rings problem had been studied. The two major private sector contractors in the case, Morton Thiokol and Rockwell, both questioned the decision to launch in cold weather. NASA decided to launch as what they called a management decision versus an engineering decision, thereby bypassing the engineering questions and complaints (safety and effectiveness). This decision was made by NASA, with strong input from George Hardy, Deputy Director of Science and Engineering, and Lawrence Malloy, Chief of the Shuttle Projects Office of NASA, even though the O rings had been designated "criticality 1" items, or components whose failure would likely cause mission failure. This designation had been in effect for over 4 years when the Challenger event unfolded (Magneson, 1986).

In brief, the paradigm shift (Kuhn, 1970) from effectiveness to efficiency, which began significantly in the early 1980s, played a large role. NASA had expanded its launch schedule, without matching it to a comparable increase in resources. It was therefore, short on: money, time, personnel, engineering and hardware, etc. This increased the risk involved (efficiency) and placed pressure for performance on NASA managers. At one point, for instance, NASA's Mulloy stated: "My God, Thiokol, when do you want me to launch, next April?" (Magneson, 1986).

The Rogers Commissions investigation made it clear, in accordance with Johnston's Entrepreneurial Management and Public Policy Model (Appendix A), that NASA had made the move from effectiveness (safety) to efficiency (risk) and in going through the grid part of the analytical model revealed that power had increased (NASA made it a management decision, so towards risk and efficiency) thus eliminating significant engineering disapproval (effectiveness and safety decision criteria). Trust among the engineers collapsed, e.g. Thiokol did not bother objecting again. And the consequences went from a flight delay due to weather (effectiveness, safety), to an efficiency based high risk situation leading to the Catalytic Event of the Challenger explosion and its serious impact on NASA and its credibility.

Along the way management scholars also demonstrated that Irving Janis' Groupthink was at work in this situation. Most, or all of the symptoms were in play: invulnerability, rationale, morality, stereotypes, pressure, self-censorship, unanimity, and mindguards. At the same time most of the known viable remedies for Groupthink were missing from NASA during the Challenger disaster. These remedies include: critical evaluator, impartial stance, outside policy planning and evaluation groups, unit discussion before consensus, outside experts, devil's advocate, survey the relevant warning signs, subgroup review under different chairs, and second chance meetings to iron out residual doubts (Janis, 1985).

NASA's response to its Challenger Catalytic Event was a Partial Re-Set. It hired an expert on organization management, systems, and groupthink, Dianne Vaughan, to be a member of its staff. Then it paid little attention to her professional expertise. It had also had safety identified as a priority on its organization chart, but that proved to be amazingly thin. NASA also proved to be almost missing in action when it came to designing a viable crisis contingency plan which could include: an escape pod, hatch, or plan to deal with crew members in both the Challenger and, without a Full Re-Set, the Columbia which followed.

The Columbia

Challenger's Catalytic Event was based on its failure to deal adequately with a long history of negative feedback regarding its O rings. It had many chances to deal with the problem and had failed. Efficiency was valued over effectiveness. NASA claimed nothing like this would ever happen again.

Columbia failed over a grossly inadequate response to a history of foam chunk impacts on the wings and, at least as important, a near total collapse of leadership, management and engineering during the over two week period from launch to disintegration of the orbiter. NASA's failure to Re-SET the model more fully from Challenger to Columbia left the model in the direction of efficiency versus effectiveness.

Effectiveness as a management, systems, and policy model is expensive in the short run. There is a struggle between the forces of efficiency and those of effectiveness to prevail. If, the safety and security risks of efficiency are acceptable, then, after the efficiency revolution launched about 1980, we are likely to default to the efficiency environment. Thus, NASA did precisely that; and the risk of another Catalytic Event was taken on, and it unfolded with the disintegration of Columbia, and the deaths of all its astronauts.

After Challenger in 1986, NASA fixed the O ring problem. It partially Re-Set the model and brought Dianne Vaughan on board to help with their management systems. Her book: *Challenger; Launch Decision* (Vaughan, 1996) was geared to that situation. Yet, even after the Partial Re-Set towards more safety (effectiveness) after Challenger, NASA ignored Vaughan and blindly chased the efficiency model again, even as Columbia unfolded over a period of time.

In brief, the Columbia Catalytic Event developed as follows. Lift off occurs. 87 seconds of ascent later, chunks of foam hit the left wing. NASA management and engineering, based on a long history of foam debris hitting the shuttle, ignore the significance of the event. Yet some among NASA's engineering and management team are alarmed by the apparent size of the foam debris (estimated at 2 pounds) striking the orbiter at about 500 to 700 miles per hour. They want clearer film to analyze, more and better photographs, and an investigation.

Structural engineer Rodney Rocha requests outside agency, e.g. military, photographs of the shuttle's wing for damage analysis. He is emphatic enough to use the term "beg" to highlight what he believes to be an urgent situation. He learns the next day that his request is not even passed on. He wonders if this could eventually lead to a wheel well burn through.

Yet NASA does assemble a team to investigate the situation. The team asks for better photographic evidence. It wants enhancements of existing photos, as was eventually done after the disaster; or, perhaps outside agency photos. These were not provided.

Boeing engineers looked at the tiles under the wings, not on the leading edge. They concluded that the damage they expected to find would not be a safety of flight issue, even though it appeared to be a huge foam hit, versus past incidents.

NASA management sent an e-mail around indicating the foam impact was not even worth mentioning. Linda Hamm, co-chair of the flight management team, at a Columbia meeting shortly thereafter, said there was no safety of flight issue and NASA would do nothing different. Structural engineer Rodney Rocha said later that he felt like he would not be listened to even if he said anything, having been ignored like he had been so far. This is precisely how groupthink (above) works. Efficiency displaces effectiveness, and risk is taken on. In this case, Dianne Vaughan's management and systems analysis and recommendations could still likely have been of assistance. NASA management, however, ignored her contributions, ignored valuable possible photo evidence, did not plan for any repair, and did not plan for a rescue. They did not even let the astronauts know of the potentially catastrophic foam damage, even though one of the astronauts, from space, thanked the "team" for all their help.

Over two weeks elapsed with the NASA ground team negligently not even getting photo evidence to be able to use to analyze the damage, asses the risk, or plan a fix or a rescue. This is efficiency at its extreme unfolding before the world.

Then the reentry. Traveling at the extreme speeds that accompany reentering the earth's atmosphere, Columbia developed the superheated gases around the orbiter that scientists often call plasma. As it descended over the southwest, plasma entered the breach at the front of the left wing and burned the wing from the inside out. Debris fell from the shuttle over Arizona and New Mexico, over a 250 mile path, until it disintegrated over Texas.

An investigative board later concluded that a 2 pound piece of foam traveling at 700 miles per hour had breached the leading edge of Columbia's left wing (smoking gun) which was made of reinforced carbon, and this caused a three foot hole that later let the super heated gases inside the wing on reentry, causing the Catalytic Event.

Dianne Vaughan, hired to prevent such management and systems breakdowns, said NASA management yet again became "comfortable," quoting Ron Dittemore, the Columbia Flight Program Manager, and noting this is virtually identical to what happened to Challenger based on the O rings, when management and systems were analyzed. She stated: "This was not just about foam. This was a failure of the system".

The post Catalytic Event Investigative Board concluded: "Safety was dangerously inadequate. There was no significant safety discovered when the board analyzed it in terms of: budget cuts, people, engineering, analysis, or expertise. NASA's claim of having 1,700 people trained on safety was only on paper. There was No there there (Gibson, 2003).

NASA, yet again, says it will change (Re-Set the JEMPP model for more safety). Linda Hamm and other senior managers were reassigned. NASA indicated: "This is not about holding individuals accountable."

The NASA Investigative Board also suggested that a space repair or even a space rescue might have been possible. But, these are products and processes of the effectiveness environment, not of efficiency. NASA's behavior and performance was a natural unfolding of efficiency. Viable contingency plans, systems integration, and the kind of leadership and management that would focus on actual safety, or effectiveness, have those standards in its DNA. Efficiency simply does not.

So, we see that NASA suffered the Challenger disaster by relying on efficiency too much. It then said it would Re-Set the model substantially towards effectiveness. But we have just seen that Columbia was the result of too much efficiency yet again.

Using the grid (Appendix A) for analysis, we see that: ...As the situation with Columbia unfolded, decisions were power based; Hamm deciding no safety of flight risk, versus listening to engineer Rodney Rocha who begged for better photo evidence. Trust diminished dramatically so even Rocha later signed off (without negative photo evidence) as ok, believing no one would ever listen to him seriously. And the consequences were severe. Indeed, the Shuttle Columbia was destroyed, all the astronauts died, and NASA'a credibility evaporated, a clear Catalytic Event for NASA.

NASA says it will fix itself in the future. An awful lot of change will have to happen before that day comes. One alternative is for NASA to use a lot more robotics and a lot less manpower. Almost an astronaut per year died, from Challenger to Columbia. Other options are: to really fund the changes required; and to seriously train NASA's leadership, management, engineers, and staff; and to genuinely develop safety based contingency plans. In brief, NASA needs to fully Re-Set the Entrepreneurial Management and Public Policy Model from efficiency to effectiveness.

RE-SETTING THE MODEL FOR THE FEDERAL EMERGENCY MANAGEMENT AGENCY

Our analysis of the public policy and business case situations: terrorism, finance, and NASA; unfolds differently with FEMA. We have seen so far with these case situations that second catalytic events occur because there has not been a relatively full Re-Set from the efficiency environment to effectiveness when applying the entrepreneurial management and public policy model.

If we start our analysis of FEMA through Hurricane Andrew in Florida in 1992, we would find FEMA at the efficiency end of the model at the top, practically inviting a Catalytic Event. Hurricane Andrew proved to be that event. It broadcast to everyone who paid attention that FEMA was broken.

Shortly after Andrew in 1992, President Bill Clinton and Vice President Al Gore initiated a program to professionalize management in the federal government. This public sector version of business' reengineering (Hammer and Champty, 1993) and total quality management (Hyde, 1995; Johnston, 1995a,b) was called reinventing government (Osborne and Gaebler, 1991; Moe, 1994; Kettl, 1994; Johnston, 1996a,b,c). It was based on the National Performance Review (NPR) that Vice President Al Gore undertook from his office (Gore, 1993, 1994, 1996). Reinventing government for FEMA came in two stages: NPR 1 which enhanced its performance and changed its culture; and NPR 2 which worked to lower the costs of national disasters through investigation efforts (Useem, Chapter 7, 2000).

President Clinton also provided FEMA with an exceptional leader and manager when he appointed James Lee Witt to be Director of the 2,700 employee agency that had been formed in 1979 to improve the federal government's disaster management efforts. Director Witt embraced the values and goals of the National Performance Review (NPR) right away. His commitment, diligence, professionalism and skills in leading and managing his employees translated into support and respect from his employees. His ability and interest in creating partnerships with other agencies of government at different levels, in accordance with the NPR, led to increased cooperation for performance and enhanced networking for team approaches to problem solving. Eventually, these cooperative ventures even became formalized as performance partnership agreements (Useem, Chapter 7, 2000).

It was in this far more serious effectiveness environment, after the relatively primitive efficiency oriented Hurricane Andrew environment, that FEMA would be tested when the 1994 Northridge, California earthquake ripped onto the scene. Based on Director Witt's priority for implementing the NPR directives within FEMA at the outset of his leadership, the Agency had already prepared a dedicated and skilled staff of emergency management employees. With substantial progress in implementing NPR 1 goals already achieved, FEMA had become a seriously professionalized and disciplined problem solving organization oriented towards empowering its workers to cut through red tape and make better decisions towards delivering its services more optimally.

In brief, FEMA was well on its way towards an effectiveness based agency, transformed from the efficiency oriented organization that was criticized so much after its poor performance in dealing with Hurricane Andrew. FEMA's outstanding performance with the Northridge Earthquake informed that the agency had indeed transformed itself (Useem, Chapter 7, 2000). It was ready to move on to even more effectiveness based challenges by developing agreements with state and local agencies. Its transformation from the efficiency based poor performance with Hurricane Andrew to its effectiveness accomplishments with the Northridge Earthquake were recognized universally by emergency management professionals. FEMA had accomplished a virtually full Re-Set of the entrepreneurial management and public policy model (Appendix A).

FEMA's efforts in accordance with NPR 2 to develop performance partnership agreements (PPA) dealing with these state and local governments, traditionally primarily responsible for their own disaster management programs, would expand and enhance the effectiveness oriented and network based mitigation efforts. Behind the scenes a clear goal was to lower and control the costs incurred with national disasters (Useem, Chapter 7, 2000).

When the terrorists attacked on September 11, 2001, we began to witness a paradigm shift unfold. With the creation of the huge 170,000 employee federal Department of Homeland Security to deal with terrorism, FEMA became part of this new mega agency, along with over 20 other federal agencies, programs and offices. We had also elected a new, more conservative president. George W. Bush was elected over President Clinton's Vice President Al Gore in a close race.

As the new, more conservative and more efficiency based policy and management environment of President George W. Bush began to be implemented, resources and professionals ebbed away from FEMA. James Lee Witt was gone. Mr. Michael Brown became the new FEMA Director.

His credentials were not in the emergency management arena. The evolution of the new Department of Homeland Security focused more on the threat of terrorism, after 9-11. The practical effect of this on FEMA was that its mission was devalued. Its budget was diminished. Its professionals were marginalized, often replaced with new employees with little or no experience in emergency management.

The George W. Bush emphasis on efficiency took over. Lowest common denominator output over input replaced the more effectiveness based values (safety and security) that FEMA had embraced after Hurricane Andrew when it performed so admirably in working on the Northridge, California Earthquake disaster. The organizational mission, training, values, networking, budgets, and infrastructure began to break down.

It did not take long before FEMA became one of the least desirable places to work in the federal government (Johnston and Schulz, The Federal Emergency Management Agency and Hurricane Katrina, Chapter 8). In brief, FEMA had regressed from a professionally developed effectiveness based emergency management agency to a marginal efficiency based organization that did not even have the respect of its own professionals.

In terms of the Entrepreneurial Management and Public Policy Model (Appendix A), FEMA had regressed from the bottom of the model (effectiveness) to the top of the model (efficiency) where it was vulnerable to a catalytic event (top right). Hurricane Katrina proved to be that Catalytic Event. Katrina turned out to be the "big one" that Gulf Coast residents had talked about for decades. This monster hurricane demonstrated that FEMA had transformed once again. However, unlike the positive Re-Set transformation of FEMA from Hurricane Andrew (efficiency) to the professional performance it demonstrated with the Northridge Earthquake (effectiveness), Hurricane Katrina so completely overwhelmed FEMA and its ability to respond meaningfully that the question for most who were looking for significant professional government emergency management performance was: "Where is FEMA?" (Morris, 2006).

The Re-Set activity with Hurricane Katrina was not the proactive positive improvement from efficiency to effectiveness based performance. It was not only not a Full Re-Set, it was not even a partial Re-Set. It was in fact quite the opposite. Having achieved close to a Full Re-Set optimizing effectiveness with its performance in the Northridge Earthquake, the collapse of FEMA precipitated by the Catalytic Event of Hurricane Katrina was almost predictable, given the severe efficiency based changes made with regard to FEMA after 9-11 and the development of the Department of Homeland Security (Useem, Chapter 7; Johnston and Schulz, Chapter 8; Haynes and Wright, Chapter 17).

It remains to be seen if FEMA will be able to recover as a viable organization. Emergency management organizations have effectiveness based missions. They focus on safety and security. It could be argued that FEMA's best hope could come with a change of national leadership which could shift the organization's emphasis once again towards effectiveness (output/standards) and Re-Set the Entrepreneurial Management and Public Policy model away from simple efficiency (output/input).

RE-SETTING THE MODEL FOR OPTIMAL EFFECTIVENESS AND EFFICIENCY

We have seen in the case examples analyzed above: terrorism; business, public policy and finance; NASA; and FEMA; that when efficiency is emphasized too much, not only does effectiveness diminish, but risk increases to levels where we can suffer serious Catalytic Events.

Efficiency is necessary to a certain extent. Without it, waste and lack of accountability can become rampant. When dealing with business and public policy problems and stakeholder issues, however, effectiveness must be a significant consideration. A balance of effectiveness and efficiency, based on the situation being managed, is necessary to have professional entrepreneurial management and public policy.

COLLABORATION VS. COMPETITION: A 21ST CENTURY CHALLENGE

In the early 21st century we are witnessing new emphasis on controlling the dysfunctions resulting from unbridled efficiency. This over reliance on market based efficiency is often regarded as the COMPETITION model of decision making in the public policy and business arena. The cases analyzed in this chapter are classic examples of the short term, bottom line, managerial practices that so often end in disaster; leaving damaged stakeholders and significant unfunded liabilities.

Emerging from this sort of excessive competition and efficiency based performance is an increasing awareness of the potential value of more COLLABORATION. This model is based on effectiveness, or output over standards. It is more time consuming. It is more participatory and inclusive. It focuses more on planning, safety, and security. Collaboration based organizational performance is increasingly well received as we move more into the 21st century. Current viable Collaboration examples include:

Denver's multi billion dollar T-REX transportation mega expansion project (Johnston, Haynes, and Schulz, 2006); Collaboration for improving rail security across America (Johnston and Plant, 2007 a); Collaboration for improving intermodal transportation security (Johnston, Seidenstat, and Johnston, 2007 b); and intersector and international collaboration by utilizing privatization and contracting out (Johnston and Seidenstat, 2007 c).

Looking at Johnston's Entrepreneurial Management and Public Policy Model, the term COMPETITION can be applied at the top, where efficiency and the deregulated environment reside. COLLABORATION can be added to the JEMPP model at the bottom, where effectiveness and the more regulated environment exist (Appendix B). This is the same model we have been exploring throughout this chapter, but with the added perspective of the competition versus collaboration interface.

The challenge for the 21st century is to optimally apply the lessons being taught in management, public policy and administration, and business schools across the country. Our current understanding demonstrates that optimal contingency applications of collaborative and competitive management models and systems, as noted in the recent collaboration examples and manuscripts cited above in this last section of this chapter, can deliver much more satisfactory results for our organizations and stakeholders if we exercise both the will and the skill necessary for quality professional organizational performance.

REFERENCES

Berman, E.M. (1997). Dealing with cynical citizens. *Public Administration Review*, *57*(2), 105-112.

Bozeman, B. (1987). *All organizations are public: Bridging public and private organizational theories*. San Francisco: Jossey-Bass.

De Leon, L. (1996). Ethics and Entrepreneurship. *Policy Studies Journal*, *24*(3), 495-510.

Donahue, J.D. (1989). *The privatization decision: Public ends, private means*. New York: Basic.

Gibson, C. (July 7, 2003). *Columbia Final Mission* [Television broadcast]. ABC News Special Report.

Gore, Jr., A.E. (1993). *From red tape to results: creating a government that works better and costs less* (National Performance Review Report). Washington, DC: U.S. Government Printing Office.

Gore, Jr., A.E. (1994). *Creating a government that works better and costs less: status report* (National Performance Review Report). Washington, DC: U.S. Government Printing Office.

Gore, Jr., A.E. (1996). *Reaching public goals: Managing government for results* (National Performance Review Report). Washington, DC: U.S. Government Printing Office.

Halachmi, A. (1996). Franchising in government: can a principal agent theory be the first step towards a theory? *Policy Studies Journal*, *24*(3), 478-494.

Halachmi, A. (1998). Franchising in government: an idea in search of a theory. In A. Halachmi, and P. B. Boorsma (Eds.), *Inter and intra government arrangements for productivity: an agency approach* (pp. 45-58). Boston: Kluwer Academic.

Hammer, M., & Champty, J. (1993). *Reengineering the corporation: a manifesto for business revolution*. New York, NY: HarperBusiness.

Hyde, A.C. (1995). Quality reengineering and performance: managing change in the public sector. In A. Halachmi, & G. Bouckaert (Eds.), *The enduring challenges in public management surviving and excelling in a changing world* (pp. 150-176). San Francisco: Jossey-Bass.

Janis, L. (1985). Groupthink in organizations. In J. L. Gibson, J. M. Ivancevich, and J. H. Donnelly (Eds.), *Organizations close-up: a book of readings*, 5th ed. (pp. 166-177). Plano: Business Publications.

Johnston, V.R. (1995a). Caveat emptor: Customers vs. citizens. *The Public Manager - The New Bureaucrat*, *24*(3), 11-14.

Johnston, V.R. (1995b). Increasing quality and productivity: strategic planning, TQM and beyond. In A. Halachmi, and G. Bouckaert (Eds.), *Public productivity through quality and strategic management* (pp. 83-97). Brussels: International Institute of Administrative Sciences.

Johnston, V.R. (1996a). Optimizing productivity through privatization and entrepreneurial management. *Policy Studies Journal*, *24*(3), 439-443.

Johnston, V.R. (1996b). Privatization and entrepreneurial management. *Policy Studies Journal*, *24*(3), 437-443.

Johnston, V.R. (1996c). The entrepreneurial transformation: from privatization, reinventing, and re-engineering, to franchising, efficiency, and entrepreneurial ethics. *Policy Studies Journal*, *24*(3), 444-463.

Johnston, V.R. (1999). *Trust, cynicism and credibility in air transportation policy and administration* (National Conference Professional Paper). Orlando: American Society for Public Administration.

Johnston, V.R. (2000). *Entrepreneurial management and public policy*. Huntington, N.Y: Nova Science Publishers.

Johnston, V.R. (2001). *Air transportation policy and administration* (National Conference Professional Paper). Newark: American Society for Public Administration.

Johnston, V.R. (2002a). Air transportation policy and administration at the millennium. *Review of Policy Research*, *19*(2), 109-127.

Johnston, V.R. (Winter,2002b). Effective security and safety vs. efficiency contracting And freedom in our transportation systems at the millennium. *Intermodal Fare*, 3-6.

Johnston, V.R. (2004). Terrorism and Transportation Policy and Administration: Balancing the Model and Equations for Optimal Security. *Review of Policy Research*, *21*(3), 263-274.

Johnston, V.R., Haynes, W., and Schulz, C.L. (2006). The T-REX Megaproject: Denver's Showcase for Innovation and Creativity, *The Public Manager*, 35(2), 3-8.

Johnston, V.R., and Plant, J.F. (2007,a). Towards Increasingly Collaborative Transportation Security: The Case of Rail Security. A Professional Paper delivered at the National Conference of the American Society for Public Administration, Washington, DC, March, 2007.

Johnston, V.R., Seidenstat, P., and Johnston, E.W. (2007b). Transportation Security Policy, Chapter 27 in the *Handbook of Transportation Policy and Administration*,

Plant, J.F. (Editor), and Johnston, V.R. (Associate Editor). Handbook 127 in the series. Boca Raton, FL: CRC Press, Taylor and Francis Group, Publishers, 525-536.

Johnston, V.R., and Seidenstat, P. (2007c). Contracting Out Government Services: Privatization at the Millenium. *International Journal of Public Administration*, (30,3), 231-247.

Kettl, D.F. (1994). *Reinventing government? Appraising the national performance review* (CPM Report 9402). Washington, D.C.: Center for Public Management, The Brookings Institution.

Kouzes, J.M., and Posner, B.Z. (1993). *Credibility: how leaders gain and lose it, why people demand it*. San Francisco: Jossey-Bass.

Kuhn, T. (1970). *The Structure of Scientific Revolutions*. Chicago: University of Chicago Press.

Landon, R. (2002). Tools for governing: Privatization, public-private partnerships, and entrepreneurial management. *Public Administration Review*, 62(1), 118-122.

Magneson, E. (March 10, 1986). A Serious Deficiency. *Time*.

Moe, R.C. (1994). The 'reinventing government' exercise: misinterpreting the problem, misjudging the consequence. *Public Administration Review*, 54(2), 111-122.

Morris, J.C. (2006). Whither FEMA? Hurricane Katrina and FEMA's Response to the Gulf Coast. *Public Works Management and Policy*, 10(4), 284-294.

Osborne, D., and Gaebler, T. (1991). *Reinventing government: how the entrepreneurial spirit is transforming the public sector*. New York: Addison-Wesley.

Savas, E.S. (1982). *Privatizing the public sector: how to shrink government*. Chatham: Chatham House.

Schiavo, M.F. (2001). *Homeland defense and crisis management*. Retrieved March 12, 2004, from http://www.e-gov.com/events/2002/hls2/downloads/hlsdec18report.pdf

Senge, P.M. (1990). *The fifth discipline: the art and practice of the learning organization*. New York: Doubleday/Currency.

U.S. State Department. (2001). *Countering the changing threat of international terrorism*. Retrieved January 21, 2001, from http://w3.access.gpo.gov/nct

Vaughan, D. (1996). *The Challenger launch decision: risky technology, culture, and deviance at NASA*. Chicago: University of Chicago Press.

Wicks, A.C., Berman, S.L., and Jones, T.M. (1999). The structure of optimal trust: moral and strategic implications. *Academy of Management Review*, 24(1), 99-116.

APPENDIX A

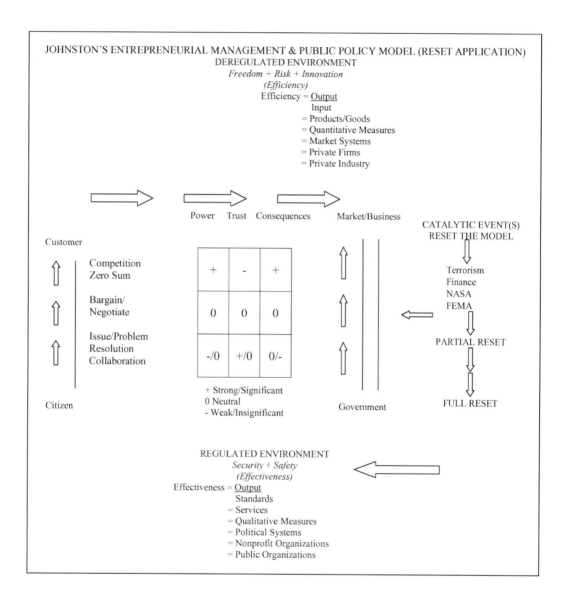

APPENDIX B

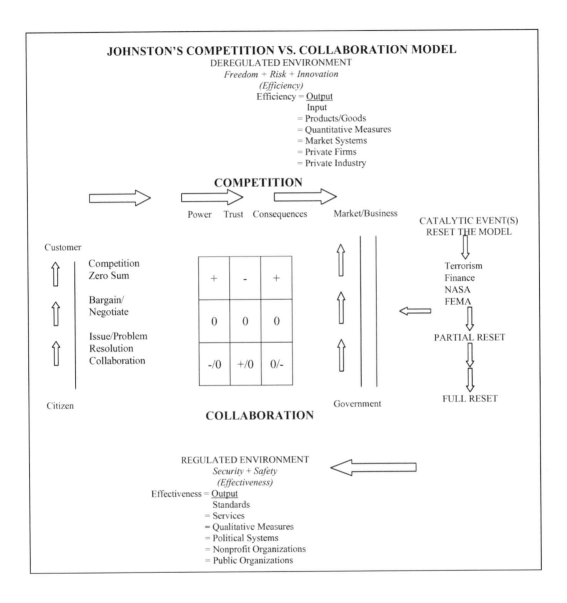

JOHNSTON'S COMPETITION VS. COLLABORATION MODEL
DEREGULATED ENVIRONMENT
Freedom + Risk + Innovation
(Efficiency)
Efficiency = Output
Input
= Products/Goods
= Quantitative Measures
= Market Systems
= Private Firms
= Private Industry

COMPETITION

Power   Trust   Consequences   Market/Business

CATALYTIC EVENT(S)
RESET THE MODEL

Customer

Competition
Zero Sum

Terrorism
Finance
NASA
FEMA

Bargain/
Negotiate

Issue/Problem
Resolution
Collaboration

+	-	+
0	0	0
-/0	+/0	0/-

PARTIAL RESET

Citizen   Government

FULL RESET

COLLABORATION

REGULATED ENVIRONMENT
Security + Safety
(Effectiveness)
Effectiveness = Output
Standards
= Services
= Qualitative Measures
= Political Systems
= Nonprofit Organizations
= Public Organizations

SELECTED BIBLIOGRAPHY

Albrecht, K. 1990. *Service Within.* Homewood, III: Dow Jones Irwin.

Ambrose, M. 1997. "A new way of thinking about customer service," *Business Communications Review,* 27 (7), 51-55.

Anders, K., et. al. 2003. "New federalism: Impact on state and local governments." *Journal of Public Budgeting, Accounting, and Financial Management,* 15, (3), 466-486.

Annandale, D., Morrison-Saunders, A., and Bouma, G. 2004. The Impact of Voluntary Environmental Instruments on Company Environmental Performance. *Business Strategy and the Environment,* 13, 1-12.

Arora, R. & Stoner, C. 1996. "The effect of perceived service quality and name familiarity on the service selection decision. *The Journal of Service Marketing,* 10 (1), 22-34.

Arrow, K.J. 1985. "The Economics of Agency," In *Principals and Agents: The Structure of American Business,* Boston: Harvard Business School Press.

Asubonteng, P., McCleary, K.J., and Swan, J.E. 1996. "SERVQUAL revisited: a Critical review of service quality," *The Journal of Services Marketing,* 10 (6), 62-81.

Axelrod, R. and Koehane, R.O. 1985. "Achieving Cooperation under Anarchy," *World Politics,* 38 (3), 226-253.

Babin, B.J. and M. Griffin. 1998. "The Nature of Satisfaction: An Updated Examination," *Journal of Business Research,* 41, 127-136.

Ban, C. 1991. "The Navy Demonstration Project: An 'Experiment in Experimentation," In Ban, C. and Riccucci, N.M. (Eds.), *Public Personnel Management – Current Concerns, Future Challenges.* White Plains, NY: Longman Publishing Group. 31-41.

Bardack, E. 1977. *The Implementation Game: What Happens After a Bill Becomes a Law.* Cambridge, MA: The MIT Press.

Barney, J. B. and Hesterly, W. 1996. "Organizational Economics: Understanding the Relationships between Organizations and Economic Analysis," In Clegg, S.R., Hardy, C., and Nord, W. R. (Eds.), *Handbook of Organizational Studies.* Thousand Oaks, CA: Sage, 115-147.

Barr, S. September 14, 2005. Morale among FEMA workers on decline for years, hits nadir. *Washington Post*, B2.

Bellone, Carl J. and Goerl, G.F. 1992. "Reconciling public entrepreneurship and democracy," *Public Administration Review,* 52 (2), 130-134.

Bellone, Carl J. and G. F. Goerl. 1993. "In defense of civic-regarding entrepreneurship, or helping the wolves to promote good citizenship," *Public Administration Review,* 53 (4), 396-398.

Berman, E. M. 1997. "Dealing with cynical citizens," *Public Administration Review,* 57 (2), 105-112.

Berman, E.M., Lynch, T.D., Lynch, C.E. and Berman, M.D. October, 2005. There was no plan – A Louisiana perspective. *PA Times,* 3-5.

Bernstein, Aaron. 1990. *Grounded: Frank Lorenzo and the Destruction of Eastern Airlines.* New York: Simon and Schuster.

Berry, L.L., Zeithaml, V.A. and Parasuraman, A. Summer, 1990. "Five Imperatives for Improving service quality," *Sloan Management Review, 29-38.*

Block, R. August 7, 2006. FEMA regroups after Katrina, but some question its readiness. *Wall Street Journal*, A1.

Block, R. September 19, 2006. Politics and Economics: FEMA revamp snubs Homeland Security Chief; Congressional negotiators unraveled some changes Chertoff had supported. *Wall Street Journal.* A8.

Bolman, L. G. and T. E. Deal, T.E. 2003. *Reframing Organizations: Artistry, Choice, and Leadership.* Third edition. San Francisco: Jossey-Bass.

Bonner, S., and Sprinkle, G. 2002. The effects of monetary incentives on effort and task performance: theories, evidence, and a framework for research. *Accounting, Organizations, and Society,* 27(4), 303-345.

Boycko, M., Schleifer, A., Vishny, R.AW. March, 1996. "A theory of privatization," *The Economic Journal,* 106, 309-319.

Boyett, I. 1996. "The public sector entrepreneur – a definition," *International Journal of Public Sector Management,* 9 (2), 36-51.

Bozeman, Barry. 1987. *All Organizations Are Public: Bridging Public and Private Organizational Theories.* San Francisco: Jossey Bass.

Bretschneider, S. 2003. "Information technology, e-government, and institutional Change," *Public Administration Review,* 63 (6), 738-741.

Brookings Publication. 2002. *Project on Homeland Security – Chapter 7: Organizing for Success.* Washington, DC: Brookings Institution, 99-124.

Brown, S. L. and Eisenhardt, K.M. 1998. *Competing on the Edge.* Boston: Harvard Business School Press.

Bryant, B. E. 1996. Customers are different: Satisfying all types is a challenge (Working paper #9690-04). University of Michigan Business School, Ann Arbor, MI, 1-1.

Butz, H.E., and Goodstein, L. Winter, 1996. "Measuring customer value: gaining the strategic advantage," *Organizational Dynamics,* 24, 63-77.

Caiden, Gerald E. 1994. "Administrative reform – American style," *Public Administration Review,* 54 (2), 123-128.

Carr, Nicholas G. 2004. *Does It Matter?* Boston: Harvard Business School Press.

Carson, T.L. 2004. "Self-interest and business ethics: Some lessons of the recent corporate scandals," *Journal of Business Ethics,* 43 (3), 389-394.

Carver, R. H. 1989. Examining the premises of contracting out," *Public Productivity and Management Review,* 13 (1), 27-40.

Carroll, J. D., and Lynn, D. B. 1995. "The rhetoric of reform and political reality in the National Performance Review," *Public Administration Review,* 55 (3), 299-304.

Casson, M.C. 1991. *The Economics of Business Culture.* Oxford, UK: Clarendon Press.

Caudle, S. 2005. "Homeland security: approaches to results management," *Public Performance & Management Review.* 28 (3): 352-375.

Chambliss, S. 2002. *Counterterrorism Intelligence Capabilities and Performance Prior to 9/11.* Report of the Subcommittee on Terrorism and Homeland Security, House Permanent Select Committee on Intelligence, U.S. House of Representatives. Washington DC: Government Printing Office.

Chandler, T. and Feuille, P. 1991. "Municipal unions and privatization," *Public Administration Review,* 51 (1), 15-21.

Chen, W. H. 1998. "Benchmarking quality goals in service systems," *The Journal of Services Marketing,* 12 (2), 113-128.

Cleveland H. 1972. *The Future Executive.* New York: Harper and Row.

Clow, K.E., Kurtz, D.L., and Ozment, J. 1998. "A longitudinal study of the stability of consumer expectations of services," *Journal of Business Research,* 42, 63-73.

Coglianese, C., and Nash, J. (Eds.). 2001. *Regulating from the Inside: Can Environmental Management Systems Achieve Policy Goals?* Washington, DC: Resources for the Future.

Cohen, M. D., and March, J.G., and Olsen, J.P. 1972. "A garbage can model of organizational choice," *Administrative Science Quarterly,* 17, 1-25.

Cohen, M.J. 2004. "George W. Bush and the Environmental Protection Agency: A Midterm Appraisal," *Society and Natural Resources,* 17.

Comfort, L.K., and Haase, T.W. April, 2006. Communication, Coherence, and Collective Action: The Impact of Hurricane Katrina on Communications Infrastructure. *Public Works Management and Policy,* 10(4), 328-343.

Courty, P., and Marschke, G. 2004. A general test of gaming. (Discussion Paper No. 4514; ISSN 0265-8003). London: Centre for Policy Research.

Dale, T.B. Summer, 2000. "Political Obstacles to the Implementation of Emissions Markets: The Lessons of RECLAIM," *Natural Resources Journal.*

Davidow, William and Malone, Michael. December 7, 1992. "The Virtual Corporation," *Forbes Technology Supplement,* 102-105.

Day, G. S. 1998. "What does it mean to be market driven?" *Business Strategy Review,* 9 (1), 1-14.

De Hoog, R. H. 1984. "Theoretical Perspectives on Contracting Out Government Services," In Edwards, G.C. III (Ed.), *Public Policy Implementation.* Greenwich, CT: JAI Press, 227-259.

de Leon, Linda. 1993. "As easy as 1,2,3...and 4: Ethics and organization structure," *Administration and Society,* 25 (3), 293-316.

de Leon, Linda. 1994. "Embracing anarchy: Network organization and interorganizational networks," *Administrative Theory and Praxis,* 16 (2), 234-252.

de Leon, Linda. 1996. "Ethics and entrepreneurship," *Policy Studies Journal,* 24 (3), 495-510.

de Leon, L. 1998. "Accountability in a 'reinvented' government," *Public Administration,* 76, (3): 539-558. Reprinted in Bill Jenkins and Edward C. Page, Eds., *The Foundations of Bureaucracy in Economic And Social Thought* (Volume II). 2004. Cheltenham, UK: Edward Elgar Publishing, Limited.

DiIulio, John J., Jr., 1987. *Governing Prisons: A Comparative Study of Correctional Management,* New York: Free Press.

DiIulio, John J., Jr., 1989. "Recovering the public management variable; Lessons from schools, prisons, armies," *Public Administration Review,* 49 (2), 127-133.

DiIulio, J.J., Jr., Garvey, G.and Kettl, D.F. 1993. *Improving Government Performance: An Owner's Manual.* Washington, DC: The Brookings Institution.

Dilworth, R. R. 1996. "Institutionalizing learning in the public sector," *Public Productivity and Management Review,* 19, June, 407-421.

Dimock, M. 1980. *Law and Dynamic Administration.* New York: Praeger Publishers.

Doig, J. W. and E.C. Hargrove. 1987. *Leadership and Innovation; A Biographical Perspective on Entrepreneurs in Government.* Baltimore: the Johns Hopkins University Press.

Dolsak, N., and E. Ostrom. 2003. *The Commons in the New Millenium Challenges And Adaptation.* Cambridge, MA: MIT Press.

Donahue, John D. 1989 *The Privatization Decision: Public Ends, Private Means.* New York: Basic Books, Inc.

Donahue, A. K. and Joyce, P.G. 2001. "A framework for analyzing emergency management with an application to federal budgeting," *Public Administration Review.* 61 (6): 728-740.

Donahue, A. K. 2004. "Managerial perceptions and the production of fire protection," *Administration & Society.* 35 (6): 717-46.

Drew, C., and Oppel, R.A. Jr., March 6, 2004. How Industry Won the Battle of Pollution Control at E.P.A. *The New York Times.*

Drucker, Peter F. 1985. *Innovation and Entrepreneurship.* New York: Harper.

Dubnick, M.J., & Romzek, B.S. 1991. *American Public Administration: Politics And the Management of Expectations.* New York: Macmillan.

Eggers, W. D. 1994. *Rightsizing Government: Lessons for America's Public Sector Innovators.* Los Angeles: The Reason Foundation.

Eichenwald, K. 2005. *Conspiracy of Fools.* New York: Broadway Books (Random House).

Eisner, M.A., April, 2004. "Corporate Environmentalism, Regulatory reform, and Industry Self-Regulation: Toward Genuine Regulatory Reinvention in the United States," *Governance: An International Journal of Policy, Administration, And Institutions,* 17(2), 145-167.

Elmore, R. F. 1986. "Graduate education in public management: Working the seams of government," *Journal of Policy Analysis and Management.* 6 (1), 69-83.

Field, Mary A. 2002. "Highway Intermodal freight Transportation: A policy And administration challenge for the new millennium," *The Review of Policy Research*, 19 (2), 33-50.

Field, Mary, A. 2004. "Highway security and terrorism," *The Review of Policy Research*, 21 (3), 317-328.

Fisher, F. 1983. "The New Entrepreneurs," In B.H. Moore, *The Entrepreneur In Local Government*. Washington, DC, International City Management Association, 9-14.

Florida, R., and Davison, D. 2001. "Why Do Firms Adopt Advanced Environmental Practices (And Do They Make A Difference)?" In C. Coglianese, and J. Nash (Eds.), *Regulating From the Inside: Can Environmental Management Systems Achieve Policy Goals?* Washington, DC: Resources for the Future.

Foster, C.D. 1992. *Privatization, Public Ownership and the Regulation of Natural Monopoly*. Oxford: Blackwell.

Fox, C. J. 1996. "Reinventing government as postmodern symbolic politics," *Public Administration Review*, 56 (3), 256-261.

Fredrickson, H.G. 1996. "Comparing the reinventing government movement with the new public administration," *Public Administration Review*, 56 (3), 263-269.

Frederickson, G. H. 2005. *Public Administration with an Attitude*. Washington, DC: American Society for Public Administration.

Gibson, Charles. 2003. Columbia: Final Mission. *ABC News Special Report*, July 7 Broadcast.

Gilbert, G. R., Nicholls, J.A.F. 1999. "Measuring public sector customer service Satisfaction," *The Public Manager*, 27 (4), 21-26.

Gilmore, J.S. III, Chairman. 2002. *Fourth annual report to the President and the Congress of the advisory panel to assess domestic response capabilities for terrorism involving weapons of mass destruction* (a.k.a. - the Gilmore Commission). Washington, DC: Government Printing Office.

Goggin, M.L., Boman, A., Lester, J.P., and O'Toole, L. 1998. *Implementation Theory and Practice: Toward a Third Generation*. New York: Harper Collins.

Golembieski, R.T., Stevenson, J., and White, M. 1997. *Cases in Public Management*. Itsaca: F. E. Peacock, p. 119.

Goodsell, Charles T. 1993. "Reinvent government or rediscover it," *Public Administration Review*, 53 (1), 85-87.

Gore, Albert E., Jr. 1993. *From Red Tape to Results: Creating a Government That Works Better And Costs Less*. Report of the *National Performance Review*. Washington DC: U.S. government Printing Office.

Gore, Albert E., Jr. 1994. *Creating a Government That Works Better And Costs Less: Status Report*. Washington DC: U.S. Government Printing Office.

Gore, Albert E., Jr. 1996 *Reaching Public Goals: Managing Government for Results*, National Performance Review. U.S. Government Printing Office.

Grunwald, M., and Glasser, S.B. December 23, 2005. Brown's turf wars sapped FEMA's strength. *Washington Post*, A1.

Gurwitt, R. 1994. "Entrepreneurial government: The morning after." *Governing*, 7 (8), 34-40.

Halachmi, Arie. 1994" The Challenge of the Competitive Sector," In *the Enduring Challenges in Public Management: Surviving and Excelling in a Changing World*. San Francisco: Jossey-Bass, 220-223.

Halachmi, Arie. 1996. "Franchising in government: Can a principal – agent perspective be the first step towards a theory?" *Policy Studies Journal,* 24 (3), 478-494.

Halachmi, Arie and R. Boydston, 1994. "The Political Economy of Outsourcing," In Kahn, A., and Hildreth, B. *Public Budgeting and Financial Management*. DuBuque, IA: Kendall Hunt Publishing Company.

Halachmi, Arie. 1998. "Franchising in Government; An Idea In Search of a Theory," Chapter 4 in Halachmi, A. and P. Boorsma (Eds.), *Inter and Intra Government Arrangements for Productivity: An Agency Approach*. Boston: Kluwer Academic Publishers, 45-58.

Halachmi, Arie. 2002. Performance Measurement: A look at some possible dysfunctions. *Work Study*. 51(5), 230-239.

Halachmi, Arie. 2005. Performance Measurement: test the water before you dive in. *International Review of Administrative Sciences*, 71(2), 255-266.

Halachmi, Arie. 2005. The Role of the Manager in Employee Motivation. In Condry, S.E. and Perry, J.L. (Eds.), *Handbook of Human Resource Management in Government*. San Francisco: Jossey-Bass, 469-498.

Hallowell, R., Schlesinger, L. A. and Zorintsky, J. 1996. "Internal service quality, customer and job satisfaction: Linkages and implications for management," *Human Resources Planning,* 19 (2), 20-32.

Hammer, Michael and J. Champty. 1993. *Reengineering the Corporation*. New York: Harper Business Books.

Handman, A. L., 2002. Intermodalism – A solution for highway congestion at the Millennium?" *The Review of Policy Research*, 19 (2), 51-61.

Hart, G., and Rudman, W. B. 2002. *America Still Unprepared—America Still in Danger*. Report of the Independent Task Force, US. Commission on National Security. New York: The Council on Foreign Relations.

Haynes, W. 2002. *An exploration of the nexus of the public and private sectors in the project management organizations for two Boston mega project: The Central Artery/ tunnel project and the Boston Harbor Cleanup*. Dissertation. *Boston: Northeastern University*. UMI.

Haynes, W. 2002. "Transportation at the millennium: In search of a megaproject lense," *The Review of Policy Research,"* 19 (2), 62-89.

Haynes, W. 2004. "Seeing around corners: Crafting the new department of homeland Security," *The Review of Policy Research,* 21, (3), 369-395.

Haynes, W., and R. Wright. 2005. Thought on the department of homeland security: Border management, students, and our communities – a holistic approach. Professional paper presented at the 66th National conference of the American Society for Public Administration in Milwaukee, WI (April 2-6).

Heppard, Kurt A., and Steve G. Green. 2007. "The Evolving Role of the Department of Defense in Homeland and Transportation Security," In Plant, J.F., Johnston, V.R., and Ciocirlan, C.E. (Eds.), *Handbook of Transportation Policy and Administration*, New York: CRC Press – Taylor and Francis Group, 579-593.

Ho, A. T. 2002. Reinventing local governments and the e-government initiative. *Public Administration Review,* (62) 4, 434-444.

Holcomb, John. 2003. "Corporate global citizenship: Conflicts between human rights and power politics," *Business and Professional Ethics Journal*, 22(2), 21-49.

Holzer, Marc and Rabin, Jack. 1987. "Public service; Problems, professionalism and policy recommendations," *Public Productivity Review,* 43, Fall.

Howard, J., Nash, J., and Ehrenfeld, J. 2000. Standard or Smokescreen? Implementation of a voluntary Environmental Code. *California Management Review,* 42 (2), 63-82.

Hyde, Albert C. 1992. "Feedback from customers, clients, and captives," *The Bureaucrat,* 22, (4), 35-40.

Hyde, Albert C. 1995. "Quality, Reengineering, and Performance: Managing Change in The Public Sector," In Halachmi, Arie, and G. Bouckaert (Eds.), *the Enduring Challenge in Public Management.* San Francisco: Jossey-Bass, 150-176.

Hyde, Albert C. 1995. "Improving customer service concepts," *The Public Manager- The New Bureaucrat,* 24 (3), 25-28.

Ingraham, P. 2005. "Performance: Promises to keep and miles to go," *Public Administration Review,* 65 (4), 390-395.

Ink, D., November/December, 2006. "An Analysis of the House Select Committee and White House Reports on Hurricane Katrina," *Public Administration Review*, 66(6), 800-807.

Ireland, R., Duane, Zahara, Shaker A., Gutierrez, Isabel, and Hitt, Michael A. 2000. Special Topic forum on "Privatization and entrepreneurial transformation," *The Academy of Management Review,* 25 (3), 508- 669.

Jablonski, Joseph R. 1991. *Implementing Total Quality Management: An Overview.* Toronto: Pfeiffer and Company.

Jacobs, J.J. 1991. *The Anatomy of an Entrepreneur.* San Francisco: ICS Press.

Janis, L. 1971. *Group Think in Organizations.* In Gibson, James L., John M. Invancevich, and James H. Donnelly, Jr. 1985. *Organizations Close-up: A Book of Readings,* 5th ed. 166-177.

Jensen, M.C. and W. H. Meckling. 1976. "Theory of firm: Managerial behavior, agency cost and ownership structure," *Journal of Financial Economics,* 3, 305-360.

Johns, N. & Tyas, P. 1997. Customer perceptions of service operations: Gestalt, incident of mythology. *The Services Industry Journal,* 17 (3), 474-488.

Johnston, Van R., et al., (Eds.). 1982. *Alternative Energy Sources: Barriers and Incentives.* Denver: American Society for Public Administration, Colorado.

Johnston, Van R., and Bright, Paul. 1982. "Diffusion of Technological Innovation: The Case of Alternative Energy Sources," In Johnston, Van R., et al., (Eds.). *Alternative Energy Sources: Barriers and Incentives*, Denver: American Society for Public Administration, Colorado.

Johnston, Van R. Winter, 1990. "Privatization of prisons: Management, productivity and governance concerns," *Public Productivity and Management Review* 14, 189-201.

Johnston, Van R. 1990. "Public – Private Partnerships," A National Conference Paper for the American Society for Public Administration, Los Angeles, April.

Johnston, Van R. 1991 "...Colorado's Privatization Experiments," A National Conference Paper for the American Society for Public Administration, Washington, DC, March.

Johnston, Van R. 1991. "Gambling with Privatization: Management and Governance Concerns," A Professional Conference Paper for the Multi-Regional American Society for Public Administration, Las Vegas, September.

Johnston, Van R. 1992. "Total Quality Management," A National Conference Paper for the American Society for Public Administration, Chicago, April.

Johnston, Van R., and Robert D'Amico. 1992. "TQM in a Reorganizing and Privatizing Military," An invited research paper presented at the Mid-Atlantic Regional Total Quality Management Conference, sponsored by the President's Council on Management Improvement, the Federal Quality Institute, and several Federal Executive Boards, Pittsburgh, September.

Johnston, Van R., and Robert D'Amico. 1993. "Integrating Innovative Entrepreneurship, Optimal Privatization, and Total Quality Management into our Defense Acquisition System," in *Acquisitions for the Future: Imagination, Innovation, And Implementation*, the 1993 Acquisition Research Symposium Proceedings Co-hosted by the Defense Systems Management College and the National Management Association, Washington, DC. 327-339.

Johnston, Van R. 1993. "Privatization Lessons from Hospital and Prison Experiences," A Professional Conference Paper for the Western Regional Science Association, Maui, February.

Johnston, Van R. 1993. "Entrepreneurial Government: Privatization's Contributions Towards Re-Inventing Partnerships for Progress," A National Conference Paper for the American Society for Public Administration, San Francisco, July.

Johnston, Van R. 1993. "Improving Quality and Productivity by Implementing TQM and Creative Entrepreneurial Organizational Innovations in Public Sector Organizations," A Professional paper presented at the International Institute of Administrative Sciences, Toluca, Mexico, July.

Johnston, Van R., and Gordon Von Stroh. 1994. "Alternatives to Quality Management and Quality Services," A professional paper for the annual conference of the Western Social Science Association, Albuquerque, April.

Johnston, Van R., and Gordon Von Stroh. 1994. "Downsizing, Performance and Productivity," A professional paper for the annual conference of the Western Governmental Research Association, San Francisco, May.

Johnston, Van R. 1994. "Beyond TQM," A National Conference Paper for the American Society for Public Administration, Kansas City, July.

Johnston, Van R. 1995. "Increasing Quality and Productivity: Strategic Planning, TQM and Beyond," In Halachmi, Arie and G. Bouckaert (Eds.) *Public Productivity Through Quality and Strategic Management.* Brussels: IOS Press, 83-97.

Johnston, Van R. 1995. "Caveat Emptor: Customers vs. Citizens," A National Conference Paper for the American Society for Public Administration, San Antonio, July.

Johnston, Van R. 1995. "Caveat emptor: Customers vs. citizens," *The Public Manager – The New Bureaucrat*, 24, 11-14.

Johnston, Van R. (Ed.), 1996. Privatization and Entrepreneurial Management," The Symposium on Reinventing Government, in *Policy Studies Journal*, 24 (3), 437-510.

Johnston, Van R. 1996. "Optimizing productivity through privatization and entrepreneurial management," *Policy Studies Journal*, 444-463.

Johnston, Van R. 1996. "The entrepreneurial management transformation: From privatization, reinventing, and reengineering, to franchising, efficiency and entrepreneurial ethics," *Policy Studies Journal*, 24 (3), 439-443.

Johnston, Van R. 1996. "Customers vs. citizens: Beware," A paper for the American Society for Public Administration, Colorado, February.

Johnston, Van R. 1997. "Professional Public Management Performance Priorities After the Reinventing and Privatization Transformation," A National Conference Paper for the American Society for Public Administration, Philadelphia, July.

Johnston, Van R. 1998. "DIA: Double Edged International Airport," A National Conference Professional Paper for the American Society for Public Administration, Seattle, May.

Johnston, Van R. 1999. "Privatization: Lessons from Hospital and Prison Experiences," In Seidenstat, Paul S. *Contracting out Government Services*. Westport, CT: Praeger, 134-150.

Johnston, Van R. 1999. "Trust, Cynicism and Credibility in Air Transportation Policy and Administration," A Professional Paper for the National Conference of the American Society for Public Administration, Orlando FL, April.

Johnston, Van R. 2000. *Entrepreneurial Management and Public Policy*. Huntington, New York: Nova Science Publishers.

Johnston, Van R. 2001. "Air Transportation Policy and Administration," A National Conference Professional Paper for the American Society for Public Administration, Newark, March.

Johnston, Van R. Winter, 2002. "Effective Security and Safety vs. Efficiency, Contracting and Freedom in our Transportation Systems at the Millennium," In *Intermodal Fare*, Van R. Johnston, (Ed.), Winter, 2002, pp.3-6.

Johnston, Van R. 2002, "Growth in Colorado:…Interrupted…," A National Conference Paper for the American Society for Public Administration, Phoenix, March.

Johnston, Van R. and Jeremy F. Plant, Symposium Editors, Intermodal Transportation in the New Millenium. *The Review of Policy Research*, 19(2), 6-127.

Johnston, Van R. 2002. "Air transportation policy and administration at the millennium. *The Review of Policy Research*," 19 (2), 109-127.

Johnston, Van R. Spring, 2003. "Airlines and economic survival: Through United's bankruptcy lens," In *Intermodal Fare*, Van R. Johnston (Ed.), 3-5.

Johnston, Van R. 2004. "Terrorism and transportation policy and administration: Balancing the model and equations for optimal security," *The Review of Policy Research.* 21 (3): 263-274.

Johnston, Van R. 2004. Editor. Terrorism and Transportation Security. A Symposium of Ten Articles, The *Review of Policy Research*, 21(3): 255-402.

Johnston, Van R., and Amala Nath . 2004. "Terrorism and transportation security," *The Review of Policy Research*, 21(3): 255-261.

Johnston, Van R. and Erik Johnston. 2004. "Notes from the Field" on Per Otsby's "Educating the Norwegian nation: Traffic engineering and technological diffusion," in *Comparative Technology and Society*, 2(3), 268-272.

Johnston, Van R. 2005. "Public Policy and Business Modeling for Transportation Policy and Administration After 9-11," A National Conference Paper for the American Society for Public Administration, Milwaukee, April.

Johnston, Van R. 2006. With Vijaya Narapareddy, Nancy Sampson and Claire Schulz. "Denver International Airport," In David, Fred R. *Cases in Strategic Management,* 11th Edition, Pearson Education, Prentice Hall, 2006.

Johnston, Van R. 2006. With Vijaya Narapareddy, Nancy Sampson and Claire Schulz. "Denver International Airport," in David, Fred R. *Strategic Management Concepts and Cases*, 11th Edition, Pearson Education, Prentice Hall.

Johnston, Van R., and Haynes, Wendy, and Schulz, Claire. 2006. "The T-REX megaproject: Denver's showcase for innovation and creativity," *The Public Manager*, 36(2), 3-8.

Johnston, Van R. and Seidenstat, Paul. 2007. "Contracting out government services: Privatization at the millenium," *International Journal of Public Administration*, 30(3), 231-247.

Johnston, Van R., and Paul Seidenstat and Erik Johnston. 2007. "Transportation Security Policy," in Plant, J.F., Johnston, V.R., and Ciocirlan, C.E. (Eds.), *Handbook of Transportation Policy and Administration,* New York: CRC Press - Taylor and Francis Group, 525-536.

Johnston, Van R. 2007. (Associate Editor) with Jeremy Plant (Editor), and Cristina Ciocirlan (Assistant Editor), *Handbook of Transportation Policy and Administration*, New York: CRC Press – Taylor and Francis Group.

Johnston, Van R., and Jeremy Plant. 2007. "Towards Increasingly Collaborative Transportation Security: The Case of Rail Security," A National Conference Professional Paper for the American Society for Public Administration, Washington, DC, March.

Keane, Thomas H. *The 9/11 Commission Report.* Final Report of the National Commission on Terrorist Attacks on the United States. New York: Norton.

Kettl, Donald F. 1993. *Sharing Power: Public Governance and Private Markets,* Washington DC: The Brookings Institution.

Kettl, Donald F. 1993. *Reinventing Government? Appraising the National Performance Review.* (CPM Report 94-2), Washington, DC: Center for Public Management, The Bookings Institution.

Kettl, Donald F. 1995. "Building Lasting Reform: Enduring Questions, Missing Answers," In Kettl, Donald F., and John J. DiIulio, Jr., *Inside Reinventing Machine: Appraising Government Reform.* Washington, DC: The Brookings Institution.

Kettl, Donald F. 2003. "Contingent coordination: Practical and theoretical puzzles for Homeland Security," Presentation at the American Society for Public Administration," Annual Conference, Washington, DC. In the Senior Scholar Spotlight: Bureaucratic Structure in a Post-9/11 Government.

Khademian, A. M. 1995. "Reinventing a government corporation: Professional priorities and a clear bottom line," *Public Administration Review,* 55 (1) 17-28.

Kincaid, J. 1990. From cooperative to coercive federalism. *Annals of the American Academy,* 509, 139-152.

King, A., and Lenox, M. 2000. "Prospects for industry self-regulation without sanctions: A study of responsible care in the chemical industry," *The Academy of Management Journal.* 43(4), 698-716.

Kobrak, P. 1996. "The Social responsibilities of a public entrepreneur," *Administration & Society,* 28 (2), 205-238.

Koch, R. 1995. "Public Managers and Entrepreneurialism." Paper presented at the Annual Meeting of the European Group in Public Administration (EGPA), Rotterdam, the Netherlands.

Kodryzcki, Y. January/February, 1994. "Privatization of local public services: Lessons for New England," *New England Economic Review,* 14, 39-50.

Kolderie, T. 1986. "The two different concepts of privatization," *Public Administration Review,* 46 (4), 285-291.

Kouzes, James M., and Barry Z. Posner. 1993. *Credibility: How Leaders Gain and Lose It; Why People Demand It.* San Francisco: Jossey-Bass.

Kuhn, Thomas S. 1970. *The Structure of Scientific Revolutions.* Chicago: University of Chicago Press.

Landon R. 2002. "Tools for governing: Privatization, public-private partnerships, and entrepreneurial management," *Public Administration Review,* 62 (1), 118-122.

La Porte, T., et al. 2002. "Democracy and bureaucracy in the age of the web; empirical findings and theoretical speculations," *Administrative & Society,* 34 (4), 441-446.

Lasswell, H.D. 1977. *Psychopathology and Politics.* Chicago: The University of Chicago Press.

Leavitt, W.M., and Kiefer, J.J. April, 2006. Infrastructure independence and the creation of a normal disaster: The case of Hurricane Katrina and the City of New Orleans. *Public Works Management and Policy,* 10(4), 306-314.

Levin, M.A. & Sanger, M.B. 1994. *Making Government Work.* San Francisco, CA: Jossey-Bass Publishers.

Lewis, E. 1980. *Public Entrepreneurship.* Bloomington, Indiana University Press.

Lewis, B.R., and Gabrielson, G.O.S. 1998. "Intra-organizational aspects of service quality management: The employee's perspective," *The Services Industry Journal,* 18 (2), 64-89.

Linowes, D. F. 1988. *Privatization: Toward More Effective Government.* President's Commission on Privatization. Washington, DC: U.S. Government Printing Office.

Lipsky, M. 1980. *Street-level Bureaucracy: Dilemmas of the Individual in Public Service.* Russell Sage Foundation.

Lowi, T. 1964. "American business, public policy, case studies and political theory," *World Politics,* 16 (3), 677-715.

Lowndes, V. 2005. "Something old, something new, something borrowed..." *Policy Studies,* 26 (3/4), 291-309.

Lynch, Thomas D. 1995. *Public Budgeting in America.* (5th ed.), Englewood Cliffs, NJ: Prentice Hall.

Lynn, L. E., Jr. 1987. *Managing Public Policy.* Boston: Little, Brown and Company.

Maccoby, M. 1976. *The Gamesman.* New York: Simon and Schuster.

MacDonald, S. 1995. "Too close for comfort? The strategic implications of getting close to the customer," *California Management Review,* 37 (4), 8-28.

Mangold, W. G., and Babakus, E. 1991. "Service quality: The front stage vs. back stage Perspective," *The Journal of Services Marketing,* 5 (4), 59-70.

Martin, John. 1993. "Reengineering government," *Governing,* 26-30.

Martin, Lawrence. 1993. "Contracting Out: A Comparative Analysis of Local Government Practices," In Lynch, Thomas D., and Lawrence Martin, (Eds.), *Comparative Public Budgeting and Financial Management.* New York: Decker, 225-239.

Martin, L. 1994. "How to Compare Costs Between in-House Contracted Services," In *Public Private Cooperation.* Denver: Colorado Municipal League.

Mazmanian, Daniel A., and Kraft, Michael E. 1999. "The Three Epochs of the Environmental Movement," In D.A. Mazmanian and M.E. Kraft (Eds.), *Toward Sustainable Communities: Transition and Transformations in Environmental Policy.* Cambridge, MA: Cambridge University Press.

Menzel, D.C. November/December, 2006. "The Katrina aftermath: A failure of federalism or leadership?" *Public Administration Review,* 66(6), 808-812.

McLean, Bethany and Peter Elkind. 2003. *The Smartest Guys in the Room: The Amazing Rise and Scandalous Fall of Enron.* New York: Portfolio – Penguin Group.

Miketa, A., and Mulder, P. 2005. "Energy productivity across developed and developing countries in 10 manufacturing sectors: Patterns of growth and convergence," *Energy Economics.* 27, 429-453.

Mintzberg, Henry. 1979. *The Structuring of Organizations: the theory of Management Policy.* Englewood Cliffs, NJ: Prentice Hall.

Mintzberg, Henry. 1994. *The Rise and Fall of Strategic Planning: Reconceiving Roles For Planning, Plans, Planners.* New York: the Free Press, A Division of McMillan, Inc.

Mintzberg, H. 1996, "Managing government, governing management," *Harvard Business Review,* (May-June), 75-83.

Miranda, R. A. 1992. "Privatization and the budget maximizing bureaucrat," *Public Productivity and Management Review,* 17 (4), 355-370.

Moe, Ron C. 1987. "Exploring the limits of privatization," *Public Administration Review,* 47 (6).

Moe, Ron C. 1994. "The 'Reinventing government" exercise: Misinterpreting the problem, misjudging the consequences," *Public Administration Review,* 54 (2), 111-122.

Moe, Ron C., and Gilmour, Robert S. 1995 "Rediscovering principles of public administration: The neglected foundation of public law," *Public Administration Review,* 49 (4).

Moe, Ron C., and Stanton, T.H. 1989. "Government sponsored enterprises as federal instruments: Reconciling private management and public accountability," *Public Administration Review,* 49 (4).

Morris, J.C. April, 2006. Whither FEMA? Hurricane Katrina and FEMA's response to the gulf coast. *Public Works Management and Policy*, 10(4), 284-294.

Murphy, J. 2004. "After 9/11: Priority focus areas for bioterrorism preparedness in hospitals," *Journal of Healthcare Management.* 49 (4): 227-35.

Nagel, Stuart S. 1989. *Higher Goals for America.* Lonham, MD, University Press of America, Inc.

Nance, John. 1986. *Blind Trust.* New York: William Marrow and Company, Inc.

National Quality Research Center, 2005. The American Customer Satisfaction Index (1999-2005). University of Michigan.

Newell, T. 1988. "Why can't government be like...government?" *Public Productivity Review,* 12 (1).

Niskanen , W.A. 1971. *Bureaucracy and Representative Government.* Chicago: Aldine-Atherton.

O'Brien, T. M. 1989. *Privatization in Colorado State Government.* Denver: Colorado Office of State Auditor.

O'Toole. L. J. 1999. American Intergovernmental Relations: An Overview. In *Public Administration: Concepts and Cases.* R.J. Stillman, Ed. 8th edition. Boston: Houghton Mifflin Company, 2005.

Osborne, David and Ted Gaebler. 1991. *Reinventing Government: How the Entrepreneurial Spirit is Transforming Government.* New York: Addison Wesley.

Osborne, D., & Gaebler, T. 1992. *Reinventing Government.* Reading, MA: Addison-Wesley Publishing Company.

Palumbo, Dennis J. 1986. "Privatization and corrections policy," *Policy Studies Review,* 5 (3).

Palumbo, Dennis J. and Maupin, J. 1989. "The Political Side of Privatization," *Journal of Management Science and Policy Analysis,* 6 (2), 25-40.

Palumbo, Dennis J. and D.J. Calista. 1990. *Implementation and the Policy Process: Opening up the Black Box.* New York: Greenwood Press.

Parasuraman, A., Zeithaml, V. A. And L. L. Berry. 1985. "A conceptual model of service quality and its implications for future research," *Journal of Marketing,* 49 (3), 41-50.

Parasuraman, A. 1997. "Reflections on gaining advantage through customer value," *Journal of the Academy of Marketing Science,* 25 (2), 154-161.

Pegnato, J.A. 1997. "Is a customer a citizen?" *Public Productivity and Management Review,* (20) 4, 397-404.

Pellikaan, H., and van der Veen, R. 2002. *Environmental Dilemmas and Policy Design.* New York: Cambridge University Press.

Perlmutter, F. D., and Cnaan, R.A.. 1995. "Entrepreneurship in the public sector: The horns of a dilemma," *Public Administration Review,* 55 (1), 29-36.

Peters, G.B., and Savoie, D. 1996. "Managing incoherence: The coordination and empowerment conundrum," *Public Administration Review,* 56 (3), 281-289.

Petroski, H. 1982. *To Engineer Human: The Role of Failure in Successful Design.* New York: St. Martin's Press.

Petzinger, Thomas, Jr. 1996. *Hard Landing: The Epic Contest for Power and Profits That Plunged the Airlines into Chaos.* New York: Times Business, Random House.

Pfaff, A., and Sanchirico, C.W. Summer, 2004. "Big field, small potatoes: An empirical assessment of EPA's self-audit policy," *Journal of Policy Analysis And Management.* 23 (3).

Plant, Jeremy F. 2002. "Railroad policy and intermodalism: Policy choices after deregulation," *The Review of Policy Research*, 19 (2), 13-32.

Plant, Jeremy F., and Johnston, Van R., (Eds). 2002. Intermodal Transportation at the New Millenium. A six article symposium in *The Review of Policy Research.* 19 (2), 6-127.

Plant, Jeremy F. 2004. "Terrorism and the railroads: Redefining security in the wake of 9/11," *The Review of Policy Research*, 21 (3), 293-305.

Plant, Jeremy F. (Editor), and Van R. Johnston (Associate Editor), and Cristina E. Ciocirlan (Assistant Editor). 2007. *Handbook of Transportation Policy and Administration.* New York: CRC Press – Taylor and Francis Group.

Plant, Jeremy F., 2007. "Enhancing Railroad Security," In Plant, J.F., Johnston, V.R., And Ciocirlan, C.E. (Eds.), *Handbook of Transportation Policy and Administration.* New York: CRC Press – Taylor and Francis Group. 595-606.

Popp, D. 2003. "Pollution control innovations and the Clean Air Act of 1990," *Journal of Policy Analysis and Management*, 22(4), 641-660.

Potoski, M., and Prakash, A. March/April, 2004. "The regulation dilemma: Cooperation and conflict in environmental governance," *Public Administration Review,* 62(2), 137-148.

Potoski, M., and Praksh, A., 2005. "Covenants with weak swords: ISO 1401 and facilities' environmental performance" *Journal of Policy Analysis and Management*, 24(4), 745-769.

Powpaka, S. 1996. "The role of outcome quality as a determinant of overall service quality in different categories of services industries: an empirical investigation," *The Journal of Services Marketing,* 10 (2), 5-24.

Prager, J. 1994. "Contracting out government services," *Public Administration Review,* 54 (2), 176-184.

Prendergast, C. 1999. "The provision of incentives in firms," *Journal of Economic Literature.* 37, 7-63.

Prendergast, C. 2002. "Uncertainty and incentives," *Journal of Labor Economics*, 20(2), 115-137.

President's Council on Management Improvement. 1991. *Federal Total Quality Handbook*. Washington, DC: U.S. Government Printing Office.

Press, Daniel, and Daniel A. Mazmanian. 2006. "The Greening of Industry: Combining Government Regulation and Voluntary Strategies," in N. J. Vig, and M.E.

Kraft, *Environmental Policy: New Directions for the Twenty First Century*. Washington, DC: CG Press, 264-287.

Pressman, Jeffrey and Aaron B. Wildavsky. 1974. *Implementation*. University of California Press.

Pressman, J. and A. Wildavsky 1984. *Implementation: How great expectations in Washington are dashed in Oakland; or, why it's amazing the federal programs work at all, this being a saga of the economic development administration as told by two sympathetic observers who seek to build morals on a foundation of ruined hopes (3rd ed.)*. Berkeley: University of California Press.

Price, Willard. 2004. "Reducing the risk of terrorism at seaports," *The Review of Policy Research*, 21 (3), 329-349.

Price, Willard. 2007. "Seaport Security from Terror: Risk and Responsibility," In Plant, J.F., Johnston, V.R., and Ciocirlan, C.E. (Eds.), *Handbook of Transportation Policy and Administration*, New York: CRC Press – Taylor and Francis Group, 557- 578.

Princen, T., and Maniates, M., and Conca, K. (Eds.). 2002. *Confronting Consumption*. Cambridge, MA: MIT Press.

Reeves, C. A., Bednar, D.A., and Lawerence, R. C. 1995. "Back to the beginning: what do customers care about in service firms," *Quality Management Journal*, 3 (1), 56-72.

Reisch, M.S. 2004. "Track Us, Trust Us: American Chemistry Council Says Will Supply the Facts to Earn the Public's Trust," *Chemical and Engineering News*, 82(23).

Reisch, M.S. 2002. "Twenty years After Bhopal: Smokescreen of True Reform? Has The Chemical Industry Changed Enough to Make another Massive Accident Unlikely?" *Chemical and Engineering News*, 82(23).

Roberts, P.S. Spring, 2006. "FEMA and the Prospects for Reputation- Based Autonomy," *Studies in American Political Development*, 20(1), 57-87.

Roberts, P.S. June/July, 2006. "FEMA After Katrina," *Policy Review*. 13(7), 15-53.

Romzek, B.S., and Dubnick, M.J. 1987. "Accountability in the public sector: Lessons from the Challenger tragedy," *Public Administration Review*, 47 (3), 227-238.

Rosenbaum, W.A. 2005. *Environmental Politics and Policy* (6th ed.). Washington, DC: CQ Press.

Rosenbloom, D. H., and R. S. Kravchuk. 2005. *Public Administration: Understanding Management, Politics, and Law in the Public Sector*. 6th edition. Boston: McGraw-Hill.

Ross, S. A. 1973. "The economic theory of agency: The principal's problem," *American Economic Review*, 63, 134-139.

Rust, R.T., Zeithaml, V. A., and Lemon, K.N. 2004. "Customer Centered Brand Management," *Harvard Business Review*, 82 (9), 110-118.

Salamon, L. M. 2005. "Training professional citizens: Getting beyond the right answer to the wrong question in public administration," *Journal of Public Affairs Education,* 11 (1), 7-19.

Sandfort, J. 2003. "Exploring the structuration of technology within human service Organizations," *Administration & Society,* 34 (6), 605-631.

Savas, E. S. 1982. *Privatizing the Public Sector.* Chatham, NJ: Chatham House.

Savas, E. S. 1987. *Privatization: The key to Better Government.* Catham NJ: Catham House.

Scheirer, J. M. 1994. Designing and Using Process Evaluation. In J. S. Wholey, H. P. Hatry, and K. E. Newcomers (eds.), *Handbook of Practical Program Evaluation.* San Francisco: Jossey-Bass

Scheirer, M. 1990. Studying Micro-Implementation Empirically: Lessons and Dilemmas, In *Implementation and the Public Policy Process: Opening Up the Black Box.* Westport, CT: Greenwood Press.

Schick, Allen. 1966. "The road to PPB: The stages of budget reform," *Public Administration Review",* 26 (6), 243-258.

Seidenstat, Paul. 1996. "Privatization: Trends, interplay of forces and lessons learned," *Policy Studies Journal,* 24 (3), 464-477.

Seidenstat, Paul. 1999. *Contracting Out Government Services.* London: Praeger.

Seidenstat, Paul. 2004. "Terrorism, airport security and the private sector," *The Review of Policy Research,* 21 (3), 275-291.

Senge, Peter. 1990. *Fifth Discipline: Mastering the Five Practices of the Learning Organization.* New York: Doubleday.

Shafritz, J. M., and E. W. Russell. 2005. *Introducing Public Administration.* 4th edition. Boston: Pearson Longman.

Smith, R. W. 2005. "What is homeland security? Developing a definition grounded in the curricula," *Journal of Public Affairs Education.* 11 (3), 233-246.

Solomon, R. C. 1992. *Ethics and Excellence.* New York: Oxford University Press.

Stever, J.A. 1988. *The End of Public Administration.* Dobbs Ferry, New York: Transnational Publishers, Inc.

Sturdy A. 1998." Customer care in a consumer society: Smiling and sometimes meaning it?" *Organization,* 5 (1), 27-53.

Sullivan, H.J. 1987. "Privatization of public services: A growing threat to constitutional rights," *Public Administration Review,* 47 (6), 461-467.

Swiss, J. E. 1992. "Adapting total quality management (TQM) to government," *Public Administration Review,* 52 (4), 356-362.

Swiss, J. E. 2005. "A Framework for assessing incentives in results-based management," *Public Administration Review* 65 (5), 592-602.

Szyliowicz, J.E. 2004. "International Transportation Security," *The Review of Policy Research,* 21 (3), 351-368.

Szyliowicz, J.E. 2007. "Globalization and Transportation Security," In Plant, J.F., Johnston, V.R., and Ciocirlan, C.E. (Eds.), *Handbook of Transportation Policy and Administration,* New York: CRC Press – Taylor and Francis Group, 537-556.

Taylor, M. 1982. *Community, Anarchy and Liberty.* Cambridge, England: Cambridge University Press.

Terry, L.D. 1993. "Why we should abandon the misconceived quest to reconcile entrepreneurship with democracy," *Public Administration Review,* 53 (4), 393-395.

Terry, L.D. 1998. "Administrative leadership, neo-managerialism, and the public management movement." *Public Administration Review,* 58 (3), 194-200.

Tewes, J.E. 1983. "The New Entrepreneurship," In B.H. Moore, *The Entrepreneur In Local Government.* Washington, DC: International City Management Association, 15-20.

Thomas J.C., and Streib, G. 2003. "The new face of government: Citizen-initiated contacts in the era of e-government," *Journal of Public Administration Research and Theory,* 13 (1), 83-102.

Thomas, R. 1990. "National-local relations and the city's dilemma," *Annals of the American Academy,* 509, 106-117.

Thompson, D.L. 1983. "Public-Private Policy: An introduction," *Policy Studies Journal,* 11 (3), 419-426.

Thompson, J.D. 1967. *Organizations in Action.* New York: McGraw-Hill.

U. S. DHS Office of Inspector General. 2004. *Major management challenges facing the Department of Homeland Security.* (OIG-05-06). December.

U. S. Government. 1994. National Performance Review. *Putting Customers First: Standards for Serving the American People,* Washington, DC: U.S. Government Printing Office.

U. S. Government. 1998. The National Performance Review. *Putting Customers First: Serving the American People.* Washington, DC: U. S. Government Printing Office.

U. S. Government. 1998. The National Performance Review. *Reinventing Performance at the IRS.* Washington, DC: U.S. Government Printing Office.

U.S. House Select Bipartisan Committee to Investigate the Preparation for and the Response to Hurricane Katrina. 2006. *A Failure of Initiative.* Washington, DC: U.S. Government Printing Office.

U.S. OMB. 2004. Expanding E-government: Partnering for a Results-Oriented Government. Washington, DC.

Vaughan, Diane. 1996. *The Challenger Launch Decision: Risky Technology, Culture And Deviance at NASA.* Chicago: University of Chicago Press.

Vinzant, J. C., and Vinzant, D.H.. 1996. "Strategic management and total quality management," *Public administration Quarterly,* 20, 201-219.

Von Hippel, E. 2005. *Democratizing Innovation.* Cambridge: MIT Press.

Waugh, W.L. 2004. "Securing Mass Transit: A challenge for Homeland Security," *The Review of Policy Research,* 21(3), 307-316.

Waugh, W.L., and Smith, R.R. August, 2006. "Economic development and reconstruction on the gulf coast after Katrina.," *Economic Development Quarterly: The Journal of American Economic Revitalization.* 20 (3), 211-218.

Waugh, W.L. 2007. "Securing Mass Transit After the Madrid and London Bombings," In Plant, J.F., Johnston, V.R. and Ciocirlan, C.E., *Handbook of Transportation Policy and Administration*, New York: CRC Press – Taylor and Francis Group, 607-616.

Wayland, R. E. and P. Cole. 1997. *Customer Connections: New Strategies for Growth.* Boston: Harvard Business School Press.

Webb, D. 1998. "Segmenting police customers on the basis of their service quality expectations," *The Service Industries Journal* 18 (1), 72-100.

West, J., Berman, E., and Milakovich, M. 1994. "Implementing TQM in local government: The leadership challenge," *Public Productivity and Management Review,* 17 (2).

Wicks, Andrew C., Berman, Shawn L., and Jones., Thomas M. 1999. "The structure of optimal trust: Moral and strategic implications," *Academy of Management Review,* 24 (1), 99-116.

Williamson, O. E. 1991. "Comparative economic organization: The analysis of discrete structural alternatives," *Administrative Science Quarterly,* 36, 269-296.

Wolf, Patrick. 1997. "Why must we reinvent the federal government?: Putting historical development claims to the test," *Journal of Public Administration Research and Theory,* 7 (3), 353-388.

Woodruff, R. B. "Customer value: The next source for competitive advantage," *Journal of the Academy of Marketing Science,* 25 (2), 139-153.

Wyden, Ron, McCain, John, Bryen, Richard H. and Snowe, Olympia J. 1999. *Airline Passenger Fairness Act.* S. 383, 106thCongress, 1st Session.

Yasai-Ardekani, M. and P. Nystrom. 1996. "Design for environmental scanning systems: Tests of a contingency theory," *Management Science,* 42 (2), 187-204.

Zahra, S. and S. Chaples. 1993. "Blind spots in competitive analysis," *Academy of Management Executive,* 7 (2), 7-28.

Zimmerman, D., Zimmerman, P., and Lund, C. 1997. "Customer service: The new battlefield for market share," *Healthcare Financial Management,* 51 (3), 51-55.

ABOUT THE AUTHORS

Peter B. Boorsma is a Professor of Public Finance in the Department for Governance, Business, and Technology at the University of Twente in the Netherlands. He is an increasingly renowned expert in the emerging field of principal-agent theory. Besides applying his expertise to solving practical problems with his innovative theoretical applications, by way of the Netherlands' Boorsma Committee, he has also traveled quite extensively professionally while developing his multi disciplinary theories. His research manuscripts are known for integrating theory and practice.

Peter J. Cruise is an Associate Professor in the Health and Community Services Department at California State University-Chico. After a 12 year career in health care in both private and public sectors, Dr. Cruise has now taught at universities in California, Florida, and Louisiana. Dr. Cruise's research interests include values-based management in the public sector and ethnographic approaches in health services planning and program evaluation. Dr. Cruise is the co-editor of the *Handbook of Organization Theory and Management: The Philosophical Approach* (2nd Edition, 2006). He has published in such peer-reviewed journals as: *Administration & Society, Evaluation and the Health Professions, International Journal of Public Administration, International Journal of Organization Theory and Behavior, International Review of Public Administration, Journal of Health and Human Services Administration, Journal of Public Administration Research and Theory, Managed Care Quarterly, Public Administration and Policy, Public Administration Quarterly*, and *Social Service Review*.

Linda de Leon is an Associate Professor and Associate Dean at the Graduate School of Public Affairs, University of Colorado at Denver, where she directs the Executive Master of Public Administration program and the Rocky Mountain MPA Program (on line). Prior to joining the SPA faculty, she was Director of Human Resources for the Irvine, California office of a national insurance-brokerage firm. She holds her Ph.D. in Political Science from the University of California at Los Angeles and has worked at the Rand Corporation and on the public affairs faculty of the University of Southern California. She has served as Associate Editor for the *Journal of Public Administration Education* and the *International Public Management Journal*. Her articles have appeared

in a variety of well-respected journals on the topics of organization theory, human
resources management, administrative reform, public sector professionals, and ethics and
values in organizations. In 2000, she and co-author Robert Denhardt won the Mosher
award for the best lead article in *Public Administration Review*. Dr. de Leon is active
with ASPA and chaired the host management committee for the 2006 National ASPA
Conference.

J. Roberto Evaristo is an Associate Professor of Information Technology and
Electronic Commerce on the faculty of the Information and Decision Sciences
Department at the University of Illinois, Chicago. He has degrees in civil and
transportation engineering and got his Ph.D. in Management Information Systems at the
University of Minnesota. Dr. Evaristo is interested in deregulation, privatization, and
competition. He is currently involved in several projects related to the management of
complex environments, with emphasis on distributed projects. He has published in
outlets such as: *Communications of the ACM*, *International Journal of Project
Management*, *Database*, *Journal of Engineering and Technology Management*,
International Journal of Emergency Management, *Business Horizons*, *European
Management Journal*, *Human Systems Management*, *Journal of Organizational
Computing and Electronic Commerce*, and elsewhere. He is an associate editor for the
International Journal of e-Collaboration and the *Journal of Global Information
Management* and also serves on the editorial board of *Information Technology and
People* and the *Journal of Global Information Technology Management*.

Arie Halachmi is the editor of *Performance and Quality Measurement in
Government*, Chatelaine Press, 1999. He is Visiting Professor at the Faculty of Public
Administration (BSK) at the University of Twente (NL) and a Professor at the Institute of
Government at Tennessee State University. He earned his Ph.D. in 1972 (with
distinction) from SUNY Buffalo. He has served as a consultant to various government
agencies in the U.S. and abroad, has twice served on the national council of the American
Society for Public Administration, and has been the chair of SECOPA. He founded and
has chaired the International Working Group on Public Sector Productivity for the
International Institute of Administrative Sciences (IIAS). He was the Associate Editor of
Public Productivity and Management Review, having served as its managing editor from
1985 to 1995. He has published over half a dozen books and several articles recently,
and has an extensive lifetime publications record.

Wendy Haynes, Ph.D., is Associate Professor and Coordinator of the Master of
Public Administration (MPA) program in the Department of Political Science at
Bridgewater State College in Massachusetts. Dr. Haynes brings nearly three decades of
dedicated public service at all levels of government to the classroom. Her professional
and scholarly work is informed significantly by her thirteen years in the Massachusetts
Inspector General's Office where she headed an interdisciplinary team charged with
monitoring megaprojects in Boston. She has written, spoken, and consulted extensively
on this and related governance topics, including performance auditing, reporting, and

strategic planning and management issues. Dr. Haynes has served on several editorial boards, including *Public Administration Review*, has also served as chair of the Section on Transportation Policy and Administration of the American Society of Public Administration, and has served two terms on ASPA's National Council. Dr. Haynes was President of ASPA in 2007.

Albert C. Hyde is a senior staff consultant with the Brookings Institution's Center for Public Policy Education in Washington, D.C. He has been with Brookings since 1992 serving as the Center's senior expert on quality management, reengineering, and business management innovation. He is overseeing several major strategic innovation projects with the U.S. Forest Service and the Department of the Interior in wildland fire management. He also directed the Center's reengineering and strategic planning initiatives with the U.S. Customs Service, the National Library of Medicine, the FAA, and the National Security Agency. Prior to working with Brookings, he had over a decade of private sector consulting experience in quality management and performance measurement with many major petrochemical and engineering corporations in the United States and Europe. Dr. Hyde also has an extensive academic background, having been a Visiting Professor at the American University's Department of Public Administration in Washington D.C. from 1992 to 1997. Prior to that, he was Director of the Policy and Public Management Departments at the University of Pittsburgh (1988-1991) and San Francisco State University (1984-1988), and was Director of the Human Resources Management program at the University of Houston-Clear Lake (1979-1984). He is co-author or co-editor of six textbooks and has published numerous articles and papers on all aspects of public management and administration in government. His Ph.D. in Political Science is from SUNY Albany.

Van R. Johnston is Professor of Management and Public Policy at the Daniels College of Business at the University of Denver. He has also taught and done research at the University of Southern California, and was a Distinguished Visiting Professor of Management and Strategy at the United States Air Force Academy. He has been on the National Council (elected at Large), and was appointed to the National Executive Committee of the American Society for Public Administration. With ASPA, he was also Chair of the Section on Transportation Policy and Administration, Chair of the Performance Steering Group, Chair of the Publications Committee, and Chapter President twice. Professor Johnston was also elected to the National Council of the Policy Studies Organization, while a Co-Editor of *Policy Studies Review*. He has been an Associate Editor of the *Review of Policy Research*, and has served on several editorial boards. He has received numerous professional awards (including ASPA's prestigious STONE Award, and the ASPA President's Citation of Merit). He has also received the Policy Studies Organization's Wildavsky Award; as well as numerous grants and fellowships. Dr. Johnston has received 4 significant research awards, in addition to receiving five graduate and undergraduate teaching awards in one five year period. Professor Johnston was Chair of the Business and Public Policy graduate and undergraduate courses and faculty group at the Daniels College of Business at the University of Denver for 10 years.

Dr. Johnston has eight books/monographs, and a hundred publications, as well as a hundred professional conference papers/presentations. Professor Johnston has articles published in the following, among others: *Policy Studies Journal, The Review of Policy Research, Policy Studies Review, Public Administration Review, Public Productivity and Management Review, Public Administration Quarterly, The International Journal of Public Administration, The Public Manager, and National Civic Review.* Professor Johnston is also the Associate Editor of the *Handbook of Transportation Policy and Administration* (2007).   Dr. Johnston has an extensive board, consulting, and training background in both the public and private sectors for over 30 years. Professor Johnston received his Ph.D. from the University of Southern California in 1976.

Cynthia E. Lynch is an Assistant Professor in the MPA program in the School of Public Policy and Urban Affairs at Southern University. She received her B.A. degree from the University of Massachusetts at Boston in Planning and Management, the M.P.A. degree from Louisiana State University, and the Ph.D. degree in Public Policy from Southern University. Dr. Lynch is an Assistant Professor at the University of Texas, Pan Am.   She is the president of Scott Balsdon Inc., a consulting company working in professional training in the areas of organizational design, ethics, performance measurement, and program evaluation. She is the current editor of the *Global Virtue Ethics Review* journal and has written several professional conference papers, book chapters, and articles in the area of ethics and spiritual wisdom. In 1998, she co-authored *The World of the Light* with her husband, Thomas D. Lynch.

Rev. Dr. Thomas D. Lynch is Professor of Public Administration in the E.J. Ourso College of Business at Louisiana State University. He received his MPA and Ph.D. Degrees from the Rockefeller College, State University of New York. He worked six years in the federal government and has taught at six universities since 1974. He has published widely and is on the editorial boards of over 10 journals world wide. He is most known for his textbook *Public Budgeting in America* which is in its 30th year and 5th edition.   He was also President of the American Society for Public Administration (ASPA). Professor Lynch has founded three journals, including the *Public Manager.* He writes primarily in the areas of public budgeting, ethics, and organization theory. He has been editor of *Global Virtue Ethics Review*, which is an electronic journal started in 1999.

Daniel A. Mazmanian is the Bedrosian Chair in Governance at the School of Policy, Planning, and Development (SPPD), at the University of Southern California. His books include: *Toward Sustainable Communities* (1999), *Beyond Superfailure: America's Toxic Policy for the 1990s* (1992), *Implementation and Public Policy* (1989), *Can Regulation Work?* (1983), *Can Organizations Change?* (1979), and *Third Parties in Presidential Elections* (1974). He served as Dean of SPPD at USC from 2000-2005, and was Dean of the School of Natural Resources and Environment at the University of Michigan from 1996-2000. Dr. Mazmanian's Ph.D. is in Political Science from Washington University. He earned his M.A. and B.A. degrees from San Francisco State University. He is a former President of the Policy Studies Organization. He is also President of the National Association of Schools of Public Affairs and Administration.

Stuart S. Nagel, Ph.D., J.D. was Professor Emeritus of Political Science at the University of Illinois. He was the Leader/Coordinator of: (1) the Policy Studies Organization, (2) The Miriam K. Mills Research Center for Super Optimizing Analysis and Developing Nationals, and (3) the Everett Dirksen – Adlai Stevenson Institute for International Policy Studies. Dr. Nagel received numerous awards, fellowships, and grants from: the Ford and Rockefeller Foundations, the National Science Foundation, the Center for Advanced Study in the Behavioral Sciences, and other policy relevant organizations and foundations. He authored and edited several hundred relevant books and articles. Dr. Nagel died shortly after the turn of the century.

Dorothy Olshfski is an Associate Professor of Public Administration at Rutgers University in Newark, New Jersey. She has published in numerous journals, some of which are: *Public Administration Review, Public Performance and Management Review,* and *Administration and Society.* She has been managing editor of *Public Performance and Management Review* and has published a book of case studies with Kathe Callahan of Rutgers and Erwin Schwella of the University of Stellensbosch in South Africa. She has just completed a book with Robert Cunningham, *Agendas and Decisions: How State Government Executives and Middle Managers Make and Administer Policy* which will be published by SUNY Albany Press.

Daniel Press is Professor and Chair of Environmental Studies at UC Santa Cruz, where he teaches environmental politics and policy. His research interests include land and species conservation as well as industrial greening. He was appointed by Governor Arnold Schwarzenegger to the Central Coast Regional Water Quality Control Board, a state agency that enforces water quality rules and regulations. His most recent book is *Saving Open Space: The Politics of Local Preservation in California*, UC Press, 2002.

Claire-Lauren Schulz is a law student at the Sturm College of Law at the University of Denver. She completed two graduate degrees (MBA Marketing, and MS in Management) at the Daniels College of Business at the University of Denver. While an undergraduate and graduate student, she collaborated with Daniels faculty on different research projects and on professional publications. She has also co-authored a case on Denver International Airport with faculty from the Daniels College of Business. As a graduate assistant, she co-authored an article for the *Public Manager* with Drs. Johnston and Haynes.

Paul Seidenstat is Associate Professor of Economics at Temple University and has been director of the graduate program in economics. Dr. Seidenstat has numerous books and articles in the field of privatization. He has co-edited: *Privatizing the United States Justice System, Privatizing Correctional Institutions, Privatizing Educational Choice,* and *Privatizing Transportation Systems.* In 1999, he edited *Contracting Out Government*

Services. A specialist in public finance, he has been a principal investigator for several research projects for federal government agencies and has served local governments as finance director and financial advisor. His recent research has been in the area of state and local government finance and management.

Judith L.J.L. Tijdink was a doctoral student in the field of Public Policy and Administration in the Department of Organization and Finance at the University of Twente in the Netherlands. Dr. Tijdink is currently working as a civil servant at the Department for Social Affairs, The Hague. She has done significant research work with Peter B. Boorsma.

Bert Useem is Professor of Sociology at the University of New Mexico. He has two books and numerous professional publications and research grants. His Ph.D. is from Brandeis University in 1980. He was also a Postdoctoral Fellow at the University of Michigan. Research interests include the areas of reinventing government and emergency management. He has also written extensively about prisons and crime.

William L. Waugh, Jr. is Professor of Public Administration at the Andrew Young School of Policy Studies at Georgia State University. He is the author of *Living with Hazards, Dealing with Disasters* (M.E. Sharpe, 2000), *Terrorism and Emergency Management* (Marcel Dekker, 1990), and *International Terrorism* (Documentary Publications, 1982); co-author of *State and Local Tax Policies* (Greenwood Press, 1995); and co-editor of *Disaster Management in the United States and Canada* (Charles C. Thomas, 1996), *Cities and Disaster* (Charles C. Thomas, 1990), and the *Handbook of Emergency Management* (Greenwood Press, 1990), as well as the author of articles, chapters, essays, and reports published in the United States, Canada, Europe, and Asia. He has numerous professional publications and has served diligently on university committees affecting governance for a number of years. He has also been a Co-Editor of *Policy Studies Review*. Entrepreneurial management, governance systems, and emergency management are among his primary writing interests. His primary focus has been on local capacities to deal with natural and technological hazards, including terrorism. Professor Waugh was Chair of ASPA's Publication Committees for in 2007.

Robert J. Wright has over 16 years of experience in the public sector where he led efforts to implement innovative programs impacting the public and private sectors. These experiences range from work with the City Council of Chicago to management roles within the Office of the State Comptroller, Commonwealth of Massachusetts. Mr. Wright is working on his doctorate in Public Administration. He holds an MPA from Suffolk University, School of Management, Boston, Massachusetts; and a BA from the University of Chicago in Political Science. Mr. Wright has collaborated with Dr. Haynes on several research projects in a variety of capacities.

INDEX

B

C

E

F

G

H

N

Q

T

U

V

W

Y